Readings in
ORGANIZATIONS

Readings in
ORGANIZATIONS

Edited by

JAMES L. GIBSON
Professor of Business Administration
University of Kentucky

JOHN M. IVANCEVICH
Professor of Organizational Behavior and Management
University of Houston

JAMES H. DONNELLY, JR.
Professor of Business Administration
University of Kentucky

Fourth Edition • 1982

BUSINESS PUBLICATIONS, INC.   Plano, Texas   75075

© BUSINESS PUBLICATIONS, INC., 1973, 1976, 1979, and 1982

ISBN 0-256-02693-9

Library of Congress Catalog Card No. 81–70927

Printed in the United States of America

1 2 3 4 5 6 7 8 9 0 ML 9 8 7 6 5 4 3 2

Preface

The study of organizations is of vital concern to many groups in society. Behavioral and social scientists have led the way in observing that modern men and women work, learn, play, worship, heal, and govern in larger and more complex institutions than their ancestors. Modern society is characterized by the existence of intricately organized firms, universities, clubs, churches, hospitals, and agencies, each carrying out specialized social functions through the combined efforts of individual specialists. The effectiveness of these organizations determines the quality of modern life.

The achievement of effective organizational performance is the essence of the managerial process. As a consequence of history and tradition, society delegates authority to use its scarce resources to the managers of its institutions. And, in return, it holds managers accountable for their actions. Thus, managers of organizations are crucial to the manner in which a modern society functions. More particularly, the decisions of managers determine to an important degree the effectiveness of society in achieving its economic, educational, leisure, religious, health, and political goals.

The subject of this fourth edition is the management of organizational behavior, structure, and processes. Our purpose is to bring together a selection of articles that bear directly on the process by which managers achieve effective organizational performance. The contributors of these articles are representative of a variety of behavioral and social sciences, including psychology, sociology, and social psychology. Though diverse in background and training, the contributors share a common interest in bringing their theory and research to bear on the practical problems of managing organizations.

The framework which we use to present the articles identifies three aspects of organizations: behavior, structure, and process. Organizational behavior emphasizes the human element of organizations and relates to the aspects of motivation, groups, and leadership. The analysis of organizations is enhanced through an understanding of each of these aspects. Organizational structure refers to the relatively fixed relationships among tasks and it derives from managerial decisions which define jobs, group jobs into

v

departments, and assign authority. Two important features of structure are job descriptions and chains of command. Organizational processes are the activities of people in the organization. These activities consist of such important elements as evaluating performance, rewarding behavior, communications, and decision making.

However, analysis of organizations implies some definite purpose. Our point of view is that the modern manager's purpose must be organizational improvement. Thus we identify a fourth aspect: modification of organizations. This aspect refers to the process by which managers improve the organization's effectiveness through the development of behavior, structure, and process. Organizational development requires knowledge of these three elements. The bases for acquiring this knowledge are provided by the articles that appear in this book.

This book is divided into six parts. The first part is introductory in that it presents articles on organizational behavior and theory, and on managerial practice. This part provides an overview of the direction and content base of these readings. Part II presents eight articles which discuss individual behavior in organizations. The articles focus on perception, personality, job satisfaction, goal setting, and stress. Part III contains five articles that look at group and leadership behavior in organizations. Part IV includes six articles, each dealing with one or more aspects of organizational structure. This section includes articles dealing with the quality of work life, matrix organizations, and information systems. Part V is comprised of five articles which discuss problems and strategies of communication, decision making, performance appraisal, and career choices. Part VI includes three articles which discuss organizational change and development and Japanese management effectiveness.

The articles which we included in this book were selected for a number of reasons. Of particular importance is that they are recent discussions of organizational behavior, structure, and process issues. Moreover, they are of high professional quality and readable by students. Yet, ultimately we had to make choices and in numerous instances excellent articles were omitted which would have been included in a larger collection. Although not arbitrarily selected, the articles do represent our judgment.

We wish to especially thank the authors and publishers of the included readings. We also wish to acknowledge Erin Sumrall for handling all the typing details in a prompt, accurate, and understandable manner.

James L. Gibson
John M. Ivancevich
James H. Donnelly, Jr.

Contributors

Baird, John G., Jr.
Beatty, Richard W.
Behling, Orlando C.
Burck, Charles G.
Burke, W. Warner
Davis, Louis E.
Drucker, Peter F.
Dyer, William G.
Galbraith, Jay R.
Hackman, J. Richard
Hall, Jay
Janis, Irving L.
Kolodny, Harvey F.
Labovitz, George H.
Latham, Gary P.
Lawler, Edward E., III
Locke, Edwin A.

Lorsch, Jay W.
Mickel, Frederick B.
Mintzberg, Henry
Pate, Larry E.
Perrow, Charles
Rice, Berkeley
Rowan, Roy
Roy, Donald F.
Rubin, Zick
Schneier, Craig Eric
Schriesheim, Chester A.
Senger, John
Tolliver, James M.
Wheeler, Dan
Wieting, Gretchen K.
Zaleznik, Abraham
Zander, Alvin

Contents

ix

PART VI.   DEVELOPING ORGANIZATIONAL EFFECTIVENESS

Cross-Reference Table

For Relating the Articles in This Reader to the Authors'
Organizations: Behavior, Structure, Processes, 4th Edition
and Other Books

Selected Organizational Behavior Oriented Books	Parts in *Readings in Organizations*					
	Part I Introduction	*Part II* Behavior Within Organizations: Individuals	*Part III* Behavior Within Organizations: Groups and Inter-personal Influences	*Part IV* Structure Within Organizations	*Part V* Processes Within Organizations	*Part VI* Developing Organizational Effectiveness
Gibson, James L., Ivancevich, John M., & Donnelly, James H., Jr. *ORGANIZATIONS: BEHAVIOR, STRUCTURE, PROCESSES*, 4th Ed. (Plano, Texas: Business Publications, Inc., 1982).	Chaps. 1 & 2	Chaps. 3, 4, 5, 6	Chaps. 7, 8, 9, 10	Chaps. 11, 12, 13	Chaps. 14, 15, 16, 17, 18	Chaps. 19, 20, Epilogue
Filley, Allan C., House, Robert J., & Kerr, Steven, *Managerial Process and Organizational Behavior* (Glenview, Ill.: Scott, Foresman and Co., 1976).	Chaps. 1, 2, 3, 4	Chaps. 4, 5, 6, 10	Chaps. 8, 9, 11, 12	Chaps. 13, 14, 15, 16, 17, 18, 19	Chap. 7	Chaps. 20, 21, 22
Hamner, W. Clay & Organ, Dennis W., *Organizational Behavior* (Dallas: Business Publications, Inc., 1978).	Chaps. 1 & 2	Chaps. 3, 4, 5, 6, 7, 8, 9, 10, 11, 12	Chaps. 13, 14, 15, 16, 17			Chap. 18
Hampton, David, Summer, Charles E., & Webber, Ross A., *Organizational Behavior and Practice of Management* (Glenview, Ill.: Scott, Foresman and Co., 1978).		Chaps. 1, 2	Chaps. 4, 5, 10, 11	Chaps. 6, 7, 8, 9	Chap. 3	Chap. 12
Hellriegel, Don and Slocum, John W., *Organizational Behavior* (St. Paul: West Publishing Co., 1979).	Chaps. 1, 2, 3	Chaps. 5, 6, 7, 11	Chaps. 9, 10, 13, 14	Chaps. 4 & 12	Chap. 8	Chaps. 1, 5, 6, 17
Luthans, Fred, *Organizational Behavior* (New York: McGraw-Hill, 1981).	Chaps. 1, 2, 3	Chaps. 4, 5, 6, 7, 8, 9, 10	Chaps. 11, 13, 14, 15	Chaps. 18, 19	Chaps. 12, 16, 17, 20	Chaps. 21, 22

Nadler, David A., Hackman, J. Richard, & Lawler, Edward E., III, *Managing Organizational Behavior* (Boston: Little, Brown, & Co., 1979).	Chaps. 1 & 13	Chap. 2	Chaps. 7, 8, 10, 13	Chaps. 6, 9, 11, 12	Chaps. 3 & 4	Chap. 14
Porter, Lyman W., Lawler, Edward E., III, and Hackman, J. Richard, *Behavior in Organizations* (New York: McGraw-Hill, 1975).	Chap. 1	Chaps. 2, 3, 4, 5, 6	Chaps. 13, 14	Chaps. 8, 9, 10	Chaps. 7, 11, 12	Chaps. 15, 16, 17
Reitz, H. Joseph, *Behavior in Organizations* (Homewood, Ill.: Richard D. Irwin, 1981).	Chaps. 1, 2	Chaps. 3, 4, 5, 7, 8, 9	Chaps. 10, 11, 14, 15, 16, 17		Chaps. 6, 12, 13	Chap. 18
Steers, Richard M., *Introduction to Organizational Behavior* (Santa Monica, California: Goodyear Publishing Co., 1981).	Chaps. 1, 2, 3	Chaps. 4, 5, 6, 7, 8	Chaps. 9, 12, 13, 14, 15	Chap. 16	Chaps. 10, 11, 17	Chap. 18
Szilagyi, Andrew D., Jr. and Wallace, Marc J., Jr. *Organizational Behavior and Performance* (Santa Monica, California: Goodyear Publishing Co., 1980).	Chaps. 1 & 2	Chaps. 3, 4, 5	Chaps. 7, 8, 9	Chaps. 6, 10, 11	Chaps. 12, 13, 14	Chaps. 15, 16, 17

Part I

INTRODUCTION

In this part, articles are presented which serve to introduce the remaining selections in the book to provide the reader with a broad overview as a foundation for understanding and appreciating what follows. Our major interest in this book will be the behavioral sciences which have produced theory, research, and generalizations concerning the behavior, structure, and processes of organizations. The articles in this book recognize these three major organizational variables which are used to classify the selections included in the book.

One of the major themes of this book is the contribution that the behavioral sciences can make to our understanding of management and organizations. The literature of psychology, sociology, social psychology, and anthropology is the source of many of the articles chosen. Other articles from the broader literature of management and business administration which use behavioral science theories, concepts, or methods of inquiry have also been included. Our purpose is to demonstrate that the behavioral sciences are rich sources of understanding about the way people behave in organizational settings.

Another major theme is that managers of organizations must come to know and to appreciate the behavioral science contributions. To this end, we have included a selection of articles which deals with the practical problems of modifying organizations. The literature of organizational development and the management of change has increased substantially in the past several years through the efforts of behavioral scientists in particular. The articles in this part are concerned with the issues that managers must confront as they engage in the process of developing the capability of their organizations.

A final important thread and one which is seemingly more concrete is that of organizational effectiveness. In fact this thread pervades the entire book. The authors whose work is represented here are concerned with various aspects of organizational effectiveness. They write about leadership effectiveness, group effectiveness, communication effectiveness, structural effectiveness, and the like. They also are concerned with conceptual and measurement problems of effectiveness. What is effectiveness? How should it be measured? These questions are not easily resolved, as the reader will come to realize as he or she reads the articles in the following part of the book.

The lead article of the book is by Jay W. Lorsch and is entitled "Making Behavioral Science More Useful." Lorsch in a logical manner explores the heat and confusion over the use of behavioral science ideas in organizations. The article is addressed to managers and academics. He is concerned about managerial use of the behavioral sciences. Lorsch also focuses on what academics need to do to make the behavioral sciences more usable for managers.

The next article, by Louis Davis, "Individuals and the Organization," introduces the field of ecology. Davis believes that a number of issues that challenge organizations must be viewed in ecological terms. Ecology is a science concerned with organisms and their environments, their interaction, and the processes which change both. The article examines various environmental impacts on organizations.

Charles Perrow's article, "The Short and Glorious History of Organizational Theory," traces the development of thinking from the advocates of the mechanical school of organizational theory—those who treat the organization as a machine—to the human relations school, which emphasizes people rather than machines as well as the contributions made by other groups along the way to the current "systems" view. Unfortunately, Perrow concludes that the "systems theory itself had not lived up to its heady predictions." Where does all this leave us? Perrow provides five very important conclusions.

The final article in Part I examines the attributes of managers. "Managerial Work: Analysis from Observation," by Henry Mintzberg describes some of the main features and characteristics of managerial work. The picture painted by the author illustrates the multiple roles a manager must play to get the job done.

Making Behavioral Science More Useful

JAY W. LORSCH

Since World War II management thought and practice have undergone great change. The computer has revolutionized information processing and, along with operations research and other quantitative techniques, has improved management decision making. New methods of market and consumer research also provide better information on which to base decisions. All these developments mean better tools for obtaining and analyzing information for more effective management.

During the same period the behavioral sciences—anthropology, psychology, social psychology, and sociology—have also contributed many potential ideas and theories to management. Unlike the first set of management tools, these ideas have focused not only on how decisions are made, but also on how employees from top management levels to the factory floor implement them. Thus these ideas should be of use to every manager: how to communicate effectively; how to give performance evaluations to employees; how to resolve conflicts between individuals or between one department and another; how to design organization structures, measurement systems, and compensation packages; how to introduce changes in organization, procedures, and strategy.

In spite of their potential for wide application, however, these ideas have been only sparingly used. Surely, General Foods, Volvo, and Procter & Gamble have introduced innovations in some factory organizations, and some management organizations have done so as well, but how many other company managements have failed to use the available knowledge? Further, why have the companies that have claimed success in one location or division been so reluctant to apply the ideas in other appropriate places?

Source: Jay W. Lorsch, "Making Behavioral Science More Useful," *Harvard Business Review,* March–April 1979, pp. 171–81. Reprinted with permission. Copyright © 1979 by the President and Fellows of Harvard College; all rights reserved.

One obvious reason seems to be the confusion, skepticism, and contro-versy about the relevance of these ideas in the minds of many managers. For example: Is participative management a suitable style for all managers? Can job enrichment be applied in a unionized factory? Will managers set realistic goals with a management by objectives program? Has laboratory training improved managerial effectiveness? And, ultimately, some hard-headed manager always asks, "What does all this psychologcal mumbo-jumbo contribute to the bottom line?" The list of such questions may seem endless, but, equally discouraging, the answers the experts provide often seem unpersuasive and even contradictory.

Another facet of the situation, however, concerns me even more. The behavioral sciences occasionally burst with enthusiasm about certain ideas. Job enlargement, T-Groups, creative thinking, participative leadership, and management by objectives are cases in point. Each set of ideas or each technique becomes almost a fad with strong advocates who tout its early successes. Then, as a growing number of companies try the ideas or tech-niques and as reports of failure and disappointment mount, the fad quickly dies. This often repeated pattern has caused many managers to lose interest in trying other behavioral science ideas which could help them.

In this article, I explore why so much heat and confusion have arisen around these behavioral science ideas and why, consequently, they have had such a limited impact on management practice. Because this is a matter of applying knowledge developed in the academic world to the problems of practicing managers, I am addressing both managers and academics. What can managers do themselves to make better use of the behavioral sciences? What can they demand from academics to get more practical knowledge? What can the academics working in this field do to provide more knowledge practitioners can use?

LURE OF THE UNIVERSAL THEORY

One major reason for the difficulties in applying behavioral science knowledge has been the interpretation that such ideas are applicable to all situations. From their earliest attempts to apply these ideas, both behav-ioral scientists developing the knowledge and managers applying it have at one time or another maintained the universality of the ideas. For example, Rensis Likert's participative-management ("Systems 4" Management) model was a call by a behavioral scientist for a universal application of ideas regardless of industry, company size, or geographic location.[1]

Over the past few years, Likert's voice has been joined by many other behavioral scientists who assume that their theories are also universally appropriate. Many of these theories were derived from studies carried out during and after World War II. The data from these studies were inter-preted as supporting, for example, the notion that all employees have strong needs for group membership at work and, consequently, the uni-

1 Rensis Likert, *New Patterns of Management* (New York: McGraw-Hill, 1961).

versal superiority of participative management. Researchers were not concerned whether these ideas were more appropriate in one setting than in another, with different groups of employees, with different jobs, and so forth.

Along with this search for the universal went a tendency to invent specific techniques for applying the theories, which it was argued would lead to improved results in all situations. Examples are management by objectives, autonomous work groups, laboratory training, job enrichment, and participative leadership.

By now many managers have tried these techniques, and their attempts have led to numerous difficulties stemming from the variable conditions existing in different companies. For example, a basic premise underlying management by objectives is that if people set their own goals, they will be committed to them. Because of the nature of the business or of the technology, however, in some situations employees can have little or no real voice in setting goals.

To illustrate, consider the case of the back office of a large bank where managers down to first-line supervisors were directed to become involved in an MBO program. The quantity, schedule, and quality of their work, however, were imposed on them by the work flow from other groups in the bank and by their customers' requests, rather than being set by the managers themselves. Moreover, upper managers trying to meet strategic goals set their cost targets. These lower-level managers had little or no leeway in which to choose their own goals. As a result, they soon saw the management by objectives program as a sham.

Another example of a situation not fitting a theory occurs when a manager's personality is not consistent with what is demanded of a participative leader. As Harry Levinson and Abraham Zaleznik, among others, have indicated, although personality development is a life-long process, a 35-year-old's character is generally stable and is unlikely to change in radically new directions.[2] Since one's style of dealing with others is closely linked to one's personality makeup, it is not surprising that some managers are comfortable with one way of managing subordinates and some with another.

To illustrate my point: Companies have faced a major difficulty in introducing autonomous work groups and similar techniques. These techniques require supervisors to involve their subordinates more heavily in decision making, and many of these managers find it difficult to adjust to this new "participative" style. Not only have they spent many years managing in a different way, but also they consciously or unconsciously chose to be foremen because their personalities were suited to the traditional, more directive role.

Such situational problems are a primary reason that so many of these

---

2 Harry Levinson, *The Exceptional Executive* (Cambridge, Mass.: Harvard University Press, 1968); Abraham Zaleznik, *Human Dilemmas of Leadership* (New York: Harper & Row, 1966).

techniques are flashes in the pan. They are applied successfully in a few companies where conditions are right and receive attention and publicity. Without considering the differences, managers, consultants, and academics alike decide the technique can be applied to other situations. Because conditions are not right, the second-generation attempts are often failures, and the enthusiasm dies.

EACH SITUATION IS UNIQUE

Neither universal theories nor the resulting techniques have been the only behavioral science ideas available to managers. Another set of ideas is built on the premise that the organization can be viewed as a social system. This approach developed out of the Hawthorne studies by Elton Mayo, F. J. Roethlisberger, and William Dickson.[3]

In this well-known study, it was learned that worker behavior is the result of a complex system of forces including the personalities of the workers, the nature of their jobs, and the formal measurement and reward practices of the organization. Workers behave in ways that management does not intend, not because they are irresponsible or lazy but because they need to cope with their work situation in a way that is satisfying and mean-ingful to them. From this perspective, what is effective management behav-ior and action depends on the specifics in each situation.

Although many scholars, including Roethlisberger and Mayo them-selves, elaborated on these ideas and taught them at many business schools, managers never gave them the attention they gave to the universal ideas. Interestingly enough, many saw the central significance of the Hawthorne studies as being either the *universal* importance of effective interpersonal communication between supervisors and workers or the so-called Haw-thorne Effect. The latter is the notion that any change in practice will *always* lead to positive results in the short run simply because of the novelty of the new practice.

In essence, this world-renowned study, which its authors saw as proving that human issues need to be viewed from a "social system," or situational perspective, was interpreted by others as a call for universal techniques of "good human relations." (For Roethlisberger's comments on this, see *The Elusive Phenomena*.)[4]

Of course, stating that one should *always* take a situational perspective could be seen as a universal prescription itself. My concern is not with universal ideas, such as this and others which I shall mention shortly, which seem to hold generally true. Rather, it is with techniques invented under a specific set of conditions, which have not been more widely tried but which their advocates argue have universal application.

---

[3] Elton Mayo, *The Human Problems of an Industrial Civilization* (New York: Viking Press, 1960); F. J. Roethlisberger and William Dickson, *Management and the Worker* (Cambridge, Mass.: Harvard University Press, 1939).

[4] F. J. Roethlisberger, *The Elusive Phenomena*, ed. George F. F. Lombard (Boston: Division of Research, Harvard Business School, 1977).

Why these social system concepts did not catch on is a matter of conjecture, but one reasonable explanation is that managers naturally prefer the simplest apparent approach to a problem. When faced with the choice between the complex and time-consuming analysis required to apply such situational ideas and the simpler, quicker prescriptions of universal theories and techniques, most managers seem to prefer the simpler universal approach. The human tendency to follow the fads and fashions also adds to the appeal of these techniques. If competitors are trying T-groups for management development, shouldn't we? If the company across the industrial park is using MBO, shouldn't we as well?

In spite of the rush to simple popular solutions in the last decade, some behavioral scientists have become aware that the universal theories and the techniques they spawned have failed in many situations where they were inappropriate. These scholars are trying to understand situational complexity and to provide managers with tools to analyze the complex issues in each specific situation and to decide on appropriate action. Examples of these efforts are listed in Exhibit 1.

These behavioral scientists do not all agree on what variables are important to understand. At this stage, people conceptualize the issues and define the variables and the important relationships among them in many different ways. Also, the "theories" they have developed often throw light on a limited set of applications.

All these behavioral scientists focusing on situational theories, however, share two fundamental assumptions. First, the proper target of behavioral science knowledge is the complex interrelationships that shape the behavior with which all mangers must deal. Harold J. Leavitt, in his well-known text *Managerial Psychology*, presents a diagram (see Exhibit 2) that illustrates clearly the basic set of relationships.[5] Behavior in an organization results, he writes, from the interaction of people's needs, their task requirements, and the organization's characteristics. He uses two-headed arrows both to suggest this complex interdependence and indicate that behavior itself can influence the other forces over time.

Although Leavitt's was an early and, from today's perspective, a simplified view of the relationships involved, it captures the essential issues in situational theories and is very close to the Roethlisberger and Dickson conception.

The second assumption that behavioral scientists focusing on situational theories seem to share is that, at this juncture, they cannot hope to provide a grand and general theory of human behavior in organizations. Rather, what the behavioral sciences can, and should, provide are what L. J. Henderson called "walking sticks" to guide the managers along complex decision-making paths about human affairs.[6] In this case, by walking sticks

---

[5] Harold J. Leavitt, *Managerial Psychology* (Chicago: University of Chicago Press, 1958), p. 286.

[6] L. J. Henderson, *On The Social System: Selected Writings* (Chicago: University of Chicago Press, 1970).

Exhibit 1
Examples of Situational Frameworks

Author	Publication	Major Focus
Fred E. Fiedler	*A Theory of Leadership Effectiveness* (New York: McGraw-Hill, 1967).	Leadership of a work unit
John P. Kotter	*Organizational Dynamics* (Reading, Mass.: Addison-Wesley, 1978).	Organizational change
Edward E. Lawler	*Pay and Organizational Effectiveness: A Psychological View* (New York: McGraw-Hill, 1971).	Employee motivation
Paul R. Lawrence and Jay W. Lorsch	*Organization and Environment* (Division of Research, Harvard Business School, Harvard University, 1967).	Organizational arrangements to fit environmental requirements
Harry Levinson	*Men, Management, and Mental Health* (Harvard University Press, 1962).	Employee motivation
Jay W. Lorsch and John Morse	*Organizations and Their Members* (New York: Harper & Row, 1975).	Organizational arrangements and leadership in functional units
Edgar H. Schein	*Career Dynamics: Matching Individual and Organizational Needs* (Reading, Mass.: Addison-Wesley, 1978).	Life stage careers, and organizational requirements
Robert Tannenbaum and Warren H. Schmidt	"How To Choose A Leadership Pattern," *Harvard Business Review*, May–June 1973.	Leadership
Victor H. Vroom and Philip W. Yetton	*Leadership and Decision Making* (University of Pittsburgh Press, 1973).	Leadership behavior for different types of decisions
Joan Woodward	*Industrial Organization: Theory and Practice* (Oxford Univeristy Press, 1965).	Organizational design

I mean conceptual models for understanding the complexity of the human issues a manager faces.

Such models represent the product these scholars have to offer managers. Universal prescriptions or techniques are like a mirage. Each situation is unique and the manager must use these conceptual models to diagnose it. With an understanding of the complex and interrelated causes of behavior in the organization, the manager can use his or her intellect and creative ability to invent a new solution or to judge what existing solutions might fit the situation.

Exhibit 2
Basic Forces Shaping Behavior

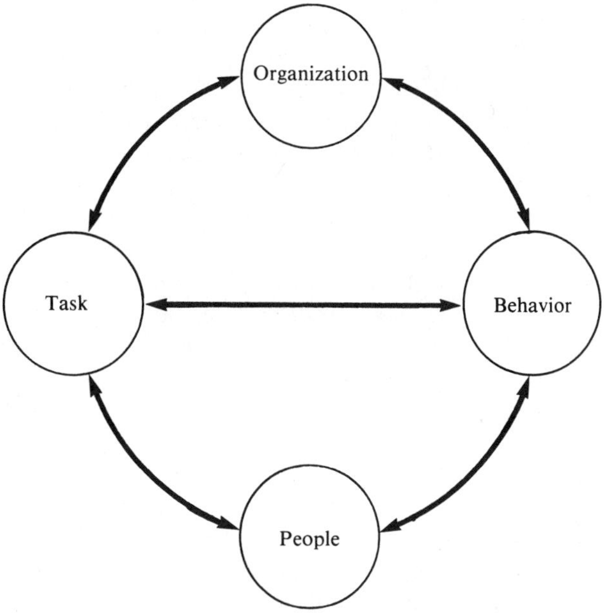

An Applied Example   The case of a major insurance company illustrates how a situational walking stick can help managers. Like many of its competitors, the top management of this company was concerned about the high rate of turnover among its younger professional staff. The managers felt that they did not understand the causes of this turnover and were unwilling to accept the conclusion that their competitors reached—namely, that the basic cause was low pay. Instead, they used an in-house consultant to help them diagnose the causes of their problem.

This consultant used a relatively simple situational model—the concept of the psychological contract as a framework for diagnosing the causes of the problem.[7] From this perspective, the relationship between a group of employees and the company is seen as an implicit, as well as explicit, contract.

While this contract is not binding in the legal sense, it is of psychological importance. Employees have certain expectations about what they are to get from their work in the company—both economically and psychologically. If these expectations are not met, the employees become dissatisfied and ultimately can express themselves by walking out the door.

With these ideas in mind, the consultant, through a series of interviews

---

[7] The concept of the psychological contract was first developed by Harry Levinson et al. in *Men, Management and Mental Health* (Cambridge, Mass.: Harvard University Press, 1966).

in offices that had varying levels of turnover, sought the answers to two basic questions: What did the employees expect from the company? And how well were these expectations being met?

He learned that these young employees considered their current salary level relatively unimportant. More important to them were future career opportunities, the chance to do their jobs with minimum interference from above, and immediate supervisors who cared about their progress and tried to facilitate their learning. Furthermore, the consultant found that staff turnover was much lower in offices where managers were meeting expectations than where they were not.

From this diagnosis, top management developed an approach to improve the skills of its middle managers in meeting the expectations of its younger staff. By discovering the basic causes of its turnover problem, the company avoided the trap its competitors with identical problems fell in of mistakenly relying on salary increases as a way of trying to buy the loyalty of its younger staff.

Potential of Situational Theories

The insurance company case illustrates the greatest potential the behavioral sciences have for managers at present. They can provide situational theories to analyze, order, understand, and deal with the complex social and human issues managers face. By their nature the universal theories make simplified assumptions about the human and business factors involved in a situation.

For example, many universal theories do not recognize that not all employees have the same career expectations. Yet we now know that while older managers may be more interested in jobs that enable them to develop subordinates and build the organization for the future, younger persons, such as the professionals just mentioned, are at a stage of life where advancement is usually critical.[8]

Similarly, different business tasks do not all lend themselves to similar leadership styles or reward schemes; running a production shop may require directive leadership, but managing a group of professional underwriters for an insurance company may require employee involvement in decisions.

Even though they neither provide ready-made solutions nor solve all classes of human problems, the situational theories are tools to understand the variety and complexity of these problems. The manager has to select the theory that seems most relevant to his or her specific problem, analyze the situation according to it, develop his or her own action alternatives, and choose among them.

A hospital laboratory provides a use analogy. It is full of diagnostic tools, but the doctor has to make the choice of the appropriate ones. Then, he makes a diagnosis and decides on the appropriate treatment. So it will

---

8 See Daniel Levinson et al., *The Seasons of A Man's Life* (New York: Alfred A. Knopf, 1978); or Edgar H. Schein, *Career Dynamics* (Reading, Mass.: Addison-Wesley, 1978).

be for managers. The behavioral sciences can provide conceptual frameworks for analyzing problems. They will indicate what data are required, on some cases how best to collect them, how the problem areas are related to each other, and the outcomes with which the managers will be concerned. With this analysis the managers can then use their experience, intuition, and intellect to decide which actions make sense.

From this description, the analytical process may seem difficult and time-consuming. How true this is will depend to some extent on the complexity of the problem and the experience that a manager has in applying these tools. A manager with experience can apply them with the same ease and skill a physician displays in using his diagnostic tools. Applying these tools to complex and infrequently encountered issues, however, may require some expertise beyond the scope of a typical line manager—a problem I shall deal with shortly.

The trend toward more situational theories signifies only a decline in emphasis on universal theories and the techniques they have spawned, not that these theories and techniques should or will disappear. Undoubtedly, on a limited number of issues, such generalizations are useful guides to actions. The problem for a manager is to identify those issues where a universal theory is helpful and not confuse them with issues where the solution depends on the situation.

For example, certain maxims about interpersonal communication seem to be generally useful in conducting performance appraisal interviews. And it seems clear that it is absolutely necessary for the top management of a unit undergoing a change to be committed to the process for it to be successful. Use of such valid generalizations from the behavioral sciences should continue and expand.

But the application of techniques and universal principles that are inappropriate in a variety of situations must decline. Because of the tendency toward fads in both managers and academics, I am not naive enough to think that the misapplications of universal theories will suddenly end. My hope is that the increasing availability and use of situational theories will gradually make universal ideas less attractive. As managers become more sophisticated diagnosticians, they will be less likely to try an idea or a technique simply because it is a fad.

Managers need also to recognize a number of current difficulties in using situational theories and must, with the help of those who are developing these ideas, seek solutions to them. In essence, in the behavioral science market they must act as consumers who influence the end product, and in their companies they must, among other things, act as teachers so that they and their associates are prepared to use these tools.

THE MANAGER AS A CONSUMER

If a manager, acting as a consumer, begins to explore the relevant literature, what is he likely to find? To what extent are the situational theories in a useful, usable form? Unfortunately, much needs to be done to make many of these tools more widely applicable. As managers become informed and demanding consumers, I hope they can influence behavioral scientists to take steps to overcome the current problems.

The Tower of Babel

One difficulty with today's situational tools is that each scholar (or group of scholars) has developed his or her own language and methods and makes interpretations based on his or her values, assumptions, and research about individual behavior. Also, in the same way physical scientists and engineers have done, each set of scholars, not surprisingly, prefers its own ideas and rejects those "not invented here." Understandably, communication among behavioral scientists and their communication with managers is confused. Different scholars use different labels to mean the same thing. Because no one relates his ideas to those of others, an academic Tower of Babel develops.

Managers and scholars alike find it difficult to understand what one label means in one model as compared to another or how the ideas developed by one group relate to those developed elsewhere. Clearly, what managers and academics can and must do is judge future studies more carefully and explicitly to determine whether they are related to each other. In this way, we will be able to see the parallels and differences in various theories and will be able to make more informed decisions about their relevance to particular problems. Similarly, such action should gradually reduce much of the variation in language and terminology that characterizes the behavioral sciences.

Lack of Parsimony

Many of these concepts are so complex that managers need to learn how to define the concepts and their relationships before they can apply them. All this takes time and, naturally, makes these ideas less appealing to the busy line executive. By their preference for complex and elegant theories that greatly exceed the needs of most managers, academics have compounded the problem. Rather than worrying about how to help managers, many academics seem preoccupied with impressing their colleagues. In my own experience, moreover, it is the relatively simple concepts that managers find most useful.

As consumers of knowledge, managers can and should reject those theories that are too complex and seek those simple enough to be understood and implemented by intelligent managers. But academics must strive to develop such theories, what Sheldon has called "friendly" models.[9] By this, he means theories that are not so complex as to intimidate potential users, yet are complete enough to enable them to deal with the real human complexities they face.

One way to ensure such a balance is for managers to encourage and for academics to conduct more research focusing on managerial issues. Experience in medicine and space technology, for example, has demonstrated

---

[9] Alan Sheldon, "Friendly Models," *Science, Medicine, and Man* 1 (1973): 49.

anew the axiom that research leading to a productive and practical payout will also likely lead to important theoretical results. Certainly, encouraging the design of research programs that tie real managerial concerns to theoretical behavioral science issues should also lead to gains in knowledge complete enough to be useful and simple enough to use.

Managers should also look for research that clarifies the conditions where findings are relevant and where they are not. In this manner, the distinction between situationally relevant ideas and universally applicable ones should be clearer. This, in turn, should reduce some of the misuses of behavioral science and also discourage academics from developing techniques in a vacuum.

An Aside
to Academics

Although HBR readers are primarily practitioners, much of my preceding argument has particular relevance to my academic colleagues. Managers can only influence us indirectly by their reactions as consumers. The responsibility for the changes in the development of knowledge for which I am calling lies directly with academics. Yet, in many centers of behavioral science research, researchers are more concerned with proving a minor but neat conceptual point or resolving a measurement issue than with tackling issues that have clear practical application. Disciplinary traditions, the promotion criteria in most universities, and the acceptance standard for most relevant publications place more emphasis on theoretical elegance and methodological perfection than on practical use of knowledge. It will, therefore, require more than just pressure from consumers to make the necessary changes in our approach to knowledge building. It is going to require dedication and courage from the behavioral scientists who believe, as I do, that our tools are still too little used.

THE MANAGER
AS MANAGER

If academics can be encouraged to move in such directions, the manager's job will be easier. He or she will gradually acquire simpler conceptual tools that are relevant to real problems, specific about the range of situations to which they apply, and related to each other.

Even today, however, a few such conceptual tools exist. The issue for managers is how to select the specific set of tools relevant to a particular type of problem. To help in this regard, in Exhibit 3 I compare the conceptual tools from Exhibit 1 as to their major focus, the type of management or organizational issues for which they are most relevant, and some of the key questions managers must be able to answer to use these tools.

In examining Exhibit 3, bear in mind some caveats. First, the list represents my personal choices. It is not exhaustive. It is based on my own and some of my colleagues' experiences in helping managers deal with these problems. Second, many of these tools are relatively new and still somewhat crude. Although, in some cases, fairly sophisticated and validated techniques have been developed for answering the key questions, in others the manager will have to rely on his or her own knowledge and judgment

Exhibit 3
Situational Frameworks and Their Applications

Framework	Major Focus	Issues								Diagnostic Questions
		Leadership	Management Selection	Career Planning	Measurement and Performance Feedback	Compensation	Job Design	Division and Coordination of Activities	Organizational Change	
Fiedler	Leadership of a work unit	●	●				●			What is the preferred leadership style of the relevant manager(s) on a continuum from permissive, passive, considerate, to controlling, active, and structuring? What is the quality of leader relations with the members of the subordinate group(s)? How well-defined and structured are the activities being performed by subordinates? How much positional authority does the leader(s) have?
Kotter	Organizational change				●			●	●	Is management concerned with short-term, moderate-term, or long-term change? If *short-term*, what is the current state of the organization's human and financial resources, its organization process and structure, its technology, and its external environment? If *moderate-term*, how well are the organization's resources, structure, and process aligned with each other and the external environment and the goals of management? If these are not well aligned, what changes have caused this? If *long-term*, are major changes likely in top management, in the organization's human and financial resources, its structure and processes, or its technology and external environment, which would make one or two of these elements out of line with the other? How malleable are the other elements so that a new alignment can be created? Is the organization inventing resources to achieve sufficient flexibility to adapt to such major changes?

Issues

Framework	Major Focus	Leadership	Management Selection	Career Planning	Measurement and Performance Feedback	Compensation	Job Design	Division and Coordination of Activities	Organizational Change	Diagnostic Questions
Lawler	Employee motivation				●	●	●			What do the relevant individuals expect to get as rewards for their behavior on the job? How valuable are these rewards to these individuals? How hard do these individuals believe it will be to achieve the results expected of them?
Lawrence and Lorsch	Organizational arrangements to fit environmental requirements				●			●		How different are the organizational practices, traditions, and the goals and time horizons of members of various organization units? To what extent are these differences consistent with the different activities each unit is performing (e.g., selling products versus manufacturing them, versus designing them)? To what extent is it necessary for these units to work collaboratively and to what extent can they perform activities independent of each other? Do the existing mechanisms for dividing and coordinating work (e.g., authority structure, coordinating rules, cross-unit committees, rewards, and measurement) facilitate the necessary division of work and coordination?
Levinson et al	Employee motivation			●	●	●	●			What is the psychological contract between the relevant individuals and the company? What does each party expect to receive from the other? How well is each party living up to its part of the contract?
Lorsch and Morse	Organizational arrangements and leadership in functional units	●	●		●		●			What is the nature of the unit's tasks? How certain are they? What goals do members have to work toward? How quickly is feedback about results available?

Exhibit 3 (continued)

Framework	Major Focus	Leadership	Management Selection	Career Planning	Measurement and Performance Feedback	Compensation	Job Design	Division and Coordination of Activities	Organizational Change	Diagnostic Questions
										What are members' shared psychological predispositions in terms of working together versus alone, preference for close supervision or not, preference for clear and predictable activities or for ambiguous ones? How well does existing leadership style, unit structure, measurement, and job design fit the unit task and members' predisposition?
Schein	Life stage, careers, and organizational requirements		•	•						At what stage of life is (are) the relevant individual(s)? Where are these people in their careers? What are their underlying career interests? What are the key dimensions of jobs available now and in the future? What are future personnel requirements for these jobs?
Vroom and Yetton	Leadership behavior for different types of decisions	•	•							Who among the boss and his subordinates have information to make a high-quality decision? Is the problem well-defined or not? Is acceptance of decisions by subordinates critical to implementation? Do subordinates share the organizational goals to be attained in making these decisions? Is conflict among subordinates likely in seeking solutions?

of the situation. Third, in such a compact article, it is obviously not possible to define the variables in each conceptual framework or state the relationships among them. For this the reader will have to refer to the original works listed in Exhibit 1.

By using tools such as these, managers will be forced to be more diagnostic. They will have to approach human problems with the same analytical rigor they devote to marketing or financial issues. This approach means less acceptance of the latest fad in management practice, whether it be management by objective, job enrichment, office of the president, sensitivity training, or whatever. Instead, managers can use these tools to identify problems and diagnose their causes. Then they can invent their own solutions or even examine what other companies are doing to see what might be relevant to their situation. In this process, managers should not ignore their intuitive hunches and past experience. Accordingly, this more rigorous analysis should be compared with such insights to arrive at the best possible judgments.

Need for Education

Because these situational tools require more skill, knowledge, and time, line managers may need help and support in the longer run to realize their full potential. Education and training, in both university courses and company management development programs, can and should aim at giving managers knowledge about these tools and the skills necessary to apply them. Such programs will have to provide not only content, but also, and equally important, practice in using these tools for anlysis and problem solving.

In calling for management education, I am not suggesting that line managers can or should develop knowledge of or skill in applying a broad range of these ideas. Rather, as Exhibit 1 shows, they should gain understanding about those concepts which are relevant to the problems they regularly encounter. For example, concepts that focus on understanding leadership issues with a small group of workers (e.g., Fiedler's) would be of value to first-level supervisors.

At the general manager level, concepts that enhance understanding of multiple-unit organizations would be more relevant (e.g., Lawrence and Lorsch). This is not to say that some of these tools will not have utility at many organizational levels. For example, managers concerned with compensation issues might find Lawler's ideas useful whether their subordinates are salesmen, blue collar workers, or general managers.

Role of Staff

In the long run, along with educational programs, corporations will need to develop staff specialists with a broader range of knowledge about the behavioral sciences. These specialists, whatever their titles—organization development agent, human resources expert, organization designer, behavioral scientist—should be able to apply their wider and deeper behavioral science knowledge to a broader range of issues.

Their role would be analogous to what market research analysts, cost analysts, and so on, perform. Their job should be first to help managers decide what concepts will be most useful in understanding the problems they face, to design studies to gather data, to analyze them, and to work with their line colleagues to develop solutions. Again, academics have an important contribution to make. They can develop courses and programs to educate the professionals to staff these functions.

Awareness of One's Values and Style

To use these tools effectively, both line and staff managers will need to be aware of their own values and their own preferred management styles. Without such awareness, one can easily and unwittingly confuse one's own sense of what is right or appropriate with what the situation seems to require and objective analysis seems to suggest. With self-knowledge about one's values and preferences, one can at least be explicit when making choices between what a situation requires and one's own preferences.

Achieving such self-awareness is not easy. It requires a willingness to be introspective and cognizant of one's limits as well as one's strengths, one's preferences as well as one's dislikes. Such probing is difficult for many managers; yet it is something that a number of seasoned, mature, and successful managers achieve. With this self-understanding, they are better able to comprehend their relationships with others around them. These same qualities must also be put to work to apply behavioral science knowledge effectively.

TOOLS ARE AVAILABLE NOW

Based on what you have read here, you may conclude that it is better to defer trying these situational tools until they have been improved, expanded, and refined. No doubt such improvements are needed. But if managers use the best of the existing situational tools now, in spite of their shortcomings, they will no doubt achieve improved effectiveness in dealing with the complex human problems of management.

The need for solving these human problems has never been more pressing. The increased size of organizations makes this so, as do the inflationary pressures on personnel costs and the rate of change in the environment of many companies. Additionally, demands from many employees for a more rewarding organizational life are growing. These situational tools offer a virtually untapped resource to provide more effective management of the human assets of most companies.

To use these tools will not be easy, and managers will have to make efforts at many levels: to be more critical consumers of behavioral science knowledge; to become more analytic and diagnostic, to gradually build educational programs and staff resources for developing skill and knowledge in using these tools; and, finally, to become more self-aware, so they can discriminate between their own preferences, current fads, and what will be most effective in their particular situations.

These efforts will be difficult, but to defer doing these things is to neglect these new and valuable tools that the behavioral sciences are making available, and this would be a tragic waste.

Individuals and the Organization*

LOUIS E. DAVIS

A number of issues challenging the future of our society—its capitalist economy, its organizational forms—must be seen in ecological terms. Ecology is a science concerned with organisms and their environments, their interaction and the processes which change both. The future survival of our economic organizations may be seen as a question of organization-evironment interactions.

There are many crises affecting our economy and its organizations. The crisis between people and organizations is a silent crisis. For our society to survive in the form that we know, acknowledgment and understanding of this crisis is required. Our society is structured for individuals but gets its work done in a variety of ways. Organizations are the frameworks through which most of society's work is executed and within which individuals seek to satisfy many of their needs. Organizations, as instruments for meeting societal and individual needs, are sensitive to changes in the expectations and demands from both quarters.

One reason for the lack of acknowledgment of the individual-organization crisis is that people are seen as employees, as members of organizations. It is forgotten that they equally are members of the social environment. They are affected by the organizations in which they work and by the social environment in which they reside. They bring aspects of that environment with them into the organization, and vice versa.

The ecology of any organization is very much affected by what its members bring from their environments. The present crisis between people and their organizations is closely related to that process. We will gain understanding of this crisis if we focus our attention on the segment of the social environment which is crucial to all of our organizations. This segment of the organizational environment is the 97 million plus people who constitute the American work force. Each of our organizations gets its members from this work force, and these are affected by what happens to this work force.

Changes in our society, particularly in the values of the work force, have seriously undermined the traditional relationship between organizations and their members. This has led to a crisis for organizations that may only be resolved by the evolution of new organizational forms.

The silent crisis has a number of manifestations, but at the moment the focus is on productivity. For the last several years the annual increase in productivity has been about 1.6 percent per year, whereas the average for the 20 years following World War II was 3.2 percent per year. Many major organizations are losing their ability to effectively utilize the human resources available to them. The decline in the historic rate of productivity improvement has lasted 10 to 12 years indicating that this is not a temporary problem, but the consequence of changes in the social environment. The statistics report the entire national economy, so we may not be comforted by the thought that this is only a problem in poorly managed firms. The issues are fundamentally societal, stemming from reactions to what all organizations are doing. What is becoming crucial is the growing inability of existing organizational forms to adapt to changing demands and constraints of our society. Those responsible for training managers are in a position to offer guidance to organizations and should encourage understanding of these changes so as to create a management community capable of meeting these new challenges with more than silent avoidance.

The Changing Values of the Work Force

What is happening in the work force? There is doubt that it can be called a work force in the 1980s, given how people are redefining themselves in relation to work. The impression of those who are professionally engaged in watching these changes is that the changes exhibited by people who work are overlooked. This is more than benign neglect. There is avoidance of work force organizational issues among scholars, business leaders, and union leaders. The views of union and business leaders are remarkably similar on these issues. Workers are seen as economic beings motivated by increases in pay and fringe benefits. What they must do to earn these rewards is largely irrelevant, as long as there is no danger to life and limb. Some have said that the durability of the conventional wisdom about work and workers derives from the fact that the workplace is perhaps the most conservative of American institutions. This may be the consequence of the enormous number of issues entangled in the workplace, including management issues of authority and control, and worker issues of reward, compensation, and equity. The meaning of work in the lives of members or organizations makes the workplace a central concern for American society. One may understand the reluctance to examine the workplace, but such conservatism will not serve society in meeting the challenges of the future.

Unfortunately, not many organizations are preparing for these challenges. Given present trends, we may predict that by the 1980s the human side of organizations will be only unsafely left to low-level personnel departments. Instead, knowledge of people and their values and needs will become an essential part of a top manager's training if he is to direct effectively large-scale institutions, as noted by Daniel Yankelovich.[1]

One aspect of the work force relates to employment. Recent data suggest much about values that are counterintuitive. Social survey data of 1976–77 indicate that the desire to hold a paid job has become a compelling need for far more Americans than those presently counted as unemployed. Independent estimates have been made by a number of serious scholars that 24 to 27 million members of our society, not now employed full-time, want jobs. Most of these are women who would take jobs if they were available. Yet our society traditionally has had a job creation rate of between 2 and 2½ million jobs per year. Much of the discourse about whether we have 6 percent or 7 percent unemployment is useless given the actual magnitude of the demand indicated by the above data.

The age of retirement from the work force provides an illustration. The mandatory retirement age was extended to 70 in 1978. The actual retirement age in the United States averages 62 to 63 years and is declining. At General Motors the average age of retirement, including managers and blue collar workers, is somewhat less than 60 years of age. Last year about half of the U.S. retirees were under the age of 65. Raising the retirement age to 70 may not mean very much except to those privileged people who love what they are doing. However, raising the retirement age becomes significant when we consider the job-holding data at the opposite end of the work force. Competition for jobs is extraordinarily strong among the young, even more so among young blacks. The unemployment rates among young blacks is estimated to be between 40 to 60 percent. It has not been below 30 percent in the last seven or eight years. The impact of this fact on our society survival is something that needs serious attention. What will the effect be if certain age groups and segments of our population never connect with modern American society in the workplace? The workplace can be seen as the locus of our strongest connection with society.

There are millions of jobs which remain unfilled. *The Los Angeles Times* recently carried an article about an experiment in providing jobs for disadvantaged youth. After a year the experimenters gave up because there were scores of unfilled jobs which people simply did not take. The jobs were considered undesirable and dead-end. These and low-paying jobs are not likely to be filled. This is not a new development. It was signaled 12 years ago in studies, done in Boston, of available jobs and unemployed blacks. The two pools remained the same. It looked as if the unemployed simply didn't care about taking the jobs. In fact, a study indicated that they did take the jobs but did not keep them because the jobs had no future. There is a minimum amount of quality that people expect from a work situation before they are willing to take and hold a job. This is a new phenomenon and it adds to the complexity of managing organizations.

---

1 Daniel Yankelovich, "Work, Value and the New Breed," in *Work in America: The Decade Ahead,* ed. C. Kerr and J. M. Rosow (New York: Van Nostrand Reinhold, 1979).

To summarize, there are millions of people who want and compete for available jobs. Young people, and especially young black people, cannot find a connection with our society for lack of a workplace. While the trend is to retire at younger ages, the retirement age has been extended. Finally, we have millions of jobs that are unfilled because no one is willing to suffer them. It appears to be more desirable to live on welfare or on unemployment compensation than to take some kinds of jobs. In California and other states, illegal workers are "imported" to do the work society cannot get its members to do.

The Employed

What are the changes occurring among the members of organizations, the people who hold the paying jobs? A survey cited in Yankelovich's "Work, Value, and the New Breed" indicates that millions of people in paying jobs find the work and its rewards so unappealing that they do not work very hard. Yet, we observe people insisting on rising increases in pay and fringe benefits. One might infer that this is compensation for the lack of appeal of the work that they are required to do. The less they are committed to do, the more they want.

This gives us a different perspective on productivity decline. A strong factor appears to be the withdrawal of workers from involvement in unrewarding jobs. What is going on among many of the employed is not very different from what we have seen among many of the unemployed. Both are members of the same society.

There is a mismatch between the carrot and stick incentives—the carrot of more pay and the stick of withdrawing security—and new motivations in the work force. While carrot and stick incentives appear to have worked well enough in the past, since the late 1960s what people expect from organizations has changed.

An important source of the mismatch arises from the uniformity of the system of rewards and incentives. It is a poor assumption that everybody wants the same thing, that money motivates everyone equally. Our systems of rewards do not reflect the diversity of expectations and goals held by people. For some, money may be the main consideration. For others leisure, status, challenge of the work, the well-being of the organization, or future rewards may be important incentives. Different segments of the work force assign greater or lesser importance to each of these goals. The workplace should afford opportunities for meeting various personal goals. At present our organizations are inflexible in their pervasive and singular reliance on economic incentives. The wildcat strikes in 1972 between the United Auto Workers local and General Motors at Lordstown, Ohio, are a good illustration. They were the first strikes in the United States in which the issue was the quality of the jobs themselves, not the kinds of jobs, the pay, or the working conditions. Both the union and the management saw increasing the pay as the solution.

Reliance on economic incentives has another drawback. Our society and the organizations within it must continuously prove their ability to meet the demands for money and security. During the 25 years of growth since World War II this ability was amply demonstrated. But in the 1970s, there has been a loss of confidence in the employer's ability to meet the needs of money and security. Withdrawal of security, once thought to be an instrument of control by the employer, is now a measure of the employer's inability to meet workers' needs.

One of the dramatic changes in our society centers on individuals. There is a widespread growth in the perception that the individual is not at fault if expectations are not met, but the institution or society is. This signifies a shift from what was called the Protestant work ethic. Success was attributed to individual endeavors and each individual had obligations to be met: "If I am not successful, something must be wrong with me." Among younger people, this value is in decline: "Something is wrong, not necessarily wrong with me. It might not have anything to do with me, but with the situation in which I find myself." People who were formerly socialized to the Protestant ethic accepted a mismatch between their needs and organizational rewards as an individual burden. Today, people thrust this mismatch back onto society, onto the organizations doing society's work.

Another important value change is the separation of success from self-fulfillment. In California, enterprises sell self-fulfillment services. They would not be in the market unless many people were not concerned with their own success and its meaning. The 1978 survey mentioned earlier indicates that about 52 percent of Americans have aspirations not fulfilled through conventional measures of success (bigger house, bigger car, higher paying job, better job title). This is more so among the young, educated, and affluent. A closely related shift is to an ethic of duty to oneself, from the traditional value on which Western societies were built, obligation to others.

Twenty-one percent of those questioned in the latest survey say work means more to them than leisure does. Sixty percent enjoy their work, but it is not the major source of their satisfaction. Nineteen percent are so exhausted by their work that they cannot conceive of it as even a minor satisfaction. There is a growing refusal to subordinate personality to the work roles. In the past, men defined their identities through their work roles. Western organizations are built on the principle of depersonalization —it is one of Weber's central criteria for bureaucratic organizations. Bureaucracies start with depersonalization, "scientific management" makes a religion out of it, but today younger people oppose it. There is aversion to becoming an object in the work role, a cog in the machine. This is producing new challenges to managerial concepts of efficiency and control.

To women, the paid job has acquired a new symbolic meaning. It is seen as a badge of membership in society and a symbol of self-worth. Women are the most rapidly growing segment of the U.S. work force, constituting 42 percent of it at present. In their quest for paid jobs, women learn the harsh reality that all work is not equally good or rewarding. Many voluntary jobs are much better than paid jobs.

A change very important to the men in the work force involves redefinition of masculinity. The definition has been very important to our society as it developed. Men saw their obligation to those who were dependent on them as taking precedence over any kind of sacrifice they would have to make. Masculinity was successfully providing for one's dependents. Men took relatively poor jobs and held them for years in order to satisfy these obligations. This sort of masculine self-esteem is dissolving, leading to grave concerns over how society will maintain itself. When balances change in society, as when more women join the work force, relationships between men and work can be expected to change. The more women in the work force, and the more security and independence they develop, the greater the shift in the meaning of masculinity will be away from sacrifice and the carrying out of obligations to one's dependents. Former symbols of masculine success—automobiles, homes, appliances—are being devalued and are now important for their use, not as status symbols. This may explain why monetary success is not the powerful motivator it was once. In addition, demand for money is often a means of revenge for lack of satisfaction with jobs. People want rewards that justly reflect the contributions they make, and if they are misused, they want to be compensated for it. It would be a gross distortion to interpret these demands for more money as signifying the growing importance of economic incentives.

Causal Factors

Why have all these changes come to pass? Why has an economic system that was demonstrably successful for so long come to be problematic in one of its fundamental relationships, that between people and organizations? To find answers we must examine organizations in the context of ecological systems. An ecological approach requires us to view organizations as systems and to inquire about the causal factors underlying changes in organizational environments. We have been discussing the changes in that environment which is particularly critical for organizations, the American work force.

According to the United States Office of Education, in 1978 the average length of schooling of the U.S. work force of approximately 97 million people was twelve years. Most of our organizations are based on the principles developed by Frederick W. Taylor in 1910, when the average educational level of the work force was three years. How much students learn in twelve years is not the issue for organizations. In the school socialization process the individual is paramount, as he should be. Twelve years of such socialization has an enormous impact on the future members of organizations: "Who am I? What am I here for? What is my engagement with work all about? What are you (the organization) doing to me?" Extended education has brought with it a rising expectation that personal needs will be met, referred to as "the psychology of entitlement." What were once seen as privileges to be earned are now seen as entitlements which are slowly becoming rights. Young people are beginning to claim the right to have an interesting, self-fulfilling, self-developing, individually-centered job. We see this expressed through the extraordinarily high value being placed on people as individuals rather than as members of organizations.

Can organizations realistically expect to find sufficient employees with the old values? Formerly many of them came from rural communities. In the early 1960s, Turner and Lawrence did some studies of industrial workers. Values of urban workers compared with those of rural workers were significantly different.[2] Professor Gerald Susman, of Pennsylvania State University, reexamined this question about 10 years later.[3] He found that the values had become so homogeneous that rural or urban background had no influence. We are a society where urban values predominate. Few workers with the old rural values are likely to be found or fitted into bureaucratic organizations.

Older workers, who remember the Great Depression of 1929–39 and experienced the effects of unemployment, are moving out of the work force. For the depression generation, economic success and security were survival issues. For today's work force, these are taken for granted. Few contemplate hunger and extreme hardship associated with some jobs, even with job security. The past cannot be recreated. "A good dose of unemployment" will not bring back old work values.

The educated "new breed of workers" have become the majority of the work force. Public and private organizations have been designed according to the principles of rational bureaucracy and scientific management, complete with fractionated, routinized jobs. We are a long way from making the necessary changes in organization design, incentives, reward systems, and performance measures that will enable organizations to cope in the society of the 1980s.[4]

Other Environmental Impacts

There are other environmental phenomena which significantly affect organizations. Two political phenomena in the United States have been little publicized. The cost of refusing to work or to take an unacceptable job has been greatly reduced due to the extensive welfare system and unemployment insurance. The economic fears that once drove millions of Americans to take any kind of job have been substantially diminished.

Second, by law and by administrative regulation the workplace has become the arena for changing American society as in areas of affirmative action and equal opportunity. The United States is saying that through the process of employment, our society will become more open, equitable, democratic. Formerly our society had placed this burden on the schools. For employing organizations this is a new burden that so far they are not prepared to perform, given their existing structures. Organizations have not done so very well in their operation that they can readily accept the

2 Arthur N. Turner and Paul R. Lawrence, *Industrial Jobs and the Workers* (Cambridge, Mass.: Harvard University Press, 1965).

3 Gerald I. Susman, "Job Enlargement: Effects of Culture on Worker Responses," *Industrial Relations* 12, no. 1 (1973): 1–15.

4 Pehr Gyllenhammer, *People at Work* (Boston: Addison-Wesley Publishing, 1977).

burden of social change now thrust upon them. No other society has made the workplace the locus for changing all of society. Yet, the United States has done this. As yet there is very little recognition of the changes needed in the structure of organizations and jobs in order to satisfy this new requirement.

The technological environment as well has had a major impact on organizations and their workplaces. The effects of advances in technology are poorly understood. Generally, they are perceived as a factor in eliminating jobs. This may not be the primary effect. Technological advances have so increased the material producing capability of our society, that scarcity as a concern has almost disappeared. The transfer payments to large segments of our population who do not have employment income are not simply money payments, but claims to goods and services. They are only possible because of the tremendous productivity that technology has helped achieve. The changes in the values and expectations of the work force and the political phenomena of reducing the cost to the individual of not working are both, to a considerable extent, results of advances in technology.

The increasing rate of technological development is causing turbulence in the economic and marketing environments of most large organizations. In a state of turbulence, environments are no longer passive, but interactive such that the actions of an organization and others may lead to unanticipated outcomes. In Western society, particularly in the United States, the rate of change is so great that individual organizations find it hard to reduce the relative uncertainty in which they have to exist, no matter what kind of long-range planning they do. Indeed, long-range planning may become a trap. Russell Ackoff has focused on the crux of the problem of the turbulent environment for organizations when he indicated that under turbulent conditions experience is not the best teacher.[5] It may even be the worst teacher, preparing us only to deal with situations that have ceased to exist. The best teacher may be experiment. But how do we design organizations that can learn from experiments?

This issue will be discussed at the close of this article. For now, let us note that the widely applied and taught theories of bureaucratic organization are all based on stability and control. Usually, lip service is paid to the need for change, and seldom is there concern with designing adaptive capabilities into organizations. In addition to the effects of turbulent environment on organizations, there has been a rapid increase in the capital investment required to use the new sophisticated technical systems. The increase has come from the application of advanced technology as well as from the requirements for controlling pollution. Even a simple product such as mayonnaise, which was once made in large-sized batches by mixing metered ingredients, is now made continuously using computer-monitored pulsating valves. A new petrochemical plant, with an organization design

---

[5] Russell Ackoff, "The Second Industrial Revolution," mimeographed, 1975.

to suit the new values, has an investment of $2.1 million per worker. There is a new energy project on the drawing boards that will cost $4 billion and take seven years to design. The old precondition for such enormous capital investment was stability and the ability to effectively plan for, at least, the useful life of the project. That is exactly what turbulent environments have denied the modern organization which must now address itself to the complex question of adaptability.

The rapidly increasing capital requirements for sophisticated technical systems have not helped managers understand the impact of such systems on the workplace. Publicists have led us to believe that automation decreases the dependence of organizations on their workers, while engineers project the image of people-proof production systems. In our mind's eye, we are asked to imagine plants spewing out products with scarcely anyone around. This simply is not the case. True, the number of employees per unit of product output is reduced. However, the dependence of the organization on its remaining members increases with the sophistication of the technical system. Why? Consider the petrochemical plant which costs over $2 million per worker. At that level of investment, every programmable or controllable task has been built into the system, taken over by machines. What remains are the unprogrammable tasks such as monitoring, diagnosing, adjusting, fine tuning, and maintaining the system. These are skilled tasks on which the organization is critically dependent if output is to be maintained. Not only are extremely large investments in sophisticated technical systems required, but the organization has high vulnerability in its increased dependence on the activities of the relatively few remaining workers.

Additionally, advancements in technology have altered the nature of work itself. Since 1900, when F. W. Taylor introduced scientific management, many millions of jobs have been fractioned into measured and programmable single elements. Efficiency was easily measurable in output-per-unit of time, and anything that could distract workers from the purely mechanical execution of their tasks was eliminated. Modern sophisticated technical systems largely absorb fractioned tasks. The easily programmable and measurable tasks are automated. What remains for people to do is radically different. People working in high technology settings live in a work world very similar to that of professionals. Their working world is one of abstractions, not of concrete objects. They work by reading dials, meters, and computer printouts, and operate valves, pumps, gates, and other devices by pressing buttons in a control room far from the objects or machines being manipulated. These activities would have absolutely no meaning to workers unless they developed certain cognitive maps of the interacting processes which cannot be seen or touched. There is no way to fit this kind of work into the principles of scientific management and bureaucracy. Skills come to have different meaning. Efficiency and productivity take on different meanings as does management direction and control. To a manager, control means being able to tell an employee when and how to do a task, and being able to measure the performance against his expectations. In advanced technical systems, the most a manager can do is ask the employee to use his best judgment in situations he is likely to understand better than the manager does. Thus, advances in technology have resulted in new kinds of work relationships which present new challenges to management and confound the principles by which our organizations have been designed traditionally.[6]

New Directions

This article began by exploring the crisis between individuals and organizations but it need not end on this note. Significant and rewarding new directions are being developed in some leading firms through new forms of organization which constitute effective and efficient alternatives to bureaucracy and scientific management. These forms provide very flexible and adaptive organizations designed to meet the challenges of the changing economic and political environments, the demands of complex technologies, as well as the expressed needs of their members for enhanced quality of their working lives. An examination of the characteristics of these organizations reveals the potentials of the new designs.

Most of the alternative forms of organization were not invented in the usual way, but are the products of deliberate organizational design or renewal activities undertaken by design teams.[7] These teams usually begin by developing organizational philosophies or charters stating the desired societal, organizational, and individual objectives. These guides for design state the values on which the organization is to be built or rebuilt. Since the design process is itself participative, the design team have representatives from all levels and functions of the organization contributing to the invention of the organization structure, its jobs, reward systems. Frequently, particularly in new organizations, all those who can contribute are not available. As little as possible of the structure is specified, leaving to those who come to the organization a maximum amount of input in inventing the specifics of their working lives.[8]

Contemplate the shift of values exhibited in the structure of the alternative organizations. The central design issue is not the maintenance of authority and control by management fundamental to scientific management and bureaucracy. Instead, individual and societal values are included and the structure of the organization is taken to be evolutionary with the specifics worked out later as needed by those who work in the organization. The design of a highly automated new paper mill serves as an illustration. The operating functions of workers in this kind of setting are to monitor, adjust, control, and maintain the equipment, to anticipate breakdowns,

---

[6] Louis E. Davis, "Evolving Alternative Organization Designs: Their Sociotechnical Bases," *Human Relations* 30, no. 3 (1977): 261–73.

[7] Louis E. Davis, "The Process of Organization-Plant Design," *Organizational Dynamics,* Winter 1980.

[8] Albert B. Cherns, "Principles of Sociotechnical Design," *Human Relations* 29, no. 8 (1976): 783–92.

and to act to minimize down time. People exercise discretion and act upon their own decisions in decentralized locations. In conventional organizations, these are management functions. The designers of this organizations perceived what they had to choose from among the following in structuring the organization:

> One supervisor for each worker so that the former can carry out the discretionary or decision part of the action while the latter acts to implement the decisions already made.
>
> Supervisors who do all the work.
>
> Workers who supervise the work.

The third choice was selected by the design team. In settings where responses to randomly occurring events cannot be specified as to time and place, people must be given the authority to do what must be done. Authority to act when, where, and how needed had never been extended to workers (except craftsmen) who in actuality have the responsibility for achieving the outcomes.

A second characteristic of the new forms of organization is the self-maintaining group as the building block of the organization. This sets aside one of the fundamental principles of scientific management and bureaucracy, that it must be possible for a supervisor or manager to hold each of his subordinates directly responsible as an individual for his performance. This requirement leads to the one-person-one-task basic organizational building block of scientific management. The new forms of organization utilizing self-maintaining units have internal boundaries selected on different principles. These are located so that the units can operate as small systems within a larger system, internally coordinating their activities and leaving to management the boundary-controlling function and integration of the units. These boundaries are located so that each organizational unit is associated with identifiable product or process outcomes, for which it takes responsibility. To be self-maintaining, the unit must be able to respond to the demands placed upon it and to the exigencies in its environments. The members of such units must possess, individually or collectively, the skills to provide a product or service, including operating skills, maintenance skills, planning and evaluation skills, and social skills needed to maintain the team or unit as a social system.

An illustration of such an organizational unit exists in the receiving and shipping team of a new food products manufacturing organization structured on alternative concepts. This team carries out the function of receiving incoming materials which are to be transformed into products by processing teams. Usually, receiving departments are designed as necessary but not quite acceptable appendages of an organization. They carry out the drudgery of bringing in, storing, and later withdrawing materials, for delivery to processing units. The activities of such departments usually require few skills and include routine and sometimes physically demanding labor. People performing this work are usually forklift drivers under the direction of supervisors who make the decisions. Any leavening of this situation, by recordkeeping or inventory control, is minimized by specializing such tasks and assigning them to clerks.

The food manufacturer, in its design, used the concept of the self-maintaining organizational unit. This led to the establishment of a shipping and receiving team that sees its responsibility as the "buying" of incoming materials and the "selling" of usable materials to the processing teams. The members of the team, while doing some routine unloading, transporting, and warehousing, also perform testing of incoming materials to determine whether they meet specifications, decide on their acceptance, and receive them (by placing them in storage) or reject them (by returning them to suppliers). Each team member performs various combinations of all these activities and associated recordkeeping. The members of the team see themselves as being in the "wholesale business" of buying and selling raw materials and supplies. They are measured and held responsible for these activities and see their reputations built upon how dependable they are as "wholesalers." How and when they carry out the activities is left to them— there is no supervisor. It is their responsibility to organize and reorganize themselves to do all the work required. By being measured on outcomes achieved, they function as a self-maintaining small organization performing the work needed to maintain themselves in a larger one. The requisite response capability of the team not only includes the necessary work and decision skills, but also the social skills for maintaining an organizational unit and its members.

A third aspect of the new designs is that they are the outcome of the effort to jointly optimize the technical systems and the social systems of the organizations, since both are interrelated in the process of achieving desired outcomes. Traditionally, engineers design technical systems and their machine and tool components so that they are optimized on the basis of economic criteria. Optimizing on the basis of social criteria is seen most often to be satisfied by designing the technical system so that it is people-proof. People, the social system, are then expected to adapt themselves to the technical system which usually has been designed to minimize the feedback of needed information and the possibilities of human intervention. Joint optimization seeks to combine the complementary advantages of the technical system and the social system and, in particular, to integrate the adaptive, problem-solving capacity of people with the productive capacity of complex technical systems which, in the short run, are rigid or nonadaptive in the face of various deviations or changes.

A newly designed chemical plant illustrates this very well.[9] The plant is operated by six teams, each with 17 workers and a team coordinator, who have operating skills and mechanical, electrical, and social maintenance

---

[9] Louis E. Davis and Charles S. Sullivan, "A Labor Management Contract and Quality of Working Life," *Journal of Occupational Behavior* 1, no. 1 (1979).

skills. Each team assigns its members to their daily tasks as limited by their skills. Flexibility and adaptability will better be served as the skill mix of each member increases. Training opportunities are built into the work program so that members may accumulate knowledge and experience. Workers are not paid according to tasks performed or job titles but for the levels of knowledge and skills each has achieved. The technical and social needs are complex so that several years will be required to master all of the operating and maintenance skills needed by team members. In contrast the fractionated tasks which constitute jobs under scientific management may be learned in a few hours. The working life of team members is not preprogrammed. Indeed, given the great variety of tasks available to the team, the team "reinvents" the working lives of its members daily. The team is responsible for its output and quality as well as for the utilization of its resources, chief of which is the effort of its members. Not only is there no such thing as one man-one job, there is no direct control of an individual's performance by a supervisor.

The technical system was designed to be integrated with the social system. Control rooms were consolidated to permit team operation, quality control procedures were built into the team's tasks, and monitoring information or feedback belonged to the teams. A critical decision in the design of the technical system was to operate the costly computer system off-line, permitting operator decision making rather than computer control. Learning will take place because the computer cannot learn, while people can. Learning how to effectively operate the complex process is the central problem for economically successful performance. By means of this design, which provides needed work authority, stimulates and rewards learning, and relies on self-management of individuals and teams, the quality of working life of individuals is strongly enhanced and technical and economic success of the organization is assured. This organization design, undertaken with cooperation and participation of the union, led to a unique union-management collective agreement emphasizing quality of working life factors.

The efficient and effective performance of these alternative organization forms and the high levels of satisfaction of most criteria of quality of working life bode well in the search for overcoming the individual-organization crisis.

The Short and Glorious History of Organizational Theory*

CHARLES PERROW

From the beginning, the forces of light and the forces of darkness have polarized the field of organizational analysis, and the struggle has been protracted and inconclusive. The forces of darkness have been represented by the mechanical school of organizational theory—those who treat the organization as a machine. This school characterizes organizations in terms of such things as: centralized authority, clear lines of authority, specialization and expertise, marked division of labor, rules and regulations, and clear separation of staff and line.

The forces of light, which by mid-20th century came to be characterized as the human relations school, emphasizes people rather than machines, accommodations rather than machine-like precision, and draws its inspiration from biological systems rather than engineering systems. It has emphasized such things as: delegation of authority, employee autonomy, trust and openness, concerns with the "whole person," and interpersonal dynamics.

THE RISE AND FALL OF SCIENTIFIC MANAGEMENT

The forces of darkness formulated their position first, starting in the early part of this century. They have been characterized as the scientific management or classical management school. This school started by parading simple-minded injunctions to plan ahead, keep records, write down policies, specialize, be decisive, and keep your span of control to about six people. These injunctions were needed as firms grew in size and complexity, since there were few models around beyond the railroads, the military, and the Catholic Church to guide organizations. And their injunctions worked. Executives began to delegate, reduce their span of control, keep records, and specialize. Planning ahead still is difficult, it seems, and the modern equivalent is Management by Objectives.

* Reprinted by permission of the publisher from *Organizational Dynamics*, Summer 1973. Copyright 1973 by AMACOM, a division of American Management Association.

But many things intruded to make these simple-minded injunctions less relevant:

1.   Labor became a more critical factor in the firm. As the technology increased in sophistication it took longer to train people, and more varied and specialized skills were needed. Thus, labor turnover cost more and recruitment became more selective. As a consequence, labor's power increased. Unions and strikes appeared. Management adjusted by beginning to speak of a cooperative system of capital, management, and labor. The machine model began to lose its relevancy.

2.   The increasing complexity of markets, variability of products, increasing number of branch plants, and changes in technology all required more adaptive organization. The scientific management school was ill-equipped to deal with rapid change. It had presumed that once the proper structure was achieved the firm could run forever without much tampering. By the late 1930s, people began writing about adaptation and change in industry from an organizational point of view and had to abandon some of the principles of scientific management.

3.   Political, social, and cultural changes meant new expectations regarding the proper way to treat people. The dark, satanic mills needed at the least a whitewashing. Child labor and the brutality of supervision in many enterprises became no longer permissible. Even managers could not be expected to accept the authoritarian patterns of leadership that prevailed in the small firm run by the founding father.

4.   As mergers and growth proceeded apace and the firm could no longer be viewed as the shadow of one man (the founding entrepreneur), a search for methods of selecting good leadership became a preoccupation. A good, clear, mechanical structure would no longer suffice. Instead, firms had to search for the qualities of leadership that could fill the large footsteps of the entrepreneur. They tacitly had to admit that something other than either "sound principles" or "dynamic leadership" was needed. The search for leadership traits implied that leaders were made, not just born, that the matter was complex, and that several skills were involved.

ENTER HUMAN RELATIONS

From the beginning, individual voices were raised against the implications of the scientific management school. *Bureaucracy* had always been a dirty word, and the job design efforts of Frederick Taylor were even the subject of a congressional investigation. But no effective counterforce developed until 1938, when a business executive with academic talents named Chester Barnard proposed the first new theory of organizations: Organizations are cooperative systems, not the products of mechanical engineering. He stressed natural groups within the organization, upward communication, authority from below rather than from above, and leaders who functioned as a cohesive force. With the spectre of labor unrest and the Great Depression upon him, Barnard's emphasis on the cooperative nature of organizations was well-timed. The year following the publication of his *Functions of the Executive* (1938) saw the publication of F. J. Roeth-lisberger and William Dickson's *Management and the Worker,* reporting on the first large-scale empirical investigation of productivity and social relations. The research, most of it conducted in the Hawthorne plant of the Western Electric Company during a period in which the work force was reduced, highlighted the role of informal groups, work restriction norms, the value of decent, humane leadership, and the role of psychological manipulation of employees through the counseling system. World War II intervened, but after the war the human relations movement, building on the insights of Barnard and the Hawthorne studies, came into its own.

The first step was a search for the traits of good leadership. It went on furiously at university centers but at first failed to produce more than a list of Boy Scout maxims: A good leader was kind, courteous, loyal, courageous, and so on. We suspected as much. However, the studies did turn up a distinction between "consideration," or employee-centered aspects of leadership, and job-centered, technical aspects labeled "initiating structure." Both were important, but the former received most of the attention and the latter went undeveloped. The former led directly to an examination of group processes, an investigation that has culminated in T-group programs and is moving forward still with encounter groups. Meanwhile, in England, the Tavistock Institute sensed the importance of the influence of the kind of task a group had to perform on the social relations within the group. The first important study, conducted among coal miners, showed that job simplification and specialization did not work under conditions of uncertainty and nonroutine tasks.

As this work flourished and spread, more adventurous theorists began to extend it beyond work groups to organizations as a whole. We now knew that there were a number of things that were bad for the morale and loyalty of groups—routine tasks, submission to authority, specialization of tasks, segregation of task sequence, ignorance of the goals of the firm, centralized decision making, and so on. If these were bad for groups, they were likely to be bad for groups of groups—i.e., for organizations. So people like Warren Bennis began talking about innovative, rapidly changing organizations that were made up of temporary leadership and role assignments, and democratic access to the goals of the firm. If rapidly changing technologies and unstable, turbulent environments were to characterize industry, then the structure of firms should be temporary and decentralized. The forces of light, of freedom, autonomy, change, humanity, creativity, and democracy were winning. Scientific management survived only in outdated text books. If the evangelizing of some of the human relations school theorists were excessive, and, if Likert's System 4, or MacGregor's Theory Y, or Blake's 9×9 evaded us, at least there was a rationale for the confusion, disorganization, scrambling, and stress: Systems should be temporary.

BUREAUCRACY'S COMEBACK   Meanwhile, in another part of the management forest, the mechanistic school was gathering its forces and preparing to outflank the forces of light. First came the numbers men—the linear programmers, the budget experts, and the financial analysts—with their PERT systems and cost-benefit analyses. From another world, unburdened by most of the scientific management ideology and untouched by the human relations school, they began to parcel things out and give some meaning to those truisms, "plan ahead" and "keep records." Armed with emerging systems concepts, they carried the "mechanistic" analogy to its fullest—and it was very productive. Their work still goes on, largely untroubled by organizational theory; the theory, it seems clear, will have to adjust to them, rather than the other way around.

Then the words of Max Weber, first translated from the German in the 1940s—he wrote around 1910, incredibly—began to find their way into social science thought. At first, with his celebration of the efficiency of bureaucracy, he was received with only reluctant respect, and even with hostility. All writers were against bureaucracy. But it turned out, surprisingly, that managers were not. When asked, they acknowledge that they preferred clear lines of communication, clear specifications of authority and responsibility, and clear knowledge of whom they were responsible to. They were as wont to say "there ought to be a rule about this," as to say "there are too many rules around here," as wont to say "next week we've got to get organized," as to say "there is too much red tape." Gradually, studies began to show that bureaucratic organizations could change faster than nonbureaucratic ones, and that morale could be higher where there was clear evidence of bureaucracy.

What was this thing, then? Weber had showed us, for example, that bureaucracy was the most effective way of ridding organizations of favoritism, arbitrary authority, discrimination, payola, and kickbacks, and, yes, even incompetence. His model stressed expertise, and the favorite or the boss's nephew or the guy who burned up resources to make his performance look good was *not* the one with expertise. Rules could be changed; they could be dropped in exceptional circumstances; job security promoted more innovation. The sins of bureaucracy began to look like the sins of failing to follow its principles.

ENTER POWER, CONFLICT, AND DECISIONS

But another discipline began to intrude upon the confident work and increasingly elaborate models of the human relations theorists (largely social psychologists) and the uneasy toying with bureaucracy of the "structionalists" (largely sociologists). Both tended to study economic organizations. A few, like Philip Selznick, were noting conflict and differences in goals (perhaps because he was studying a public agency, the Tennessee Valley Authority), but most ignored conflict or treated it as a pathological manifestation of breakdowns in communication or the ego trips of unreconstructed managers.

But in the world of political parties, pressure groups, and legislative bodies, conflict was not only rampant, but to be expected—it was even functional. This was the domain of the political scientists. They kept talking about power, making it a legitimate concern for analysis. There was an open acknowledgment of "manipulation." These were political scientists who were "behaviorally" inclined—studying and recording behavior rather than constitutions and formal systems of government—and they came to a much more complex view of organized activity. It spilled over into the area of economic organizations, with the help of some economists like R. A. Gordon and some sociologists who were studying conflicting goals of treatment and custody in prisons and mental hospitals.

The presence of legitimately conflicting goals and techniques of preserving and using power did not, of course, sit well with a cooperative systems view of organizations. But it also puzzled the bureaucratic school (and what was left of the old scientific management school), for the impressive Weberian principles were designed to settle questions of power through organizational design and to keep conflict out through reliance on rational-legal authority and systems of careers, expertise, and hierarchy. But power was being overtly contested and exercised in covert ways, and conflict was bursting out all over, and even being creative.

Gradually, in the second half of the 1950s and in the next decade, the political-science view infiltrated both schools. Conflict could be healthy, even in a cooperative system, said the human relationists; it was the mode of resolution that counted, rather than prevention. Power became reconceptualized as "influence," and the distribution was less important, said Arnold Tannenbaum, than the total amount. For the bureaucratic school—never a clearly defined group of people, and largely without any clear ideology—it was easier to just absorb the new data and theories as something else to be thrown into the pot. That is to say, they floundered, writing books that went from topic to topic, without a clear view of organizations, or better yet, producing "readers" and leaving students to sort it all out.

Buried in the political-science viewpoint was a sleeper that only gradually began to undermine the dominant views. This was the idea, largely found in the work of Herbert Simon and James March, that because man was so limited—in intelligence, reasoning powers, information at his disposal, time available, and means of ordering his preferences clearly—he generally seized on the first acceptable alternative when deciding, rather than looking for the best; that he rarely changed things unless they really got bad, and even then he continued to try what had worked before; that he limited his search for solutions to well-worn paths and traditional sources of information and established ideas; that he was wont to remain preoccupied with routine, thus preventing innovation. They called these characteristics "cognitive limits on rationality" and spoke of "satisficing" rather than maximizing or optimizing. It is now called the "decision-making" school and is concerned with the basic question of how people make decisions.

This view had some rather unusual implications. It suggested that if managers were so limited, then they could be easily controlled. What was necessary was not to give direct orders (on the assumption that subordinates were idiots without expertise) or to leave them to their own devices (on the assumption that they were supermen who would somehow know what was best for the organization, how to coordinate with all the other supermen, how to anticipate market changes, and so on). It was necessary to control only the *premises* of their decisions. Left to themselves, with those premises set, they could be predicted to rely on precedent, keep things stable and smooth, and respond to signals that reinforce the behavior desired of them.

To control the premises of decision making, March and Simon outline a variety of devices, all of which are familiar to you, but some of which you may not have seen before in quite this light. For example, organizations develop vocabularies, and this means that certain kinds of information are highlighted, and others are screened out—just as Eskimos (and skiers) distinguish many varieties of snow, while Londoners see only one. This is a form of attention-directing. Another is the reward system. Change the bonus for salesmen and you can shift them from volume selling to steady-account selling, or to selling quality products or new products. If you want to channel good people into a different function (because, for example, sales should no longer be the critical functions as the market changes, but engineering applications should), you may have to promote mediocre people in the unrewarded function in order to signal to the good people in the rewarded one that the game has changed. You cannot expect most people to make such decisions on their own because of the cognitive limits on their rationality, nor will you succeed by giving direct orders, because you yourself probably do not know whom to order where. You presume that once the signals are clear and the new sets of alternatives are manifest they have enough ability to make the decision but you have had to change the premises for their decisions about their career lines.

It would take too long to go through the dozen or so devices, covering a range of decision areas (March and Simon are not that clear or systematic about them, themselves, so I have summarized them in my own book), but I think the message is clear.

It was becoming clear to the human relations school, and to the bureaucratic school. The human relationists had begun to speak of changing stimuli rather than changing personality. They had begun to see that the rewards that can change behavior can well be prestige, money, comfort, and the like, rather than trust, openness, self-insight, and so on. The alternative to supportive relations need not be punishment, since behavior can best be changed by rewarding approved behavior rather than by punishing disapproved behavior. They were finding that although leadership may be centralized, it can function best through indirect and unobtrusive means such as changing the premises on which decisions are made, thus giving the impression that the subordinate is actually making a decision when he has only been switched to a different set of alternatives. The implications of this work were also beginning to filter into the human relations school, through an emphasis on behavioral psychology (the modern version of the much maligned stimulus-response school) that was supplanting personality theory (Freudian in its roots and drawing heavily, in the human relations school, on Maslow).

For the bureaucratic school, this new line of thought reduced the heavy weight placed upon the bony structure of bureaucracy by highlighting the muscle and flesh that make these bones move. A single chain of command, precise division of labor, and clear lines of communication are simply not enough in themselves. Control can be achieved by using alternative communication channels, depending on the situation; by increasing or decreasing the static or "noise" in the system; by creating organizational myths and organizational vocabularies that allow only selective bits of information to enter the system; and through monitoring performance through indirect means rather than direct surveillance. Weber was all right for a starter, but organizations had changed vastly, and the leaders needed many more means of control and more subtle means of manipulation than they did at the turn of the century.

THE TECHNOLOGICAL QUALIFICATION

By now the forces of darkness and forces of light had moved respectively from midnight and noon to about 4 A.M. and 8 P.M. But any convergence or resolution would have to be on yet new terms, for soon after the political-science tradition had begun to infiltrate the established schools, another blow struck both of the major positions. Working quite independently of the Tavistock Group, with its emphasis on sociotechnical systems, and before the work of Burns and Stalker on mechanistic and organic firms, Joan Woodward was trying to see whether the classical scientific principles of organization made any sense in her survey of a hundred firms in South Essex. She tripped and stumbled over a piece of gold in the process. She picked up the gold, labeled it "technology," and made sense out of her otherwise hopeless data. Job-shop firms, mass-production firms, and continuous-process firms all had quite different structures because the type of tasks, or the "technology," was different. Somewhat later, researchers in America were coming to very similar conclusions based on studies of hospitals, juvenile correctional institutions, and industrial firms. Bureaucracy appeared to be the best form of organization for routine operations; temporary work groups, decentralization, and emphasis on interpersonal processes appeared to work best for nonroutine operations. A raft of studies appeared and are still appearing, all trying to show how the nature of the task affects the structure of the organization.

This severely complicated things for the human relations school, since it suggested that openness and trust, while good things in themselves, did not have much impact, or perhaps were not even possible in some kinds of work situations. The prescriptions that were being handed out would have to be drastically qualified. What might work for nonroutine, high-status, interesting, and challenging jobs performed by highly educated people might not be relevant or even beneficial for the vast majority of jobs and people.

It also forced the upholders of the revised bureaucratic theory to qualify their recommendations, since research and development units should obviously be run differently from mass-production units, and the difference between both of these and highly programmed and highly sophisticated continuous-process firms was obscure in terms of bureaucratic theory. But the bureaucratic school perhaps came out on top, because the forces of evil—authority, structure, division of labor, and the like—no longer looked evil, even if they were not applicable to a minority of industrial units.

The emphasis on technology raised other questions, however. A can company might be quite routine, and a plastics division nonroutine, but there were both routine and nonroutine units within each. How should they be integrated if the prescription were followed that, say, production should be bureaucratized and R&D not? James Thompson began spelling out different forms of interdependence among units in organizations, and Paul Lawrence and Jay Lorsch looked closely at the nature of integrating mechanisms. Lawrence and Lorsch found that firms performed best when the differences between units were *maximized* (in contrast to both the human relations and the bureaucratic school), as long as the integrating mechanisms stood half-way between the two—being neither strongly bureaucratic nor nonroutine. They also noted that attempts at participative management in routine situations were counterproductive, that the environments of some kinds of organizations were far from turbulent and customers did not want innovations and changes, that cost reduction, price and efficiency were trivial considerations in some firms, and so on. The technical insight was demolishing our comfortable truths right and left. They were also being questioned from another quarter.

ENTER GOALS, ENVIRONMENTS, AND SYSTEMS

The final seam was being mined by the sociologists while all this went on. This was the concern with organizational goals and the environment. Borrowing from the political scientists to some extent, but pushing ahead on their own, this "institutional school" came to see that goals were not fixed; conflicting goals could be pursued simultaneously, if there were enough slack resources, or sequentially (growth for the next four years, then cost-cutting and profit-taking for the next four); that goals were up for grabs in organizations, and units fought over them. Goals were, of course, not what they seemed to be, the important ones were quite unofficial; history played a big role; and assuming profit as the preeminent goal, explained almost nothing about a firm's behavior.

They also did case studies that linked the organization to the web of influence of the environment; that showed how unique organizations were in many respects (so that, once again, there was no one best way to do things for all organizations); how organizations were embedded in their own history, making change difficult. Most striking of all, perhaps, the case studies revealed that the stated goals usually were not the real ones; the official leaders usually were not the real ones; the official leaders usually were not the powerful ones; claims of effectiveness and efficiency were deceptive or even untrue; the public interest was not being served; political influences were pervasive; favoritism, discrimination, and sheer corruption were commonplace. The accumulation of these studies presented quite a pill for either the forces of light or darkness to swallow, since it was hard to see how training sessions or interpersonal skills were relevant to these problems, and it was also clear that the vaunted efficiency of bureaucracy was hardly in evidence. What could they make of this wad of case studies?

We are still sorting it out. In one sense, the Weberian model is upheld because organizations are not, *by nature,* cooperative systems; top managers must exercise a great deal of effort to control them. But if organizations are tools in the hands of leaders, they may be very recalcitrant ones. Like the broom in the story of the sorcerer's apprentice, they occasionally get out of hand. If conflicting goals, bargaining, and unofficial leadership exists, where is the structure of Weberian bones and Simonian muscle? To what extent are organizations tools, and to what extent are they products of the varied interests and group strivings of their members? Does it vary by organization, in terms of some typological alchemy we have not discovered? We don't know. But at any rate, the bureaucratic model suffers again; it simply has not reckoned on the role of the environment. There are enormous sources of variations that the neat, though by now quite complex, neo-Weberian model could not account for.

The human relations model has also been badly shaken by the findings of the institutional school, for it was wont to assume that goals were given and unproblematical and that anything that promoted harmony and efficiency for an organization also was good for society. Human relationists assumed that the problems created by organizations were largely limited to the psychological consequences of poor interpersonal relations within them, rather than their impact on the environment. Could the organization really promote the psychological health of its members when by necessity it had to define psychological health in terms of the goals of the organization itself? The neo-Weberian model at least called manipulation "manipulation" and was skeptical of claims about autonomy and self-realization.

But on one thing all the varied schools of organizational analysis now seemed to be agreed: organizations are systems—indeed, they are open systems. As the growth of the field has forced ever more variables into our consciousness, flat claims of predictive power are beginning to decrease and research has become bewilderingly complex. Even consulting groups need more than one or two tools in their kit-bag as the software multiplies.

The systems view is intuitively simple. Everything is related to everything else, though in uneven degrees of tension and reciprocity. Every unit, organization, department, or work group takes in resources, transforms them, and sends them out, and thus interacts with the larger system. The psychological, sociological, and cultural aspects of units interact. The systems view was explicit in the institutional work, since they tried to study whole organizations; it became explicit in the human relations school, because they were so concerned with the interactions of people. The political science and technology viewpoints also had to come to this realization, since they deal with parts affecting each other (sales affecting production; technology affecting structure).

But as intuitively simple as it is, the systems view has been difficult to put into practical use. We still find ourselves ignoring the tenets of the open-systems view, possibly because of the cognitive limits on our rationality. General systems theory itself had not lived up to its heady predictions; it remains rather nebulous. But at least there is a model for calling us to account and for stretching our minds, our research tools, and our troubled nostrums.

SOME CONCLUSIONS

Where does all this leave us? We might summarize the prescriptions and proscriptions for management very roughly as follows:

1. A great deal of the "variance" in a firm's behavior depends on the environment. We have become more realistic about the limited range of change that can be induced through internal efforts. The goals of organizations, including those of profit and efficiency, vary greatly among industries and vary systematically by industries. This suggests that the impact of better management by itself will be limited, since so much will depend on market forces, competition, legislation, nature of the work force, available technologies and innovations, and so on. Another source of variation is, obviously, the history of the firm and its industry and its traditions.

2. A fair amount of variation in both firms and industries is due to the type of work done in the organization—the technology. We are now fairly confident in recommending that if work is predictable and routine, the necessary arrangement for getting the work done can be highly structured, and one can use a good deal of bureaucratic theory in accomplishing this. If it is not predictable, if it is nonroutine and there is a good deal of uncertainty as to how to do a job, then one had better utilize the theories that emphasize autonomy, temporary groups, multiple lines of authority and communications, and so on. We also know that this distinction is important when organizing different parts of an organization.

We are also getting a grasp on the question of what is the most critical function in different types of organizations. For some organizations, it is production; for others, marketing; for still others, development. Furthermore, firms go through phases whereby the initial development of a market or a product or manufacturing process or accounting scheme may require a nonbureaucratic structure, but once it comes on stream, the structure should change to reflect the changed character of the work.

3. In keeping with this, management should be advised that the attempt to produce change in an organization through managerial grids, sensitivity training, and even job enrichment and job enlargement is likely

to be fairly ineffective for all but a few organizations. The critical reviews of research in all these fields show that there is no scientific evidence to support the claims of the proponents of these various methods; that research has told us a great deal about social psychology, but little about how to apply the highly complex findings to actual situations. The key word is *selectivity:* We have no broad-spectrum antibiotics for interpersonal relations. Of course, managers should be sensitive, decent, kind, courteous, and courageous, but we have known that for some time now, and beyond a minimal threshold level the payoff is hard to measure. The various attempts to make work and interpersonal relations more humane and stimulating should be applauded, but we should not confuse this with solving problems of structure, or as the equivalent of decentralization or participatory democracy.

4.   The burning cry in all organizations is for "good leadership," but we have learned that beyond a threshold level of adequacy it is extremely difficult to know what good leadership is. The hundreds of scientific studies of this phenomenon come to one general conclusion: Leadership is highly variable or "contingent" upon a large variety of important variables such as nature of task, size of the group, length of time the group has existed, type of personnel within the group and their relationships with each other, and amount of pressure the group is under. It does not seem likely that we'll be able to devise a way to select the best leader for a particular situation. Even if we could, that situation would probably change in a short time and thus would require a somewhat different type of leader.

Furthermore, we are beginning to realize that leadership involves more than smoothing the paths of human interaction. What has rarely been studied in this area is the wisdom or even the technical adequacy of a leader's decision. A leader does more than lead people; he also makes decisions about the allocation of resources, type of technology to be used, the nature of the market, and so on. This aspect of leadership remains very obscure, but it is obviously crucial.

5.   If we cannot solve our problems through good human relations or through good leadership, what are we then left with? The literature suggests that changing the structures of organizations might be the most effective and certainly the quickest and cheapest method. However, we are now sophisticated enough to know that changing the formal structure by itself is not likely to produce the desired changes. In addition, one must be aware of a large range of subtle, unobtrusive, and even covert processes and change devices that exist. If inspection procedures are not working, we are now unlikely to rush in with sensitivity training, nor would we send down authoritative communications telling people to do a better job. We are more likely to find out where the authority really lies, whether the degree of specialization is adequate, what the rules and regulations are, and so on, but even this very likely will not be enough.

According to the neo-Weberian bureaucratic model—it has been influenced by work on decision making and behavioral psychology—we should find out how to manipulate the reward structure, change the premises of the decision makers through finer controls on the information received and the expectations generated, search for interdepartmental conflicts that prevent better inspection procedures from being followed, and after manipulating these variables, sit back and wait for two or three months for them to take hold. This is complicated and hardly as dramatic as many of the solutions currently being peddled, but I think the weight of organizational theory is in its favor.

We have probably learned more, over several decades of research and theory, about the things that do *not* work (even though some of them obviously *should* have worked) than we have about things that do work. On balance, this is an important gain and should not discourage us. As you know, organizations are extremely complicated. To have as much knowledge as we do have in a fledgling discipline that has had to borrow from the diverse tools and concepts of psychology, sociology, economics, engineering, biology, history, and even anthropology is not really so bad.

REFERENCES

This paper is an adaptation of the discussion to be found in Charles Perrow, *Complex Organizations: A Critical Essay* (Glenview, Ill.: Scott, Foresman, 1972). All the points made in this paper are discussed thoroughly in that volume.

The best overview and discussion of classical management theory, and its changes over time is by Joseph Massie, "Management Theory" in *Handbook of Organizations*, ed. James March (Chicago: Rand McNally, 1965), pp. 387–422.

The best discussion of the changing justifications for managerial rule and worker obedience as they are related to changes in technology, and the like, can be found in Reinhard Bendix's *Work and Authority in Industry* (New York: John Wiley & Sons, 1956). See especially the chapter on the American experience.

Some of the leading lights of the classical view—F. W. Taylor, Colonel Urwick, and Henri Fayol—are briefly discussed in *Writers on Organizations* by D. S. Pugh, D. J. Hickson, and C. R. Hinings (Baltimore: Penguin, 1971). This brief, readable, and useful book also contains selections from many other schools that I discuss, including Weber, Woodward, Cyert and March, Simon, the Hawthorne Investigations, and the Human Relations Movement as represented by Argyris, Herzberg, Likert, McGregor, and Blake and Mouton.

As good a place as any to start examining the human relations tradition is Rensis Likert, *The Human Organization* (New York: McGraw-Hill, 1967). See also his *New Patterns of Management* (New York: McGraw-Hill, 1961).

The Buck Rogers school of organizational theory is best represented by Warren Bennis. See his *Changing Organizations* (New York: McGraw-Hill, 1966), and his book with Philip Slater, *The Temporary Society* (New York: Harper & Row, 1968). Much of this work is linked into more general studies, e.g., Alvin Toffler's very popular paperback *Future Shock* (New York: Random House, 1970), and Bantam Paperbacks; or Zibigniew Brzezinsky's *Between Two Ages: America's Role in the Technitronic Era* (New York: Viking Press, 1970). One of the first intimations of the new type of environment and firm and still perhaps the most perceptive is to be found in the volume by Tom Burns and G. Stalker, *The Management of Innovation* (London: Tavistock, 1961), where they distinguished between "organic" and "mechanistic" systems. The introduction, which is not very long, is an excellent and very tight summary of the book.

The political science tradition came in through three important works. First, Herbert Simon's *Administrative Behavior* (New York: Macmillan, 1948), followed by the second half of James March and Herbert Simon's *Organizations* (New York: John Wiley & Sons, 1958), then Richard M. Cyert and James March's *A Behavioral Theory of the Firm* (Englewood Cliffs, N.J.: Prentice-Hall, 1963). All three of these books are fairly rough going, though chapters 1, 2, 3, and 6 of the last volume are fairly short and accessible. A quite interesting book in this tradition, though somewhat heavy-going, is Michael Crozier's *The Bureaucratic Phenomenon* (Chicago: University of Chicago, and London: Tavistock Publications, 1964). This is a striking description of power in organizations, though there is a somewhat dubious attempt to link organization processes in France to the cultural traits of the French people.

The book by Joan Woodward, *Industrial Organisation: Theory and Practice* (London: Oxford University Press, 1965), is still very much worth reading. A fairly popular attempt to discuss the implications for this for management can be found in my own book *Organizational Analysis: A Sociological View* (London: Tavistock, 1970), chaps. 2 and 3. The impact of technology on structure is still fairly controversial. A number of technical studies have found both support and nonsupport, largely because the concept is defined so differently, but there is general agreement that different structures and leadership techniques are needed for different situations. For studies that support and document this viewpoint see James Thompson, *Organizations in Action* (New York: McGraw-Hill, 1967), and Paul Lawrence and Jay Lorsch, *Organizations and Environment* (Cambridge, Mass.: Harvard University Press, 1967).

The best single work on the relation between the organization and the environment and one of the most readable books in the field is Philip Selznick's short volume *Leadership in Administration* (Evanston, Ill.: Row, Peterson, 1957). But the large number of these studies are scattered about. I have summarized several in my *Complex Organizations: A Critical Essay.*

Lastly, the most elaborate and persuasive argument for a systems view of organizations is found in the first 100 pages of the book by Daniel Katz and Robert Kahn, *The Social Psychology of Organizations* (New York: John Wiley & Sons, 1966). It is not easy reading, however.

Managerial Work: Analysis from Observation*

HENRY MINTZBERG

What do managers do? Ask this question and you will likely be told that managers plan, organize, coordinate, and control. Since Henri Fayol [9][1] first proposed these words in 1916, they have dominated the vocabulary of management. (See, for example, [8], [12], [17].) How valuable are they in describing managerial work? Consider one morning's work of the president of a large organization:

As he enters his office at 8:23, the manager's secretary motions for him to pick up the telephone. "Jerry, there was a bad fire in the plant last night, about $30,000 damage. We should be back in operation by Wednesday. Thought you should know."

At 8:45 a Mr. Jamison is ushered into the manager's office. They discuss Mr. Jamison's retirement plans and his cottage in New Hampshire. Then the manager presents a plaque to him commemorating his 32 years with the organization.

Mail processing follows: An innocent-looking letter, signed by a Detroit lawyer, reads: "A group of us in Detroit has decided not to buy any of your products because you used that anti-flag, anti-American pinko, Bill Lindell, upon your Thursday night TV show." The manager dictates a restrained reply.

The 10:00 meeting is scheduled by a professional staffer. He claims that his superior, a high-ranking vice president of the organization, mistreats his staff and that if the man is not fired they will all walk out. As soon as the meeting ends, the manager rearranges his schedule to investigate the claim and to react to this crisis.

Which of these activities may be called planning, and which may be called organizing, coordinating, and controlling? Indeed, what do words

---

* Reprinted by permission, Henry Mintzberg, "Managerial Work: Analysis from Observation," *Management Science*, October 1971, B 97–B 110.

1 Numbers refer to references at the end of the article.

such as "coordinating" and "planning" mean in the context of real activity? In fact, these four words do not describe the actual work of managers at all; they describe certain vague objectives of managerial work. ". . . they are just ways of indicating what we need to explain." [1, p. 537]

Other approaches to the study of managerial work have developed, one dealing with managerial decision-making and policy-making processes, another with the manager's interpersonal activities. (See, for example, [2] and [10].) And some empirical researchers, using the "diary" method, have studied, what might be called, managerial "media"—by what means, with whom, how long, and where managers spend their time.[2] But in no part of this literature is the actual content of managerial work systematically and meaningfully described.[3] Thus, the question posed at the start—what do managers do?—remains essentially unanswered in the literature of management.

This is indeed an odd situation. We claim to teach management in schools of both business and public administration; we undertake major research programs in management; we find a growing segment of the management science community concerned with the problems of senior management. Most of these people—the planners, information and control theorists, systems analysts, and the like—are attempting to analyze and change working habits that they themselves do not understand. Thus, at a conference called at M.I.T. to assess the impact of the computer on the manager and attended by a number of America's foremost management scientists, a participant found it necessary to comment after lengthy discussion [20, p. 198]:

> I'd like to return to an earlier point. It seems to me that until we get into the question of what the top manager does or what the functions are that define the top management job we're not going to get out of the kind of difficulty that keeps cropping up. What I'm really doing is leading up to my earlier question which no one really answered. And that is: Is it possible to arrive at a specification of what constitutes the job of a top manager?

His question was not answered.

RESEARCH STUDY ON MANAGERIAL WORK

In late 1966, I began research on this question, seeking to replace Fayol's words by a set that would more accurately describe what managers do. In essence, I sought to develop by the process of induction a statement of managerial work that would have empirical validity. Using a method called "structured observation," I observed for one-week periods the chief executives of five medium to large organizations (a consulting firm, a

---

[2] Carlson [6] carried out the classic study just after World War II. He asked nine Swedish managing directors to record on diary pads details of each activity in which they engaged. His method was used by a group of other researchers, many of them working in the U.K. (See [4], [5], [15], [25].)

[3] One major project, involving numerous publications, took place at Ohio State University and spanned three decades. Some of the vocabulary used followed Fayol. The results have generated little interest in this area. (See, for example, [13].)

school system, a technology firm, a consumer goods manufacturer, and a hospital).

Structured as well as unstructured (i.e., anecdotal) data were collected in three "records." In the *chronology record,* activity patterns throughout the working day were recorded. In the *mail record,* for each of 890 pieces of mail processed during the five weeks, were recorded its purpose, format and sender, the attention it received, and the action it elicited. And recorded in the *contact record,* for each of 368 verbal interactions, were the purpose, the medium (telephone call, scheduled or unscheduled meeting, tour), the participants, the form of initiation, and the location. It should be noted that all categorizing was done during and after observation so as to ensure that the categories reflected only the work under observation. [Mintzberg's study] [19] contains a fuller description of this methodology and a tabulation of the results of the study.

Two sets of conclusions are presented below. The first deals with certain characteristics of managerial work, as they appeared from analysis of the numerical data (e.g., How much time is spent with peers? What is the average duration of meetings? What proportion of contacts are initiated by the manager himself?) The second describes the basic content of managerial work in terms of ten roles. This description derives from an analysis of the data on the recorded *purpose* of each contact and piece of mail.

The liberty is taken on referring to these findings as descriptive of managerial, as opposed to chief executive, work. This is done because many of the findings are supported by studies of other types of managers. Specifically, most of the conclusions on work characteristics are to be found in the combined results of a group of studies of foremen [11], [16], middle managers [4], [5], [15], [25], and chief executives [6]. And although there is little useful material on managerial roles, three studies do provide some evidence of the applicability of the role set. Most important, Sayles' empirical study of production managers [24] suggests that at least five of the ten roles are performed at the lower end of the managerial hierarchy. And some further evidence is provided by comments in Whyte's study of leadership in a street gang [26] and Neustadt's study of three U.S. presidents [21]. (Reference is made to these findings where appropriate.) Thus, although most of the illustrations are drawn from my study of chief executives, there is some justification in asking the reader to consider when he sees the terms "manager" and his "organization" not only "presidents" and their "companies," but also "foremen" and their "shops," "directors" and their "branches," "vice presidents" and their "divisions." The term *manager* shall be used with reference to all those people in charge of formal organizations or their subunits.

SOME CHARACTERISTICS OF MANAGERIAL WORK

Six sets of characteristics of managerial work derive from analysis of the data of this study. Each has a significant bearing on the manager's ability to administer a complex organization.

Characteristic 1. The Manager Performs a Great Quantity of Work at an Unrelenting Pace

Despite a semblance of normal working hours, in truth managerial work appears to be very taxing. The five men in this study processed an average of 36 pieces of mail each day, participated in eight meetings (half of which were scheduled), engaged in five telephone calls, and took one tour. In his study of foremen, Guest [11] found that the number of activities per day averaged 583, with no real break in the pace.

Free time appears to be very rare. If by chance a manager has caught up with the mail, satisfied the callers, dealt with all the disturbances, and avoided scheduled meetings, a subordinate will likely show up to usurp the available time. It seems that the manager cannot expect to have much time for leisurely reflection during office hours. During "off" hours, our chief executives spent much time on work-related reading. High-level managers appear to be able to escape neither from an environment which recognizes the power and status of their positions nor from their own minds which have been trained to search continually for new information.

Characteristic 2. Managerial Activity Is Characterized by Variety, Fragmentation, and Brevity

There seems to be no pattern to managerial activity. Rather, variety and fragmentation appear to be characteristic, as successive activities deal with issues that differ greatly both in type and in content. In effect the manager must be prepared to shift moods quickly and frequently.

A typical chief executive day may begin with a telephone call from a director who asks a favor (a "status request"); then a subordinate calls to tell of a strike at one of the facilities (fast movement of information, termed "instant communication"); this is followed by a relaxed scheduled event at which the manager speaks to a group of visiting dignitaries (ceremony); the manager returns to find a message from a major customer who is demanding the renegotiation of a contract (pressure); and so on. Throughout the day, the managers of our study encountered this great variety of activity. Most surprisingly, the significant activities were interspersed with the trivial in no particular pattern.

Furthermore, these managerial activities were characterized by their brevity. Half of all the activities studied lasted less than 9 minutes and only 10 percent exceeded one hour's duration. Guest's foremen averaged 48 seconds per activity, and Carlson [6] stressed that his chief executives were unable to work without frequent interruption.

In my own study of chief executives, I felt that the managers demonstrated a preference for tasks of short duration and encouraged interruption. Perhaps the manager becomes accustomed to variety, or perhaps the flow of "instant communication" cannot be delayed. A more plausible explanation might be that the manager becomes conditioned by his workload. He develops a sensitive appreciation for the opportunity cost of his own time. Also, he is aware of the ever-present assortment of obligations associated with his job—accumulations of mail that cannot be delayed, the callers that must be attended to, the meetings that require his participation. In other words, no matter what he is doing, the manager is plagued by what he must do and what he might do. Thus, the manager is forced to treat issues in an abrupt and superficial way.

Characteristic 3. Managers Prefer Issues That Are Current, Specific, and Ad Hoc

Ad hoc operating reports received more attention than did routine ones; current, uncertain information—gossip, speculation, hearsay—which flows quickly was preferred to historical, certain information; "instant communication" received first consideration; few contacts were held on a routine or "clocked" basis; almost all contacts concerned well-defined issues. The managerial environment is clearly one of stimulus-response. It breeds, not reflective planners, but adaptable information manipulators who prefer the live, concrete situation, men who demonstrate a marked action orientation.

Characteristic 4. The Manager Sits between His Organization and a Network of Contacts

In virtually every empirical study of managerial time allocation, it was reported that managers spent a surprisingly large amount of time in horizontal or lateral (nonline) communication. It is clear from this study and from that of Sayles [24] that the manager is surrounded by a diverse and complex web of contacts which serves as his self-designed external information system. Included in this web can be clients, associates and suppliers, outside staff experts, peers (managers of related or similar organizations), trade organizations, government officials, independents (those with no relevant organizational affiliation), and directors or superiors. (Among these, directors in this study and superiors in other studies did *not* stand out as particularly active individuals.)

The managers in this study received far more information than they emitted, much of it coming from contacts, and more from subordinates who acted as filters. Figuratively, the manager appears as the neck of an hour-glass, sifting information into his own organization from its environment.

Characteristic 5. The Manager Demonstrates a Strong Preference for the Verbal Media

The manger has five media at his command—mail (documented), telephone (purely verbal), unscheduled meeting (informal face-to-face), scheduled meeting (formal face-to-face), and tour (observational). Along with all the other empirical studies of work characteristics, I found a strong predominance of verbal forms of communication.

Mail. By all indications, managers dislike the documented form of communication. In this study, they gave cursory attention to such items as operating reports and periodicals. It was estimated that only 13 percent of the input mail was of specific and immediate use to the managers. Much of the rest dealt with formalities and provided general reference data. The managers studied initiated very little mail, only 25 pieces in the five weeks. The rest of the outgoing mail was sent in reaction to mail received—a reply to a request, an acknowledgment, some information forwarded to a part of the organization. The managers appeared to dislike this form of communication, perhaps because the mail is a relatively slow and tedious medium to use.

Telephone and Unscheduled Meetings. The less formal means of verbal communication—the telephone, a purely verbal form, and the unscheduled meeting, a face-to-face form—were used frequently (two-thirds of the contacts in the study) but for brief encounters (average duration of

6 and 12 minutes, respectively). They were used primarily to deliver requests and to transmit pressing information to those outsiders and subordinates who had informal relationships with the manager.

Scheduled Meetings.   These tended to be of long duration, averaging 68 minutes in this study and absorbing over half the managers' time. Such meetings provided the managers with their main opportunities to interact with large groups and to leave the confines of their own offices. Scheduled meetings were used when the participants were unfamiliar to the manager (e.g., students who request that he speak at a university), when a large quantity of information had to be transmitted (e.g., presentation of a report), when ceremony had to take place, and when complex strategy making or negotiation had to be undertaken. An important feature of the scheduled meeting was the incidental, but by no means irrelevant, information that flowed at the start and end of such meetings.

Tours.   Although the walking tour would appear to be a powerful tool for gaining information in an informal way, in this study tours accounted for only 3 percent of the managers' time.

In general, it can be concluded that the manager uses each medium for particular purposes. Nevertheless, where possible, he appears to gravitate to verbal media since these provide greater flexibility, require less effort, and bring faster response. It should be noted here that the manager does not leave the telephone or the meeting to get back to work. Rather, communication is his work, and these media are his tools. The operating work of the organization—producing a product, doing research, purchasing a part—appears to be undertaken infrequently by the senior manager. The manager's productive output must be measured in terms of information, a great part of which is transmitted verbally.

Characteristic 6. Despite the Preponderance of Obligations, the Manager Appears to Be Able to Control His Own Affairs

Carlson suggested in his study of Swedish chief executives that these men were puppets, with little control over their own affairs. A cursory examination of our data indicates that this is true. Our managers were responsible for the initiation of only 32 percent of their verbal contacts and a smaller proportion of their mail. Activities were also classified as to the nature of the managers' participation, and the active ones were outnumbered by the passive ones (e.g., making requests versus receiving requests). On the surface, the manager is indeed a puppet, answering requests in the mail, returning telephone calls, attending meetings initiated by others, yielding to subordinates' requests for time, reacting to crises.

However, such a view is misleading. There is evidence that the senior manager can exert control over his own affairs in two significant ways: (1) It is he who defines many of his own long-term commitments by developing appropriate information channels which later feed him information, by initiating projects which later demand his time, by joining committees or outside boards which provide contacts in return for his services, and so on. (2) The manager can exploit situations that appear as obligations. He can lobby at ceremonial speeches; he can impose his values on his organization when his authorization is requested; he can motivate his subordinates whenever he interacts with them; he can use the crisis situation as an opportunity to innovate.

Perhaps these are two points that help distinguish successful and unsuccessful managers. All managers appear to be puppets. Some decide who will pull the strings and how, and they then take advantage of each move that they are forced to make. Others, unable to exploit this high-tension environment, are swallowed up by this most demanding of jobs.

THE MANAGER'S WORK ROLES

In describing the essential content of managerial work, one should aim to model managerial activity, that is, to describe it as a set of programs. But an undertaking as complex as this must be preceded by the development of a useful typological description of managerial work. In other words, we must first understand the distinct components of managerial work. At the present time we do not.

In this study, 890 pieces of mail and 368 verbal contacts were categorized as to purpose. The incoming mail was found to carry acknowledgments, requests and solicitations of various kinds, reference data, news, analytical reports, reports on events and on operations, advice on various situations, and statements of problems, pressures, and ideas. In reacting to mail, the managers acknowledged some, replied to the requests (e.g., by sending information), and forwarded much to subordinates (usually for their information). Verbal contacts involved a variety of purposes. In 15 percent of them activities were scheduled, in 6 percent ceremonial events took place, and a few involved external board work. About 34 percent involved requests of various kinds, some insignificant, some for information, some for authorization of proposed actions. Another 36 percent essentially involved the flow of information to and from the manager, while the remainder dealt specifically with issues of strategy and with negotiations. (For details, see [19].)

In this study, each piece of mail and verbal contact categorized in this way was subjected to one question: Why did the manager do this? The answers were collected and grouped and regrouped in various ways (over the course of three years) until a typology emerged that was felt to be satisfactory. While an example, presented below, will partially explain this process to the reader, it must be remembered that (in the words of Bronowski [3, p. 62]): "Every induction is a speculation and it guesses at a unity which the facts present but do not strictly imply."

Consider the following sequence of two episodes: A chief executive attends a meeting of an external board on which he sits. Upon his return to his organization, he immediately goes to the office of a subordinate, tells of a conversation he had with a fellow board member, and concludes with the statement: "It looks like we shall get the contract."

The purposes of these two contacts are clear—to attend an external board meeting and to give current information (instant communication) to a subordinate. But why did the manager attend the meeting? Indeed, why does he belong to the board? And why did he give this particular information to his subordinate?

Basing analysis on this incident, one can argue as follows: The manager belongs to the board in part so that he can be exposed to special information which is of use to his organization. The subordinate needs the information but has not the status which would give him access to it. The chief executive does. Board memberships bring chief executives in contact with one another for the purpose of trading information.

Two aspects of managerial work emerge from this brief analysis. The manager serves in a "liaison" capacity because of the status of his office, and what he learns here enables him to act as "disseminator" of information into his organization. We refer to these as *roles*—organized sets of behaviors belonging to identifiable offices or positions [23]. Ten roles were chosen to capture all the activities observed during his study.

All activities were found to involve one or more of three basic behaviors —interpersonal contact, the processing of information, and the making of decisions. As a result, our ten roles are divided into three corresponding groups. Three roles—labeled *figurehead, liaison,* and *leader*—deal with behavior that is essentially interpersonal in nature. Three others—*nerve center, disseminator,* and *spokesman*—deal with information-processing activities performed by the manager. And the remaining four—*entrepreneur, disturbance handler, resource allocator,* and *negotiator*—cover the decision-making activities of the manager. We describe each of these roles in turn, asking the reader to note that they form a *gestalt,* a unified whole whose parts cannot be considered in isolation.

The Interpersonal Roles

Three roles relate to the manager's behavior that focuses on interpersonal contact. These roles derive directly from the authority and status associated with holding managerial office.

Figurehead.   As legal authority in his organization, the manager is a symbol, obliged to perform a number of duties. He must preside at ceremonial events, sign legal documents, receive visitors, make himself available to many of those who feel, in the words of one of the men studied, "that the only way to get something done is to get to the top." There is evidence that this role applies at other levels as well. Davis [7, pp. 43–44] cites the case of the field sales manager who must deal with those customers who believe that their accounts deserve his attention.

Leader.   Leadership is the most widely recognized of managerial roles. It describes the manager's relationship with his subordinates—his attempts to motivate them and his development of the milieu in which they work. Leadership actions pervade all activity—in contrast to most roles, it is possible to designate only a few activities as dealing exclusively with leadership (these mostly related to staffing duties). Each time a manager encourages a subordinate, or meddles in his affairs, or replies to one of his requests, he is playing the *leader* role. Subordinates seek out and react to the leadership clues, and, as a result, they impart significant power to the manager.

Liaison. As noted earlier, the empirical studies have emphasized the importance of lateral or horizontal communication in the work of managers at all levels. It is clear from our study that this is explained largely in terms of the *liaison* role. The manager establishes his network of contacts essentially to bring information and favors to his organization. As Sayles notes in his study of production supervisors [24, p. 258], "The one enduring objective [of the manager] is the effort to build and maintain a predictable, reciprocating system of relationships. . . ."

Making use of his status, the manager interacts with a variety of peers and other people outside his organization. He provides time, information, and favors in return for the same from others. Foremen deal with staff groups and other foremen; chief executives join boards of directors and maintain extensive networks of individual relationships. Neustadt notes this behavior in analyzing the work of President Roosevelt [21, p. 150]:

> His personal sources were the product of a sociability and curiosity that reached back to the other Roosevelt's time. He had an enormous acquaintance in various phases of national life and at various levels of government; he also had his wife and her variety of contacts. He extended his acquaintanceships abroad; in the war years Winston Churchill, among others, become a "personal source." Roosevelt quite deliberately exploited these relationships and mixed them up to widen his own range of information. He changed his sources as his interests changed, but no one who had ever interested him was quite forgotten or immune to sudden use.

The Informational Roles

A second set of managerial activities relates primarily to the processing of information. Together they suggest three significant managerial roles, one describing the manager as a focal point for a certain kind of organizational information, the other two describing relatively simple transmission of this information.

Nerve Center. There is indication, both from this study and from those by Neustadt and Whyte, that the manager serves as the focal point in his organization for the movement of nonroutine information. Homans, who analyzed Whyte's study, draws the following conclusions [14, p. 187]:

> Since interaction flowed toward [the leaders], they were better informed about the problems and desires of group members than were any of the followers and therefore better able to decide on an appropriate course of action. Since they were in close touch with other gang leaders, they were also better informed than their followers about conditions in Cornerville at large. Moreover, in their positions at the focus of the chains of interaction, they were better able than any follower to pass on to the group decisions that had been reached.

The term *nerve center* is chosen to encompass those many activities in which the manager receives information.

Within his own organization, the manager has legal authority that formally connects him—and only him—to *every* member. Hence, the manager emerges as *nerve center* of internal information. He may not know as much about any one function as the subordinate who specializes in it, but he comes to know more about his total organization than any other member. He is the information generalist. Furthermore, because of the manager's status and its manifestation in the *liaison* role, the manager gains unique access to a variety of knowledgeable outsiders including peers who are themselves *nerve centers* of their own organizations. Hence, the manager emerges as his organization's *nerve center* of external information as well.

As noted earlier, the manager's nerve center information is of a special kind. He appears to find it most important to get his information quickly and informally. As a result, he will not hesitate to by pass formal information channels to get it, and he is prepared to deal with a large amount of gossip, hearsay, and opinion which has not yet become substantial fact.

Disseminator. Much of the manager's information must be transmitted to subordinates. Some of this is of a *factual* nature, received from outside the organization or from other subordinates. And some is of a *value* nature. Here, the manager acts as the mechanism by which organizational influencers (owners, governments, employee groups, the general public, and the like, or simply the "boss") makes their preferences known to the organization. It is the manager's duty to integrate these value positions and to express general organizational preferences as a guide to decision made by subordinates. One of the men studied commented: "One of the principal functions of this position is to integrate the hospital interests with the public interests." Papandreou describes his duty in a paper published in 1952, referring to management as the "peak coordinator" [22].

Spokesman. In his *spokesman* role, the manager is obliged to transmit his information to outsiders. He informs influencers and other interested parties about his organization's performance, its policies, and its plans. Furthermore, he is expected to serve outside his organization as an expert in its industry. Hospital administrators are expected to spend some time serving outside as public experts on health, and corporation presidents, perhaps as chamber of commerce executives.

The Decisional Roles   The manager's legal authority requires that he assume responsibility for all of his organization's important actions. The *nerve center* role suggests that only he can fully understand complex decisions, particularly those involving difficult value trade-offs. As a result, the manager emerges as the key figure in the making and interrelating of all significant decisions in his organization, a process that can be referred to as *strategy making*. Four roles describe the manager's control over the strategy-making system in his organization.

Entrepreneur. The *entrepreneur* role describes the manager as initiator and designer of much of the controlled change in his organization. The manager looks for opportunities and potential problems which may cause him to initiate action. Action takes the form of *improvement projects*

—the marketing of a new product, the strengthening of a weak department, the purchasing of new equipment, the reorganization of formal structure, and so on.

The manager can involve himself in each improvement project in one of three ways: (1) He may *delegate* all responsibility for its design and approval, implicitly retaining the right to replace that subordinate who takes charge of it. (2) He may delegate the design work to a subordinate, but retain the right to *approve* it before implementation. (3) He may actively *supervise* the design work himself.

Improvement projects exhibit a number of interesting characteristics. They appear to involve a number of subdecisions, consciously sequenced over long periods of time and separated by delays of various kinds. Furthermore, the manager appears to supervise a great many of these at any one time—perhaps 50 to 100 in the case of chief executives. In fact, in his handling of improvement projects, the manager may be likened to a juggler. At any one point, he maintains a number of balls in the air. Periodically, one comes down, receives a short burst of energy, and goes up again. Meanwhile, an inventory of new balls waits on the sidelines and, at random intervals, old balls are discarded and new ones added. Both Lindblom [2] and Marples [18] touch on these aspects of strategy making, the former stressing the disjointed and incremental nature of the decisions, and the latter depicting the sequential episodes in terms of a stranded rope made up of fibres of different lengths each of which surfaces periodically.

Disturbance Handler.   While the *entrepreneur* role focuses on voluntary change, the *disturbance handler* role deals with corrections which the manager is forced to make. We may describe this role as follows: The organization consists basically of specialist operating programs. From time to time, it experiences a stimulus that cannot be handled routinely, either because an operating program has broken down or because the stimulus is new and it is not clear which operating program should handle it. These situations constitute disturbances. As generalist, the manager is obliged to assume responsibility for dealing with the stimulus. Thus, the handling of disturbances is an essential duty of the manager.

There is clear evidence for this role both in our study of chief executives and in Sayles study of production supervisors [24, p. 162]:

> The achievement of this stability, which is the manager's objective, is a never-to-be-attained ideal. He is like a symphony orchestra conductor, endeavoring to maintain a melodious performance in which contributions of the various instruments are coordinated and sequenced, patterned and paced, while the orchestra members are having various personal difficulties, stage hands are moving music stands, alternating excessive heat and cold are creating audience and instrument problems, and the sponsor of the concert is insisting on irrational changes in the program.

Sayles goes further to point out the very important balance that the manager must maintain between change and stability. To Sayles, the manager seeks "a dynamic type of stability" (p. 162). Most disturbances elicit short-term adjustments which bring back equilibrium; persistent ones require the introduction of long-term structural change.

Resource Allocator. The manager maintains ultimate authority over his organization's strategy-making system by controlling the allocation of its resources. By deciding who will get what (and who will do what), the manager directs the course of his organization. He does this in three ways:

1. *In selecting his own time,* the manager allocates his most precious resource and thereby determines organizational priorities. Issues that receive low priority do not reach the *nerve center* of the organization and are blocked for want of resources.

2. In designing the organizational structure and in carrying out many improvement projects, the manager *programs the work of his subordinates.* In other words, he allocates their time by deciding what will be done and who will do it.

3. Most significantly, the manager maintains control over resource allocation by the requirement that he *authorize all significant decisions* before they are implemented. By retaining this power, the manager ensures that different decisions are interrelated—that conflicts are avoided, that resource constraints are respected and that decisions complement one another.

Decisions appear to be authorized in one of two ways. Where the costs and benefits of a proposal can be quantified, where it is competing for specified resources with other known proposals, and where it can wait for a certain time of year, approval for a proposal is sought in the context of a formal *budgeting* procedure. But these conditions are most often not met—timing may be crucial, nonmonetary costs may predominate, and so on. In these cases, approval is sought in terms of an *ad hoc request for authorization.* Subordinate and manager meet (perhaps informally) to discuss one proposal alone.

Authorization choices are enormously complex ones for the manager. A myriad of factors must be considered (resource constraints, influencer preferences, consistency with other decisions, feasibility, payoff, timing, subordinate feelings, and so on). But the fact that the manager is authorizing the decision rather than supervising its design suggests that he has little time to give to it. To alleviate this difficulty, it appears that managers use special kinds of *models* and *plans* in their decision making. These exist only in their minds and are loose, but they serve to guide behavior. Models may answer questions such as, "Does this proposal make sense in terms of the trends that I see in tariff legislation?" or "Will the EDP department be able to get along with marketing on this?" Plans exist in the sense that, on questioning, managers reveal images (in terms of proposed improvement projects) of where they would like their organizations to go: "Well, once I get these foreign operations fully developed, I would like to begin to look into a reorganization," said one subject of this study.

Negotiator. The final role describes the manager as participant in negotiation activity. To some students of the management process [8, p. 343], this is not truly part of the job of managing. But such distinctions are arbitrary. Negotiation is an integral part of managerial work, as this study notes for chief executives and as that of Sayles made very clear for production supervisors [24, p. 131]: "Sophisticated managers place great stress on negotiations as a way of life. They negotiate with groups who are setting standards for their work, who are performing support activity for them, and to whom they wish to 'sell' their services."

The manager must participate in important negotiation sessions because he is his organization's legal authority, its *spokesman,* and its *resource allocator.* Negotiation is resource trading in real time. If the resource commitments are to be large, the legal authority must be present.

These ten roles suggest that the manager of an organization bears a great burden of responsibility. He must oversee his organization's status system; he must serve as a crucial informational link between it and its environment; he must interpret and reflect its basic values; he must maintain the stability of its operations; and he must adapt it in a controlled and balanced way to a changing environment.

MANAGEMENT AS A PROFESSION AND AS A SCIENCE

Is management a profession? To the extent that different managers perform one set of basic roles, management satisfies one criterion for becoming a profession. But a profession must require, in the words of the *Random House Dictionary,* "knowledge of some department of learning or science." Which of the 10 roles now requires specialized learning? Indeed, what school of business or public administration teaches its students how to disseminate information, allocate resources, perform as figurehead, make contacts, or handle disturbances? We simply know very little about teaching these things. The reason is that we have never tried to document and describe in a meaningful way the procedures (or programs) that managers use.

The evidence of this research suggests that there is as yet no science in managerial work—that managers do not work according to procedures that have been prescribed by scientific analysis. Indeed, except for his use of the telephone, the airplane, and the dictating machine, it would appear that the manager of today is indistinguishable from his predecessors. He may seek different information, but he gets much of it in the same way—from word-of-mouth. He may make decisions dealing with modern technology but he uses the same intuitive (that is, nonexplicit) procedures in making them. Even the computer, which has had such a great impact on other kinds of organizational work, has apparently done little to alter the working methods of the general manager.

How do we develop a scientific base to understand the work of the manager? The description of roles is a first and necessary step. But tighter forms of research are necessary. Specifically, we must attempt to model managerial work—to describe it as a system of programs. First, it will be necessary to decide what programs managers actually use. Among a great number of programs in the manager's repertoire, we might expect to find a time-scheduling program, an information-disseminating program, and a disturbance-handling program. Then, researchers will have to devote a considerable amount of effort to studying and accurately describing the content of each of these programs—the information and heuristics used. Finally, it will be necessary to describe the interrelationships among all of these programs so that they may be combined into an integrated descriptive model of managerial work.

When the management scientist begins to understand the programs that managers use, he can begin to design meaningful systems and provide help for the manager. He may ask: Which managerial activities can be fully reprogrammed (i.e., automated)? Which cannot be reprogrammed because they require human responses? Which can be partially reprogrammed to operate in a man-machine system? Perhaps scheduling, information-collecting, and resource-allocating activities lend themselves to varying degrees of reprogramming. Management will emerge as a science to the extent that such efforts are successful.

IMPROVING THE MANAGER'S EFFECTIVENESS

Fayol's 50-year-old description of managerial work is no longer of use to us. And we shall not disentangle the complexity of managerial work if we insist on viewing the manager simply as a decision maker or simply as a motivator of subordinates. In fact, we are unlikely to overestimate the complexity of the manager's work, and we shall make little headway if we take over simple or narrow points of view in our research.

A major problem faces today's manager. Despite the growing size of modern organizations and the growing complexity of their problems (particularly those in the public sector), the manager can expect little help. He must design his own information system, and he must take full charge of his organization's strategy-making system. Furthermore, the manager faces what might be called the *dilemma of delegation*. He has unique access to much important information, but he lacks a formal means of disseminating it. As much of it is verbal, he cannot spread it around in an efficient manner. How can he delegate a task with confidence when he has neither the time nor the means to send the necessary information along with it?

Thus, the manager is usually forced to carry a great burden of responsibility in his organization. As organizations become increasingly large and complex, this burden increases. Unfortunately, the man cannot significantly increase his available time or significantly improve his abilities to manage. Hence, in the large, complex bureaucracy, the top manager's time assumes an enormous opportunity cost, and he faces the real danger of becoming a major obstruction in the flow of decisions and information.

Because of this, as we have seen, managerial work assumes a number of distinctive characteristics. The quantity of work is great; the pace is unrelenting; there is great variety, fragmentation, and brevity in the work activities; the manager must concentrate on issues that are current, specific, and ad hoc, and to do so, he finds that he must rely on verbal forms of communications. Yet it is on this man that the burden lies for designing and operating strategy-making and information-processing systems that are to solve his organization's (and society's) problems.

The manager can do something to alleviate these problems. He can learn more about his own roles in his organization, and he can use this information to schedule his time in a more efficient manner. He can recognize that only he has much of the information needed by his organization. Then, he can seek to find better means of disseminating it into the organization. Finally, he can turn to the skills of his management scientists to help reduce his workload and to improve his ability to make decisions.

The management scientist can learn to help the manager to the extent he can develop an understanding of the manager's work and the manager's information. To date, strategic planners, operations researchers, and information system designers have provided little help for the senior manager. They simply have had no framework available by which to understand the work of the men who employed them, and they have had poor access to the information which has never been documented. It is folly to believe that a man with poor access to the organization's true *nerve center* can design a formal management information system. Similarly, how can the long-range planner, a man usually uninformed about many of the *current* events that take place in and around his organization, design meaningful strategic plans? For good reason, the literature documents many manager complaints of naïve planning and many planner complaints of disinterested managers. In my view, our lack of understanding of managerial work has been the greatest block to the progress of management science.

The ultimate solution to the problem—to the overburdened manager seeking meaningful help—must derive from research. We must observe, describe, and understand the real work of managing; then and only then shall we significantly improve it.

REFERENCES

1. Braybrooke, David. "The Mystery of Executive Success Re-examined." *Administrative Science Quarterly* 8 (1964): 533–60.

2. Braybrooke, David, and Charles E. Lindblom. *A Strategy of Decision.* New York: Free Press, 1963.

3. Bronowski, J. "The Creative Process." *Scientific American,* September 1958, pp. 59–65.

4. Burns, Tom. "The Directions of Activity and Communications in a Departmental Executive Group." *Human Relations* 7 (1954): 73–97.

5. Burns, Tom. "Management in Action." *Operational Research Quarterly* 8 (1957): 45–60.

6. Carlson, Sune. *Executive Behavior.* Stockholm: Strömbergs, 1951.

7. Davis, Robert T. *Performance and Development of Field Sales Managers.*

Boston: Division of Research, Graduate School of Business Administration, Harvard University, 1957.

8. Drucker, Peter F. *The Practice of Management.* New York: Harper & Row, 1954.

9. Fayol, Henri. *Administration industrielle et générale.* Paris: Dunods, 1950 (first published 1916).

10. Gibb, Cecil A. "Leadership." *The Handbook of Social Psychology.* 2d ed., edited by Gardner Lindzey and Elliott A. Aronson. Reading, Mass.: Addison-Wesley, 1969, vol. 4, chap. 31.

11. Guest, Robert H. "Of Time and the Foreman." *Personnel* 32 (1955–56): 478–86.

12. Gulick, Luther H. "Notes on the Theory of Organization." In *Papers on the Science of Administration,* edited by Luther Gulick and Lyndall Urwick. New York: Columbia University Press, 1937.

13. Hemphill, John K. *Dimensions of Executive Positions.* Columbus: Bureau of Business Research Monograph on Number 98, The Ohio State University, 1960.

14. Homans, George C. *The Human Group.* New York: Harcourt Brace Jovanovich, 1950.

15. Horne, J. H., and Tom Lupton. "The Work Activities of Middle Managers—An Exploratory Study." *The Journal of Management Studies,* February 1965, pp. 14–33.

16. Kelly, Joe. "The Study of Executive Behavior by Activity Sampling." *Human Relations,* August 1964, pp. 277–87.

17. Mackenzie, R. Alex. "The Management Process in 3D." *Harvard Business Review,* November–December 1969, pp. 80–87.

18. Marples, D. L. "Studies of Managers—A Fresh Start?" *The Journal of Management Studies,* October 1967, pp. 282–99.

19. Mintzberg, Henry. "Structured Observation as a Method to Study Managerial Work." *The Journal of Management Studies,* February 1970, pp. 87–104.

20. Myers, Charles A., ed. *The Impact of Computers on Management.* Cambridge, Mass.: The MIT Press, 1967.

21. Neustadt, Richard E. *Presidential Power: The Politics of Leadership.* New York: New American Library, 1964.

22. Papandreou, Andreas G. "Some Basic Problems in the Theory of the Firm." In *A Survey of Contemporary Economics,* Vol. II, edited by Bernard F. Haley. Homewood, Ill.: Richard D. Irwin, 1952, pp. 183–219.

23. Sarbin, T. R. and V. L. Allen. "Role Theory." In *The Handbook of Social Psychology,* Vol. I, 2d ed., edited by Elliott A. Aronson. Reading, Mass.: Addison-Wesley, 1968, pp. 488–567.

24. Sayles, Leonard R. *Managerial Behavior: Administration in Complex Enterprises.* New York: McGraw-Hill, 1964.

25. Stewart, Rosemary. *Managers and Their Jobs,* London: Macmillan, 1967.

26. Whyte, William F. *Street Corner Society.* 2d ed. Chicago: University of Chicago Press, 1955.

Part II

BEHAVIOR WITHIN ORGANIZATIONS: INDIVIDUALS

Attempts are continually being made by psychologists, social psychologists, sociologists, and anthropologists to understand human behavior. Administrators and entrepreneurs want to know what caused a person to behave in a particular way. Theory and research have provided managers with some general knowledge about behavior that can be used in real-world situations.

It is generally agreed that behavior is the product of two things: the nature of the individual who behaves and the nature of the situation in which individuals find themselves. The nature of an individual depends on heredity, group affiliations, culture, and the situations that a person has faced throughout life. These different background factors cause differences in perceptions, attitudes, motivations, and personalities.

The psychologist advances the premise that there is a causal sequence of behavior that a manager should understand. This sequence is briefly presented in Figure 1.

Figure 1
Psychological View of a Causal Sequence of Behavior

Stimulus ⟵⟶	Individual ⟶	Behavioral ⟶ Pattern	Goal Achievement
a. Action of managers or informal leaders	a. Heredity	a. Talking	a. Productivity
b. Climate of the unit	b. Cultural background	b. Expressions	b. Absenteeism
c. Group pressures	c. Situation	c. Thinking	c. Quitting
d. Working conditions	d. Group membership		

The double-headed arrows in Figure 1 indicate that the individual interacts with the environment and interprets the various stimuli. Thus, in order to explain behavior, one must be concerned with the stimuli as well as the individual.

This part concentrates upon the stimulus-individual interaction, as well as the behavior and goal achievement which results from this interaction. Specifically, three major organizational concepts are analyzed in the selected readings—motivation, groups, and leadership. These three facets of organizational life in businesses, hospitals, schools, and government agencies are stimuli that definitely interact with individuals and result in various levels of goal achievement.

The first article examines individual differences. In the article "The Individual Organization: Problems and Promise," Edward E. Lawler, III examines the notion of individual differences and how organizations respond to them. The differences among people are viewed in terms of pay systems, leadership, training, selection, and structuring jobs. It is Lawler's contention that the research on individual differences indicates that the shaping of organizations to people should be developed and tested.

John Senger in "Seeing Eye to Eye: Practical Problems of Perceptions" emphasizes that people do not see things alike. These perceptual differences can mislead and result in problems for any manager. Examples of perceptual problems are highlighted in the article.

The next article by Zick Rubin is entitled "Does Personality Change after 20?" Rubin raises the issue of personality change in adulthood—is it fact or fiction? The stability or instability of personality is widely debated in the literature. Rubin's belief is that personality may change depending on a person's own ideas about what is possible and about what is valuable.

Donald F. Roy in "Banana Time: Job Satisfaction and Informal Interaction" describes the social interaction which took place in a small work group in a factory. Some of the mysteries about the influence of the small group are presented in an interesting fashion.

Larry E. Pate presents an article entitled "Cognitive versus Reinforcement Views of Intrinsic Motivation." In the article Pate discusses cognitive and reinforcement in terms of intrinsic motivation. He also presents some implications and potential areas of application of these views of intrinsic motivation.

Goal setting is currently a widely cited and practical approach in organizations. Gary P. Latham and Edwin A. Locke conclude in "Goal Setting—A Motivational Technique That Works" that managers could benefit from the use of goal-setting practices. They first introduce the goal-setting concept and some related research. Production, absenteeism, and accidents all seem to be positively influenced by goal setting.

Frederick B. Mickel introduces dramatically a real example of stress-related problems—his heart attack. Mickel in "Stress: Race to the Bottom Line" clearly discusses the notion of stress, Type A behavior, and occupationl factors that are stress related. His own story is interesting reading and food for thought.

In another stress article entitled "Can Companies Kill?" Berkeley Rice discusses legal cases against employers. Is an employer legally implicated in psychiatric injury to employees? This is today becoming a major new area of organizational concern. In California alone there are now 3,000 to 4,000 claims for psychiatric injury each year. Rice proposes that emotional security guarantees may become a reality in organizations in the future.

The Individual Organization:
Problems and Promise*

EDWARD E. LAWLER, III

Two easily identified and distinctly different approaches to the study of behavior in organizations have dominated the organizational behavior literature for the past half century. One emphasizes the differences among people, the other the similarities.

The first and least dominant approach has its foundation in differential psychology and is concerned with the study of individual differences. The basic assumptions underlying this approach are that people differ in their needs, skills, and abilities; that these differences can be measured; that valid data about people's competence and motivation can be obtained by organizations; and that these data can be used to make organizations more effective.

When behavioral scientists who take this approach look at organizations, they tend to see selection and placement. Their concern is with selecting those people who are right for a given job by measuring the characteristics of both the people and jobs and then trying to achieve the best fit. Their paradigm of the ideal organization would seem to be one where everyone has the ability and motivation to do the job to which he is assigned. Rarely do behavioral scientists with this orientation try to change the design of jobs or of organizations. Jobs are taken as a given and the focus is on finding the right people for them. Where efforts at job redesign have been made, they typically are instituted in the tradition of human engineering. That is, jobs have been made simpler so that more people can do them.

What is needed if this approach is to work?

1. People must differ in meaningful ways.
2. Valid data about the characteristics of people must exist.
3. People who are suited for the jobs must apply.

---

* Copyright 1974 by the Regents of the University of California. Reprinted from *California Management Review* 16, no. 4, pp. 31–39.

4. A favorable selection ratio must exist (a large number of qualified applicants must apply for the job).

The second approach has generally assumed that all employees in an organization are similar in many ways and that certain general rules or principles can and should be developed for the design of organizations. It is universalistic, propounding that there is a right way to deal with all people in organizations. This type of thinking is present in the work of such traditional organization theorists as Urwick and Taylor. It is also present in the writings of human relations theorists such as Mayo and in the work of the human resource theorists such as McGregor and Likert. As John Morse notes, all these approaches contain either implicitly or explicitly the assumption that there is a right way to manage people.[1]

Douglas McGregor's discussion of Theory X and Theory Y points out that, although scientific management and the more modern theories make different assumptions about the nature of man, both emphasize the similarities among people rather than the differences.[2] Based upon the Theory Y view of the nature of people, McGregor develops a normative organization theory that, like, Theory X, stresses universal principles of management. For any of the universality theories to be generally valid, a certain type of person must populate society: one that fits its assumptions about the nature of people. In the case of the human resource theorists, this universal person will respond favorably to such things as enriched jobs, participative leadership, and interpersonal relationships characterized by openness, trust, and leveling. For the scientific management theorists, the universal type responds well to the use of financial rewards and the simplification of work. Thus, the validity of these theories rests upon the correctness of the assumptions about the nature of people.

The work of those behavioral scientists who are concerned with individual differences suggests that the assumptions of all the universal theorists are dangerous oversimplifications for one very important reason: They fail to acknowledge the significant differences (in needs, personalities, and abilities) that cause individuals to react differently to organization practices concerned with job design, pay systems, leadership, training, and selection. Although many studies of individual behavior in organizations have not looked for individual differences, there are some that have found significant diversities. They are worth reviewing briefly since they clearly illustrate what is wrong with all organization theories which make universal assumptions about the nature of people.

JOB DESIGN

Job enrichment is one of the key ideas in most of the recent human resource theories of organization. According to the argument presented by

---

[1] John J. Morse, "A Contingency Look at Job Design," *California Management Review,* Fall 1973, pp. 67–75.

[2] Douglas McGregor, *The Human Side of Enterprise* (New York: McGraw-Hill, 1960).

Frederick Herzberg and others, job enrichment can lead to appreciable increases in employee motivation, performance, and satisfaction.[3] In fact, there is a fairly large body of evidence to support this view.[4]

There is, however, also a considerable amount of evidence that all individuals do not respond to job enrichment with higher satisfaction, productivity, and quality. In many studies the researchers have not been concerned with explaining these individual differences and have treated them as error variance. In others, however, attempts have been made to find out what distinguishes those people who respond positively to job enrichment. It has been pointed out that the type of background a person comes from may be related to how he or she responds to an enriched job.[5] According to some analyses, employees from rural backgrounds are more likely to respond positively to enrichment than are workers from urban environments.

More recent findings have shown that individual differences in need strength determine how people respond to jobs; the reason previous researchers have found urban-rural differences to be important lies in the kind of needs that people from these backgrounds have.[6] Rural background people have stronger higher-order needs (self-actualization, competence, self-esteem), and people with these needs respond positively to job enrichment, while those who don't fail to respond. It is argued that job enrichment creates conditions under which people can experience growth and self-esteem, motivating them to perform well. Clearly, for those employees who do not want to experience competence and growth, the opportunity to experience them will not be motivating, and not everyone should be expected to respond well to enriched jobs.[7]

PAY SYSTEMS

The scientific management philosophy strongly emphasizes the potential usefulness of pay as a motivator as in many piece rate, bonus, profit-sharing, and other pay incentive plans. There is abundant evidence to support the point that, when pay is tied to performance, motivation and performance are increased.[8] However, there is also evidence to indicate that not everyone responds to pay incentive plans by performing better. In one study, certain

---

3 Frederick Herzberg, *Work and the Nature of Man* (Cleveland: World, 1966).

4 Robert Blauner, *Alienation and Freedom* (Chicago: University of Chicago, 1964); and Edward E. Lawler, "Job Design and Employee Motivation," *Personnel Psychology* 22 (1969): 426–35.

5 Arthur Turner and Paul R. Lawrence, *Industrial Jobs and the Worker* (Boston: Division of Research, Harvard Business School, 1965); and Charles L. Hulin and Milton R. Blood, "Job Enlargement, Individual Differences, and Worker Responses," *Psychological Bulletin* 69 (1968): 41–55.

6 J. Richard Hackman and Edward E. Lawler, "Employee Reactions to Job Characteristics," *Journal of Applied Psychology* 55 (1971): 259–86.

7 John J. Morse, "A Contingency Look at Job Design."

8 Edward E. Lawler, *Pay and Organizational Effectiveness: A Psychological View* (New York: McGraw-Hill, 1971).

types of employees responded to a piece rate incentive system while others did not.[9] Who responded? Workers from rural backgrounds who owned their homes, were Protestants, and social isolates—workers who, in short, saw money as a way of getting what they wanted and for whom social relations were not highly important.

There are many different kinds of pay incentive systems; and the kind of pay system that will motivate one person often does not motivate others. For example, group plans apparently work best with people who have strong social needs.[10] This suggests that not only do the members of an organization have to be treated differently according to whether they will or will not respond to a pay incentive, but that those who will respond to pay systems may have to be subdivided according to the type of system to which they will respond.

There is abundant evidence that individuals differ in their responses to the fringe benefits they receive. Large differences, determined by such things as age, marital status, education, and so on, exist among individuals in the kind of benefits they want and need.[11] Most organizations ignore this and give everyone the same benefits, thereby often giving high cost benefits to people who do not want them. Maximizing individual satisfaction with fringe benefits would require a unique plan for each employee.

LEADERSHIP

Research on leadership style during the past two decades has stressed the advantages that can be gained from the use of the various forms of power equalization. Participation, flat organizations, decentralization, and group decision making are all power equalization approaches to motivating and satisfying employees. There is a considerable body of evidence to suggest that power equalization can lead to higher subordinate satisfaction, greater subordinate motivation, and better decision making.[12] Unfortunately, much of this literature has only given brief mention to the fact that not all subordinates respond in the same way to power equalization and the fact that not all superiors can practice power equalization.

Victor Vroom was one of the first to point out that at least one type of subordinate does not respond positively to participative management.[13] His data show that subordinates who are high on the F-scale (a measure of authoritarianism) do not respond well when they are subordinates to a boss who is oriented toward participative management. Later studies have shown that at times the majority of the membership of a work group may

---

[9] William F. Whyte, *Money and Motivation* (New York: Harper, 1955).

[10] Edward E. Lawler, *Pay and Organizational Effectiveness.*

[11] Stanley Nealy, "Pay and Benefit Preferences," *Industrial Relations* 3 (1963): 17–28.

[12] Chris Argyris, "Personality and Organization Revisited," *Administrative Science Quarterly* 18 (1973): 141–67.

[13] Victor H. Vroom, *Some Personality Determinants of the Effects of Participation* (Englewood Cliffs, N.J.: Prentice-Hall, 1960).

not respond positively to power equalization efforts on the part of superiors.[14]

Many superiors cannot manage in a democratic manner.[15] This, combined with the poor responses of many employees to democratic management styles, raises the question of whether it is advisable even to think of encouraging most managers to lead in a democratic manner. Many superiors probably *cannot* adopt a democratic leadership style, and because of the likely responses of some of their subordinates they *shouldn't*— regardless of task and situational considerations.

TRAINING

To most modern organization theorists, training is an important element of organization design. It is particularly helpful in resolving individual differences. T-groups, managerial grid seminars, and leadership courses are some examples of the kinds of human relations training that organizations use. These training approaches help assure that most people in the organization have certain basic skills and abilities and that some valid assumptions about the capacity of the people in the organization can be made.

Once again, the problem is that the very individual employee differences greatly affect the ability to learn from things such as T-groups and managerial grid seminars; this type of training is simply wasted on many people.[16] In fact, the training may end up increasing the range of individual differences in an organization rather than reducing it. It is also likely that while one type of human relations training may not affect a person another type could have a significant impact. The same point can be made with respect to training people in the area of occupational skills. One person may learn best from a teaching machine while another learns the same material best from a lecture format.

SELECTION

In the work on selection the assumption has typically been made that people are sufficiently similar so that the same selection instruments can be used for everyone. Thus, all applicants for a job are often given the same battery of selection criteria—overlooking the fact that different instruments might work better as predictors for some groups than for others. This would not be a serious problem if individual difference factors were not related to the ability of the selection instruments to predict performance; but recent evidence suggests that they are. Certain kinds of tests

---

14 John R. P. French, J. Israel, and Dagfin As, "An Experiment on Participation in a Norwegian Factory," *Human Relations* 13 (1960): 3–19; and George Strauss, "Some Notes on Power Equalization," in *The Social Science of Organizations,* ed. H. J. Leavitt (Englewood Cliffs, N.J.: Prentice-Hall, 1963).

15 Frederick E. Fiedler, "Predicting the Effects of Leadership Training and Experience from the Contingency Model," *Journal of Applied Psychology* 56 (1972): 114–19.

16 John P. Campbell and Marvin D. Dunnette, "Effectiveness of T-Group Experiences in Managerial Training and Development," *Psychological Bulletin* 70 (1968): 73–104.

work better for some segments of the population than for others.[17] However, this uniformity in selection testing is not the only reason for poor job performance prediction.

Differential psychologists have developed numerous valid tests of people's ability to perform jobs, but they have failed to develop tests that measure how empolyees will fit into particular organizational climates and how motivated they will be in particular organizations. All too often they have tried to predict individual behavior in organizations without measuring the characteristics of the organization. Trying to predict behavior by looking only at personal characteristics must inevitably lead to predictions whose validity is questionable.

All this is beginning to change, but it is doubtful if highly accurate predictions will ever be obtained. The measurement problems are too great, and both organizations and people change too much. The research evidence also shows that people sometimes don't give valid data in selection situations and that some important determinants of individual behavior in organizations are difficult to measure.[18]

INDIVIDUAL DIFFERENCES

One clear implication of the research on individual differences is that for any of the universalistic theories to operate effectively in a given organization or situation one of two things must occur: either the organization must deal with the individuals it hires so that they will change to meet the assumptions of the theory, or it must hire only those individuals who fit the kind of system that the organization employs. Unfortunately, there is no solid evidence that individuals can be trained or dealt with in ways that will increase the degree to which they respond to such things as enriched jobs and democratic supervision. Proponents of job enrichment often stress that people will come to like it once they have tried it, but this point remains to be proven.

The validity of most selection instruments is so low that organizations should not count on finding instruments that will allow them to select only those who fit whatever system they use. There is always the prospect that the differential psychologist can develop appropriate measures and that this will lead to organizations being able to select more homogenous work forces. This, in turn, would allow approaches such as the human resources approach to be effectively utilized in some situations. However, it seems unlikely that they could ever be used in large complex organizations. Even if measures are developed, it may not be possible for large homogenous populations of workers to be selected by organizations. Effective selection depends on favorable selection ratios, which are rare, and on the legal ability of organizations to run selection programs. It is also obvious that

---

[17] Edwin E. Ghiselli, "Moderating Effects and Differential Reliability and Validity," *Journal of Applied Psychology* 47 (1963): 81–86.

[18] Robert M. Guion, *Personnel Testing* (New York: McGraw-Hill, 1965).

there has been and will continue to be a large influx into the labor market and into organizations of people from different socioeconomic backgrounds. This has and will continue to create more diversity rather than homogeneity in the work forces of most organizations, decreasing the likelihood that large organizations can ever be completely staffed by people who fit the assumptions of scientific management, Theory X, Theory Y, or any other organization theory that is based upon the view that people are similar in important ways.

Further, it soon may not be legally possible for organizations to conduct the kind of selection programs that will by themselves produce good individual-organization fits. The federal government restrictions on testing for selection purposes soon could create conditions under which testing will no longer be practical. Organizations may find themselves in a situation where they must randomly select from among the "qualified applicants" for a job. Thus, even if valid tests were developed, work forces probably could not be selected that would contain only people that fit either the human resources or the scientific management assumptions about people.

There is evidence in the literature that some organization theorists are moving away from the view that one style of management or one organization design is right for most organizations.[19] However, the focus so far has been on environmental variables, such as degree of uncertainty and stability, and production variables, such as whether the task is predictable and whether the product can be mass, process, or unit produced. The researchers point out that different structures and different management styles are appropriate under different conditions. Some of the evidence they present is persuasive: products and environmental factors need to be considered when organizations are being designed. However, they often fail to point out that the nature of the work force also needs to be considered and they fail to suggest organization structures that allow for the fact that the people in any organization will vary in their response to such things as tight controls, job enrichment, and so on.

What seems to be needed is an organization theory based upon assumptions like the following, which recognize the existence of differences among individuals:

1. Most individuals are goal oriented in their behavior, but there are large differences in the goals people pursue.
2. Individuals differ both in what they enjoy doing and in what they can do.
3. Some individuals need to be closely supervised while others can exercise high levels of self-control.

---

19 Joan Woodward, *Industrial Organization: Theory and Practice* (London: Oxford University Press, 1965); Paul R. Lawrence and Jay W. Lorsch, *Organization and Environment* (Boston: Division of Research, Harvard Business School, 1967); Chris Argyris, *Integrating the Individual and the Organization* (New York: John Wiley & Sons, 1964); and Tom Burns and G. M. Stalker, *The Management of Innovation* (London: Tavistock, 1961).

In order to design an organization based on these assumptions, it is necessary to utilize various normative theories as guides to how different members of the same organization should be treated. In addition measures of individual needs and abilities, like those developed by differential psychologists, are needed. As will become apparent, it probably also is necessary to depend on the ability of individuals to help make decisions about where and how they will work. In short, it requires a synthesis of the individual differences approach and the work of the organization theorists into a new paradigm of how organizations should be designed—a new paradigm that emphasizes structuring organizations so that they can better adapt themselves to the needs, desires, and abilities of their members.

STRUCTURING THE INDIVIDUALIZED ORGANIZATION

The research on job design, training, reward systems, and leadership provides a number of suggestions about what an organization designed on the basis of individual differences assumptions would look like. A brief review will help to illustrate how an individualized organization might operate and identify some of the practical problems of approach.

The research on job design shows that jobs can be fit to people if organizations can tolerate having a wide range of jobs and tasks. One plant in Florida has done this by having an assembly line operating next to a bench assembly of the same product. Employees are given a choice of which kind of job they want. The fact that some want to work on each kind is impressive evidence of the existence of individual differences. Robert Kahn has suggested that the fit process can be facilitated by allowing individuals to choose among different groups of tasks or modules that would be several hours long.[20] In his system, workers would bid for those tasks which they would like to do. For this system to work, all individuals would, of course, have to know a considerable amount about the nature of the different modules, and the approach would probably have to take place in conjunction with some job enrichment activities. Otherwise, the employee might be faced with choosing among modules made up of simple repetitive tasks, thus giving them no real choice. As Kahn notes, the work module concept is also intriguing because it should make it easier for individuals to choose not to work a standard 40-hour work week. This is important because of the difference in people's preferences with respect to hours of work. The whole module approach rests on the ability of individuals to make valid choices about when and where they should work.

The leadership research shows that people respond to different types of leadership. This could be handled by fitting the superior's style to the personality of subordinates—the superior who can only behave in an authoritarian manner will be given subordinates who perform well under that type of supervision; the superior who can only behave participatively could be

---

[20] Robert Kahn, "The Work Module—A Tonic for Lunchpail Lassitude," *Psychology Today* 6 (1973): 94–95.

given only people who respond to that style; and the superior who is capable of varying his style could be given either people who respond to different styles in different conditions or a mix of people with which he or she would be encouraged to behave differently.

The research shows that training needs to be individualized so that it will fit the needs and abilities of the employee. Implementation requires careful assessment of the individual's abilities and motivation, and good career counseling. Once it has been accepted that not everyone in the organization can profit from a given kind of training then training becomes a matter of trying to develop people as much as possible with the kind of training to which they will respond. It requires accepting the fact that people may develop quite different leadership styles or ways of behaving in general and trying to capitalize on these by fitting the job the person holds and the groups he supervises to his style.

The research shows that pay systems need to be fit to the person. Fringe benefit packages are a good example of this; several companies have already developed cafeteria-style fringe benefit packages that allow employees to select the benefits they want. The research also suggests that those individuals whose desire for money is strong should be placed on jobs that lend themselves to pay incentive plans.

In summary, an organization based on individual differences assumptions would have a job environment for each person which fits his or her unique skills and abilities. It would accomplish this by a combination of good selection and self-placement choices in the areas of fringe benefits. job design, hours of work, style of supervision, and training programs. But creating truly individualized job situations presents many practical problems in organization design—it is difficult to create gratifying jobs for both the person who responds to an enriched job and the person who responds to a routinized job. One way of accomplishing this could be by creating relatively autonomous subunits that vary widely in climate, job design, leadership style, and so on. For example, within the same organization the same product might be produced by mass production in one unit and by unit production using enriched jobs in another. One subunit might have a warm, supportive climate while another might have a cold, demanding one. The size of the subunit would also vary depending upon the type of climate that is desired and the type of production it uses. This variation is desirable as long as the placement process is able to help people find the modules that fit them.

An organization would have to have an immense number of subunits if it were to try to have one to represent each of the possible combinations of climate, leadership style, incentive systems, and job design. Since such a large number is not practical, a selection should be made based on a study of the labor market, attention to the principles of motivation and satisfaction, and the nature of the product and market. A study of the labor market to see what type of people the organization is likely to attract should help determine what combinations will be needed to fit the characteristics of most of the workers. In most homogenous labor markets, this may be only a few of the many possible combinations. Traditional selection instruments can help the organization decide who will fit into the subunits; and, if individuals are given information about the nature of the subunits, they can often make valid decisions themselves.

Motivation theory argues that when important rewards are tied to performance, it is possible to have both high satisfaction and high performance.[21] This suggests that all new work modules must meet one crucial condition: Some rewards that are valued by members of that part of the organization must be tied to performance. This rules out many situations. For example, a situation in which no extrinsic rewards such as pay and promotion are tied to performance and which has authoritarian management and repetitive jobs should not exist. Finally, the research on job design and organization structures shows that the type of product and type of market limit the kind of subunit which can be successful. For example, authoritarian management, routine jobs, and tall organization structures are not effective when the product is technically sophisticated and must be marketed in a rapidly changing environment.

Creating subunits with distinctly different climates and practices is one way, but not the only way, to create an individualized organization. In small organizations this probably is not possible; thus, it is important to encourage differences within the same unit. This may mean training supervisors to deal differently with subordinates who have distinctly different personal characteristics. It may also mean designing jobs that can be done in various ways. For example, in one group a product must be built by a team and passed from one member to another while in another group everyone might build the entire product without help. Obviously, this approach generally will not allow for as much variation as does the approach of building distinctive subunits, but it permits some degree of individualization.

It is not yet entirely clear how such divergent organization practices as work modules, cafeteria-style pay plans, and job enrichment that is guided by individual difference measures can be integrated in practice. Research on how organizations can be individualized and on how individual differences affect behavior in organizations is sorely needed.

RESEARCH ON INDIVIDUAL DIFFERENCES

The work on measuring individual differences that has been done so far has focused largely on measuring the "can do" aspects of behavior for the purpose of selection. The effective individualization of organizations depends on the development of measures which tap the "will do" aspects of behavior, such as measures of motivation and reactions to different organizational climates, and measures that can be used for placing people in positions that best fit their needs.

---

[21] Victor Vroom, *Work and Motivation* (New York: John Wiley & Sons, 1964).

This is not to say that selection should be ignored; the kinds of individual differences that exist in an organization should be kept at a manageable number, and those who clearly cannot do the job should be excluded. But it is important that, in selection, measures of such things as motivation, reactions to different leadership styles, and preferred organization climate be collected and evaluated in relationship to the climate of the organization, the psychological characteristics of the jobs in the organizations, and the leadership style of various managers. The same measures are obviously relevant when consideration is given to placing new employees in different parts of the organization or in different jobs. The difficulty in doing this kind of selection and placement is that there are few measures of the relevant individual differences, of the organization climate, and of the psychological characteristics of jobs. In many cases, it is not even known what the relevant individual difference variables are when consideration is being given to predicting how people will react to different administrative practices, policies, and to different organization climates. This is where the differential psychologist can make a major contribution.

Also needed is research on selection that is responsive to the new demands that society is placing on organizations and which recognizes that individuals can contribute to better selection decisions. Since organizations are rapidly losing the ability to select who their members will be, research is needed on how the selection situation can be turned into more of a counseling situation so that enlightened self-selection will operate. There is evidence that when job applicants are given valid information about the job, they will make better choices. Joseph Weitz showed this long ago with insurance agents, and more recently it has been illustrated with West Point cadets and telephone operators.[22] In the future the most effective selection programs will have to emphasize providing individuals with valid data about themselves and about the nature of the organization. After this information is presented to the applicants, they will make the decision of whether to join the organization. Before this kind of "selection" system can be put into effect, however, much research is needed to determine how this process can be handled. We need to know, for example, what kind of information should be presented to individuals and how it should be presented. However, the problems involved in the approach are solvable, and given the current trends in society, this approach represents the most viable selection approach in many situations.

CONCLUSIONS

The research on reward systems, job design, leadership, selection, and training shows that significant individual differences exist in how individuals respond to organizational policies and practices. Because of this,

---

[22] Joseph Weitz, "Job Expectancy and Survival," *Journal of Applied Psychology* 40 (1956): 245–47; and John P. Wanous, "Effect of a Realistic Job Preview on Job Acceptance, Job Survival, and Job Attitudes," *Journal of Applied Psychology* 58 (1973: 327–32.

an effective normative organization theory has to suggest an organization design that will treat individuals differently. Existing normative theories usually fail to emphasize this point. There are, however, a number of things that organizations can do now to deal with individual differences. These include cafeteria-style pay plans and selective job enrichment. Unfortunately, a fully developed practical organization theory based upon an individual difference approach can not be yet stated. Still, it is important to note that approaches to shaping organizations to individuals are developing. It seems logical, therefore, to identify these and other similar efforts as attempts to individualize organizations. It is hoped that the identification of these efforts and the establishment of the concept of individualization will lead to two very important developments: the generation of more practices that will individualize organizations and work on how these different practices can simultaneously be made operational in organizations. Only if these developments take place will individualized organizations ever be created.

Seeing Eye to Eye: Practical Problems of Perception*

JOHN SENGER

Byron Cartwright, plant superintendent, ran his fingers worriedly through his thick, greying hair. He had a tough decision on his hands. With Frank Bauer's retirement he was faced with the problem of selecting a new foreman for the machine shop. But instead of the usual problem of a dearth of qualified people to promote, Byron felt that he had two equally well-qualified men to take over. Pete Petroni and Sam Johansen were both highly skilled machinists, conscientious workers, liked and respected by the other men in the department.

To help make up his mind, Byron called Pete and Sam into his office separately to talk to them about how they thought the shop should be run. He didn't actually say to either of them that he was considering them for the foremanship, but they knew why they were there. In fact the other men in the shop had been talking for some time about which one of them would succeed "Mr. Bauer." Both Pete and Sam were aware of these discussions and their own obvious qualifications for the job.

Byron even felt that either man had so much potential talent that one of them could succeed him as superintendent some day. With the new equipment orders in, it looked like a bright future for the machine shop—a great opportunity for the man he selected. That's what was bothering him so much. Which man?

But this was Byron's perception of the matter: opportunity, advancement, achievement, getting ahead. He didn't know what was going on inside Pete's head. Pete, as a matter of fact, was very upset by the prospect. He recognized the "opportunity" and the extra 100 bucks every month, a chance to get his wife Marge a car of her own, and additionally put something away in the bank. But Pete just doesn't like to tell other people

---

what to do; he doesn't want the responsibility for planning the shop's work and keeping everyone busy. He doesn't want to be involved in paperwork—he doesn't even do that at home. Marge pays all the bills and figures the taxes and does the family planning.

What Pete loves is being a machinist. He likes the odor of the hot metal as it curls, shining away from the cutting edge of the turning tool. He likes the "feel" of the calipers as he slips them over the surface of a finished part, checking dimensions. He likes the precision, the craftsmanship, the sense of productiveness of his occupation. Pete likes to use his long, strong fingers for something besides shuffling papers. He doesn't want to tell other guys what to do. He doesn't want the responsibility for somebody else's work.

Byron Cartwright finally does make the decision to promote Sam, and he feels guilty every time he passes Pete hunched over his lathe. But, boy, is Pete relieved! He tells Byron how pleased he is that Sam is going to be the new foreman. But Byron doesn't really believe him. Pete, however, could take a deep breath for the first time in weeks without the worried tightness across his chest. Marge, his wife, is a little disappointed. She thought he deserved the promotion—he'd been there longer than Sam. But she had also been aware of Pete's edginess the past several weeks, and his noticeable relief since the announcement.

People's actions, emotions, thoughts, and feelings are triggered by their perceptions of their surrounding situations. In the instance above, Byron Cartwright perceived the shop foremanship situation in one way—as a reward, a chance to get ahead, an opportunity to exercise authority, an achievement. Pete Petroni perceived it in quite a different way—as a threat, taking responsibility for others' mistakes, forcing his will on others, being separated from his lathe. Pete, while friendly and well-liked, preferred doing his own thing—alone.

Pete's perception is somewhat unusual in our "achieving society," but by no means rare. Even at that, Pete would have probably accepted the promotion. He was expected to, and Pete is enough of a child of his culture not to question that it is important to accept promotions and "get ahead," much as he might dislike it. That, after all, was his conflict.

But the point here is not about attitudes toward achievement, but about kinds of perception. The same set of circumstances can result in widely divergent perceptions. And differences in perception between managers and their subordinates make managing a tougher job.

We sense that people do see things differently. But we are at times so much a captive of our own perceptual sets that it becomes virtually impossible to see things as others see them. Part of the difference in what people perceive can be explained by the fact that they do see *different* things. Some of what is there to be seen may be physically obscured or unavailable knowledge to one perceiver. After all, Pete had never supervised and couldn't really accurately assess the situation. It might not be as bad as he thinks. But the important thing is that this information was not available to him, and this affected his perception.

Even greater differences in perception are the result of selectivity. One's senses are so overwhelmed by the mass of stimuli vying for attention that in order to carry on any directed activity we must somehow decide what we want most to attend to and block out or sublimate perceptual inputs that aren't related to that activity. If we go too far with selectivity, however, we block out some useful information and make it much more difficult to understand, or even be aware of, another's perception. Cartwright is an achiever, and to be an achiever he has to block out and sublimate distracting nonachievement oriented stimuli. In the process, he blocks out a perception of how someone like Pete Petroni sees things.

ORGANIZATION OF PERCEPTION

Selectivity is an important means of handling the perceptual overload. We further attempt to handle the myriad of perceptual inputs by various manners of organizing perceptions. A group of German psychologists, identified with the organization of perceptions, called themselves Gestalt psychologists and placed great emphasis upon the organization and interrelationship of perceptions. No, Virginia, there was no one named Wolfgang Gestalt. *Gestalt* is a German word essentially meaning to organize.

Common methods of organizing perceptions include grouping, figure-ground and closure. These techniques which we unconsciously utilize in an effort to cope with the mass of stimuli were first identified in connection with visual perception, but they help explain nearly as well much of social perception, as will be seen in the following illustrations.

FIGURE-GROUND

When Doris Graham started to work as secretary to Myron Green in the accounting department, the whole place and the people in it were a kind of amorphous blur in her mind. Slowly, it seemed, features of her new environment began to emerge. At first she was only really aware of chief accountant Myron Green's name and face and employment manager Dave Brigg's name and face. As she began taking dictation and typing, she began to realize Mr. Portley was an important figure to Myron Green and, therefore, to her. Otto Kowalski seemed helpful and Bill Crandell nice, but she didn't really define them against the background of the rest of the accounting department at first. Then, after a couple of weeks or so, they began to emerge as people as well as important contacts in her job as secretary.

Here we see the figure-ground phenomenon at work. Certain "figures," Myron Green, Dave Briggs, Mr. Portley, Otto Kowalski and Bill Crandell emerge from the "ground" represented by the people and things that make up the rest of the accounting department and the company. Then, slowly, the entire department begins to emerge as a "figure" against the "ground" of the entire company. Dave Briggs was the person to emerge as a "figure." (She had memorized his name from the slip of paper given her at White Collar Employment Agency before she ever got out to the company.) He had made her feel comfortable and a little as if she belonged. But now, only several weeks later, because of lack of contact, he was fading into the general company "ground" as the accounting department became a more distinct entity. Here we see the phenomenon of figure-ground reversal, not unlike the visual eye trick which occurs when silhouetted designs can been seen to reverse themselves, so that when, for example, the design is looked at one way, a white vase (the figure) appears against a dark background, and when the white portion of the design is perceived as the ground, the dark portions appear to represent a new figure, two faces.

This reversal was also seen by Doris, back when she was identified by the rest of the office as attached to Mr. Green, and she herself identified with Myron Green more than she did with the others. As time went on, she and the rest of the office got to know one another better. Sometimes when she knew Mr. Green and Mr. Portley were going to be away from the office for a certain period of time, she would pass the information along to the gang and they could all relax a little. A mutual trust developed and the office group began to emerge as the figure, while Myron Green and Mr. Portley tended to become a part of the general company background.

Figure-ground, a phenomenon long known as a visual parlor stunt, is a useful means of organizing our perceptions. It is a helpful way to think about what we see and experience and why we happen to perceive some things the way we do.

GROUPING

Stan Menke eased the Mustang to a stop in one of the lines of traffic funneling out of the south parking lot, and half turned to address Allyn White in the back seat. "Whaddya think the raise is going to be this time, Allyn?" "Gee, I dunno," replied Allyn. But Allyn, by now, wasn't surprised that Stan should ask him about details of important company decisions. So did Pete Petroni and Juan Fernandez, the other guys in the pool. All were older and had been with the company much longer than Allyn. Stan was a foreman and Allyn just a clerk. Juan was active in the union and knew a lot about how the wage negotiations were going. But Stan asked Allyn. Why?

Because Allyn worked in the accounting department, and the accounting department was on the second floor with the executive offices. Allyn wore a coat and tie, as did Mr. Portley and the rest of the executives. So Allyn was being "grouped" with the seat of the power in the company and was thought to be privy to important information. The fact that this was not the case didn't prevent the grouping from taking place.

This tendency to group persons or things that appear to be similar in certain ways, but not in all, is a common means of organizing our perceptions. Because these persons and things are similar in certain ways, but not all, distortion of perception can take place, as was the case with Allyn. Grouping helps us learn, it helps us remember, it is a valuable cognitive device, but it does carry with it the not infrequent cost of perceptual distortion.

A common example of grouping in the organization: The design engineers, the industrial engineers, the production engineers, the cost people, the production control group, who may be every bit as realistic and shop-problem oriented as the people on the shop floor, are viewed by the shop as "unrealistic," "too theoretical," "head-in-the-clouds," "ivory tower" and generally unconcerned with the shop. Why? Because they operate out of the second floor, don't wear blue collars (though some wear sport shirts and no ties), and are educated differently. They are up there with the sales people, the administrative people, the office girls, and others less involved with production. They are *grouped* with those less involved with the factory floor. Proximity and similarity contribute strongly to grouping. Some lack of awareness of shop problems among the engineers, cost ac-countants, and production control people is perhaps justified, but certainly not to the degree the grouping indicates.

It should be reemphasized, on the other hand, that *grouping*, like *figure-ground*, helps us organize and cope with our environment. Without such aids we would be overwhelmed by detail, forced to make too many deci-sions. When the guys in the shop see somebody wandering around in a coat and tie and assume he's somebody pretty important, they are *usually* right. It's just that more than occasionally such generalizations can be misleading if followed blindly.

CLOSURE

Otto Kowalski is big and broad shouldered. He has a thick neck and a jutting jaw. He never wears a coat in the office and works with his sleeves rolled up, his tie pulled down, and his collar open. He walks like a bear with a slight charley horse. His voice is very deep and coarse. He looks tough, although he's not tough at all. Otto is not a stevedore, but an ac-countant. On Saturday afternoons he listens to the symphony on FM, not the excited voice of a television sports announcer. Or he tends his roses. People who know Otto only casually find this all very confusing. Why? Because Otto's appearance, voice, and bearing send out certain perceptual signals from which the observer begins building a perceptul image of Otto. Big, loud guys with rolling gaits are "jocks," right? Tough, right? Aggres-sive, insensitive, kinda dumb, right? Wrong. Otto isn't any of these things. He is sensitive, intelligent, not particularly athletic, and gentle. Then why is almost everyone wrong about Otto on first impression?

Because of the perceptual phenomenon of "closure." Big, muscular guys are frequently stereotyped as athletic, aggressive, tough, insensitive, and, often, not too smart. It doesn't make any difference if this is the case or not. It's a common belief, and when we meet someone who looks like Otto, we start with those parts of his apparent behavior we observe and then fill in the gaps left by those parts we don't observe; that is, we "close." It is just like seeing a line that curves around until it almost meets itself. We see it as a circle with a gap in it, not a curved line. We meet someone and like several things about him. So we go right ahead and close and as-sume that we also like the many other characteristics of this person. The tendency to assume that because we like someone, almost everything about him is good, is referred to as a "halo effect," a special case of closure.

And then there's Myron Green. He has a sallow complexion, round shoulders, a bald head, wears rimless glasses, terribly conservative clothes, and a perpetual scowl. Myron Green is, therefore, cold, aloof, overmeticulous, inhibited, unathletic, has a "Friden for a brain," and is kind of sneaky, right? Right! You see we don't miss them all. But it's seductively easy to fill in an image based upon incomplete evidence and come up with the *wrong* answer.

Organization of our perceptions helps us cope with an overabundance of perceptual information, but it also misleads us sometimes, and we should be aware of this possibility, both in ourselves and others. We don't react equally to all stimuli that bombard us but select or attend to certain of them.

ATTENTION: EXTERNAL FACTORS

Industrial engineer Eldon Peavey's clothes are *not* conservative. Some people refer to them as "far out," some say "flashy," some say "too much." But no one can really ignore them—or Eldon. And that's Eldon's intent. He wants to attract attention to himself, and we do find ourselves attending to guys like Eldon. The biggest, brightest, loudest things clamor for our attention. Over in accounting, Otto Kowalski attracts our attention because he is so big, like six feet four, and 235. We therefore will perceive Otto and Eldon before we perceive others less large or more mousey. If two objects are competing for our attention at the same time, we shall perceive the more intense first. The safety department was thinking about this when they painted the exposed moving parts of machines red, in contrast to the drab grey of the rest of the machine. Size and intensity are important attention-getters.

Why did the Peabody Company finally close a deal with Harry Balou, even though Harry's price on the pumps was higher than that of the competition? Largely because Harry kept beating away at them about the superiority of "his" pumps—monthly, sometimes weekly visits, brochures, telephone calls, personal letters. He constantly reiterated the advantage of the pumps. Peabody finally had to pay attention. *Repetition* has been known for a long time by salesmen, and particularly advertisers, as an excellent means of attracting attention. When the company was big on the "Zero Defects" campaign in an attempt to cut down on scrap costs and improve quality, the term was seen everywhere, taped to machines, on every bulletin board, in the company magazine, under windshield wipers in the parking lot, on the sign board in front of the factory, over the loud speaker system, in the cafeteria—repeated and repeated and repeated. And it did appear to have an effect on quality and scrap. Certainly everyone was aware of the campaign.

The noticeability of coats and ties in the shop was previously mentioned. And the men who go up to the office from the shop are just as noticeable because of their clothes. Contrast also attracts attention. Byron Cartwright is usually pretty subdued and quiet-spoken at the weekly foreman's meetings, so when he's upset about something and raises his voice a little, everyone snaps to. If he shouted all the time, his change of tone wouldn't be as effective. Contrast again. And it works the other way. Myron Green keeps a very close eye on everything and everyone in the accounting office, and when he steps into Mr. Portley's office or is preoccupied with someone or something else, his subordinates immediately sense it. The termination of a stimulus can be nearly as attention-provoking as its onset.

ATTENTION: INTERNAL FACTORS

Bleeding us! Taking what rightfully belongs to us workers. How can Portley have that big fat smile on his face with his right hand stuffed so deep into my wallet? Look at this picture in the paper. Look at him! Proud that he's taking 18 percent profit out of the company. Bragging about it. Look at my hands. Look at your own hands. That's what makes the pumps—and the money—for this company! Not Portley sitting around on his big fat chair in his big fancy office! Not the stockholders! What have they ever done to turn out one single pump? Little old ladies doing nothing but pampering their dogs are the ones who get all that profit, doing nothing. And their dogs eat better than I do!

Sean O'Flaretty, fiery old unreconstructed Trotskyite, was very upset by Mr. Portley's announcement in the company paper that profits were up for the year. Holding forth to the luncheon crowd lounging on the castings pile outside the foundry, as orange peels, egg shells, and "baggies" were gathered up and stuffed back into lunch boxes, Sean continued,

I ask you guys why is it we do all the work around here and Portley and the little old ladies take all the money out of the place? It's not fair, never been fair, and one of these days you guys will quit sitting around doing nothing and demand your rightful share.

Obviously Sean—and maybe several others—was upset by the increased profit announcement. Why? Because the word "profit" to Sean is like a red flag to a bull. The word to him is filtered through a set of values which perceive profits as money taken away from the workers. Mr. Portley doesn't see it that way at all. He has a different set of filters. And he sees profits as evidence of a healthy organization, a feedback as to how well he is running the company, a source of income to those persons who had risked their savings in his enterprise, the generation of new wealth which can cause the company to expand and flourish.

The values, interests, beliefs, and motivations that people have tend to distort their perceptions. It is little wonder people have difficulty understanding one another when the values they hold cause them to perceive the same word quite differently. To Mr. Portley, "profit" is a very satisfying terms; to Sean O'Flaretty, a threat.

Postman, Bruner, and McGinnies tested people to find what their major value orientations were. Then for a brief millisecond they flashed the words representing these values on a screen. The time the word remained on the screen was gradually increased until it was there long enough to be recognized by all the participants in the experiment. It was found, for example, that those persons with a strong religious value orientation were able to see the word "religion" when it was on the screen for a very brief instant. Others, less religiously oriented, required that the word be on the screen for a longer period before they recognized it. Things that are important to us, those which we value, are the ones we perceive.

SET

Sam Johansen looked up from the schedule board to see Pete Petroni bending over his lathe, while beside him the tote pan for finished parts contained only a dozen of the countershafts Pete was making up for a special order, No. 5008. Sam stood beside Pete and watched for a while. "Say, Pete," he asked, "what's wrong with this job that it's taking you so long to get it out?" "Long?" from Pete, "I only got started on this job just this morning." "Well, then you oughta be half done. I only see twelve in the tote pan. Are the rest of them someplace else?" Sam wanted to know. "Ye gods, no, Sam," replied Pete, "whaddaya mean? It takes a little while to make all these double-oh-one cuts." ".001? Are you holding those things to a .001 tolerance?" blurts Sam. "Lemme see the print. Yeah, see here, it says .01. Right there. See?" "Oh, my pet cow!" grumbled Pete, "you mean all these little deals are only supposed to be held to .01. How could I have done that? I'll tell you how I did it. I haven't done anything to that loose a tolerance in five years. I just simply read another 'oh' in there. Oh, my pet cow!" "Yeah, that's probably it, Pete," replied Sam. "The new guys who normally do this kind of work were tied up on long runs, so I simply scheduled it over here." "I sure didn't see there was just one 'oh' behind that point. Well, yah got a dozen nice expensive countershafts, Sam. I'm awful sorry," said Pete dejectedly. Pete had a *preparatory set,* an expectancy, to see what he saw: one more order for highly skilled, close tolerance work of the kind he was accustomed to doing. We go through life having our perceptions influenced by such preparatory sets. Our previous experience prepares us to see something such as we have seen before, and it's not just a matter of past experience, either. What we need and want to see also causes a perceptual set.

We all have sets, as the result of previous experiences and as the result of personal needs and interests. What might simply look like an old letter to you or me may be an object of intense interest to a stamp collector. An automobile enthusiast may pick out the exhaust tone of a Ferrari which is lost in the cacophony of traffic noises to someone else. To see Juan Fernandez take a couple of quick steps from his turret lathe to deposit a finished part in a tote pan and then move briskly back to start work on the next piece appears to be efficient performance to most people. But the fellows in industrial engineering immediately identify the action as evidence of an inefficient job layout. The way they see it, *no* steps should be taken, and better yet, the part should come out of the chuck and drop immediately into a tote pan untouched by Juan. The industrial engineers have a set to perceive wasted motion which most of us miss. We are set to perceive what we value, what we're interested in, what we are trained to see, and what we've seen before.

PROJECTION

Allyn White turned into the accounting office and was just about to close the door behind him when the tail of his eye caught a glimpse of Eldon Peavey coming down the hall behind him. He didn't close the door all the way, but left it slightly ajar. Now Eldon was quite obviously not coming into the accounting department, but was headed for his desk in the industrial engineering department two doors down. But Allyn just couldn't shut the door in his face. Why? Because Allyn felt that Eldon would perceive the act as a personal rejection. Eldon probably wouldn't even have noticed, and had he noticed, he wouldn't look upon a closing door as an act of rejection. You had to get a lot more blunt than that before Eldon felt rejected. But Allyn, in the same situation, would have felt rejected. So what Allyn was doing was *projecting* his own feelings.

We can misinterpret others' actions and motives rather markedly as a result of projection. Our perceptions are distorted in the direction of our own needs and attitudes which we tend to assume are needs and attitudes shared by others. If one tends to be insincere, he perceives others as being insincere. Sears and Frenkel-Brunswick found that to be true in experimentation with both American and Austrian students.

Myron Green tends to be a sneaky sort and, sure enough, he distrusts everyone else a good deal. We saw Byron Cartwright assuming that because he liked achieving, directing, and taking responsibility, Pete Petroni did, too. Otto Kowalski likes to help people and so assumes that nearly everyone else does also, to his frequent disillusionment. Projection is a very common, internalized perception distorter. An acute form of perceptual distortion, through oversimplification, is stereotyping.

STEREOTYPE

Dave Briggs, employment manager, was working his way down through the pile of recently received application letters, when he came to a resume that caused him to emit a low whistle and reach for the telephone. Dialing quickly, Dave got Ed Yamamoto, chief engineer, on the phone. "Ed," enthused Dave, "I think I have the group leader for the bi-valve pump section." The bi-valve pump design section had been getting along without a direct supervisor since last February, when Hal Coombs had left the company. Herb Borgfeldt, senior man in the section, had twice refused the job, saying he was a designer, not a straw boss, and no one among the rest of the men in the section was experienced enough to take over as supervisor. The job really needed an expert pump designer, preferably with some supervisory experience.

"Graduated from Cal Tech, honors, three years with Livermore Radiation Lab, seven years with Cleveland Pump, last two and a half as supervisor of the bi-valve section. Lessee, two patents in own name, paper in 'Hydraulic Occlusion' at last year's SME meeting—" "Wow!" from Ed. "—and her letter says she wants to relocate here to be close to her mother, and since we are the only pump manufacturer in town, I can't see why we can't get her." "Wait one minute," Ed burst forth, "you said 'her'?" "Yeah," replied Dave, "Ann Farmer. She apparently grew up here. Lessee, went to Horace Mann High School, where she was salutatorian and editor of the year book." "A woman!" snorted Ed. "Look, I'm no male chauvinist, you understand, but this is no job for a girl! There's lots of pressure. She'll be too emotional to run things, too illogical to think through design problems, too absorbed with details to see the big picture, too—" "W-a-i-t," protested Dave. "I'm not insisting you hire this engineer, but you did sound enthusiastic when I read her qualifications." "Well, *sure,* who wouldn't be? Cal Tech, supervisory experience, patents, papers, honors. But you hadn't told me he's a her!"

Ed is going through a form of perceptual distortion known as *stereotyping,* a form of categorization. Categorization is, of course, an extremely useful cognitive device, permitting us to handle and understand large bodies of complex information. Used restrictively, however, it causes the observer to draw conclusions from too narrow a range of information and to generalize too many other traits from this minimal data, usually relating to the categorization of people. The way it works is for the perceiver to have established several ready-made, oversimplified categories of people who he thinks possess a few distinctive characteristics. Then he classifies the people he meets into one of these categories. The classification is made on the basis of one of a very few characteristics. The person so classified is then assumed to have all the characteristics thought to represent the category. Ed classified Ann Farmer as a woman, not as an engineer. Under Ed's "woman" classification are the characteristics of emotionalism, illogic, detail-mindedness, and the like. Ed's prejudiced, but then there are those who would stereotype Ed as an engineer, which to them would tend to mean that he is unemotional, socially inept, and so on. Stereotypes are usually learned young and go unquestioned. The learning usually takes place out of intimate contact with those assigned to the stereotyped category; therefore, the resulting attributed characteristics cannot help but be distorted.

SELECTIVE PERCEPTION AND BEHAVIORAL REVERSAL

Mabel Lindsey, typing pool supervisor, is aware that the girls in the typing pool don't like the clatter and din of working together in one big noisy room; she knows they prefer doing work for one or a few people rather than typing whatever is parceled out to them, that they dislike the lack of individuality being a member of the pool implies. She is aware that Charlotte Bettendorf's loudness and exhibitionism irritates the rest of the girls in the pool and that her own perfectionism is often hard to live with. She is aware of all these irritants *at the subconscious level.* To protect her own sanity, she has sublimated her awareness of these irritants and does not really perceive them anymore at the conscious level. If she were consciously to perceive and be sensitive to all the needs of her girls, she wouldn't have time to do anything else. In order to get on with her work, she must selectively stifle those perceptions of disturbing stimuli which don't contribute to what she perceives as important to her job as typing pool supervisor. This phenomenon has been described by Harold Leavitt as a self-imposed psychological blindness which helps persons maintain their equilibrium as they pursue their goals.

If, on the other hand, all in the same week, first Betty and then Claudine and then Hope were to complain that the noise, the irritation might break through Mabel's selective defense. She might then immediately burst in upon office manager Clyde Ferguson and demand that the ceiling be insulated. Selective perception, with its blackout of mild disturbances, can suddenly change to acute perception when the irritant exceeds a certain threshold. At this point, the individual shifts his attention sharply and fully to the irritant. As Leavitt puts it, "The distant irritation increases to a point at which it becomes so real, so imminent, and so threatening that we reverse our course, discard the blindfold and preoccupy ourselves completely with the thing we previously ignored." The phenomenon is a complex one because if things are threatening, they must be fended off, but in order to fend them off they must first be seen. Therefore, in order for one to protect himself from threat, he must first perceive the threat and then manage to deny to himself that he has seen it. This combination of selective perception and defensive behavior helps explain some actions on the part of others that would otherwise be extremely puzzling.

SELF-PERCEPTION   Bill Crandell, senior accountant, doesn't really think much of Bill Crandell. The company's personnel records show Bill's intelligence to be in the upper 98th percentile of the general population. He has clear-eyed good looks, with an open, ingenuous expression appealing to everyone. He moves with an easy grace. No one else can put others at their ease as readily as Bill does. His MBA is from a prestigious business school. He is vice president of Midwestern division of the CPA Association. He has an adoring wife and two happy kids doing well in Lakeside Heights Elementary School. Everyone likes Bill. But Bill doesn't like himself very much.

He doesn't feel that he's doing nearly as well as he should professionally. He doesn't feel that he is providing adequately for his family. He can't afford household help, nor the riding lessons his daughter wants so much, and he can only just manage to rent a place at the lake for the family during the summer.

If only he had the ability to concentrate like Otto Kowalski. If he only had Myron Green's coldly efficient approach. If he could only speak in public like Eldon Peavey. If he could acquire Mr. Portley's ability to see the big picture.

So, bright, charming Bill Crandell sees himself as plodding, ineffectual Bill Crandell. He has a self-percept that is not at all realistic, but realistic or not it's the one he has. It causes him to be depressed a lot of the time, and it seems to be developing into a self-fulfilling prophecy. Bill sees himself as pleasant but ineffectual, and as a result he is becoming pleasant but ineffectual. He doesn't extend himself much anymore. He just takes orders from Myron Green. His intelligence and training permit him to do an adequate job, but he shows very little initiative. He loves being with people because it takes his mind off his own problems. But even this tends to be self-defeating. He spends more and more time talking and less time working. A low self-percept is a difficult cross to bear.

Low self-percept? Not so with Gordon Green. Although no brighter than Bill Crandell and not nearly as charming, Gordon thinks of himself as a real winner. He chose industrial engineering in college because he figured this would be the place he could learn more about the operation of a company faster than from any other starting point. As he saw it, he could quickly move up to chief, then shift over into line management as superintendent, then VP of production and right on up. Gordon thinks he's good and he is, though probably not *that* good. But as a result he probes every opportunity to see where he can make his impact. Gordon's self-percept is high, but not excessively high. He *may* accomplish many of his goals. In the case where one's perception is too high, the accompanying lack of realism can often cause a poor social adjustment. It can also result in a series of too-ambitious undertakings that can't end up anywhere but in failure. Still, society probably has more to gain from those with high self-percepts than from those with low ones. The high self-perceivers will at least *try* many things, and some are bound to be successful.

Does Personality Really Change after 20?*

ZICK RUBIN

"In most of us," William James wrote in 1887, "by the age of 30, the character has set like plaster and will never soften again." Though our bodies may be bent by the years and our opinions changed by the times, there is a basic core of self—a personality—that remains basically unchanged.

The doctrine of personality stability has been accepted psychological dogma for most of the past century. The dogma holds that the plaster of character sets by one's early 20s, if not even sooner than that.

Within the past decade, however, this traditional view has come to have an almost archaic flavor. The rallying cry of the 1970s has been people's virtually limitless capacity for change—not only in childhood but through the span of life. Examples of apparent transformation are highly publicized: Jerry Rubin enters the 1970s as a screaming, war-painted Yippie and emerges as a sedate Wall Street analyst wearing a suit and tie. Richard Alpert, an ambitious assistant professor of psychology at Harvard, tunes into drugs, heads for India, and returns as Baba Ram Dass, a long-bearded mystic in a flowing white robe who teaches people to "be here now." And Richard Raskind, a successful ophthalmologist, goes into the hospital and comes out as Renée Richards a tall, well-muscled athlete on the women's tennis circuit.

Even for those of us who hold on to our original appearance (more or less) and gender, "change" and "growth" are now the bywords. The theme was seized upon by scores of organizations formed to help people change, from Weight Watchers to EST. It was captured—and advanced—by Gail Sheehy's phenomenally successful book *Passages*, which emphasized people's continuing openness to change throughout the course of adulthood. At the same time, serious work in psychology was coming along—building on earlier theories of Carl Jung and Erik Erikson—to buttress the belief that adults keep on developing. Yale's Daniel Levinson, who provided

* Reprinted from *Psychology Today Magazine*, May 1981, pp. 18–20, 23–27. Copyright © 1981, Ziff-Davis Publishing Company.

much of Sheehy's intellectual inspiration, described, in *The Seasons of a Man's Life,* an adult life structure that is marked by periods of self-examination and transition. Psychiatrist Roger Gould, in *Transformations,* wrote of reshapings of the self during the early and middle adult years, "away from stagnation and claustrophobic suffocation toward vitality and an expanded sense of inner freedom."

The view that personality keeps changing throughout life has picked up so many adherents recently that it has practically become the new dogma. Quantitative studies have been offered to document the possibility of personality change in adulthood, whether as a consequence of getting married, changing jobs, or seeing one's children leave home. In a new volume entitled *Constancy and Change in Human Development,* two of the day's most influential behavioral scientists, sociologist Orville G. Brim, Jr., and psychologist Jerome Kagan, challenge the defenders of personality stability to back up their doctrine with hard evidence. "The burden of proof," Brim and Kagan write, "is being shifted to the larger group, who adhere to the traditional doctrine of constancy, from the minority who suggest that it is a premise requiring evaluation."

And now we get to the newest act in the battle of the dogmas. Those who uphold the doctrine of personality stability have accepted the challenge. In the past few years they have assembled the strongest evidence yet available for the truth of their position—evidence suggesting that on several central dimensions of personality, including the ones that make up our basic social and emotional style, we are in fact astoundingly stable throughout the course of adult life.

THE 'LITTER-ATURE' ON PERSONALITY

Until recently there was little firm evidence for the stability of personality, despite the idea's intuitive appeal. Instead, most studies showed little predictability from earlier to later times of life—or even, for that matter, from one situation to another within the same time period—thus suggesting an essential lack of consistency in people's personalities. Indeed, many researchers began to question whether it made sense to speak of "personality" at all.

But whereas the lack of predictability was welcomed by advocates of the doctrine of change through the life span, the defenders of stability have another explanation for it: Most of the studies are lousy. Referring derisively to the "litter-ature" on personality, Berkeley psychologist Jack Block estimates that "perhaps 90 percent of the studies are methodologically inadequate, without conceptual implication, and even foolish."

Block is right. Studies of personality have been marked by an abundance of untested measures (anyone can make up a new "scale" in an afternoon), small samples, and scatter-gun strategies ("Let's throw it into the computer and get some correlations"). Careful longitudinal studies, in which the same people are followed over the years, have been scarce. The conclusion that people are not predictable, then, may be a reflection not of human nature but of the haphazard methods used to study it.

Block's own research, in contrast, has amply demonstrated that people *are* predictable. Over the past 20 years Block has been analyzing extensive personality reports on several hundred Berkeley and Oakland residents that were first obtained in the 1930s, when the subjects were in junior high school. Researchers at Berkeley's Institute of Human Development followed up on the students when the subjects were in their late teens, again when they were in their mid-30s, and again in the late 1960s, when the subjects were all in their mid-40s.

The data archive is immense, including everything from attitude checklists filled out by the subjects to transcripts of interviews with the subjects, their parents, teachers, and spouses, with different sets of material gathered at each of the four time periods.

To reduce all the data to manageable proportions, Block began by assembling separate files of the information collected for each subject at each time period. Clinical psychologists were assigned to immerse themselves in individual dossiers and then to make a summary rating of the subject's personality by sorting a set of statements (for instance, "Has social poise and presence," and "Is self-defeating") into piles that indicated how representative the statement was of the subject. The assessments by the different raters (usually three for each dossier) were found to agree with one another to a significant degree, and they were averaged to form an overall description of the subject at that age. To avoid potental bias, the materials for each subject were carefully segregated by age level; all comments that referred to the person at an earlier age were removed from the file. No psychologist rated the materials for the same subject at more than one time period.

Using this painstaking methodology, Black found a striking pattern of stability. In his most recent report, published earlier this year, he reported that on virtually every one of the 90 rating scales employed, there was a statistically significant correlation between subjects' ratings when they were in junior high school and their ratings 30 to 35 years later, when they were in their 40s. The most self-defeating adolescents were the most self-defeating adults; cheerful teenagers were cheerful 40-year-olds; those whose moods fluctuated when they were in junior high school were still experiencing mood swings in midlife.

"STILL STABLE AFTER ALL THESE YEARS"

Even more striking evidence for the stability of personality, extending the time frame beyond middle age to late adulthood, comes from the work of Paul T. Costa, Jr., and Robert R. McCrae, both psychologists at the Gerontology Research Center of the National Institute on Aging in Baltimore. Costa and McCrae have tracked people's scores over time on standardized self-report personality scales, including the Sixteen Personality

Factor Questionnaire and the Guilford-Zimmerman Temperament Survey, on which people are asked to decide whether or not each of several hundred statements describes them accurately. (Three sample items: "I would prefer to have an office of my own, not sharing it with another person." "Often I get angry with people too quickly." "Some people seem to ignore or avoid me, although I don't know why.")

Costa and McCrae combined subjects' responses on individual items to produce scale scores for each subject on such overall dimensions as extraversion and neuroticism, as well as on more specific traits, such as gregariousness, assertiveness, anxiety, and depression. By correlating over time the scores of subjects tested on two or three occasions—separated by 6, 10, or 12 years—they obtained estimates of personality stability. The Baltimore researchers have analyzed data from two large longitudinal studies, the Normative Aging Study conducted by the Veterans Administration in Boston and the Baltimore Longitudinal Study of Aging. In the Boston study, more than 400 men, ranging in age from 25 to 82, filled out a test battery in the mid-1960s and then completed a similar battery 10 years later, in the mid-1970s. In the Baltimore study, more than 200 men between the ages of 20 and 76 completed test batteries three times, separated by six-year intervals. Less extensive analyses, still unpublished, of the test scores of women in the Baltimore study point to a similar pattern of stability.

In both studies, Costa and McCrae found extremely high correlations, which indicated that the ordering of subjects on a particular dimension on one occasion was being maintained to a large degree a decade or more later. Contrary to what might have been predicted, young and middle-aged subjects turned out to be just as unchanging as old subjects were.

"The assertive 19-year-old is the assertive 40-year-old is the assertive 80-year-old," declares Costa, extrapolating from his and McCrae's results, which covered shorter time span. For the title of a persuasive new paper reporting their results, Costa and McCrae rewrote a Paul Simon song title, proclaiming that their subjects were "Still Stable after All These Years."

Other recent studies have added to the accumulating evidence for personality stability throughout the life span. Gloria Leon and her coworkers at the University of Minnesota analyzed the scores on the Minnesota Multiphasic Personality Inventory (MMPI) of 71 men who were tested in 1947, when they were about 50 years old, and again in 1977, when they were close to 80. They found significant correlations on all 13 of the MMPI scales, with the highest correlation over the 30-year period on the scale of "Social Introversion." Costa and McCrae, too, found the highest degrees of stability, ranging from .70 to .84, on measures of introversion-extraversion, which assess gregariousness, warmth, and assertiveness. And Paul Mussen and his colleagues at Berkeley, analyzing interviewers' ratings of 53 women who were seen at ages 30 and 70, found significant correlations on such aspects of introversion-extraversion as talkativeness, excitability, and cheerfulness.

Although character may be most fixed in the domain of introversion-extraversion, Costa and McCrae found almost as much constancy in the domain of "nuroticism," which includes such specific traits as depression, anxiety, hostility, and impulsiveness. Neurotics are likely to be complainers throughout life. They may complain about different things as they get older—for example, worries about love in early adulthood, a "midlife crisis" at about age 40, health problems in late adulthood—but they are still complaining. The less neurotic person reacts to the same events with greater equanimity. Although there is less extensive evidence for its stability, Costa and McCrae also believe that there is an enduring trait of "openness to experience," including such facets as openness to feelings, ideas, and values.

Another recent longitudinal study of personality, conducted by University of Minnesota sociologist Jeylan Mortimer and her coworkers, looked at the self-ratings of 368 University of Michigan men who were tested in 1962–63, when they were freshmen, in 1966–67, when they were seniors, and in 1976, when they were about 30. At each point the subjects rated themselves on various characteristics, such as relaxed, strong, warm, and different. The ratings were later collapsed into overall scores for well-being, competence, sociability, and unconventionality. On each of these dimensions, Mortimer found a pattern of persistence rather than one of change. Mortimer's analysis of the data also suggested that life experiences such as the nature of one's work had an impact on personality. But the clearest message of her research is, in her own words, "very high stability."

IS EVERYBODY CHANGING?

The high correlations between assessments made over time indicate that people in a given group keep the same rank order on the traits being measured, even as they traverse long stretches of life. But maybe *everyone* changes as he or she gets older. If, for example, everyone turns inward to about the same extent in the latter part of life, the correlations—representing people's *relative* standing—on measures of introversion could still be very high, thus painting a misleading picture of stability. And, indeed, psychologist Bernice Neugarten concluded as recently as five years ago that there was a general tendency for people to become more introverted in the second half of life. Even that conclusion has been called into question, however. The recent longitudinal studies have found only slight increases in introversion as people get older, changes so small that Costa and McCrae consider them to be of little practical significance.

Specifically, longitudinal studies have shown slight drops over the course of adulthood in people's levels of excitement seeking, activity, hostility, and impulsiveness. The Baltimore researchers find no such changes in average levels of gregariousness, warmth, assertiveness, depression, or anxiety. Costa summarizes the pattern of changes as "a mellowing—but the person isn't so mellowed that you can't recognize him." Even as this mellowing occurs, moreover, people's relative ordering remains much the same—on the average, everyone drops the same few standard points. Thus, an "impulsive" 25-year-old may be a bit less impulsive by the time he or she is 70 but is still likely to be more impulsive than his or her agemates.

The new evidence of personality stability has been far too strong for the advocates of change to discount. Even in the heart of changeland, in Brim and Kagan's *Constancy and Change in Human Development,* psychologists Howard Moss and Elizabeth Susman review the research and conclude that there is strong evidence for the continuity of personality.

PEOPLE WHO GET STUCK

The new evidence has not put the controversy over personality stability and change to rest, however. If anything, it has sharpened it. Although he praises the new research, Orville Brim is not convinced by it that adults are fundamentally unchanging. He points out that the high correlations signify strong associations between measures, but not total constancy. For example, a .70 correlation between scores obtained at two different times means that half of the variation (.70 squared, or .49) between people's later scores can be predicted from their earlier scores. The apostles of stability focus on this predictability, which is all the more striking because of the imperfect reliability of the measures employed. But the prophets of change, like Brim, prefer to dwell on the half of the variability that cannot be predicted, which they take as evidence of change.

Thus, Costa and McCrae look at the evidence they have assembled, marvel at the stability that it indicates, and call upon researchers to explain it: to what extent may the persistence of traits bespeak inherited biological predispositions, enduring influences from early childhood, or patterns of social roles and expectations that people get locked into? And at what age does the plaster of character in fact begin to set? Brim looks at the same evidence, acknowledges the degree of stability that it indicates, and then calls upon researchers to explain why some people in the sample are changing. "When you focus on stability," he says, "you're looking at the dregs— the people who have gotten stuck. You want to look at how a person grows and changes, not at how a person stays the same."

Brim, who is a president of the Foundation for Child Development in New York, also emphasizes that only certain aspects of personality—most clearly, aspects of social and emotional style, such as introversion-extraversion, depression, and anxiety—have been shown to be relatively stable. Brim himself is more interested in other parts of personality, such as people's self-esteem, sense of control over their lives, and ultimate values. These are the elements of character that Brim believes undergo the most important changes over the course of life. "Properties like gregariousness don't interest me," he admits; he does not view such traits as central to the fulfillment of human possibilities.

If Brim is not interested in some of the personality testers' results, Daniel Levinson is even less interested. In his view, paper-and-pencil measures like those used by Costa and McCrae are trivial, reflecting, at best, peripheral aspects of life. (Indeed, critics suggest that such research indicates only that people are stable in the way they fill out personality scales.) Levinson sees the whole enterprise of "rigorous" studies of personality stability as another instance of psychologists' rushing in to measure whatever they have measures for before they have clarified the important issues. "I think most psychologists and sociologists don't have the faintest idea what adulthood is about," he says.

Levinson's own work at the Yale School of Medicine (see "Growing Up with the Dream," *Psychology Today,* January 1978) has centered on the adult's evolving life structure—the way in which a person's social circumstances, including work and family ties, and inner feelings and aspirations fit together in an overall picture. Through intensive interviews of a small sample of men in the middle years of life—he is now conducting a parallel study of women—Levinson has come to view adult development as marked by an alternating sequence of relatively stable "structure-building" periods and periods of transition. He has paid special attention to the transition that occurs at about the age of 40. Although this midlife transition may be either smooth or abrupt, the person who emerges from it is always different from the one who entered it.

The midlife transition provides an important opportunity for personal growth. For example, not until we are past 40, Levinson believes, can we take a "universal" view of ourselves and the world rising above the limited perspective of our own background to appreciate the fullest meaning of life. "I don't think anyone can write tragedy—real tragedy—before the age of 40," Levinson declares.

DISAGREEMENT OVER METHODS

As a student of biography, Levinson does not hesitate to take a biographical view of the controversy at hand. "To Paul Costa," he suggests in an understanding tone, "the most important underlying issue is probably the specific issue of personality stability or change. I think the question of *development* is really not important to him personally. But he's barely getting to 40, so he has time." Levinson himself began his research on adult development when he was 46, as part of a way of understanding the changes he had undergone in the previous decade. He is now 60.

Costa, for his part, thinks that Levinson's clinical approach to research, based on probing interviews with small numbers of people, lacks the rigor needed to establish anything conclusively. "It's only 40 people, for crying out loud!" he exclaims. And Costa doesn't view his own age (he is 38) or that of his colleague McCrae (who is 32) as relevant to the questions under discussion.

Jack Block, who is also a hardheaded quantitative researcher—and, for the record, is fully 57 years old—shares Costa's view of Levinson's method. "The interviews pass through the mind of Dan Levinson and a few other people," Block grumbles, "and he writes it down." Block regards Levinson as a good psychologist who should be putting forth his work as speculation, and not as research.

As this byplay suggests, some of the disagreement between the upholders of stability and the champions of change is methodological. Those who argue for the persistence of traits tend to offer rigorous personality test evidence, while those who emphasize the potential for change often offer more qualitative, clinical descriptions. The psychometricians scoff at the clinical reports as unreliable, while the clinicians dismiss the psychometric data as trivial. This summary oversimplifies the situation, though, because some of the strongest believes in change, like Brim, put a premium on statistical, rather than clinical, evidence.

When pressed, people on both sides of the debate agree that personality is characterized by *both* stability and change. But they argue about the probabilities assigned to different outcomes. Thus, Costa maintains that "the assertive 19-year-old is the assertive 40-year-old is the assertive 80-year-old . . . *unless something happens to change it.*" The events that would be likely to change deeply ingrained patterns would have to be pretty dramatic ones. As an example, Costa says that he would not be surprised to see big personality changes in the Americans who were held hostage in Iran.

From Brim's standpoint, in contrast, people's personalities—and especially their feelings of mastery, control, and self-esteem—will keep changing through the course of life . . . *unless they get stuck.* As an example, he notes that a coal miner who spends 10 hours a day for 50 years down the shaft may have little opportunity for psychological growth. Brim believes that psychologists should try to help people get out of such ruts of stability. And he urges researchers to look more closely at the ways in which life events—not only the predictable ones, such as getting married or retiring, but also the unpredictable ones, such as being fired or experiencing a religious conversion—may alter adult personality.

At bottom, it seems, the debate is not so much methodological as ideological, reflecting fundamental differences of opinion about what is most important in the human experience. Costa and McCrae emphasize the value of personality constancy over time as a central ingredient of a stable sense of identity. "If personality were not stable," they write, "our ability to make wise choices about our future lives would be severely limited." We must know what we are like—and what we will continue to be like—if we are to make intelligent choices, whether of careers, spouses, or friends. Costa and McCrae view the maintenance of a stable personality in the face of the vicissitudes of life as a vital human accomplishment.

Brim, however, views the potential for growth as the hallmark of humanity. "The person is a dynamic organism," he says, "constantly striving to master its environment and to become something more than it is." He adds, with a sense of purpose in his voice, "I see psychology in the service of liberation, not constraint."

Indeed, Brim suspects that we are now in the midst of a "revolution in human development," from a traditional pattern of continuity toward greater discontinuity throughout the life span. Medical technology (plastic surgery and sex-change surgery, for example), techniques of behavior modification, and the social supports for change provided by thousands of groups "from TA to TM, from AA to Zen" are all part of this revolution. Most important, people are trying, perhaps for the first time in history, to change *themselves.*

Some social critics, prominent among them Christopher Lasch in *The Culture of Narcissism,* have decried the emphasis on self-improvement as a manifestation of the "Me" generation's excessive preoccupation with self. In Brim's view, these critics miss the point. "Most of the concern with oneself going on in this country," he declares, "is not people being selfish, but rather trying to be better, trying to be something more than they are now." If Brim is right in his reading of contemporary culture, future studies of personality that track people through the 1970s and into the 1980s may well show less stability and more change than the existing studies have shown.

THE TENSION IN EACH OF US

In the last analysis, the tension between stability and change is found not only in academic debates but also in each of us. As Brim and Kagan write,

> There is, on the one hand, a powerful drive to maintain the sense of one's identity, a sense of continuity that allays fears of changing too fast or of being changed against one's will by outside forces. . . . On the other hand, each person is, by nature, a purposeful, striving organism with a desire to be more than he or she is now. From making simple new year's resolutions to undergoing transsexual operations, everyone is trying to become something that he or she is not, but hopes to be.

A full picture of adult personality development would inevitably reflect this tension between sameness and transformation. Some aspects of personality, such as a tendency to be reclusive or outgoing, calm or anxious, may typically be more stable than other aspects, such as a sense of mastery over the environment. Nevertheless, it must be recognized that each of us reflects, over time, both stability and change. As a result, observers can look at a person as he or she goes through a particular stretch of life and see either stability or change or—if the observer looks closely enough—both.

For example, most people would look at Richard Alpert, the hard-driving psychology professor of the early 1960s, and Ram Dass, the bearded, free-flowing guru of the 1970s, and see that totally different persons are here now. But Harvard psychologist David McClelland, who knew Alpert well, spent time with the Indian holy man and said to himself, "It's the same old Dick!"—still as charming, as concerned with inner experience, and as power-oriented as ever. And Jerry Rubin can view his own transformation from Yippie to Wall Streeter in a way that recognizes the underlying continuity: "Finding out who I really was was done in typical Jerry Rubin way. I tried everything, jumped around like crazy with boundless energy and curiosity." If we look closely enough, even Richard Raskind and Renée Richards will be found to have a great deal in common.

Whether a person stays much the same or makes sharp breaks with the past may depend in large measure on his or her own ideas about what is possible and about what is valuable. Psychological research on adult development can itself have a major impact on these ideas by calling attention to what is "normal" and by suggesting what is desirable. Now that researchers have established beyond reasonable doubt that there is often considerable stability in adult personality, they may be able to move on to a clearer understanding of how we can grow and change, even as we remain the same people we always were. It may be, for example, that if we are to make significant changes in ourselves, without losing our sense of identity, it is necessary for some aspects of our personality to remain stable. "I'm different now," we can say, "but it's still me."

As Jack Block puts it in his characteristically judicious style: "Amidst change and transformation, there is an essential coherence to personality development."

Banana Time: Job Satisfaction and Informal Interaction*

DONALD F. ROY

This paper undertakes description and exploratory analysis of the social interaction which took place within a small work group of factory machine operatives during a two-month period of participant observation. The factual and ideational materials which it presents lie at an intersection of two lines of research interest and should, in their dual bearing, contribute to both. Since the operatives were engaged in work which involved the repetition of very simple operations over an extra-long workday, six days a week, they were faced with the problem of dealing with a formidable "beast of monotony." Revelation of how the group utilized its resources to combat the "beast" should merit the attention of those who are seeking solution to the practical problem of job satisfaction, or employee morale. It should also provide insights for those who are trying to penetrate the mysteries of the small group.

Convergence of these two lines of interest is, of course, no new thing. Among the host of writers and researchers who have suggested connections between "group" and "joy in work" are Walker and Guest, observers of social interaction on the automobile assembly line.[1] They quote assembly-line workers as saying, "We have a lot of fun and talk all the time,"[2] and, "If it weren't for talking and fooling, you'd go nuts."[3]

My account of how one group of machine operators kept from "going nuts" in a situation of monotonous work activity attempts to lay bare the tissues of interaction which made up the content of their adjustment. The talking, fun, and fooling which provided solution to the elemental problem

---

* Reproduced by permission of the Society for Applied Anthropology from *Human Organization* 18, no. 4 (1960).

[1] Charles R. Walker and Robert H. Guest, *The Man on the Assembly Line* (Cambridge, Mass.: Harvard University Press, 1952).

[2] Ibid., p. 77.

[3] Ibid., p. 68.

of "psychological survival" will be described according to their embodiment in intragroup relations. In addition, an unusual opportunity for close observation of behavior involved in the maintenance of group equilibrium was afforded by the fortuitous introduction of a "natural experiment." My unwitting injection of explosive materials into the stream of interaction resulted in sudden, but temporary, loss of group interaction.

My fellow operatives and I spent our long days of simple repetitive work in relative isolation from other employees of the factory. Our line of machines was sealed off from other work areas of the plant by the four walls of the clicking room. The one door of this room was usually closed. Even when it was kept open, during periods of hot weather, the consequences were not social; it opened on an uninhabited storage room of the shipping department. Not even the sound of work activity going on elsewhere in the factory carried to this isolated workplace. There were occasional contacts with "outside" employees, usually on matters connected with the work; but, with the exception of the daily calls of one fellow who came to pick up finished materials for the next step in processing, such visits were sporadic and infrequent.

Moreover, face-to-face contact with members of the managerial hierarchy were few and far between. No one bearing the title of foreman ever came around. The only company official who showed himself more than once during the two-month observation period was the plant superintendent. Evidently overloaded with supervisory duties and production problems which kept him busy elsewhere, he managed to pay his respects every week or two. His visits were in the nature of short, businesslike, but friendly, exchanges. Otherwise he confined his observable communications with the group to occasional utilization of a public address system. During the two-month period, the company president and the chief chemist paid one friendly call apiece. One man, who may or may not have been of managerial status, was seen on various occasions lurking about in a manner which excited suspicion. Although no observable consequences accrued from the peculiar visitations of this silent fellow, it was assumed that he was some sort of efficiency expert, and he was referred to as "The Snooper."

As far as our work group was concerned, this was truly a situation of laissez-faire management. There was no interference from staff experts, no hounding by time-study engineers or personnel men hot on the scent of efficiency or good human relations. Nor were there any signs of industrial democracy in the form of safety, recreational, or production committees. There was an international union, and there was a highly publicized union-management cooperation program; but actual interactional processes of cooperation were carried on somewhere beyond my range of observation and without participation of members of my work group. Furthermore, these union-management get-togethers had no determinable connection with the problem of "toughing out" a 12-hour day at monotonous work.

Our work group was thus not only abandoned to its own resources for creating job satisfaction, but left without that basic reservoir of ill-will toward management which can sometimes be counted on to stimulate the development of interesting activities to occupy hand and brain. Lacking was the challenge of intergroup conflict, that perennial source of creative experience to fill the otherwise empty hours of meaningless work routine.[4]

The clicking machines were housed in a room approximately thirty by twenty-four feet. They were four in number, set in a row, and so arranged along one wall that the busy operator could, merely by raising his head from his work, freshen his reveries with a glance through one of three large barred windows. To the rear of one of the end machines sat a long cutting table; here the operators cut up rolls of plastic materials into small sheets manageable for further processing at the clickers. Behind the machine at the opposite end of the line sat another table which was intermittently the work station of a female employee who performed sundry scissors operations of a more intricate nature on raincoat parts. Boxed in on all sides by shelves and stocks of materials, this latter locus of work appeared a cell within a cell.

The clickers were of the genus punching machines; of mechanical construction similar to that of the better known punch presses, their leading features were hammer and block. The hammer, or punching head, was approximately eight inches by twelve inches at its flat striking surface. The descent upon the block was initially forced by the operator, who exerted pressure on a handle attached to the side of the hammer head. A few inches of travel downward established electrical connection for a sharp, power-driven blow. The hammer also traveled, by manual guidance, in a horizontal plane to and from, and in an arc around, the central column of the machine. Thus the operator, up to the point of establishing electrical connections for the sudden and irrevocable downward thrust, had flexibility in maneuvering his instrument over the larger surface of the block. The latter, approximately twenty-four inches wide, eighteen inches deep, and ten inches thick, was made, like a butcher's block, of inlaid hardwood; it was set in the machine at a convenient waist height. On it the operator placed his materials, one sheet at a time if leather, stacks of sheets if plastc to be cut with steel dies of assorted sizes and shapes. The particular die in use would be moved, by hand, from spot to spot over the material each time a cut was made; less frequently, materials would be shifted on the block as the operator saw need for such adjustment.

Introduction to the new job, with its relatively simple machine skills and work routines, was accomplished with what proved to be, in my experience, an all-time minimum of job training. The clicking machine assigned to me was situated at one end of the row. Here the superintendent and one of the operators gave a few brief demonstrations, accompanied by bits of advice which included a warning to keep hands clear of the descending hammer. After a short practice period, at the end of which the super-

---

4 Donald F. Roy, "Work Satisfaction and Social Reward in Quota Achievement: An Analysis of Piecework Incentive," *American Sociological Review*, October 1953, pp. 507–14.

intendent expressed satisfaction with progress and potentialities, I was left to develop my learning curve with no other supervision than that afforded by members of the work group. Further advise and assistance did come, from time to time, from my fellow operatives, sometimes upon request, sometimes unsolicited.

THE WORK GROUP

Absorbed at first in three related goals of improving my clicking skill, increasing my rate of output, and keeping my left hand unclicked, I paid little attention to my fellow operatives save to observe that they were friendly, middle-aged, foreign-born, full of advice, and very talkative. Their names, according to the way they addressed each other, were George, Ike, and Sammy.[5] George, a stocky fellow in his late fifties, operated the machine at the opposite end of the line; he, I later discovered, had emigrated in early youth from a country in Southeastern Europe. Ike, stationed at George's left, was tall, slender, in his early fifties, and Jewish; he had come from Eastern Europe in his youth. Sammy, number three man in the line, and my neighbor, was heavy set, in his late fifties, and Jewish; he had escaped from a country in Eastern Europe just before Hitler's legions had moved in. All three men had been downwardly mobile as to occupation in recent years. George and Sammy had been proprietors of small businesses; the former had been "wiped out" when his uninsured establishment burned down; the latter had been entrepreneuring on a small scale before he left all behind him to flee the Germans. According to his account, Ike had left a highly skilled trade which he had practiced for years in Chicago.

I discovered also that the clicker line represented a ranking system in descending order from George to myself. George not only had top seniority for the group, but functioned as a sort of lead man. His superior status was marked in the fact that he received five cents more per hour than the other clickermen, put in the longest workday, made daily contact outside the workroom with the superintendent on work matters which concerned the entire line, and communicated to the rest of us the directives which he received. The narrow margin of superordination was seen in the fact that directives were always relayed in the superintendent's name; they were on the order of, "You'd better let that go now and get on the green. Joe says they're running low on the fifth floor," or "Joe says he wants two boxes of the 3–1 die today." The narrow margin was also seen in the fact that the superintendent would communicate directly with his operatives over the public address system; and, on occasion, Ike or Sammy would leave the workroom to confer with him for decisions or advice in regard to work orders.

Ike was next to George in seniority, then Sammy. I was, of course, low man on the totem pole. Other indices to status differentiation lay in informal interaction to be described later.

---

[5] All names used are fictitious.

With one exception job status tended to be matched by length of work-day. George worked a 13-hour day, from 7 A.M. to 8:30 P.M. Ike worked 11 hours, from 7 A.M. to 6:30 P.M.; occasionally he worked until 7 or 7:30 for an 11½- or a 12-hour day. Sammy put in a 9-hour day, from 8 A.M. to 5:30 P.M. My 12 hours spanned from 8 A.M. to 8:30 P.M. We had a half hour for lunch, from 12 to 12:30.

The female who worked at the secluded table behind George's machine put in a regular plantwide eight-hour shift from 8 to 4:30. Two women held this job during the period of my employment: Mable was succeeded by Baby. Both were Negroes and in their late 20s.

A fifth clicker operator, an Arabian emigré called Boo, worked a night shift by himself. He usually arrived about 7 P.M. to take over Ike's machine.

THE WORK

It was evident to me, before my first workday drew to a weary close, that my clicking career was going to be a grim process of fighting the clock, the particular timepiece in this situation being an old-fashioned alarm clock which ticked away on a shelf near George's machine. I had struggled through many dreary rounds with the minutes and hours during the various phases of my industrial experience, but never had I been confronted with such a dismal combination of working conditions as the extra-long work-day, the infinitesimal cerebral excitation, and the extreme limitation of physical movement. The contrast with a recent stint in the California oil fields was striking. This was no eight-hour day of racing hither and yon over desert and foothills with a rollicking crew of "roustabouts" on a variety of repair missions at oil wells, pipe lines, and storage tanks. Here there was no afternoon dallying to search the sands for horned toads, tarantulas, and rattlesnakes or to climb old wooden derricks for raven's nests, with an eye out, of course, for the tell-tale streak of dust in the distance which gave ample warning of the approach of the boss. This was standing all day in one spot beside three old codgers in a dingy room looking out through barred windows at the bare walls of a brick warehouse, leg movements largely restricted to the shifting of body weight from one foot to the other, hand and arm movement confined, for the most part, to a simple repetitive sequence of place the die, _____ punch the clicker, _____ place the die, _____ punch the clicker, and intellectual activity reduced to computing the hours to quitting time. It is true that from time to time a fresh stack of sheets would have to be substituted for the clicked-out old one; but the stack would have been prepared by someone else, and the exchange would be only a minute or two in the making. Now and then a box of finished work would have to be moved back out of the way, and an empty box brought up; but the moving back and the bringing up involved only a step or two. And there was the half hour for lunch, and occasional trips to the lavatory or the drinking fountain to break up the day into digestible parts. But after each momentary respite, hammer and die were moving again: click, _____ move die, _____ click, _____ move die.

Before the end of the first day, Monotony was joined by his twin brother, Fatigue. I got tired. My legs ached, and my feet hurt. Early in the afternoon I discovered a tall stool and moved it up to my machine to "take the load off my feet." But the superintendent dropped in to see how I was "doing" and promptly informed me that "we don't sit down on this job." My reverie toyed with the idea of quitting the job and looking for other work.

The next day was the same: the monotony of the work, the tired legs and sore feet, and thoughts of quitting.

THE GAME OF WORK

In discussing the factory operative's struggle to "cling to the remnants of joy in work," Henri de Man makes the general observations that "it is psychologically impossible to deprive any kind of work of all its positive emotional elements," that the worker will find some meaning in any activity assigned to him, a "certain scope for initiative which can satisfy after a fashion the instinct for play and the creative impulse," that "even in the Taylor system there is found luxury of self-determination."[6] De Man cites the case of one worker who wrapped 13,000 incandescent bulbs a day; she found her outlet for creative impulse, her self-determination, her meaning in work by varying her wrapping movements a little from time to time.[7]

So did I search for some meaning in my continuous mincing of plastic sheets into small ovals, fingers, and trapezoids. The richness of possibility for creative expression previously discovered in my experience with the "Taylor system"[8] did not reveal itself here. There was no piecework, so no piecework game. There was no conflict with management, so no war game. But, like the light bulb wrapper, I did find a "certain scope for initiative," and out of this slight freedom to vary activity, I developed a game of work.

The game developed was quite simple, so elementary in fact, that its playing was reminiscent of rainy-day preoccupations in childhood, when attention could be centered by the hour on colored bits of things of assorted sizes and shapes. But this adult activity was not mere pottering and piddling; what it lacked in the earlier imaginative content, it made up for in clean-cut structure. Fundamentally involved were: (a) variation in color of the materials cut (b) variation in shape of the dies used, and (c) a process called "scraping the block." The basic procedure which ordered the particular combination of components employed could be stated in the form: "As soon as I do so many of these, I'll get to do those." If, for example, production scheduled for the day featured small, rectangular strips in three colors, the game might go: "As soon as I finish a thousand of the green ones, I'll click some brown ones." And, with success in attaining

---

[6] Henri de Man, *The Psychology of Socialism* (New York: Henry Holt and Company, 1927), pp. 80—81.

[7] Ibid., p. 81.

[8] Roy, "Work Satisfaction."

the objective of working with brown materials, a new goal of "I'll get to do the white ones" might be set. Or the new goal might involve switching dies.

Scraping the block made the game more interesting by adding to the number of possible variations in its playing; and what was perhaps more important, provided the only substantial reward, save for going to the lavatory or getting a drink of water, on days when work with one die and one color of material was scheduled. As a physical operation, scraping the block was fairly simple; it involved application of a coarse file to the upper surface of the block to remove roughness and unevenness resulting from the wear and tear of die penetration. But, as part of the intellectual and emotional content of the game of work, it could be in itself a source of variation in activity. The upper left-hand corner of the block could be chewed up in the clicking of 1,000 white trapezoid pieces, then scraped. Next, the upper right-hand corner, and so until the entire block had been worked over. Then, on the next round of scraping by quadrants, there was the possibility of a change of color or die to green trapezoid or white oval pieces.

Thus the game of work might be described as a continuous sequence of short-range production goals with achievement rewards in the form of activity change. The superiority of this relatively complex and self-determined system over the technically simple and outside-controlled job satisfaction injections experienced by Milner at the beginner's table in a shop of the feather industry should be immediately apparent: "Twice a day our work was completely changed to break the monotony. First Jennie would give us feathers of a brilliant green, then bright orange or a light blue or black. The "ohs" and "ahs" that came from the girls at each change was proof enough that this was an effective way of breaking the monotony of the tedious work."[9]

But a hasty conclusion that I was having lots of fun playing my clicking game should be avoided. These games were not as interesting in the experiencing as they might seem to be from the telling. Emotional tone of the activity was low, and intellectual currents weak. Such rewards as scraping the block or "getting to do the blue ones" were not very exciting, and the stretches of repetitive movement involved in achieving them were long enough to permit lapses into obsessive reverie. Henri de Man speaks of "clinging to the remnants of joy in work," and this situation represented just that. How tenacious the clinging was, how long I could have "stuck it out" with my remnants, was never determined. Before the first week was out, this adjustment to the work situation was complicated by other developments. The game of work continued, but in a different context. Its influence became decidedly subordinated to, if not completely overshadowed by, another source of job satisfaction.

---

[9] Lucille Milner, *Education of an American Liberal* (New York: Horizon Press, 1954), p. 97.

**INFORMAL
SOCIAL ACTIVITY
OF THE WORK
GROUP: TIMES
AND THEMES**

The change came about when I began to take serious note of the social
activity going on around me; my attentiveness to this activity came with
growing involvement in it. What I heard at first, before I started to listen,
was a stream of disconnected bits of communication which did not make
much sense. Foreign accents were strong and referents were not joined to
coherent contexts of meaning. It was just "jabbering." What I saw at first,
before I began to observe, was occasional flurries of horseplay so simple
and unvarying in pattern and so childish in quality that they made no
strong bid for attention. For example, Ike would regularly switch off the
power at Sammy's machine whenever Sammy made a trip to the lavatory
or the drinking fountain. Correlatively, Sammy invariably fell victim to
the plot by making an attempt to operate his clicking hammer after returning to the shop. And, as the simple pattern went, this blind stumbling into
the trap was always followed by indignation and reproach from Sammy,
smirking satisfaction from Ike, and mild paternal scolding from George.
My interest in this procedure was at first confined to wondering when Ike
would weary of his tedious joke or when Sammy would learn to check his
power switch before trying the hammer.

But, as I began to pay closer attention, as I began to develop familiarity
with the communication system, the disconnected became connected, the
nonsense made sense, the obscure became clear, and the silly actually
funny. And, as the content of the interaction took on more meaning, the
interaction began to reveal structure. There were "times" and "themes,"
and roles to serve their enaction. The interaction had subtleties, and I
began to savor and appreciate them. I started to record what hitherto had
seemed unimportant.

Times

This emerging awareness of structure and meaning included recognition
that the long day's grind was broken by interruptions of a kind other than
the formally instituted or idiosyncratically developed disjunctions in work
routine previously described. These additional interruptions appeared in
daily repetition in an ordered series of informal interactions. They were,
in part, but only in part and in very rough comparison, similar to those
common fractures of the production process known as the coffee break,
the coke break, and the cigarette break. Their distinction lay in frequency
of occurrence and in brevity. As phases of the daily series, they occurred
almost hourly, and so short were they in duration that they disrupted work
activity only slightly. Their significance lay not so much in their function
as rest pauses, although it cannot be denied that physical refreshment was
involved. Nor did their chief importance lie in the accentuation of progress
points in the passage of time, although they could perform that function
far more strikingly than the hour hand on the dull face of George's alarm
clock. If the daily series of interruptions be likened to a clock, then the
comparison might best be made with a special kind of cuckoo clock, one
with a cuckoo which can provide variation in its announcements and can
create such an interest in them that the intervening minutes become filled

with intellectual content. The major significance of the interactional inter-ruptions lay in such a carryover of interest. The physical interplay which momentarily halted work activity would initiate verbal exchanges and thought processes to occupy group members until the next interruption. The group interactions thus not only marked off the time; they gave it content and hurried it along.

Most of the breaks in the daily series were designated as "times" in the parlance of the clicker operators, and they featured the consumption of food or drink of one sort or another. There was coffee time, peach time, banana time, fish time, coke time, and, of course, lunch time. Other inter-ruptions, which formed part of the series but were not verbally recog-nized as times, were window time, pickup time, and the staggered quitting times of Sammy and Ike. These latter unnamed times did not involve the partaking of refreshments.

My attention was first drawn to this times business during my first week of employment when I was encouraged to join in the sharing of two peaches. It was Sammy who provided the peaches; he drew them from his lunch box after making the announcement, "Peach time!" On this first occasion I refused the proffered fruit, but thereafter regularly consumed my half peach. Sammy continued to provide the peaches and to make the "Peach time!" announcement, although there were days when Ike would remind him that it was peach time, urging him to hurry up with the mid-morning snack. Ike invariably complained about the quality of the fruit, and his complaints fed the fires of continued banter between peach donor and critical recipient. I did find the fruit a bit on the scrubby side but felt, before I achieved insight into the function of peach time, that Ike was showing poor manners by looking a gift horse in the mouth. I wondered why Sammy continued to share his peaches with such an ingrate.

Banana time followed peach time by approximately an hour. Sammy again provided the refreshments, namely, one banana. There was, how-ever, no four-way sharing of Sammy's banana. Ike would gulp it down by himself after surreptitiously extracting it from Sammy's lunch box, kept on a shelf behind Sammy's work station. Each morning, after making the snatch, Ike would call out, "Banana time!" and proceed to down his prize while Sammy made futile protests and denunciations. George would join in with mild remonstrances, sometimes scolding Sammy for making so much fuss. The banana was one which Sammy brought for his own con-sumption at lunch time; he never did get to eat his banana, but kept bring-ing one for his lunch. At first this daily theft startled and amazed me. Then I grew to look forward to the daily seizure and the verbal interaction which followed.

Window time came next. It followed banana time as a regular conse-quence of Ike's castigation by the indignant Sammy. After "taking" re-peated references to himself as a person badly lacking in morality and character, Ike would "finally" retaliate by opening the window which faced Sammy's machine, to let the "cold air" blow in on Sammy. The slandering which would, in its echolalic repetition, wear down Ike's patience and forbearance usually took the form of the invidious comparison. "George is a good daddy! Ike is a bad man! A very bad man!" Opening the window would take a little time to accomplish and would involve a great deal of verbal interplay between Ike and Sammy, both before and after the event. Ike would threaten, make feints toward the window, then finally open it. Sammy would protest, argue, and make claims that the air blowing in on him would give him a cold; he would eventually have to leave his machine to close the window. Sometimes the weather was slightly chilly, and the draft from the window unpleasant; but cool or hot, windy or still, window time arrived each day. (I assume that it was originally a cold season development.) George's part in this interplay, in spite of the "good daddy" laudations, was to encourage Ike in his window work. He would stress the tonic values of fresh air and chide Sammy for his unappreciativeness.

Following window time came lunch time, a formally designated half-hour for the midday repast and rest break. At this time, informal interaction would feature exchanges between Ike and George. The former would start eating his lunch a few minutes before noon, and the latter, in his role as straw boss, would censure him for malobservance of the rules. Ike's off-beat luncheon usually involved a previous tampering with George's alarm clock. Ike would set the clock ahead a few minutes in order to maintain his eating schedule without detection, and George would discover these small daylight saving changes.

The first "time" interruption of the day I did not share. It occurred soon after I arrived on the job, at eight o'clock. George and Ike would share a small pot of coffee brewed on George's hot plate.

Pickup time, fish time, and coke time came in the afternoon. I name it pickup time to represent the official visit of the man who made daily calls to cart away boxes of clicked materials. The arrival of the pickup man, a Negro, was always a noisy one, like the arrival of a daily passenger train in an isolated small town. Interaction attained a quick peak of intensity to crowd into a few minutes all communications, necessary and otherwise. Exchanges invariably included loud depreciations by the pickup man of the amount of work accomplished in the clicking department during the preceding 24 hours. Such scoffing would be on the order of "Is that all you've got done? What do you boys do all day?" These devaluations would be countered with allusions to the "soft job" enjoyed by the pickup man. During the course of the exchanges news items would be dropped, some of serious import, such as reports of accomplished or impending layoffs in the various plants of the company, or of gains or losses in orders for company products. Most of the news items, however, involved bits of information on plant employees told in a light vein. Information relayed by the clicker operators was usually told about each other, mainly in the form of summaries of the most recent kidding sequences. Some of this material was repetitive, carried over from day to day. Sammy would be the butt of most of this newscasting, although he would make occasional counterreports on Ike and George. An invariable part of the interactional content of pickup time was Ike's introduction of the pickup man to George. "Meet Mr. Papeatis!" Ike would say in mock solemnity and dignity. Each day the pickup man "met" Mr. Papeatis, to the obvious irritation of the latter. Another pickup time invariably would bring Baby (or Mable) into the interaction. George would always issue the loud warning to the pickup man: "Now I want you to stay away from Baby! She's Henry's girl!" Henry was a burly Negro with a booming bass voice who made infrequent trips to the clicking room with lift-truck loads of materials. He was reputedly quite a ladies' man among the colored population of the factory. George's warning to "Stay away from Baby!" was issued to every Negro who entered the shop. Babys' only part in this was to laugh at the horseplay.

About mid-afternoon came fish time. George and Ike would stop work for a few minutes to consume some sort of pickled fish which Ike provided. Neither Sammy nor I partook of this nourishment, nor were we invited. For this omission I was grateful; the fish, brought in a newspaper and with the head and tail intact, produced a reverse effect on my appetite. George and Ike seemed to share a great liking for fish. Each Friday night, as a regular ritual, they would enjoy a fish dinner together at a nearby restaurant. On these nights Ike would work until 8:30 and leave the plant with George.

Coke time came late in the afternoon, and was an occasion for total participation. The four of us took turns in buying the drinks and in making the trip for them to a fourth floor vending machine. Through George's manipulation of the situation, it eventually became my daily chore to go after the cokes; the straw boss had noted that I made a much faster trip to the fourth floor and back than Sammy or Ike.

Sammy left the plant at 5:30, and Ike ordinarily retired from the scene an hour and a half later. These quitting times were not marked by any distinctive interaction save the one regular exchange between Sammy and George over the former's "early washup." Sammy's tendency was to crowd his washing up toward five o'clock, and it was George's concern to keep it from further creeping advance. After Ike's departure came Boo's arrival. Boo's was a striking personality productive of a change in topics of conversation to fill in the last hour of the long workday.

Themes

To put flesh, so to speak, on this interactional frame of "times," my work group had developed various "themes" of verbal interplay which had become standardized in their repetition. These topics of conversation ranged in quality from an extreme of nonsensical chatter to another extreme of serious discourse. Unlike the times, these themes flowed one into the other in no particular sequence of predictability. Serious conversation could suddenly melt into horseplay, and vice versa. In the middle of a serious discussion on the high cost of living, Ike might drop a weight behind the easily startled Sammy, who hit him over the head with a dusty paper sack. Interaction would immediately drop to a low comedy exchange of slaps, threats, guffaws, and disapprobations which would invariably include a ten-minute echolalia of "Ike is a bad man, a very bad man! George is a good daddy, a very fine man!" Or, on the other hand, a stream of such invidious comparisons as followed a surreptitious switching-off of Sammy's machine by the playful Ike might merge suddenly into a discussion of the pros and cons of saving for one's funeral.

"Kidding themes" were usually started by George or Ike, and Sammy was usually the butt of the joke. Sometimes Ike would have to "take it," seldom George. One favorite kidding theme involved Sammy's alleged receipt of $100 a month from his son. The points stressed were that Sammy did not have to work long hours, or did not have to work at all, because he had a son to support him. George would always point out that he sent money to his daughter; she did not send money to him. Sammy received occasional calls from his wife, and his claim that these calls were requests to shop for groceries on the way home were greeted with feigned disbelief. Sammy was ribbed for being closely watched, bossed, and henpecked by his wife, and the expression "Are you a man or mouse?" became an echolalic utterance, used both in and out of the original context.

Ike, who shared his machine and the work scheduled for it with Boo, the night operator, came in for constant invidious comparison on the subject of output. The socially isolated Boo, who chose work rather than sleep on his lonely night shift, kept up a high level of performance, and George never tired of pointing this out to Ike. It so happened that Boo, an Arabian Moslem from Palestine, had no use for Jews in general; and Ike, who was Jewish, had no use for Boo in particular. Whenever George would extol Boo's previous night's production, Ike would try to turn the conversation into a general discussion on the need for educating the Arabs. George, never permitting the development of serious discussion on the topic, would repeat a smirking warning, "You watch out for Boo! He's got a long knife!"

The "poom poom" theme was one that caused no sting. It would come up several times a day to be enjoyed as unbarbed fun by the three older clicker operators. Ike was usually the one to raise the question, "How many times you go poom poom last night?" The person questioned usually replied with claims of being "too old for poom poom." If this theme did develop a goat, it was I. When it was pointed out that I was a younger man, this provided further grist for the poom poom mill. I soon grew weary of this poom poom business, so dear to the hearts of the three old satyrs, and, knowing where the conversation would inevitably lead, winced whenever Ike brought up the subject. . . .

Serious themes included the relating of major misfortunes suffered in the past by group members. George referred again and again to the loss, by fire, of his business establishment. Ike's chief complaints centered around a chronically ill wife who had undergone various operations and periods of hospital care. Ike spoke with discouragement of the expenses attendant upon hiring a housekeeper for himself and his children; he referred with disappointment and disgust to a teen-age son, an inept lad who "couldn't even fix his own lunch. He couldn't even make himself a sandwich!" Sammy's reminiscences centered on the loss of a flourishing business when he had to flee Europe ahead of Nazi invasion.

But all serious topics were not tales of woe. One favorite serious theme which was optimistic in tone could be called either "Danelly's future" or "getting Danelly a better job." It was known that I had been attending "college," the magic door to opportunity, although my specific course of study remained somewhat obscure. Suggestions poured forth on good lines of work to get into, and these suggestions were backed with accounts of friends, and friends of friends, who had made good via the academic route. My answer to the expected question, "Why are you working here?" always stressed the "lots of overtime" feature, and this explanation seemed to suffice for short-range goals.

There was one theme of especially solemn import, the "professor theme." This theme might also be termed "George's daughter's marriage theme"; for the recent marriage of George's only chld was inextricably bound up with George's connection with higher learning. The daughter had married the son of a professor who instructed in one of the local colleges. This professor theme was not in the strictest sense a conversation piece; when the subject came up, George did all the talking. The two Jewish operatives remained silent as they listened with deep respect, if not actual awe, to George's accounts of the Big Wedding which, including the wedding pictures, entailed an expense of $1,000. It was monologue, but there was listening, there was communication, the sacred communication of a temple, when George told of going for Sunday afternoon walks on the Midway with the professor, or of joining the professor for a Sunday dinner. Whenever he spoke of the professor, his daughter, the wedding, or even of the new son-in-law, who remained for the most part in the background, a sort of incidental like the wedding cake, George was complete master of the interaction. His manner, in speaking to the rank-and-file of clicker operators, was indeed that of master deigning to notice his underlings. I came to the conclusion that it was the professor connection, not the straw-boss-ship or the extra nickel an hour, which provided the fount of George's superior status in the group.

If the professor theme may be regarded as the cream of verbal inter-action, the "chatter themes" should be classed as the dregs. The chatter themes were hardly themes at all; perhaps they should be labeled "verbal states," or "oral autisms." Some were of doubtful status as communication; they were like the howl or cry of an animal responding to its own physio-logical state. They were exclamations, ejaculations, snatches of song or doggerel, talkings-to-oneself, mutterings. Their classification as themes would rest on their repetitive character. They were echolalic utterances, repeated over and over. An already mentioned example would be Sammy's repetition of "George is a good daddy, a very fine man! Ike is a bad man, a very bad man!" Also, Sammy's repetition of "Don't bother me! Can't you see I'm busy? I'm a very busy man!" for ten minutes after Ike had dropped a weight behind him would fit the classification. Ike would shout "Ma-mariba!" at intervals between repetition of bits of verse, such as

> Mama on the bed,
> Papa on the floor,
> Baby in the crib
> Says giver some more!

Sometimes the three operators would pick up one of these simple chatter-ings in a sort of chorus. "Are you man or mouse? I ask you, are you man or mouse?" was a favorite of this type.

So initial discouragement with the meagerness of social interaction I now recognized as due to lack of observation. The interaction was there in constant flow. It captured attention and held interest to make the long day pass. The 12 hours of "click, _____ move die, _____ click, _____ move die" became as easy to endure as eight hours of varied activity in the oil fields. The "beast of boredom" was gentled to the harmlessness of a kitten.

BLACK FRIDAY: DISINTEGRATION OF THE GROUP

But all this was before "Black Friday." Events of that dark day shattered the edifice of interaction, its framework of times and mosaic of themes, and reduced the work situation to a state of social atomization and machine-tending drudgery. The explosive element was introduced deliberately, but without prevision of its consequences.

On Black Friday, Sammy was not present; he was on vacation. There was no peach time that morning, of course, and no banana time. But George and Ike held their coffee time, as usual, and a steady flow of themes was filling the morning quite adequately. It seemed like a normal day in the making, at least one which was going to meet the somewhat reduced expectations created by Sammy's absence.

Suddenly I was possessed of an inspiration for modification of the pro-fessor theme. When this idea struck, I was working at Sammy's machine, clicking out leather parts for billfolds. It was not difficult to get the atten-tion of close neighbor Ike to suggest sotto voice, "Why don't you tell him you saw the professor teaching in a barber college on Madison Street? . . . Make it near Halsted Street."

Ike thought this one over for a few minutes and caught the vision of its possibilities. After an interval of steady application to his clicking, he informed the unsuspecting George of his near West Side discovery; he had seen the professor busy at his instructing in a barber college in the lower reaches of Hobohemia.

George reacted to this announcement with stony silence. The burden of questioning Ike for further details on his discovery fell upon me. Ike had not elaborated his story very much before we realized that the show was not going over. George kept getting redder in the face and more tight-lipped; he slammed into his clicking with increased vigor. I made one last weak attempt to keep the play on the road by remarking that barber colleges paid pretty well. George turned to hiss at me, "You'll have to go to Kankakee with Ike" I dropped the subject. Ike whispered to me, "George is sore!"

George was indeed sore. He didn't say another word the rest of the morning. There was no conversation at lunchtime, nor was there any after lunch. A pall of silence had fallen over the clicker room. Fish time fell a casualty. George did not touch the coke I brought for him. A very long, very dreary afternoon dragged on. Finally, after Ike left for home, George broke the silence to reveal his feelings to me: "Ike acts like a five-year-old, not a man! He doesn't even have the respect of the niggers. But he's got to act like a man around here! He's always fooling around! I'm going to stop that! I'm going to show him his place! . . . Jews will ruin you, if you let them. I don't care if he sings, but the first time he mentions my name, I'm going to shut him up! It's always 'Meet Mr. Papeatis! George is a good daddy!" And all that. He's paid to work! If he doesn't work, I'm going to tell Joe!"

Then came a succession of dismal workdays devoid of times and barren of themes. Ike did not sing, nor did he recite bawdy verse. The shop songbird was caught in the grip of icy winter. What meager communication there was took a sequence of patterns which proved interesting only in retrospect.

For three days, George would not speak to Ike. Ike made several weak attempts to break the wall of silence which George had put between them, but George did not respond; it was as if he did not hear. George would speak to me, on infrequent occasions, and so would Ike. They did not speak to each other.

On the third day George advised me of his new communication policy, designed for dealing with Ike, and for Sammy, too, when the latter returned to work. Interaction was now on a "strictly business" basis, with emphasis to be placed on raising the level of shop output. The effect of this new policy on production remained indeterminate. Before the fourth day had ended, George got carried away by his narrowed interests to the point of making sarcastic remarks about the poor work performances of the absent Sammy. Although addressed to me, these caustic depreciations were obviously for the benefit of Ike. Later in the day Ike spoke to me, for George's benefit, of Sammy's outstanding ability to run out billfold parts. For the next four days, the prevailing silence of the shop was occasionally broken by either harsh criticism or fulsome praise of Sammy's outstanding workmanship. I did not risk replying to either impeachment or panegyric for fear of involvement in further situational deteriorations.

Twelve-hour days were creeping again at snails' pace. The strictly business communications were of no help, and the sporadic bursts of distaste or enthusiasm for Sammy's clicking ability helped very little. With the return of boredom, came a return of fatigue. My legs tired as the afternoons dragged on, and I became engaged in conscious efforts to rest one by shifting my weight to the other. I would pause in my work to stare through the barred windows at the grimy brick wall across the alley; and, turning my head, I would notice that Ike was staring at the wall too. George would do very little work after Ike left the shop at night. He would sit in a chair and complain of weariness and sore feet.

In desperation, I fell back on my game of work, my blues and greens and whites, my ovals and trapezoids, and my scraping the block. I came to surpass Boo, the energetic night worker, in volume of output. George referred to me as a "day Boo" (dayshift Boo) and suggested that I "keep" Sammy's machine. I managed to avoid this promotion, and consequent estrangement with Sammy, by pleading attachment to my own machine.

When Sammy returned to work, discovery of the cleavage between George and Ike left him stunned. "They were the best of friends!" he said to me in bewilderment.

George now offered Sammy direct, savage criticisms of his work. For several days the good-natured Sammy endured these verbal aggressions without losing his temper, but when George shouted at him, "You work like a preacher!" Sammy became very angry, indeed. I had a few anxious moments when I thought that the two old friends were going to come to blows.

Then, 13 days after Black Friday, came an abrupt change in the pattern of interaction. George and Ike spoke to each other again in friendly conversation: I noticed Ike talking to George after lunch. The two had newspapers of fish at George's cabinet. Ike was excited; he said, "I'll pull up a chair!" The two ate for 10 minutes. . . . It seems that they went up to the 22nd Street Exchange together during lunch period to cash pay checks.

That afternoon Ike and Sammy started to play again, and Ike burst once more into song. Old themes reappeared as suddenly as the desert flowers in spring. At first, George managed to maintain some show of the dignity of superordination. When Ike started to sing snatches of "You Are My Sunshine," George suggested that he get "more production." Then Ike backed up George in pressuring Sammy for more production. Sammy turned this exhortation into low comedy by calling Ike a "slave driver" and by shouting over and over again, "Don't bother me! I'm a busy man!" On one occasion, as if almost overcome with joy and excitement, Sammy cried out, "Don't bother me! I'll tell Rothman! [the company president] I'll tell the union! Don't mention my name! I hate you!"

I knew that George was definitely back into the spirit of the thing when he called to Sammy, "Are you man or mouse?" He kept up the "man or mouse" chatter for some time.

George was for a time reluctant to accept fruit when it was offered to him, and he did not make a final capitulation to coke time until five days after renewal of the fun and fooling. Strictly speaking, there never was a return to banana time, peach time, or window time. However, the sharing and snitching of fruit did go on once more, and the window in front of Sammy's machine played a more prominent part than ever in the renaissance of horseplay in the clicker room. In fact, the "rush to the window" became an integral part of increasingly complex themes and repeated sequences of interaction. This window rushing became especially bound up with new developments which featured what may be termed the *anal gesture*.[10] Introduced by Ike, and given backing by an enthusiastic, very playful George, the anal gesture became a key component of fun and fooling during the remaining weeks of my stay in the shop: Ike broke wind, and put his head in his hand on the block as Sammy grabbed a rod and made a mock rush to open the window. He beat Ike on the head, and George threw some water on him, playfully. In came the Negro head of the leather department; he remarked jokingly that we should take out the machines and make a playroom out of the shop.

Of course, George's demand for greater production was metamorphized into horseplay. His shout of "Production please" became a chatter theme to accompany the varied antics of Ike and Sammy.

The professor theme was dropped completely. George never again mentioned his Sunday walks on the Midway with the professor.

CONCLUSION

Speculative assessment of the possible significance of my observations on informal interaction in the clicking room may be set forth in a series of general statements.

Practical Application

First, in regard to possible practical application to problems of industrial management, these observations seem to support the generally accepted notion that one key source of job satisfaction lies in the informal interaction shared by members of a work group. In the clicking room situation the spontaneous development of a pattern combination of horseplay, serious conversation, and frequent sharing of food and drink reduced the monotony of simple, repetitive operations to the point where a regular schedule of long work days became livable. This kind of group interplay may be termed "consumatory" in the sense indicated by Dewey, when he makes a basic distinction between "instrumental" and "consumatory" communication.[11] The enjoyment of communication "for its own sake" as "mere sociabilities," as "free, aimless social intercourse," brings job satisfaction, at least job endurance, to work situations largely bereft of creative experience.

In regard to another managerial concern, employee productivity, any appraisal of the influence of group interaction upon clicking room output could be no more than roughly impressionistic. I obtained no evidence to warrant a claim that banana time, or any of its accompaniments in consumatory interaction, boosted production. To the contrary, my diary recordings express an occasional perplexity in the form of "How does this

---

[10] I have been puzzled to note widespread appreciation of this gesture in the "consumatory" communication of the working men of this nation. For the present I leave it to clinical psychologists to account for the nature and pervasiveness of this social bond.

[11] John Dewey, *Experience and Nature* (Chicago: Open Court Publishing, 1925), pp. 202–6.

company manage to stay in business?" However, I did not obtain sufficient evidence to indicate that, under the prevailing conditions of laissez-faire management, the output of our group would have been more impressive if the playful cavorting of three middle-aged gentlemen about the barred windows had never been. As far as achievement of managerial goals is concerned, the most that could be suggested is that leavening the deadly boredom of individualized work routines with a concurrent flow of group festivities had a negative effect on turnover. I left the group, with sad reluctance, under the pressure of strong urgings to accept a research fellowship which would involve no factory toil. My fellow clickers stayed with their machines to carry on their labors in the spirit of banana time.

Theoretical Considerations

Secondly, possible contribution to ongoing sociological inquiry into the behavior of small groups, in general, and factory work groups, in particular, may lie in one or more of the following ideational products of my clicking room experience.

1. In their day-long confinement together in a small room spatially and socially isolated from other work areas of the factory the clicking department employees found themselves ecologically situated for development of a "natural" group. Such a development did take place; from worker intercommunications did emerge the full-blown sociocultural system of consumatory interactions which I came to share, observe, and record in the process of my socialization.

2. These interactions had a content which could be abstracted from the total existential flow of observable doings and sayings for labeling and objective consideration. That is, they represented a distinctive subculture, with its recurring patterns of reciprocal influencings which I have described as times and themes.

3. From these interactions may also be abstracted a social structure of statuses and roles. This structure may be discerned in the carrying out of the various informal activities which provide the content of the subculture of the group. The times and themes were performed with a system of roles which formed a sort of pecking hierarchy. Horseplay had its initiators and its victims, its amplifiers and its chorus; kidding had its attackers and attacked, its least attacked and its most attacked, its ready acceptors of attack and its strong resistors to attack. The fun went on with the participation of all, but within the controlling frame of status, a matter of who can say or do what to whom and get away with it.

4. In both the cultural content and the social structure of clicker group interaction could be seen the permeation of influences which flowed from the various multiple group memberships of the participants. Past and present "other-group" experiences or anticipated "outside" social connections provided significant materials for the building of themes and for the establishment and maintenance of status and role relationships. The impact of reference group affiliations on clicking room interaction was notably revealed in the sacred, status-conferring expression of the professor theme.

This impact was brought into very sharp focus in developments which followed my attempt to degrade the topic and, correlatively, to demote George.

5. Stability of the clicking room social system was never threatened by immediate outside pressures. Ours was not an instrumental group, subject to disintegration in a losing struggle against environmental obstacles or oppositions. It was not striving for corporate goals; nor was it faced with the enmity of other groups. It was strictly a consumatory group, devoted to the maintenance of patterns of self-entertainment. Under existing conditions, disruption of unity could come only from within.

Potentials for breakdown were endemic in the interpersonal interactions involved in conducting the group's activities. Patterns of fun and fooling had developed within a matrix of frustration. Tensions born of long hours of relatively meaningless work were released in the mock aggressions of horseplay. In the recurrent attack, defense, and counterattack there continually lurked the possibility that words or gestures harmless in conscious intent might cross the subtle boundary of accepted, playful aggression to be perceived as a real assault. While such an occurrence might incur displeasure no more lasting than necessary for the quick clarification or creation of kidding norms, it might also spark a charge of hostility sufficient to disorganize the group.

A contributory potential for breakdown from within lay in the dissimilar "other-group" experiences of the operators. These other-group affiliations and identifications could provide differences in tastes and sensitivities, including appreciation of humor, differences which could make maintenance of consensus in regard to kidding norms a hazardous process of trial and error adjustments.

6. The risk involved in this trial and error determination of consensus on fun and fooling in a touchy situation of frustration—mock aggression—was made evident when I attempted to introduce alterations in the professor theme. The group disintegrated, *instanter*. That is, there was an abrupt cessation of the interactions which constituted our groupness. Although both George and I were solidly linked in other-group affiliations with the higher learning, there was not enough agreement in our attitudes toward university professors to prevent the interactional development which shattered our factory play group. George perceived my offered alterations as a real attack, and he responded with strong hostility directed against Ike, the perceived assailant, and Sammy, a fellow traveler.

My innovations, if accepted, would have lowered the tone of the sacred professor theme, if not to "Stay Away from Baby" ribaldry, then at least to the verbal slapstack level of "finding Danelly an apartment." Such a downgrading of George's reference group would in turn, have downgraded George. His status in the shop group hinged largely upon his claimed relations with the professor.

7. Integration of our group was fully restored after a series of changes in the patterning and quality in clicking-room interaction. It might be

said that reintegration took place in these changes, that the series was a progressive one of step-by-step improvement in relations, that reequilibration was in process during the three weeks that passed between initial communication collapse and complete return to "normal" interaction.

The cycle of loss and recovery of equilibrium may be crudely charted according to the following sequence of phases: *(a)* the stony silence of "not speaking"; *(b)* the confining of communication to formal matters connected with work routines; *(c)* the return of informal give-and-take in the form of harshly sarcastic kidding, mainly on the subject of work performance, addressed to a neutral go-between for the "benefit" of the object of aggression; *(d)* highly emotional direct attack, and counterattack, in the form of criticism and defense of work performance; *(e)* a sudden rapprochement expressed in serious, dignified, but friendly conversation; *(f)* return to informal interaction in the form of mutually enjoyed mock aggression; *(g)* return to informal interaction in the form of regular patterns of sharing food and drink.

The group had disintegrated when George withdrew from participation; and, since the rest of us were at all times ready for rapprochement, reintegration was dependent upon his "return." Therefore, each change of phase in interaction on the road to recovery could be said to represent an increment of return on George's part. Or, conversely, each phase could represent an increment of reacceptance of punished deviants. Perhaps more generally applicable to description of a variety of reunion situations would be conceptualization of the phase changes as increments of reassociation without an atomistic differentiation of the "movements" of individuals.

8.   To point out that George played a key role in this particular case of reequilibration is not to suggest that the homeostatic controls of a social system may be located in a type of role or in a patterning of role relationships. Such controls could be but partially described in terms of human interaction; they would be functional to the total configuration of conditions within the field of influence. The automatic controls of a mechanical system operate as such only under certain achieved and controlled conditions. The human body recovers from disease when conditions for such homeostasis are "right." The clicking room group regained equilibrium under certain undetermined conditions. One of a number of other possible outcomes could have developed had conditions not been favorable for recovery.

For purposes of illustration, and from reflections on the case, I would consider the following as possibly necessary conditions for reintegration of our group: *(a)* Continued monotony of work operations; *(b)* Continued lack of a comparatively adequate substitute for the fun and fooling release from work tensions; *(c)* Liability of the operatives to escape from the work situation or from each other, within the work situation. George could not fire Ike or Sammy to remove them from his presence, and it would have been difficult for the three middle-aged men to find other jobs if they were to quit the shop. Shop space was small, and the machines close together. Like a submarine crew, they had to "live together"; (d) Lack of conflicting definitions of the situation after Ike's perception of George's reaction to the "barber college" attack. George's anger and his punishment of the offenders were perceived as justified; (e) Lack of introduction of new issues or causes which might have carried justification for new attacks and counterattacks, thus leading interaction into a spiral of conflict and crystallization of conflict norms. For instance, had George reported his offenders to the superintendent for their poor work performance; had he, in his anger, committed some offense which would have led to reporting of a grievance to local union officials; had he made his anti-Semitic remarks in the presence of Ike or Sammy, or had I relayed these remarks to them; had I tried to "take over" Sammy's machine, as George had urged; then the interactional outcome might have been permanent disintegration of the group.

9.   Whether or not the particular patterning of interactional change previously noted is somehow typical of a "reequilibration process" is not a major question here. My purpose in discriminating the seven changes is primarily to suggest that reequilibration, when it does occur, may be described in observable phases and that the emergence of each succeeding phase should be dependent upon the configuration of conditions of the preceding one. Alternative eventual outcomes may change in their probabilities, as the phases succeed each other, just as prognosis for recovery in sickness may change as the disease situation changes.

10.   Finally, discrimination of phase changes in social process may have practical as well as scientific value. Trained and skillful administrators might follow the practice in medicine of introducing aids to reequilibration when diagnosis shows that they are needed.

Cognitive versus Reinforcement Views of Intrinsic Motivation*

LARRY E. PATE

A central thrust of managerial psychology has been to determine the motivating forces that energize, direct, and sustain individual work behavior (59). Lewin's (37) conceptualization that behavior is the result of interactions between individual and environmental factors is still widely accepted; but this approach is too global from a research standpoint, and there is disagreement on the composition of these factors. A major controversy historically surrounds the relative importance of each factor as a determinant of behavior and the extent to which other concepts (such as needs and drives) are innate or learned. Cognitive theorists argue that the individual's cognitive processes play an important role in determining behavior, while reinforcement theorists retort that it is unnecessary, if not impossible, to examine such thought processes, and therefore our central concern should be the behavior itself. Each theoretical position specifies alternative mixes and categories of variables.

This article makes no attempt to resolve such debate, but rather explicates the positions of mechanistic-reinforcement theorists (such as Scott) and organismic-cognitive theorists (like Deci), specifically as they relate to the current controversy regarding intrinsic motivation. Briefly, this controversy centers on Deci's research, a departure from the central thrust of the cognitive school and one which has provided a convenient target for reinforcement theorists like Scott. First the theoretical roots of each group of theorists will be traced, and then specific points of disagreement on the measurement of intrinsic motivation and on potential areas of application in organizations will be highlighted.

* Reproduced by permission of *Academy of Management Review,* July 1978, pp. 505–19.

REINFORCEMENT THEORY BACKGROUND

The work of Watson (65) and his commitment to the concept of learning is said to mark the formal beginning of behaviorism (38, 66). Watson's emphasis on stimulus-response (S-R) mechanisms extended the earlier classical-conditioning work of Russian psychologists, notably Pavlov. Behavioral learning theorists traditionally draw a distinction between *respondent* (unlearned: controlled or elicited by prior stimulation) and *operant* (learned: influenced by events which follow) behavior (see 24, 30, 54, 55, for detailed reviews of reinforcement theory and research).

The earliest reinforcement theory of learning, Thorndike's (61) "law of effect," states that satisfying consequences serve to reinforce S-R connections. In essence, reinforcement theories are an extension of Watson's S-R paradigm and posit that external or internal stimuli (goads) determine behavior through mechanistic S-R bonds and reinforcement histories. All behavior is said to be learned and solely a function of its consequences, so that behavior toward an object will persist only when the individual performing the behavior is adequately reinforced; in the absence of removal of either continuous or intermittent reinforcement, extinction of the behavior is said to occur.

These and other theories, such as Hull's (29) drive-reduction theory and Spence's (56) refinement of it, influenced the work of current reinforcement theorists, notably Skinner (54, 55). Skinner first made the important distinction between operant and respondent behavior and focused upon the conditioning aspects of operant behavior (38). Table 1 compares neo-

Table 1
Summary of Mechanistic Theories*

Theory Classification	Theory Structure	Description
Behaviorist	S-R	Behavior explained in terms of stimulus-response connections. Intervening hypothetical constructs are not employed in the analysis of action. Proponents include Skinner, Watson, other associationists, and behaviorists.
Neobehaviorist	S-Construct-R	Behavior explained in terms of stimulus-response connections. Intervening constructs also are employed in the analysis of action, such as drive, incentive, and so on. Proponents include Spence, Hull, Miller, Brown, and other neobehaviorists.

* Adapted from B. Weiner, *Theories of Motivation: From Mechanisms to Cognition* (Chicago: Rand McNally, 1972).

behaviorist and behaviorist classes of mechanistic-reinforcement theories that explain behavior with and without the use of intervening (but noncognitive) constructs.

Behavior modification, a scientifically derived set of behavioristic principles and techniques, represents a major attempt to apply operant and respondent conditioning techniques for the purpose of achieving effective behavior change and control. While the use of behavior modification principles has largely been neglected in the management and organizational behavior (OB) literature (cf. 44), there have been several recent attempts to test these principles in natural and organizational settings (2, 34, 38, 43, 46, 47, 52, 60).

COGNITIVE THEORY BACKGROUND

Following Weiner, "there are types of reinforcement theories, types of cognitive theories, and all shades of grey in between" (66, p. 7). The cognitive versus reinforcement dichotomy is artificial. Weiner refers to the theories of Lewin and Atkinson as only quasi-cognitive, for reinforcement concepts seem to have had a greater influence on these theorists than cognitive constructs. The common element shared by cognitive theorists is the belief that it is necessary to examine a particular class of intervening variables when explaining behavior; cognitive theories posit that an antecedent stimuli is separated from the final behavior response by a mediating cognitive event. These theories differ on what constitutes the cognitive act as well as on how the cognition influences behavior. The intervening cognition may be a perceived path to the goal (37), expectancy (64), or subjective probability of success (3).

The theoretical foundation of a cognitive approach is traceable to the writings of Kant (31) and to phenomenological thinking; Lewin, for example, was greatly influenced by Cassirer, a prominent neo-Kantian (66). Van de Geer and Jaspers (63) note that cognitive theory ranges from neobehavioristic mediation to phenomenological interpretation. Baldwin defines the approach as follows:

> A cognitive theory of behavior assumes that the first stage in the chain of events initiated by the stimulus situation and resulting in the behavioral act is the construction of a cognitive representation of the distal environment. The later events in the chain are instigated, modified, and guided by this cognitive representation. The cognitive representation thus acts as the effective environment which arouses motives and emotions, and guides overt behavior toward its target or goal (4, p. 321).

One type of cognitive theory, expectancy theory, limits the range of cognitive constructs by focusing on anticipatory end states or goals. The theories of Lewin (37), Rotter (50), Tolman (62), Edwards (19), Atkinson (3), Vroom (64), and Porter and Lawler (48) fall within this category. Expectancy models have been thoroughly reviewed and criticized elsewhere (27, 28, 41, 42, 57) and will not be discussed here.

A second class of cognitive theories, referred to here as extraexpectancy, examines cognitive concepts, such as causal attributions and social comparisons, in addition to anticipatory end states. The theories of Freud (21), Festinger (20), Heider (26), Adams (1), and Deci (12) are included in this

Table 2
Summary of Cognitive Theories

Theory Classification	Theory Structure	Description
Expectancy .... S-Cognition-R		Thoughts intervene between incoming information and the final behavioral response. The main cognitive determinant of action is an "expectancy." Proponents include Atkinson, Lewin, Porter, Rotter, Tolman, and Vroom.
Extraexpectancy .... S-Cognition-R		Thoughts intervene between incoming information and the final behavioral response. Many cognitive processes determine action, such as information seeking, causal attributions, and the like. Proponents include Adams, Deci, Festinger, Heider, Kelley, and Lazarus.

category. Table 2 compares these two classes of cognitive theories. Other distinctions, such as the humanistic approaches typified by Maslow, Mc-Gregor, and Rogers, could also be made.

In terms of the motivation construct, the writing of deCharms (8) is often cited as a more recent point of departure of cognitive theory. He distinguishes between behavior that is intrinsically motivated and behavior that is extrinsically motivated and argues that intrinsic and extrinsic motivation may interact rather than summate, counter to other cognitive theorists (e.g., 48, 64). Further, deCharms predicts an interaction between intrinsic and extrinsic dimensions if rewards are withheld. Although the meaning of *intrinsic motivation* remains obscure (cf. 17, 53), it generally refers to the pleasure of value associated with the content of the task itself, while *extrinsic motivation* refers to the value an individual derives from the environment surrounding the context of the work. Regardless of what intrinsic motivation actually is, the crucial issues are whether individuals distinguish between intrinsic and extrinsic causes (57) and how to determine the consequences of such distinctions (7).

Research stimulated by deCharms' theorizing, particularly that conducted by Deci and associates (5, 9, 10, 11, 12, 13, 14, 15, 16), raises important questions regarding the effects of extrinsic rewards, such as pay, on intrinsic motivation and on subsequent behavioral acts. With this brief background, let us now turn to Deci's cognitive framework, which makes predictions counter to reinforcement and other cognitive theorists.

RESEARCH ON INTRINSIC MOTIVATION

Essentially, Deci's argument is that individuals who are paid to perform an interesting task will attribute their behavior to external forces and thus reduce their intrinsic interest in the task itself. Deci conducted a series of laboratory studies (and a tangentially related field study with an N = 4) in which subjects, under varying degrees of contingent and noncontingent reward conditions, engaged in a presumably interesting task (such as completing the Soma puzzle), after which behavioral measures of the subject's intrinsic motivation were obtained. Subjects in most of these studies were students who participated in the experiment to satisfy requirements for an introductory course in psychology. The dependent measure of intrinsic motivation was the amount of time subjects continued to engage in the puzzle-completion task during a free-choice period following the experimental time period; Deci's assumption was that subjects' intrinsic motivation could be aroused during the experiment and that the presence of contingent versus noncontingent rewards would systematically alter these internal motivation states. Deci also hypothesized that verbal reinforcement would increase intrinsic motivation (9, 10), but that noncontingent monetary rewards would not affect intrinsic motivation (11).

Although slight variations exist in each study, Deci found consistent differences between experimental and control groups on the dependent measures when rewards were given contingent upon desired behavior (12, 14). He interpreted these findings as support for deCharms' hypothesis that extrinsic rewards can decrease intrinsic motivation. Similar findings have been reported in studies conducted by other investigators (18, 22, 23, 32, 35, 36, 49), lending some support to this position. To account for such findings, and perhaps even in anticipation of the charge that he has not contributed to theoretical development of the intrinsic motivation construct (53), Deci has proposed a cognitive evaluation theory (12, 13, 14) which equates intrinsic motivation with Heider's (26) concept of perceived locus of causality (see Figure 1).

Deci's research has been criticized in a number of recent papers (6, 25, 39, 45, 51, 53, 57). Salancik (51) discusses two procedural limitations to Deci's work: (a) his failure to report performance data as an indication of the difficulty of the task, and (b) his reliance on task persistence as the sole dependent measure. In an attempt to control for these limitations, Salancik

Figure 1
A Schematic Representation of a Cognitive System of Intrinsically and Extrinsically Motivated Behavior

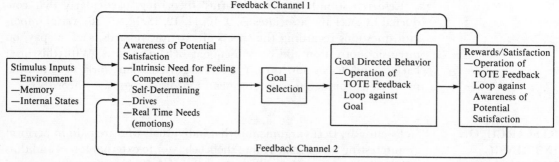

Source: E. L. Deci. "Notes on the Theory and Metatheory of Intrinsic Motivation," *Organizational Behavior and Human Performance,* vol. 15 (1975): 130–45.

tested the interaction effects of pay and level of performance of an interesting task by using an innovative road racing task; his results contradicted Deci's and suggested that subjects are less intrinsically motivated when the task is perceived as easy relative to their ability.

Further methodological problems exist with the magnitude and timing of Deci's rewards and the question of whether or not these rewards were expected by subjects (6). Research by Lepper, Greene, and Nisbett (36) suggests that intrinsic motivation may decrease only when extrinsic rewards are expected, yet there is no mention of subjects' expectations in Deci's research. Calder and Staw (6) point out that Deci's conclusions regarding the effects of noncontingent rewards on intrinsic motivation are not justified by his data, since Deci has essentially affirmed the null hypothesis.

Perhaps the strongest attack on Deci's work is that of Scott (53), who effectively argues that uncontrolled and differential conditioning was taking place and that even Deci's statistical procedures were inappropriate. Deci used difference scores between experimental and free-time periods minus the time spent on the puzzle by control group subjects, rather than simply the average numbers of seconds for all subjects in the experimental session, as Scott suggests. But Scott's attack centers on the conditioning aspects of Deci's experiments:

> ... not only were the reinforcing events different in the third study, but more importantly, they were also contingent upon persisting at the task rather than upon successful solutions of the task as in the first study. Deci concluded that social approval does not seem to impair intrinsic motivation as does money. However, we cannot be certain that the differences between the experimental group and the control group in any of the sessions were not due to differences in conditioning treatments prior to the observations (53, p. 123).

Scott also notes Deci's failure to provide sufficient information on the nature of these different conditioning treatments.

Scott's position is that suitably scheduled reinforcers increase the rate of responding, although such behavior-maintaining reinforcers are not easily discerned. He suggests that since "an additional reinforcer may not produce behavior incompatible with operants maintained by other reinforcers" then "*other* conditions may produce a significant increment in the probability or rate of operant responding" (53, p. 127). Thus, even discarding the methodological limitations surrounding Deci's data, the logic of his interpretations is still open to serious question. Essentially, Scott maintains there is a more logical (better tested) theory which is not consistent with Deci's interpretations:

> It is possible that the addition of contingent reinforcers would produce a rather intricate interaction effect. On the one hand, the additional reinforcer might retard habituation to the response-produced sensory stimuli and might even enhance their reinforcing effectiveness by virtue of their being classically paired with the added reinforcing event. However, should

the additional reinforcer be administered on an effective interval or ratio schedule, the consequent increase in rate of responding may result in a reduction in the reinforcing effectiveness of response-produced sensory reinforcers if they, in turn, occurred more frequently. The performance effects under these circumstances would be difficult to predict, and it may be that Deci's contribution was in alerting us to this particular complexity and its potential significance (53, p. 127).

Similar criticism and discussion of alternative reinforcement explanations of Deci's findings are forwarded by Luthans, Martinko, and Kess (39) —notably the impact of satiation, stimulus control, reinforcement contrast, and punishing consequences.

In response, Deci (13) argues that the essential disagreement between himself and others centers on their discrepant philosophical orientations regarding the causes of behavior—namely, the reinforcement-cognitive split. Deci also argues that Scott confuses intrinsic motivation with behavior, presumably a result of Scott's reinforcement position. In his cognitive evaluation theory (see Figure 1), Deci maintains that extrinsic rewards have two aspects—a controlling aspect and an informational aspect. Implicit in Deci's response to Scott is the notion that reinforcement theorists have focused narrowly on the controlling aspect and have neglected the informational aspect. Conversely, the cognitive framework allows for the situation where extrinsic rewards, such as pay, serve as feedback about how past behavior has been received, rather than as reinforcement per se. Deci (13) also provides performance data previously omitted from his published reports; these data show no significant differences between paid and unpaid subjects during the manipulation phase of his earlier (9, 10) experiments.

A problem with Deci's remarks is that alternative cognitive explanations for his findings exist and have been discussed in other critiques. Luthans, et al. (39), for example, offer both expectancy and locus of control explanations. An expectancy theory explanation is that paid subjects did not expect to receive payments beyond the third experimental period, thereby decreasing the amount of time they engaged in the free-time task. The combined effects of these criticisms cast serious doubt on the accuracy of Deci's research and theorizing.

IMPLICATIONS AND POTENTIAL AREAS OF APPLICATION

Perhaps the major areas of disagreement are with respect to the controlling aspects of organizational reward systems and the design of jobs themselves. Some kinds of organizational rewards, such as pay and promotion, are intentionally based on performance. There must be evidence that the worker is deserving of the reward before it is supplied. The merits of such a practice generally have been espoused by both cognitive and reinforcement theorists (33), although for different reasons.

But Deci argues that such contingent reward practices may run counter to the interests and intentions of the organizations using them. People may begin to like their work less when their organizational rewards are made contingent upon it. The rationale for Deci's position lies in his theory, which states that when extrinsic rewards are interpreted as a form of control, intrinsic motivation may suffer; when interpreted as a form of feedback that also informs the worker that she or he is competent and self-determining, then intrinsic motivation may increase. Such reasoning is not completely counter to existing studies of pay in organizational settings (33), but determining how such rewards are interpreted is a key issue Deci neglects.

The issue for reinforcement theorists is whether or not the reward is a reinforcer of desired behaviors. To the extent that pay is such a reinforcer, reinforcement theorists would argue that job behaviors should be made contingent upon it. But they would also argue that rewards are a form of environmental stimuli which can reinforce undesired behaviors. To be truly effective, immediate reinforcement should be provided for desired behaviors; withdrawal of such reinforcers is punishing to the individual. Several research efforts in nonorganizational settings support this contention (54, 55), but there is insufficient evidence to indicate that principles of reinforcement can be applied effectively in complex organizational settings, although a few notable exceptions exist (2, 34, 38, 43, 46, 47, 52).

Meyer (40) argues that some of the more important rewards, specifically those associated with intrinsic motivation, are not under the control of management and thus cannot be administered according to reinforcement schedules. One could argue that a central goal of leaders is to manage the reinforcement contingencies of their workers and that such control can be obtained through task and job design efforts. Since the reinforcing properties of a given reinforcer may vary across individuals, perhaps a cafeteria-style reward system, as suggested long ago by Lawler, is appropriate. These considerations should probably be included in any organizational analysis prior to committing resources to reinforcement practices in work settings.

Deci suggests that organizations should supply rewards on a noncontingent basis or expect possible negative effects (14). To attempt to counter these effects, he suggests that jobs be designed to offer the potential for intrinsic motivation. In a sense, such sentiment parallels the job enrichment movement and argues that jobs can be made intrinsically motivating. The implicit assumption in some of the literature is that cognitive processes are important in intrinsic motivation but not in extrinsic (i.e., extrinsic motivation is the sole province of reinforcement theorists). Vroom, Porter, Lawler, and other recognized cognitive theorists probably would disagree.

The issue here is not to resolve such debate, for debate can be a healthy exercise for any science. For example, Herzberg's motivation-hygiene theory has received much criticism, yet in the process it has stimulated thought and research on the motivation constructs (59). More research on the effects of extrinsic rewards on intrinsic motivation, as advocated by both Deci and Scott, needs to be conducted before knowing with any precision the outcomes for the individual or the organization. The effects Deci describes may exist, but this has not yet been demonstrated unambiguously.

In spite of the methodological limitations of Deci's studies, one clear prescription can be offered to researchers and practitioners. Provision must be made for interpretation of findings, consequences, and causation from *both* cognitive and reinforcement positions. Given the state of the art, the researcher who hastily opts for a single interpretation and excludes consideration of the other does science a disservice. The practitioner who relies on prescriptions solely from one position may commit major organizational errors. These views provide a firm basis for true theory-testing research, an unusual occurrence in the behavioral sciences.

Future efforts should attempt to overcome the methodological limitations noted in Deci's research and focus on the multidimensional tasks one might find in actual organizational settings (25). Further work also is needed to determine the conditions under which the effects of extrinsic rewards on intrinsic motivation are limited in scope (e.g., to voluntary or intentionally motivated behaviors). For example, Calder and Staw (7) showed that the effect is limited to interesting tasks; more recently, Staw, Calder, and Hess (58) showed that payment must be counter to situational norms. The issue at present is to answer the question: When is a reward a genuine reward or a cue that one is attempting to control another or to obtain compliance? The answer may lie in the situational cues present or in subtle cues given off by the allocator of rewards, and so on. This is potentially a difficult question, but certainly not an either-or proposition as presented in past studies.

REFERENCES

1. Adams, J. S. "Inequity in Social Exchange." In *Advances in Experimental Social Psychology,* Vol. 2 edited by L. Berkowitz. New York: Academic Press, 1965.

2. "At Emery Air Freight: Positive Reinforcement Boosts Performance," *Organizational Dynamics,* Winter 1973.

3. Atkinson, J. W. *An Introduction to Motivation.* Princeton, N.J: Van Nostrand Reinhold, 1964.

4. Baldwin, A. L. "A Cognitive Theory of Socialization." In *Handbook of Socialization Theory and Research* edited by D. Goslin. Chicago: Rand McNally, 1969.

5. Benware, C., and E. L. Deci. "Attitude Change as a Function of the Inducement for Espousing a Pro-Attitudinal Communication." *Journal of Experimental Social Psychology* 11 (1975): 271–78.

6. Cadler, B. J., and B. M. Staw. "Interaction of Intrinsic and Extrinsic Motivation: Some Methodological Notes." *Journal of Personality and Social Psychology* 31 (1975): 76–80.

7. Calder, B. J., and B. M. Staw. "Self-perception of Intrinsic and Extrinsic Motivation." *Journal of Personality and Social Psychology* 31 (1975): 599–605.

8. DeCharms, R. *Personal Causation: The Internal Affective Determinants of Behavior.* New York: Academic Press, 1968.

9. Deci, E. L. "Effects of Externally Mediated Rewards on Intrinsic Motivation." *Journal of Personality and Social Psychology* 18 (1971): 105–15.

10. Deci, E. L. "Intrinsic Motivation, Extrinsic Reinforcement, and Inequity." *Journal of Personality and Social Psychology* 22 (1972): 113–20.

11. Deci, E. L. "The Effects of Contingent and Non-Contingent Rewards and Controls on Intrinsic Motivation." *Organizational Behavior and Human Performance* 8 (1972): 217–29.

12. Deci, E. L. *Intrinsic Motivation* (New York: Plenum, 1975).

13. Deci, E. L. "Notes on the Theory and Metatheory of Intrinsic Motivation." *Organizational Behavior and Human Performance* 15 (1975): 130–45.

14. Deci, E. L. "The Hidden Costs of Rewards." *Organizational Dynamics* 4, no. 3 (1976); 61–72.

15. Deci, E. L., and W. F. Cascio. "Changes in Intrinsic Motivation as a Function of Negative Feedback and Threats." Paper presented at the 43rd Annual Meeting of the Eastern Psychological Association, Boston, 1972.

16. Deci, E. L.; W. F. Cascio; and J. Krusell. "Cognitive Evaluation Theory and Some Comments on the Calder, Staw Critique." *Journal of Personality and Social Psychology* 31 (1975): 81–85.

17. Dyer, L., and D. F. Parker. "Classifying Outcomes in Work Motivation Research: An Examination of the Intrinsic-Extrinsic Dichotomy." *Journal of Applied Psychology* 60 (1975): 455–58.

18. Eden, D. "Intrinsic and Extrinsic Rewards Both Have Motivating and Demotivating Effects." *Journal of Applied Social Psychology,* in press.

19. Edwards, W. "The Prediction of Decision among Bets." *Journal of Experimental Psychology* 50 (1955): 201–14.

20. Festinger, L. *A Theory of Cognitive Dissonance.* Stanford, Calif.: Stanford University Press, 1957.

21. Freud, S. *Collected Papers.* London: Hogarth Press, 1948.

22. Greene, D. *Immediate and Subsequent Effects of Differential Reward Systems on Intrinsic Motivation in Public School Classrooms.* Ph.D. dissertation, Stanford University, 1974.

23. Greene, D., and M. R. Lepper. "Effects of Extrinsic Rewards on Children's Subsequent Intrinsic Interest." *Child Development* 45 (1974): 1141–45.

24. Hamner, W. C. "Reinforcement Theory and Contingency Management in Organizational Settings." In *Organizational Behavior and Management: A Contingency Approach,* edited by H. L. Tosi and W. C. Hamner. Chicago: St. Clair Press, 1974, pp. 86–112.

25. Hamner, W. C., and L. W. Foster. "Are Intrinsic and Extrinsic Rewards Additive: A Test of Deci's Cognitive Evaluation Theory of Task Motivation." *Organizational Behavior and Human Performance* 14 (1975): 398–415.

26. Heider, F. *The Psychology of Interpersonal Relations.* New York: John Wiley & Sons, 1958.

27. Heneman, H. G., III, and D. P. Schwab. "Expectancy Theory Predictions of Employee Performance: A Review of the Theory and Evidence." *Psychological Bulletin* 78 (1972): 1–9.

28. House, R. J.; H. J. Shapiro; and M. A. Wahba. "Expectancy Theory as a Predictor of Work Behavior and Attitude: A Reevaluation of Empirical Evidence." *Decision Sciences* 5 (1974): 481–506.

29. Hull, C. L. *Principles of Behavior*. New York: Appleton-Century-Crofts, 1943.

30. Jablonsky, S. F., and D. L. DeVries. "Operant Conditioning Principles Extrapolated to the Theory of Management." *Organizational Behavior and Human Performance* 7 (1972): 340–58.

31. Kant, I. "The Critique of Pure Reason" (1781). In *Great Books of the Western World*, Vol. 42, edited by R. M. Hutchins. Chicago: Encyclopaedia Britannica, 1952.

32. Kruglanski, A. W.; S. Alon; and T. Lewis. "Retrospective Mis-Attribution and Task Enjoyment." *Journal of Experimental Social Psychology* 8 (1972): 493–501.

33. Lawler, E. E. *Pay and Organizational Effectiveness*. New York: McGraw-Hill, 1971.

34. Lawler, E. E., and J. R. Hackman. "Impact of Employee Participation in the Development of Pay Incentive Plans: A Field Experiment." *Journal of Applied Psychology* 53 (1969): 467–71.

35. Lepper, M. R., and D. Greene. "Turning Play into Work: Effects of Adult Surveillance and Extrinsic Rewards on Children's Intrinsic Motivation." *Journal of Personality and Social Psychology* 31 (1975): 479–86.

36. Lepper, M. R.; D. Greene; and R. E. Nisbett. "Undermining Children's Intrinsic Interest with Extrinsic Rewards: A Test of the 'Overjustification' Hypothesis." *Journal of Personality and Social Psychology* 28 (1973): 129–37.

37. Lewin, K. *The Conceptual Representation and the Measurement of Psychological Forces*. Durham, N.C.: Duke University Press, 1938.

38. Luthans, F., and R. Kreitner. *Organizational Behavior Modification*. Glenview, Ill.: Scott Foresman, 1975.

39. Luthans, F.; M. Martinko; and T. Kess. "An Analysis of the Impact of Contingent Monetary Rewards on Intrinsic Motivation." *Proceedings of the 19th Annual Meeting of the Midwest Academy of Management*, 1976, pp. 209–21.

40. Meyer, H. H. "The Pay for Performance Dilemma." *Organizational Dynamics,* Winter 1973, pp. 39–50.

41. Mitchell, T. R. "Expectancy Models of Job Satisfaction, Occupational Preference and Effort: A Theoretical, Methodological and Empirical Appraisal." *Psychological Bulletin* 81 (1974): 1096–1112.

42. Mitchell, T. R., and A. Biglan. "Instrumentality Theories: Current Uses in Psychology." *Psychological Bulletin* 76 (1971): 432–54.

43. "New Tool: Reinforcement for Good Works." *Psychology Today,* April 1972, pp. 68–69.

44. Nord, W. R. "Beyond the Teaching Machine: Operant Conditioning in Management." *Organizational Behavior and Human Performance* 4 (1969): 375–401.

45. Notz, W. W. "Work Motivation and the Negative Effects of Extrinsic Rewards: A Review with Implications for Theory and Practice." *American Psychologist* 30 (1975): 884–91.

46. Ottemann, R., and F. Luthans. "An Experimental Analysis of the Effectiveness of an Organizational Behavior Modification Program in Industry."

Proceedings of the 35th Annual Meeting of the Academy of Management, 1975, pp. 140–42.

47. Pedalino, E., and V. U. Gamboa. "Behavior Modification and Absenteeism: Intervention in One Industrial Setting." *Journal of Applied Psychology* 59 (1974): 694–98.

48. Porter, L. W., and E. E. Lawler. *Managerial Attitudes and Performance.* Homewood, Ill.: Irwin-Dorsey, 1968.

49. Ross, M. "Salience of Reward and Intrinsic Motivation." *Journal of Personality and Social Psychology* 32 (1975): 245–54.

50. Rotter, J. B. *Social Learning and Clinical Psychology.* Englewood Cliffs, N.J.: Prentice-Hall, 1954.

51. Salancik, G. R. "Interaction Effects of Performance and Money on Self-Perception of Intrinsic Motivation." *Organizational Behavior and Human Performance* 13 (1975): 339–51.

52. Scheflen, K. C.; E. E. Lawler; and J. R. Hackman. "Long Term Impact of Employee Participation in the Development of Pay Incentive Plans: A Field Experiment Revisited." *Journal of Applied Psychology* 55 (1971): 182–86.

53. Scott, W. E. "The Effects of Extrinsic Rewards on Intrinsic Motivation." *Organizational Behavior and Human Performance* 15 (1975): 117–29.

54. Skinner, B. F. *Contingencies of Reinforcement.* New York: Appleton-Century-Crofts, 1969.

55. Skinner, B. F. "The Steep and Thorny Way to a Science of Behavior." *American Psychologist* 30 (1975): 42–49.

56. Spence, K. W. *Behavior Theory and Conditioning.* New Haven, Conn.: Yale University Press, 1956.

57. Staw, B. M. *Intrinsic and Extrinsic Motivation.* Morristown, N.J.: General Learning Press, 1976.

58. Staw, B. M.; B. J. Calder; and R. K. Hess. "Intrinsic Motivation and Norms About Payment." Unpublished paper, Northwestern University, 1976.

59. Steers, R. M., and L. W. Porter. *Motivation and Work Behavior.* New York: McGraw-Hill, 1975.

60. Tharp, R. G., and R. J. Wetzel. *Behavior Modification in the Natural Environment.* New York: Academic Press, 1969.

61. Thorndike, E. L. *Animal Intelligence.* New York: Macmillan, 1911.

62. Tolman, E. C. "Principles of Performance." *Psychological Review* 62 (1955): 315–26.

63. Van de Geer, J. P., and J. M. F. Jaspers. "Cognitive Functions." *Annual Review of Psychology* 17 (1966): 145–76.

64. Vroom, V. H. *Work and Motivation.* New York: John Wiley & Sons, 1964.

65. Watson, J. B. "Psychology as the Behaviorist Views It." *Psychological Review* 20 (1913): 158–77.

66. Weiner, B. *Theories of Motivation: From Mechanism to Cognition.* Chicago: Rand McNally, 1972.

Goal Setting—A Motivational Technique That Works*

GARY P. LATHAM and EDWIN A. LOCKE

The problem of how to motivate employees has puzzled and frustrated managers for generations. One reason the problem has seemed difficult, if not mysterious, is that motivation ultimately comes from within the individual and therefore cannot be observed directly. Moreover, most managers are not in a position to change an employee's basic personality structure. The best they can do is try to use incentives to direct the energies of their employees toward organizational objectives.

Money is obviously the primary incentive, since without it few if any employees would come to work. But money alone is not always enough to motivate high performance. Other incentives, such as participation in decision making, job enrichment, behavior modification, and organizational development, have been tried with varying degrees of success. A large number of research studies have shown, however, that one very straightforward technique—goal setting—is probably not only more effective than alternative methods, but may be the major mechanism by which these other incentives affect motivation. For example, a recent experiment on job enrichment demonstrated that, unless employees in enriched jobs set higher, more specific goals than do those with unenriched jobs, job enrichment has absolutely no effect on productivity. Even money has been found most effective as a motivator when the bonuses offered are made contingent on attaining specific objectives.

THE GOAL-SETTING CONCEPT

The idea of assigning employees a specific amount of work to be accomplished—a specific task, a quota, a performance standard, an objective, or a deadline—is not new. The task concept, along with time and motion

* Reprinted, by permission of the publisher, from *Organizational Dynamics*, Autumn 1979, pp. 68–80. © 1979 by AMACOM, a division of American Management Associations. All rights reserved.

study and incentive pay, was the cornerstone of scientific management, founded by Frederick W. Taylor more than 70 years ago. He used his system to increase the productivity of blue collar workers. About 20 years ago the idea of goal setting reappeared under a new name, management by objectives, but this technique was designed for managers.

In a 14-year program of research, we have found that goal setting does not necessarily have to be part of a wider management system to motivate performance effectively. It can be used as a technique in its own right.

Laboratory and Field Research

Our research program began in the laboratory. In a series of experiments, individuals were assigned different types of goals on a variety of simple tasks—addition, brainstorming, assembling toys. Repeatedly it was found that those assigned hard goals performed better than did people assigned moderately difficult or easy goals. Furthermore, individuals who had specific, challenging goals outperformed those who were given such vague goals as to "do your best." Finally, we observed that pay and performance feedback led to improved performance only when these incentives led the individual to set higher goals.

While results was quite consistent in the laboratory, there was no proof that they could be applied to actual work settings. Fortunately, just as Locke published a summary of the laboratory studies in 1968, Latham began a separate series of experiments in the wood products industry that demonstrated the practical significance of these findings. The field studies did not start out as a validity test of a laboratory theory, but rather as a response to a practical problem.

In 1968, six sponsors of the American Pulpwood Association became concerned about increasing the productivity of independent loggers in the South. These loggers were entrepreneurs on whom the multimillion-dollar companies are largely dependent for their raw materials. The problem was twofold. First, these entrepreneurs did not work for a single company; they worked for themselves. Thus they were free to (and often did) work two days one week, four days a second week, five half-days a third week, or whatever schedule they preferred. In short, these workers could be classified as marginal from the standpoint of their productivity and attendance, which were considered highly unsatisfactory by conventional company standards. Second, the major approach taken to alleviate this problem had been to develop equipment that would make the industry less dependent on this type of worker. A limitation of this approach was that many of the logging supervisors were unable to obtain the financing necessary to purchase a small tractor, let alone a rubber-tired skidder.

Consequently, we designed a survey that would help managers determine "what makes these people tick." The survey was conducted orally in the field with 292 logging supervisors. Complex statistical analyses of the data identified three basic types of supervisor. One type stayed on the job with their men, gave them instructions and explanations, provided them with training, read the trade magazines, and had little difficulty financing the equipment they needed. Still, the productivity of their units was at best mediocre.

The operation of the second group of supervisors was slightly less mechanized. These supervisors provided little training for their work force. They simply drove their employees to the woods, gave them a specific production goal to attain for the day or week, left them alone in the woods unsupervised, and returned at night to take them home. Labor turnover was high and productivity was again average.

The operation of the third group of supervisors was relatively unmechanized. These leaders stayed on the job with their men, provided training, gave instructions and explanations, and in addition, set a specific production goal for the day or week. Not only was the crew's productivity high, but their injury rate was well below average.

Two conclusions were discussed with the managers of the companies sponsoring this study. First, mechanization alone will not increase the productivity of logging crews. Just as the average taxpayer would probably commit more mathematical errors if he were to try to use a computer to complete his income tax return, the average logger misuses, and frequently abuses, the equipment he purchases (for example, drives a skidder with two flat tires, doesn't change the oil filter). This increases not only the logger's downtime, but also his costs which, in turn, can force him out of business. The second conclusion of the survey was that setting a specific production goal combined with supervisory presence to ensure goal commitment will bring out a significant increase in productivity.

These conclusions were greeted with the standard, but valid, cliché, "Statistics don't prove causation." And our comments regarding the value of machinery were especially irritating to these managers, many of whom had received degrees in engineering. So one of the companies decided to replicate the survey in order to check our findings.

The company's study placed each of 892 independent logging supervisors who sold wood to the company into one of three categories of supervisory styles our survey had identified—namely, (1) stays on the job but does not set specific production goals; (2) sets specific production goals but does not stay on the job; and (3) stays on the job and sets specific production goals. Once again, goal setting, in combination with the on-site presence of a supervisor, was shown to be the key to improved productivity.

TESTING FOR THE HAWTHORNE EFFECT

Management may have been unfamiliar with different theories of motivation, but it was fully aware of one label—the Hawthorne effect. Managers in these wood products companies remained unconvinced that anything so simple as staying on the job with the men and setting a specific production goal could have an appreciable effect on productivity. They pointed out that the results simply reflected the positive effects any supervisor would have on the work unit after giving his crew attention. And they were unimpressed by the laboratory experiments we cited—experiments showing that individuals who have a specific goal solve more arithmetic problems or assemble more tinker toys than do people who are told to "do your best." Skepticism prevailed.

But the country's economic picture made it critical to continue the study of inexpensive techniques to improve employee motivation and productivity. We were granted permission to run one more project to test the effectiveness of goal setting.

Twenty independent logging crews who were all but identical in size, mechanization level, terrain on which they worked, productivity, and attendance were located. The logging supervisors of these crews were in the habit of staying on the job with their men, but they did not set production goals. Half the crews were randomly selected to receive training in goal setting; the remaining crews served as a control group.

The logging supervisors who were to set goals were told that we had found a way to increase productivity at no financial expense to anyone. We gave the ten supervisors in the training group production tables developed through time-and-motion studies by the company's engineers. These tables made it possible to determine how much wood should be harvested in a given number of manhours. They were asked to use these tables as a guide in determining a specific production goal to assign their employees. In addition, each sawhand was given a tallymeter (counter) that he could wear on his belt. The sawhand was asked to punch the counter each time he felled a tree. Finally, permission was requested to measure the crew's performance on a weekly basis.

The 10 supervisors in the control group—those who were not asked to set production goals—were told that the researchers were interested in learning the extent to which productivity is affected by absenteeism and injuries. They were urged to "do your best" to maximize the crew's productivity and attendance and to minimize injuries. It was explained that the data might be useful in finding ways to increase productivity at little or no cost to the wood harvester.

To control for the Hawthorne effect, we made an equal number of visits to the control group and the training group. Performance was measured for 12 weeks. During this time, the productivity of the goal-setting group was significantly higher than that of the control group. Moreover, absenteeism was significantly lower in the groups that set goals than in the groups who were simply urged to do their best. Injury and turnover rates were low in both groups.

Why should anything so simple and inexpensive as goal setting influence the work of these employees so significantly? Anecdotal evidence from conversations with both the loggers and the company foresters who visited them suggested several reasons.

Harvesting timber can be a monotonous, tiring job with little or no meaning for most workers. Introducing a goal that is difficult, but attainable, increases the challenge of the job. In addition, a specific goal makes it clear to the worker what it is he is expected to do. Goal feedback via the tallymeter and weekly recordkeeping provide the worker with a sense of achievement, recognition, and accomplishment. He can see how well he is doing now as against his past performance and, in some cases, how well he is doing in comparison with others. Thus the worker not only may expend greater effort, but may also devise better or more creative tactics for attaining the goal than those he previously used.

NEW APPLICATIONS

Management was finally convinced that goal setting was an effective motivational technique for increasing the productivity of the independent woods worker in the South. The issue now raised by the management of another wood products company was whether the procedure could be used in the West with company logging operations in which the employees were unionized and paid by the hour. The previous study had involved employees on a piece-rate system, which was the practice in the South.

The immediate problem confronting this company involved the loading of logging trucks. If the trucks were underloaded, the company lost money. If the trucks were overloaded, however, the driver could be fined by the Highway Department and could ultimately lose his job. The drivers opted for underloading the trucks.

For three months management tried to solve this problem by urging the drivers to try harder to fill the truck to its legal net weight and by developing weighing scales that could be attached to the truck. But this approach did not prove cost effective, because the scales continually broke down when subjected to the rough terrain on which the trucks traveled. Consequently, the drivers reverted to their former practice of underloading. For the three months in which the problem was under study the trucks were soldom loaded in excess of 58 to 63 percent of capacity.

At the end of the three-month period, the results of the previous goal-setting experiments were explained to the union. They were told three things—that the company would like to set a specific net weight goal for the drivers, that no monetary reward or fringe benefits other than verbal praise could be expected for improved performance, and that no one would be criticized for failing to attain the goal. Once again, the idea that simply setting a specific goal would solve a production problem seemed too incredible to be taken seriously by the union. However, they reached an agreement that a difficult, but attainable, goal of 94 percent of the trucks' legal net weight would be assigned to the drivers, provided that no one could be reprimanded for failing to attain the goal. This latter point was emphasized to the company foremen in particular.

Within the first month, performance increased to 80 percent of the truck's net weight. After the second month, however, performance decreased to 70 percent. Interviews with the drivers indicated that they were testing management's statement that no punitive steps would be taken against them if their performance suddenly dropped. Fortunately for all concerned, no such steps were taken by the foremen, and performance exceeded 90 percent of the truck's capacity after the third month. Their performance has remained at this level to this day, seven years later.

The results over the nine-month period during which this study was conducted saved the company $250,000. This figure, determined by the company's accountants, is based on the cost of additional trucks that would have been required to deliver the same quantity of logs to the mill if goal setting had not been implemented. The dollars-saved figure is even higher when you factor in the cost of the additional diesel fuel that would have been consumed and the expenses incurred in recruiting and hiring the additional truck drivers.

Why could this procedure work without the union's demanding an increase in hourly wages? First, the drivers did not feel that they were really doing anything differently. This, of course, was not true. As a result of goal setting, the men began to record their truck weight in a pocket notebook, and they found themselves bragging about their accomplishments to their peers. Second, they viewed goal setting as a challenging game: "It was great to beat the other guy."

Competition was a crucial factor in bringing about goal acceptance and commitment in this study. However, we can reject the hypothesis that improved performance resulted solely from competition, because no special prizes or formal recognition programs were provided for those who came closest to, or exceeded, the goal. No effort was made by the company to single out one "winner." More important, the opportunity for competition among drivers had existed before goal setting was instituted; after all, each driver knew his own truck's weight, and the truck weight of each of the 36 other drivers every time he hauled wood into the yard. In short, competition affected productivity only in the sense that it led to the acceptance of, and commitment to, the goal. It was the setting of the goal itself and the working toward it that brought about increased performance and decreased costs.

PARTICIPATIVE GOAL SETTING

The inevitable question always raised by management was raised here: "We know goal setting works. How can we make it work better?" Was there one best method for setting goals? Evidence for a "one best way" approach was cited by several managers, but it was finally concluded that different approaches would work best under different circumstances.

It was hypothesized that the woods workers in the South who had little or no education would work better with assigned goals, while the educated workers in the West would achieve higher productivity if they were allowed to help set the goals themselves. Why the focus on education? Many of the uneducated workers in the South could be classified as culturally disadvantaged. Such persons often lack self-confidence, have a poor sense of time, and are not very competitive. The cycle of skill mastery, which in turn guarantees skill levels high enough to prevent discouragement, doesn't apply to these employees. If, for example, these people were allowed to participate in goal setting, the goals might be too difficult or they might be too easy. On the other hand, participation for the educated worker was considered critical in effecting maximum goal acceptance. Since these conclusions appeared logical, management initially decided that no research was necessary. This decision led to hours of further discussion.

The same questions were raised again and again by the researchers. What if the logic were wrong? Can we afford to implement these decisions without evaluating them systematically? Would we implement decisions regarding a new approach to tree planting without first testing it? Do we care more about trees than we do about people? Finally, permission was granted to conduct an experiment.

Logging crews were randomly appointed to either participative goal setting, assigned (nonparticipative) goal setting, or a do-your-best condition. The results were startling. The uneducated crews, consisting primarily of black employees who participated in goal setting, set significantly higher goals and attained them more often than did those whose goals were assigned by the supervisor. Not surprisingly, their performance was higher. Crews with assigned goals performed no better than did those who were urged to do their best to improve their productivity. The performance of white, educationally advantaged workers was higher with assigned rather than participatively set goals, although the difference was not statistically significant. These results were precisely the opposite of what had been predicted.

Another study comparing participative and assigned goals was conducted with typists. The results supported findings obtained by researchers at General Electric years before. It did not matter so much *how* the goal was set. What mattered was *that* a goal was set. The study demonstrated that both assigned and participatively set goals led to substantial improvements in typing speed. The process by which these gains occurred, however, differed in the two groups.

In the participative group, employees insisted on setting very high goals regardless of whether they had attained their goal the previous week. Nevertheless, their productivity improved—an outcome consistent with the theory that high goals lead to high performance.

In the assigned-goal group, supervisors were highly supportive of employees. No criticism was given for failure to attain the goals. Instead, the supervisor lowered the goal after failure so that the employee would be certain to attain it. The goal was then raised gradually each week until the supervisor felt the employee was achieving his or her potential. The result? Feelings of accomplishment and achievement on the part of the worker and improved productivity for the company.

These basic findings were replicated in a subsequent study of engineers and scientists. Participative goal setting was superior to assigned goal setting only to the degree that it led to the setting of higher goals. Both participative and assigned-goal groups outperformed groups that were simply told to "do your best."

An additional experiment was conducted to validate the conclusion that participating in goal setting may be important only to the extent that it leads to the setting of difficult goals. It was performed in a laboratory setting in which the task was to brainstorm uses for wood. One group was asked to "do your best" to think of as many ideas as possible. A second group took part in deciding, with the experimenter, the specific number of ideas each person would generate. These goals were, in turn, assigned to individuals in a third group. In this way, goal difficulty was held constant between the assigned-goal and participative groups. Again, it was found that specific, difficult goals—whether assigned or set through participation—led to higher performance than did an abstract or generalized goal such as "do your best." And, when goal difficulty was held constant, there was no significant difference in the performance of those with assigned as compared with participatively set goals.

These results demonstrate that goal setting in industry works just as it does in the laboratory. Specific, challenging goals lead to better performance than do easy or vague goals, and feedback motivates higher performance only when it leads to the setting of higher goals.

It is important to note that participation is not only a motivational tool. When a manager has competent subordinates, participation is also a useful device for increasing the manager's knowledge and thereby improving decision quality. It can lead to better decisions through input from subordinates.

A representative sample of the results of field studies of goal setting conducted by Latham and others is shown in Figure 1. Each of these ten studies compared the performance of employees given specific challenging

Figure 1
Representative Field Studies of Goal Setting

Researcher(s)	Task	Duration of Study or of Significant Effects	Percent of Change in Performance*
Blumenfeld and Leidy	Servicing soft drink coolers	Unspecified	+27
Dockstader	Keypunching	3 months	+27
Ivancevich	Skilled technical jobs	9 months	+15
Ivancevich	Sales	9 months	+24
Kim and Hamner	5 telephone service jobs	3 months	+13
Latham and Baldes	Loading trucks	9 months†	+26
Latham and Yukl	Logging	2 months	+18
Latham and Yukl	Typing	5 weeks	+11
Migliore	Mass production	2 years	+16
Umstot, Bell, and Mitchell	Coding land parcels	1–2 days‡	+16

* Percentage changes were obtained by subtracting pregoal-setting performance from postgoal-setting performance and dividing by pregoal-setting performance. Different experimental groups were combined where appropriate. If a control group was available, the percentage figure represents the difference of the percentage changes between the experimental and control groups. If multiple performance measures were used, the median improvement on all measures was used. The authors would like to thank Dena Feren and Vicki McCaleb for performing these calculations.

† Performance remained high for seven years.

‡ Simulated organization.

goals with those given "do best" or no goals. Note that goal setting has been successful across a wide variety of jobs and industries. The effects of goal setting have been recorded for as long as seven years after the onset of the program, although the results of most studies have been followed up for only a few weeks or months. The median improvement in performance in the ten studies shown in Figure 1 was 17 percent.

A CRITICAL INCIDENTS SURVEY

To explore further the importance of goal setting in the work setting, Dr. Frank White conducted another study in two plants of a high-technology, multinational corporation on the East Coast. Seventy-one engineers, 50 managers, and 31 clerks were asked to describe a specific instance when they were especially productive and a specific instance when they were especially unproductive on their present jobs. Responses were classified according to a reliable coding scheme. Of primary interest here are the external events perceived by employees as being responsible for the high-productivity and low-productivity incidents. The results are shown in Figure 2.

The first set of events—pursuing a specific goal, having a large amount of work, working under a deadline, or having an uninterrupted routine—accounted for more than half the high-productivity events. Similarly, the converse of these—goal blockage, having a small amount of work, lacking a deadline, and suffering work interruptions—accounted for nearly 60 percent of the low-productivity events. Note that the first set of four categories are all relevant to goal setting and the second set to a lack of goals or goal blockage. The goal category itself—that of pursuing an attainable goal or goal blockage—was the one most frequently used to describe high- and low-productivity incidents.

Figure 2
Events Perceived as Causing High and Low Productivity*

Event	Percent of Times Event Caused	
	High Productivity	*Low Productivity*
Goal pursuit/goal blockage	17.1	23.0
Large amount of work/small amount of work	12.5	19.0
Deadline or schedule/no deadline	15.1	3.3
Smooth work routine/interrupted routine	5.9	14.5
Intrinsic/extrinsic factors	50.6	59.8
Interesting task/uninteresting task	17.1	11.2
Increased responsibility/decreased responsibility	13.8	4.6
Anticipated promotion/promotion denied	1.3	0.7
Verbal recognition/criticism	4.6	2.6
People/company conditions	36.8	19.1
Pleasant personal relationships/unpleasant personal relationships	10.5	9.9
Anticipated pay increase/pay increase denied	1.3	1.3
Pleasant working conditions/unpleasant working conditions	0.7	0.7
Other (miscellaneous)	—	9.3

* $N = 152$ in this study by Frank White.

The next four categories, which are more pertinent to Frederick Herzberg's motivator-hygiene theory—task interest, responsibility, promotion, and recognition—are less important, accounting for 36.8 percent of the high-productivity incidents (the opposite of these four categories accounted for 19.1 percent of the lows). The remaining categories were even less important.

Employees were also asked to identify the responsible agent behind the events that had led to high and low productivity. In both cases, the employees themselves, their immediate supervisors, and the organization were the agents most frequently mentioned.

The concept of goal setting is a very simple one. Interestingly, however, we have gotten two contradictory types of reaction when the idea was introduced to managers. Some claimed it was so simple and self-evident that everyone, including themselves, already used it. This, we have found, is not true. Time after time we have gotten the following response from subordinates after goal setting was introduced: "This is the first time I knew what my supervisor expected of me on this job." Conversely, other managers have argued that the idea would not work, precisely *because* it is so simple (implying that something more radical and complex was needed). Again, results proved them wrong.

But these successes should not mislead managers into thinking that goal setting can be used without careful planning and forethought. Research and experience suggest that the best results are obtained when the following steps are followed:

Setting the Goal.   The goal set should have two main characteristics. First, it should be specific rather than vague: "Increase sales by 10 percent" rather than "Try to improve sales." Whenever possible, there should be a time limit for goal accomplishment.: "Cut costs by 3 percent in the next six months."

Second, the goal should be challenging yet reachable. If accepted, difficult goals lead to better performance than do easy goals. In contrast, if the goals are perceived as unreachable, employees will not accept them. Nor will employees get a sense of achievement from pursuing goals that are never attained. Employees with low self-confidence or ability should be given more easily attainable goals than those with high self-confidence and ability.

There are at least five possible sources of input, aside from the individual's self-confidence and ability, that can be used to determine the particular goal to set for a given individual.

The scientific management approach pioneered by Frederick W. Taylor uses time and motion study to determine a fair day's work. This is probably the most objective technique available, but it can be used only where the task is reasonably repetitive and standardized. Another drawback is that this method often leads to employee resistance, especially in cases where the new standard is substantially higher than previous performance and where rate changes are made frequently.

More readily accepted, although less scientific than time and motion study, are standards based on the average past performance of employees. This method was used successfully in some of our field studies. Most employees consider this approach fair, but naturally, in cases where past performance is far below capacity, beating that standard will be extremely easy.

Since goal setting is sometimes simply a matter of judgment, another technique we have used is to allow the goal to be set jointly by supervisor and subordinate. The participative approach may be less scientific than time and motion study, but it does lead to ready acceptance by both employee and immediate superior in addition to promoting role clarity.

External constraints often affect goal setting, especially among managers. For example, the goal to produce an item at a certain price may be dictated by the actions of competitors, and deadlines may be imposed externally in line with contract agreements. Legal regulations, such as attaining a certain reduction in pollution levels by a certain date, may affect goal setting as well. In these cases, setting the goal is not so much the problem as is figuring out a method of reaching it.

Finally, organizational goals set by the board of directors or upper management will influence the goals set by employees at lower levels. This is the essence of the MBO process.

Another issue that needs to be considered when setting goals is whether they should be designed for individuals or for groups. Rensis Likert and a number of other human relations experts argue for group goal setting on grounds that it promotes cooperation and team spirit. But one could argue that individual goals better promote individual responsibility and make it easier to appraise individual performance. The degree of task interdependence involved would also be a factor to consider.

Obtaining Goal Commitment. If goal setting is to work, then the manager must ensure that subordinates will accept and remain committed to the goals. Simple instruction backed by positive support and an absence of threats or intimidation were enough to ensure goal acceptance in most of our studies. Subordinates must perceive the goals as fair and reasonable and they must trust management, for if they perceive the goals as no more than a means of exploitation, they will be likely to reject the goals.

It may seem surprisingly that goal acceptance was achieved so readily in the field studies. Remember, however, that in all cases the employees were receiving wages or a salary (although these were not necessarily directly contingent on goal attainment). Pay in combination with the supervisor's benevolent authority and supportiveness were sufficient to bring about goal acceptance. Recent research indicates that whether goals are assigned or set participatively, supportiveness on the part of the immediate superior is critical. A supportive manager or supervisor does not use goals to threaten subordinates, but rather to clarify what is expected of them. His or her role is that of a helper and goal facilitator.

As noted earlier, the employee gets a feeling of pride and satisfaction from the experience of reaching a challenging but fair performance goal. Success in reaching a goal also tends to reinforce acceptance of future goals. Once goal setting is introduced, informal competition frequently arises among the employees. This further reinforces commitment and may lead employees to raise the goals spontaneously. A word of caution here, however: We do not recommend setting up formal competition, as this may lead employees to place individual goals ahead of company goals. The emphasis should be on accomplishing the task, getting the job done, not "beating" the other person.

When employees resist assigned goals, they generally do so for one of two reasons. First, they may think they are incapable of reaching the goal because they lack confidence, ability, knowledge, and the like. Second, they may not see any personal benefit—either in terms of personal pride or in terms of external rewards like money, promotion, recognition—in reaching assigned goals.

There are various methods of overcoming employee resistance to goals. One possibility is more training designed to raise the employee's level of skill and self-confidence. Allowing the subordinate to participate in setting the goal—deciding on the goal level—is another method. This was found most effective among uneducated and minority group employees, perhaps because it gave them a feeling of control over their fate. Offering monetary bonuses or other rewards (recognition, time off) for reaching goals may also help.

The last two methods may be especially useful where there is a history of labor-management conflict and where employees have become accustomed to a lower level of effort than currently considered acceptable. Group incentives may also encourage goal acceptance, especially where there is a group goal, or when considered cooperation is required.

Providing Support Elements. A third step to take when introducing goal setting is to ensure the availability of necessary support elements. That is, the employee must be given adequate resources—money, equipment, time, help—as well as the freedom to utilize them in attaining goals, and company policies must not work to block goal attainment.

Before turning an employee loose with these resources, however, it's wise to do a quick check on whether conditions are optimum for reaching the goal set. First, the supervisor must make sure that the employee has sufficient ability and knowledge to be able to reach the goal. Motivation without knowledge is useless. This, of course, puts a premium on proper selection and training and requires that the supervisor know the capabilities of subordinates when goals are assigned. Asking an employee to formulate an action plan for reaching the goal, as in MBO, is very useful, as it will indicate any knowledge deficiencies.

Second, the supervisor must ensure that the employee is provided with precise feedback so that he will know to what degree he's reaching or falling short of his goal and can thereupon adjust his level of effort or strategy accordingly. Recent research indicates that, while feedback is not a sufficient condition for improved performance, it is a necessary condition. A useful way to present periodic feedback is through the use of charts or graphs that plot performance over time.

Elements involved in taking the three steps described are shown in Figure 3, which illustrates in outline form our model of goal setting.

Figure 3
Goal-setting Model

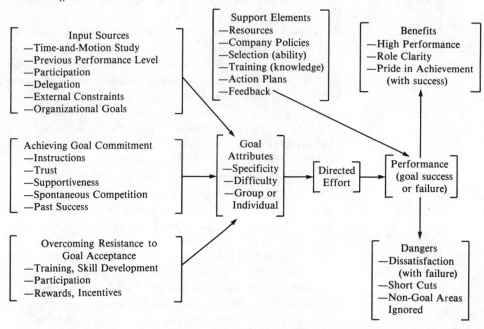

CONCLUSION   We believe that goal setting is a simple, straightforward, and highly effective technique for motivating employee performance. It is a basic technique, a method on which most other methods depend for their motivational effectiveness. The current popular technique of behavior modification, for example, is mainly goal setting plus feedback, dressed up in academic terminology.

However, goal setting is no panacea. It will not compensate for underpayment of employees or for poor management. Used incorrectly, goal setting may cause rather than solve problems. If, for example, the goals set are unfair, arbitrary, or unreachable, dissatisfaction and poor performance may result. If difficult goals are set without proper quality controls, quantity may be achieved at the expense of quality. If pressure for immediate results is exerted without regard to how they are attained, short-term improvement may occur at the expense of long-run profits. That is, such pressure often triggers the use of expedient and ultimately costly methods —such as dishonesty, high-pressure tactics, postponing of maintenance expenses, and so on—to attain immediate results. Furthermore, performance goals are more easily set in some areas than in others. It's all too easy, for example, to concentrate on setting readily measured production goals and ignore employee development goals. Like any other management tool, goal setting works only when combined with good managerial judgment.

SELECTED BIBLIOGRAPHY

A summary of the early (mainly laboratory) research on goal setting may be found in E. A. Locke's "Toward a Theory of Task Motivation and Incentives" (*Organization Behavior and Human Performance,* May 1968). More recent reviews that include some of the early field studies are reported by G. P. Latham and G. A. Yukl's "Review of Research on the Application of Goal Setting in Organizations" (*Academy of Management Journal,* December 1975) and in R. M. Steers and L. W. Porter's "The Role of Task-Goal Attributes in Employee Performance" (*Psychological Bulletin,* July 1974).

An excellent historical discussion of management by objectives, including its relationship to goal-setting research, can be found in G. S. Odiorne's "MBO: A Backward Glance" (*Business Horizons,* October 1978).

A thorough review of the literature on participation, including the relationship of participation and goal setting, can be found in a chapter by E. A. Locke and D. M. Schweiger, "Participation in Decision-Making: One More Look," in B. M. Staw's edited work, *Research in Organizational Behavior* (Vol. 1, Greenwich, JAI Press, 1979). General Electric's famous research on the effect of participation in the appraisal interview is summarized in H. H. Meyer, E. Kay, and J. R. P. French, Jr.'s "Split Roles in Performance Appraisal" (*Harvard Business Review,* January-February 1965).

The relationship of goal setting to knowledge of results is discussed in E. A. Locke, N. Cartledge, and J. Koeppel's "Motivational Effects of Knowledge of Results: A Goal Setting Phenomenon?" (*Psychological Bulletin,* December 1968) and L. J. Becker's "Joint Effect of Feedback and Goal Setting on Performance: A Field Study of Residential Energy Conservation" (*Journal of Applied Psychology,* August 1978). Finally, the role of goal setting in virtually all theories of work motivation is documented in E. A. Locke's "The Ubiquity of the Technique of Goal Setting in Theories of and Approaches to Employee Motivation" (*Academy of Management Review,* July 1978).

Stress: Race to the Bottom Line*

FREDERICK B. MICKEL

A coronary care unit is a strange place. It is a vast jungle of electronic equipment, with medical technicians who move around the unit very quietly so that the most noticeable noise is that of various unseen beeps and buzzes apparently coming from the huge computerized console in the center of the unit. As you lie there watching the incessant display of your heartbeat on the monitor beside your bed (I wonder if doctors know how disconcerting those things are to the patient), you realize that you can alter the pattern traced on the screen just by raising and lowering your arm (it's amazing what you will do to entertain yourself when there is very little to do). You never realize just how much salt adds to the taste of food until you sample the hospital's salt-free "cuisine."

You constantly are told to rest, but I never did figure out how they thought that was possible since they check your blood pressure and temperature quite frequently. I did figure out how they entertain themselves. They wait until you fall asleep, and then they send in the lab technicians for a blood sample. Wild thoughts race through your mind. You wonder if their work performance is measured in average patients cared for and if they are keeping your blood supply purposely low so they can keep you from moving to the regular care unit and not hurt their performance statistics. I've always loved to sleep on my stomach, but you learn quickly that you can't roll over completely without half-strangling yourself in the assorted wires and intravenous tubes attached to you. You also would be surprised at how long you can go when a bed pan is your only source of relief. What you do is stare at the ceiling a lot and wonder how you got there and how it is going to affect your life. According to my cardiologist, I got there because of too much stress.

In retrospect, I should have seen some of the symptoms, such as the periods of extreme hypertension and several incidents of severe vertigo, but I ignored them, falsely assuming I was indestructible. I was slightly past 40 at the time of my attack—mild coronary problems—the first week of October 1979.

As I found out, stress affects the individual and the organization he or she works for. What is work-induced stress and what can be done to minimize it?

What Is Stress?

From a medical standpoint, stress is the common result of exposure to any stimulus. In other words, the bodily changes produced by stimuli such as injury, nervous tension, infection, heat, cold, and the like are called stress. It also is the rate of "wear and tear" on the body. Dr. Hans Selye classifies the general concept of stress, which would include all responses to stressors, into *distress*, which is always unpleasant, and *eustress*, which is always pleasant. During both "distress" and "eustress" the body undergoes the same "nonspecific response" to the stressors acting upon it, yet eustress results in much less "wear and tear" on the body. How well a person likes

---

* Reprinted by permission of *Management Accounting*, April 1981, pp. 15–20.

what is happening to him (his ability to adapt) determines the degree of effect on his physiological and psychological condition.

The effects of stress, or what Dr. Selye calls "diseases of adaption," are numerous. They include many nervous and emotional disturbances, high blood pressure, gastric and duodenal ulcers, diseases of the heart and of the blood vessels, diseases of the kidney, rheumatic and rheumatoid arthritis, inflammatory diseases of the skin and eyes, sexual derangements, metabolic diseases, cancer, and diseases of resistance in general.

Some persons react to even mild life stresses with an excessive rise in blood pressure, indicating that over a period of time their bodies get used to responding to daily life as if it were a series of emergencies. These persons usually develop hypertension. Early symptoms of excessive stress include sleeping problems and inability to relax, irritability, trouble concentrating, very little interest in recreation, tiring more quickly, taking too much work home (physically and mentally), drinking too much on a regular basis, or overindulgence in sedatives. Stress, however, does not occur from outside sources alone. Much of it has to do with what goes on within the person.

Type A's Annoy Their Co-workers

We have all heard of the Type A and Type B people Drs. Meyer Friedman and Ray E. Rosenman classified. Type A is characterized as aggressive, having excessive drive, ambition, and a sense of time urgency. This group seemed to be fighting time itself. Type B did not display these characteristics. The researchers predicted that Type A persons were more prone to coronaries, and—sure enough—of those in the study group that subsequently had coronaries, 85 percent had been previously classified as Type A persons.

Ironically, a curious sidelight of their research indicated that the Type A "hard driver" usually did not become president of his firm. Rather, it was the more relaxed Type B person, who was able to use the Type A's below him. Typical Type A's have trouble delegating because they find it difficult to sit back and let employees struggle with tasks they believe they can accomplish more quickly.

Although many executives attribute their success to their high level of drive, physicians and psychologists point out that Type A behavior quite often is self-defeating. The "one-man band," the compulsive competitor, the person always in a hurry, is not always the most efficient or effective business person. Type A's certainly could improve their physiological condition by managing their time and strength with the same care they manage their work and by analyzing the kinds of situations that make them angry, anxious, or unproductively tense.

People who are excessively competitive against their own standards of time urgency are more likely to have physiological and psychological difficulties. Professor William E. Henry, of the University of Chicago, says men in the 30–40 age range view their outer world primarily as "achievement-demanding." (According to recent studies, business women are prey to the same pressures.) They believe the outside world demands accomplishment, and they follow the cues which the outside world provides. By focusing primarily on the outer world, they fail to pay adequate attention to their own feelings and their intimate personal relationships. Driven by deep-seated personality factors, they are compelled to compete continuously to achieve and lead. These competitive impulses are fanned by cultural and organizational demands and expectations. Unfortunately, those persons who are so possessed by motivation that they cannot voluntarily choose to relax or do something different and feel comfortable with themselves, never get any real pleasure from the achievements they worked so hard to obtain.

Although it is difficult to admit, the type just described is a fairly accurate portrait of myself before October 1979. I would certainly classify myself as a Type A person, and while I am aware of the problems this behavior creates, both for myself and the people around me, I find that I still constantly have to force myself to slow down.

Workaholics Usually Are Type A's

The popular term *workaholic* is, for the most part, synonymous with Type A behavior. Here, all the anxiety and drive are focused on the person's work, with all other activities (social, family) nearly shut out of his life. Temporary success achieved as a result of overachievement at work is quite often overshadowed by collapse of an individual's physical or mental resources.

While many organizations will seek "bright young people" and initially laud their aggressiveness and accomplishments, the eager beaver stalls after reaching a certain level on the corporate ladder. A combination of lack of creativity, typically snap decisions, and a tendency to annoy and intimidate co-workers too often add up to major shortcomings for these types. Another irritating fault of workaholics is their propensity for alienating and "burning out" subordinates. They neither understand nor tolerate less intensive lifestyles. They occasionally are exploited themselves, however, when managers, knowing the workaholic's receptivity to assignments, pile on the projects. One middle manager explains: "Workaholics come in handy when you have 100 things to do and not enough time for them."

Highly related to the Type A workaholic behavior is independence, which manifests itself in a type of role playing wherein the individual has convinced himself he must show little emotion in any situation and must never admit he is dependent on anyone. In other words, regardless of what happens, he must be a "rock," a real "fortress of strength."

Here I deviated from "typical" Type A behavior in that I also had many outside activities I enjoyed. I was president of NAA's Johnstown Chapter from June 1977 to May 1978. (The month after I assumed the presidency, our city suffered a major disaster in the flood of July 20, 1977.) Right before my coronary problems I also was: involved in the Executive Board of Greater Johnstown Committee, director of the Cambria County War Memorial Arena, chairman of the Computer Craft Committee of the Greater Johnstown Area Vocational-Technical School, on the Pennsylvania Human Relations Commission, and a part-time MBA student (six credit hours per semester). I was spending approximately 70 hours a week on work, school, and civic activities.

Involvement in so many activities, however, has a tendency to cause stress, just as many jobs do.

Certain Jobs Cause Added Stress

Many job situations create stress. Any kind of job *change* always means some disruption of ties or relationships—some alteration in the characteristic way of coping. It can be a transfer across the country or a simple change in the steps of a work process. Also, many people find *responsibility* difficult. Reasons range from overcontrol by parents on one hand to being pushed too hard before they were ready on the other. The result is that persons who shun responsibility are likely to be more frightened of failure than others, and the image they carry for themselves is one of incompetence. As one expert says, "self-doubt probably is the greatest crippler of executive ability."

Another factor is *role ambiguity*. Despite extensive use of performance appraisals and job descriptions, there is a great deal of disparity between what a person thinks his job is and what his superiors expect of him.

Even with modern testing and screening procedures, many people end up in jobs that are *wrong* for them. People are "in over their heads," "bored to tears," or just can't stand their work environment. How do people get into the "wrong" job in the first place? The reasons are numerous, but the major ones are strong attraction of external rewards with little consideration given to the required tasks or expected performance criteria, organizational pressures, the inability to say "no," and lack of self-knowledge or self-assessment. Wider use of psychological testing, attitude surveys, and vocational guidance can greatly relieve this problem, experts say.

When a person finds himself in such a stressful situation, he must always ask himself if what he is "killing" himself for is really worth all the pain and aggravation it is causing. An example is "career burnout" in which a person, quite simply, feels that what he's doing is not important anymore. If the situation is one that is likely to continue for an extended period of time, such as a poor work environment or job dissatisfaction, a person has to realize that he literally may kill himself attempting to adapt to the situation and that a radical change such as a transfer, new job, or new career may be the only step that will save his life—or at least change *existence* into *living*.

What the Organization Can Do about Stress

Through their work people channel their aggressive and constructive drives into meaningful directions. Managers must realize that for many employees work often is the "psychological glue" that holds them together. What can be done to maximize the good stress and minimize the bad stress within the organization? Your organization might find these guidelines helpful:

• Managers can determine what aspects of each job will bring pride to the worker and recognition from his co-workers and family and then encourage, support, and recognize the socially acceptable aspects of that behavior on the job.

• Managers can structure work rewards and work achievements in such a way that employees responsible to them will feel that what they do is worth spending part of their lives on.

• Managers can increase the opportunity for employees to master and control their work, in keeping with the task to be done, thus giving them more competence and security in their work.

• Managers must understand that the work process should, insofar as possible, emulate the style and family relationships typical of their employees. For example, a person accustomed to close family relationships will be very unhappy in a mechanized work process in which people cannot communicate with each other due to high noise levels.

• If a manager is a "Type A" personality, he must be extremely careful that, in his own natural desire to suppress anxiety within himself, he does not become insensitive to those circumstances which arouse anxiety in others.

• Managers should plan all changes together with the people who are going to be involved in them, to whatever extent is possible.

• Managers should make the collective goal the target, not employee competition. In other words, reward individual achievement for its own merits. Don't introduce guilt feelings into one person for his achievements by making his accomplishment the condition of failure for another.

• Supervisors should keep in constant touch with subordinates to define in practice the limits of their work tasks and to give them support in accomplishing their various jobs.

• Supervisors should provide the opportunity and the atmosphere for employees to talk things over whenever they feel they need to talk. By maintaining an "open door" and "open mind" policy, people will be more prone to talk about their actions before undertaking them and less prone to let subconscious feelings govern their behavior.

• Managers must realize that anger is a part of every person's personality, and they must try especially to reduce their tendency toward excessive anger and the harmful effects it can have on their work group. Obviously, not all anger should be eliminated because overcontrolled anger will reflect itself in equally harmful ways such as tension and irritability. By dealing constructively with rising aggression (i.e., recognizing it and deciding how to handle it), managers can actually improve their communication and problem solving.

• Managers can help their staffs by encouraging them not to be consumed by their career objectives. I don't mean that drive and ambition are not important, but employees must know that the company feels that well-rounded people who are interested in both their work and off-work activities make happier and more productive employees.

• Organizations need to create more differentiated reward mechanisms and career paths to allow room for technical and creative people who do not aspire to general management to grow within the organization.

• Managers can help their employees by giving them honest performance appraisals, thus aiding them in self-assessment and reducing the possibility they will move into positions for which they are not suited. Promoting someone to his "Peter Principle" level of incompetence is certainly not doing him any favor because people in such positions are certain to encounter, as well as create for others, more stress than existed before.

• Management must reduce organizational uncertainty and its resultant stress by protecting employees from worry about events over which they have no control. In other words, the organization, through its managers, must act as a shock absorber for the emotional impact of the many local, regional, and national economic crises that could, if unchecked, overload the company gossip mill as well as the emotional capacity of many workers and their families.

• Organizations can provide healthy and desirable working conditions and encourage employees to live healthy lives. As heart disease is a leading result of excess stress, it makes sense that people should not add to the heart's burden by smoking, overeating, not exercising, and the like. Some companies even are offering employees a chance to join health clubs; are setting up company health facilities such as tracks or exercise rooms; or are offering health exams as perquisites.

The real functions of a manager are to organize people to perform a task together and to create the environment that will allow the job to be completed successfully. Preventing unnecessary anxiety in the organization not only will aid in getting the task done more efficiently, but it will contribute to the employees' well-being.

Employees, on the other hand, can:

• Avoid too rigid a schedule. When possible, vary your schedule and eliminate most of those self-imposed deadlines.

• Try to develop what is known as a positive attitude. The curious thing about attitude is that it can be changed over time with practice, much like a muscle can be enlarged through exercise. At first, force yourself to see every event in its most positive light.

• Make a list of those events that regularly cause excessive stress, and carefully identify what it is about each event that is causing the stress. Next, map out a strategy for consciously attempting to lessen the stress each successive time the event occurs.

• Get on with the task, no matter how painful and get it over with rather than making yourself sick worrying about it.

Find Your Right Job and Avoid Stress

There are no ready prescriptions for solving most of life's problems, but everyone can learn from what happens to him each day. Managers can learn something about themselves and the way they live and become aware of experiences that trouble them. By trying alternative ways of carrying on their daily tasks, they can find ways of easing some of the most burdensome stresses and increase their sense of well-being. Managers also can learn something about what their work means to them and to others by attempting to examine their feelings during the various "crisis events" that occur on the job.

Company managers must understand stress and its effect on them and their organizations. Much of the literature about stress is based on its physiological aspects, with too little written about the psychological implications on the individual, especially with regard to the impact of organizational structure, morale, leadership, and other organizational variables. From the standpoint of human welfare and productivity, it is in everyone's best interest to eliminate as many sources of stress as possible. I believe that the most progress will be achieved by changing work environments that induce stress.

What Happened to Me

Mine was the classic case: I found too many things were finding their way to me for decisions—decisions that rightfully needed to be made by other officers or managers. I was one of the persons who founded Data Consultants, Inc., in 1966. At the time I was elected president in 1970, the company was not doing well. I felt that in order to "turn the company around" it would be necessary for us to stop trying to be all things to all people in the area of computer services and that we should concentrate on the vertical market we knew best, which was retailing. This strategy was implemented and has been successful. I tried to keep in touch with all major activities in the company, and I made most decisions in the areas of pricing, personnel, capital items, marketing policy, and software product capabilities, as well as the normal planning and financial decisions.

Then came my coronary problem. I was off work for less than a month, and I worked only half-days for about two weeks after I returned. I also dropped my two graduate school courses that term, but returned to school in January 1980.

While I was off work, and during my period of half-day sessions, I was quite astounded at how well the business ran and how well my managers made decisions on matters I usually either handled directly or where I customarily made the final decision. Since then, I have continued the practice of delegating as many items as possible, and in most instances the results have been excellent. The growth in ability and self-esteem of most of my managers has more than offset the few mistakes.

Delegation was forced on me—I probably would not have done it to this extent without some similar accident occurring. Regarding the temptation to take on too much work, I have to constantly remind myself that delegation of authority is good for the organization and helps to reduce my involvement in matters that are better handled by others.

I'm still involved in all the same civic activities I mentioned previously, plus I've since been named a trustee of the Johnstown Savings Bank. However, I've learned to limit my involvement in all activities, except for graduate school, to an advisory role whenever possible.

I've tried to limit my working hours to no more than 40 per week, and most of my civic activities occur within that 40-hour week. I've been carrying six credit hours per term in graduate school, which takes about 15 hours a week including travel and study. In total, my time devoted to work, civic activities, and school has been cut from about 70 hours a week to approximately 55.

Now I have stopped trying to be all things to all people. By concentrating my efforts on those things only I can do, I believe I am doing a better job for my firm, as well as building a much stronger organization which can handle the growth we are experiencing. In this process, I have found that my key people are much stronger, and the "bottom line" hasn't turned to red ink as I once thought it would.

SOME READINGS ON STRESS

Bartolome, Fernando, and Paul A. Lee Evans. "Must Success Cost So Much?" *Harvard Business Review,* March–April 1980, pp. 137–48.

Benner, Susan. "Stress: How One CEO Is Learning to Cope with it." *Inc.,* October 1979, pp. 57–60.

"Clues to Stress Overload." *Boardroom Reports,* November 15, 1979, p. 17.

Galton, Lawrence. *The Silent Disease: Hypertension.* New York: New American Library, 1973.

Levinson, Harry. "Stress Vs. Stimulus in the Executive Suite." *The Wharton Magazine,* Spring 1980, pp. 13–14.

Levinson, Harry. *Executive Stress.* New York: Harper & Row, 1964.

Mason, Stephen B., and Ida W. Mason. "Warning: Computers May Be Hazardous to Your Health." *Infosystems,* April 1980, pp. 72–76.

McLean, Alan A. *Work Stress.* Reading, Mass.: Addison-Wesley Publishing, 1979.

Peter, Laurence J., and Raymond Hull. *The Peter Principle.* New York: Bantam Books, 1969.

Price, Margaret. "Workaholism: Fears a Job Can't Solve." *Industry Week,* March 3, 1980.

Selye, Hans. *Stress without Distress.* New York: New American Library, 1974.

Selye, Hans. *The Stress of Life.* New York: McGraw-Hill, 1976.

Toffler, Alvin. *Future Shock.* New York: Random House, 1970.

Vaillant, George E. *Adaption to Life.* Boston: Little, Brown, 1977.

Warshaw, Leon J. *Managing Stress.* Reading, Mass.: Addison-Wesley Publishing, 1979.

"Workaholism: A Good Disease . . . Often." *Boardroom Reports,* March 24, 1980, p. 12.

Can Companies Kill?*

BERKELEY RICE

On the morning of January 31, 1979, Roger Berman left for work early, as usual, and drove into the city to his office at the corporate headquarters of a large international conglomerate. Instead of putting in his customary long day, however, he left the office abruptly during the morning. He may have driven around for some time, but eventually he went home and pulled into his garage. With the motor still running, he got out of the car, closed the garage door, and apparently sat down to wait. His body was found there later, slumped on the floor. The autopsy report listed carbon monoxide as the cause of death, but in this case "cause" is a matter of some dispute.

Though tragic, suicides are not uncommon. Berman's is, because his widow is suing his former employer for $6 million, claiming it caused her husband's death by failing to respond to his repeated complaints of overwork and by displaying a "callous and conscious disregard" for his mental health.

The case raises the question of whether an employer can, in effect, by its own action or inaction, kill with stress. At issue, besides a great deal of money, is the extent to which a company may be held responsible beyond the provisions of workers' compensation laws, for a psychiatric injury to one of its employees.

Since the case has not yet come to trial lawyers for both sides are understandably reluctant to discuss the details. The account of Roger Berman's career and death that follows is largely based on—and therefore limited by—information in the legal complaint filed by the lawyer representing his widow. Names and certain details have been changed to protect the identities of the parties involved.

Nevertheless, the case is real—and important; corporate lawyers will no doubt be watching it closely. The reader should bear in mind that none of the charges against the company have been proved and that if the case

* Reprinted from *Psychology Today Magazine,* June 1981, pp. 78, 80–85. Copyright © 1981, Ziff-Davis Publishing Company.

comes to trial the company may deny or contest most of the allegations. My purpose here is not to determine the accuracy of the charges but to explore the profoundly difficult issues in assessing corporate responsibility for employee mental health.

Berman joined the company as a management trainee soon after he graduated from high school. A hard worker, he put himself through college at night while rising steadily through the ranks of the giant corporation. Eventually he became manager of a large department with a salary of about $50,000, plus substantial fringe benefits. In time, however, the job became increasingly difficult for him, demanding more and more of his evening and weekend hours. The pressure became so great that he asked several times to have his work load lightened. According to the legal complaint, his superiors promised to ease up on him, but nothing changed.

Approaching 50, and with 30 years of service to the company, Berman decided in 1978 to take early retirement, largely to escape from the strain of his job. According to the suit, his superiors talked him into staying on, promising to ease his work load. Relying on those promises, he agreed, but again, the complaint charges, no relief came. Some time after that, Berman discovered that he would not become eligible again for early retirement and pension for another five years.

With escape by retirement thus effectively blocked, Berman became increasingly anxious about his ability to accomplish his work. His company doctor referred him to an outside psychiatrist. According to the suit, the psychiatrist reported back to the company, warning that Berman's mental health was "precarious" and would be "further impaired" without some relief in the conditions of his work. Still, apparently, nothing changed.

On January 10, 1979, Berman's colleagues found him sitting at his desk in a dazed stupor. They could not snap him out of it nor could the company doctor. During this "catatonic" episode, according to the complaint, he was not sent to a hospital; he was not sent home; no one called his wife. After a few hours, he came out of it on his own. He stayed in the office for the rest of that day and left for home, alone. Three weeks later he committed suicide.

The company is seeking to have the Berman suit dismissed, not by contesting the charges, but on the grounds that if his mental distress or death were caused by the conditions of his work, any resulting claims should be covered by the state's workers' compensation law—and therefore not subject to a damage suit. But that is precisely the point of this case. The suit contends that the workers' compensation law covers only accidental injuries and that Berman's death was not an accident as defined under the workers' compensation law.

Workers' compensation laws, which have been passed in every state, have been hailed as a major victory by the labor movement. The laws provide financial coverage for employees disabled by industrial accidents without their having to bring the employer to court. When disputes arise, state compensation appeal boards determine the extent of the disability and the award. Awards are limited to a percentage of the injured party's lost wages, which usually run to less than $10,000 and are rarely more than $50,000—nowhere near the Berman claim of $6 million. Thus, while the law aids the worker, it also protects the employer from damage suits for larger amounts.

For many years worker compensation awards were limited to cases of physical injury, in which disability is relatively easy to determine. Since 1960, however, court decisions have either forced or led 15 states to allow workers compensation payments in job-related cases of anxiety, depression, and other mental disorders severe enough to be disabling.

At first, the cases tended to involve a single dramatic incident: for example, the trauma of seeing a fellow worker crushed by a machine or plunging to death. But in six states, courts have extended coverage to cases of emotional or mental illness caused by gradual or "cumulative" injury from work stress. The Michigan Supreme Court upheld a compensation award to a machine operator who claimed his mental illness was caused by the daily pressure of work on an assembly line. A secretary in Detroit won a $7,000 award for emotional distress caused by her boss's continual criticism and prying questions about her family life. A California court upheld an award to a legal secretary who claimed her breakdown was caused by the pressure of her heavy work load. The court ruled that in such cases the "central consideration isn't the actual work environment, but how the employee reacts to it." In Washington, D.C., a clerical employee who had worked for 20 years with no prior sign of emotional distress walked off the job one day and was hospitalized for a mental disorder that his attorney claimed was caused by "the pressures of his job." The court allowed the claim because the employer was "unable to disprove a causal relationship." Other court decisions have established that regardless of fault, an employer can be held liable under the workers' compensation laws for an employee's mental illness if it has been "aggravated, accelerated, precipitated, or triggered" by the conditions of the job.

In all these decisions, the courts have considered psychiatric injuries as "accidents," which is all the workers' compensation laws were meant to cover. In the Berman case, however, his widow's attorney argues that Berman's "injuries" and death were not accidents within the meaning and intent of the workers' compensation law. The suit claims his company knew his mental health was "impaired and precarious, and would be further impaired" without some relief. It states that the company's failure to arrange such relief, either in the form of a reduced work load, reassignment, or a leave of absence—particularly after the psychiatrist's report and the catatonic episode—was both "reckless" and "inhumane." The workers' compensation law, Berman's lawyer holds, "should not be a shield for an employer when it acts inhumanely, in complete disregard for the safety of the employee."

One way to understand the issue involved in the dispute over what constitutes an industrial accident is to imagine a factory worker whose finger is chopped off by the machine to which he or she is assigned. That can certainly be called an industrial accident. Now suppose the worker goes back to the job a week later and loses another finger in the machine. Maybe the worker is clumsy or just stupid. But if it keeps happening, or if the machine begins lopping off the fingers of the workers who replace the injured one, it can reasonably be argued that the factory is guilty of reckless or inhumane disregard of its employees' safety. By allowing them to continue working at a machine that is clearly dangerous without effective safety precautions, the factory might be justly accused of causing the injuries. At that point, one can ask whether such injuries should be called accidents, and whether the factory's liability—and the employee's claim for damages—should be limited by a law governing industrial accidents.

Of course, the effect of prolonged stress is not as visible and not as dramatic as the loss of a finger, nor is the cause as simple to isolate. But is stress any less incapacitating or demoralizing? One reason the question has not been raised more often, particularly in cases of psychiatric distress at the executive level, is that most managers recognize that a claim for emotional disability hardly enhances their future prospects at their own or any other company. Franklin Grady, a state official who supervises California's industrial-accident claims, points out that most of them involve rank-and-file employees, not managers. A psychiatric claim, he says, "would pretty well kill an executive's career."

That is partly what happened to Roland Webster, a former vice president of a large financial corporation. Webster is suing the company for $2 million for allegedly causing him "severe mental distress" and damaging his "psychological well-being." In his case, also pending, the suit charges not only that Webster's company failed to provide relief but that it intentionally acted so as to cause psychiatric injury.

The account of Webster's career that follows is also based on, and limited by, official court papers. Neither side will discuss the matter while it is in litigation, but Webster's former employer has denied most of the allegations in the complaint. Again, because the charges remain unproved, names and identifyng details have been changed.

Like Berman, Webster had spent most of his career with his company. He started as a management trainee in 1957 and rose steadily with regular salary increases, promotions, and commendations, becoming one of the regional vice presidents. His salary was $40,000, plus a yearly bonus of several thousand dollars. Unlike Berman, Webster had no wife and children and few outside interests. For him, as later psychiatric evaluations confirmed, his work was his life.

In 1975, a new management team took over his company. Webster's complaint argues that his new superior, William Bishop, arrived with the apparent intent of forcing his resignation. Soon after taking charge, according to Webster's suit, Bishop told him his work was going to become more difficult and suggested that someone his age—he was then 50—would be better off in another job. Bishop reportedly said Webster looked "old" for the job and suggested that he get a "dye job" for his graying hair. Webster recalls Bishop's saying that the new management wanted a "young person's company" and that old-timers like Webster would soon be "recycled" or discharged. "These comments were particularly painful," Webster later recounted in an affidavit, "because, as Bishop well knew, I felt that I had to stay with the job and take abuse because at my age it would have been difficult for me to get another job."

For the next year and a half, Webster claims, Bishop subjected him to frequent harassment and humiliation. At department meetings Bishop would ask him unexpectedly for detailed data or arcane information, such as the number of checks cashed by a particular bank in a particular city during a particular period. When Webster could not respond, Bishop would berate him in front of his colleagues. He began to countermand Webster's orders, changing his budgets and reassigning his subordinates without Webster's knowledge or consent.

In February 1976 at a big company management meeting, Bishop publicly announced that he was taking over all of Webster's duties and that he would be reassigned to another position. Webster was eventually given the title of vice president of development, but he never received a description of his new duties. Soon afterward, he says, his name was taken off the distribution list for interoffice memos, and he was no longer invited to department meetings.

Previously in good physical and mental health, according to the suit, Webster began to deteriorate under the harassment. He developed a variety of symptoms of emotional distress: headaches, dizziness, diarrhea, insomnia, loss of confidence, fear, and anxiety. In the fall of 1976 after he reported his symptoms to the medical department, a company doctor gave him some sleeping pills. When the pills provided no relief, he was referred to an outside psychologist who treated him on several visits with various relaxation techniques that also had little effect.

As Webster's symptoms worsened, he claims he felt unable to work and feared a "nervous breakdown." Around Christmas of 1976, the company sent him to a clinical psychologist for an evaluation. The referral memo from the personnel department reported that Webster was "not functioning well" in his job and asked for advice about the effect of a change in his position, a reduction in his responsibilities, or a transfer to new location.

In his report to the company, the psychologist said Webster's inability to function was due to "a loss of self-esteem and a sense of extreme worthlessness," which, together with other symptoms, he diagnosed as depression. The psychologist felt Webster's condition had begun as a reaction to Bishop's harassment. As his condition had deteriorated, so had his job performance, thereby adding to his feeling of inadequacy.

By then, Webster had considered quitting, but the psychologist urged him not to. He recommended that the company give Webster a two-month medical leave of absence for a treatment of medication and extended psychotherapy. The report specifically warned the company: "No decision should be made at this time regarding the transfer or termination, as this is a period of extreme stress. These decisions should be put off until his therapeutic program has taken effect."

Within a week of receiving that specific recommendation, the company set in motion the mechanics of Webster's dismissal. They called it an extended "leave of absence," with one-third pay until he reached age 55 and became eligible for early retirement and a pension. However, the letter formally notifying him of these plans referred to his "termination." By the end of February, Webster worked his last day. He was told to turn in his company credit card and identification card. "As a practical matter," he later stated in an affidavit, "I was fired . . . put out to pasture."

Webster claims his dismissal further undermined his health. He eventually moved to California, where the held a job for three months as manager of a plant store; he later worked part time as a building manager. Today he is unemployed. According to several psychiatric evaluations included among the documents filed in the suit, Webster is "petrified of authority," "emotionally castrated," and suffering from "chronic anxiety" comparable to "shell shock."

According to the psychiatrist who has treated him in California, if the company had followed the clinical psychologist's recommendations and if Webster "had received therapy and could have worked without undue harassment, he could have continued to be a valuable contributor to the company."

If Webster's case does come to trial, the company would be likely to produce expert psychiatric witnesses to contest the claim that Webster was still "salvageable" at the time of his dismissal. However, regardless of his psychological condition or its causes, the company is seeking to have the case dismissed on the grounds that any psychiatric injury suffered in the course of employment should be covered by the workers' compensation law.

In reply, Webster's lawyer argues that what happened to his client was neither accidental nor natural and was, in fact, quite avoidable. He describes the company's behavior as "willfull" and "outrageous." He charges that it went "far beyond mere negligence" and "beyond reasonable bounds of decency." The company, he charged, "transformed a happy, healthy, productive human being into one totally incapable of functioning effectively or supporting himself."

When I tell the stories of Berman and Webster to my fellow commuters on the train, most of them corporate executives, I get no uniform response. Some are outraged, calling the cases "corporate muggings." Some shrug, saying, "It happens all the time." Many, however, are dubious. They wonder why Berman and Webster weren't able to persuade their superiors to ease up on them. They wonder why the two men were unable to get support from their colleagues. They wonder why the two men held on until their suffering incapacitated them, instead of quitting. Most agree, how-ever, quitting a company in emotional distress after 20 or 30 years, at the age of 50, does not make it easy to find another job.

Whatever psychiatric injuries Webster or Berman may have suffered, their cases will not come to trial if the judges decide that their claims should be governed by the workers' compensation law. Or, the cases may be settled out of court, thus heading off any discussion of corporate responsi-bility. Any court decisions could prompt appeals from either side that could drag on for years.

If the two cases do come to trial, the corporate employers may raise a number of arguments that cannot be easily dismissed. Berman's company, for example, may attempt to prove that his work load was no greater than that of other managers and that he simply couldn't handle it effectively. Webster's company may try to show that he simply couldn't get along with Bishop because of his own personality problems; it may also claim that he really was deadwood, no longer capable of performing his job well. The company lawyers in both cases will undoubtedly attempt to show that the mental and emotional problems of the two executives were due not merely, or perhaps not even mostly, to the stress of their work, but rather to problems in their private lives—problems not yet raised in the preliminary court papers.

Industry lawyers will be following the cases of Berman and Webster attentively, since their outcome could significantly expand corporate lia-bility for employee mental health. A favorable decision in either case could stimulate hundreds of similar suits. After all, we live in a litigious age, with more and more people suing doctors and lawyers for malpractice, commer-cial institutions for negligence.

The same spirit has led to a sharp rise in the total cost of company pay-ments for workers' compensation coverage from $2.9 billion in 1965 to more than $20 billion in 1980. In California there are now 3,000 to 4,000 claims for psychiatric injury each year; about half result in awards. A Ventura law firm solicits cases with ads that ask: "Does your job make you sick?"

Many employers have grown cynical about what they see as a wave of dubious claims for psychiatric injury under the workers' compensation laws. They point out that many claims are made just before retirement by employees who have spent years at a job they suddenly claim has been causing them severe emotional distress.

Even if most of these claims represent legitimate cases of emotional or mental illness, the problems may be due as much to individual personality or to stress at home as to stress at work. Although the term "stress" is tossed around loosely these days, it remains an exceedingly complex phe-nomenon. Recent research has shown that people's reactions to potentially stressful situations on and off the job vary greatly, depending on their per-sonalities. Some people are psychologically more resilient or "stress re-sistant" than others. Some executives thrive on a level of stress that could lead to physical or mental disorder in others. (See "Psychological Hardiness," *Psychology Today*, December 1980.)

Psychiatrist Alan McLean, the eastern medical director for IBM and one of the country's foremost authorities on occupational health, believes that the legal interpretations of "cause" in psychiatric injury cases have become unreasonably narrow. He says recent court decisions have ignored preexisting emotional conditions as well as personality or family factors, all of which may underlie or contribute to an employee's mental illness.

McLean's argument is persuasive, particularly when applied to claims due to stress from what he calls "regularly expected performance." As he points out, many managers and executives work under intense pressure without suffering from stress-related symptoms or developing mental illness. Should an employer be held liable for psychiatric injury if a particular manager just can't seem to handle that same amount of pressure?

Despite McLean's view, many companies now offer their employees stress-reduction programs or psychological counseling either by in-house experts or by outside firms. But some employers are reluctant to get involved in such programs. They wonder why they should assume responsibility for psychological problems that may be largely dependent on nonjob factors like personality and family life. The company, in their view, has no business meddling in the private lives of its employees or trying to solve their personal problems.

Drilco, a Texas tool manufacturer, recently reevaluated its stress-management program and decided to discontinue it. Jimmy Gray, Drilco's vice president for personnel, explained: "A lot of stress is job related, but a lot of it is personal, too, and we decided that this should be handled outside the company on an individual level." IBM, a company otherwise noted for its generous and humane employee policies, has no psychological counseling program for employees. Those who need such help are encouraged to seek it outside the company (as they are the companies Berman and Webster worked for). Alan McLean of IBM refers to the spread of corporate psychological-counseling programs for employees as "deadly paternalism."

Other critics, looking at the programs from an entirely different angle, argue that they divert attention from the causes of work stress for which the company can reasonably be held responsible. Sidney Lecker, a New York psychiatrist who serves as a consultant to several major corporations, says: "It's nonsense to say it's completely a matter of how the individual employee reacts to stress. The big factor is the overall quality of work life and the organizational climate." To illustrate his point, Lecker compares a typical American "Theory X" company that runs on fear as the basic motivator, with every boss "kicking ass," and a typical Japanese company, which assumes an almost parental responsibility for its employees and encourages a similar relationship between superiors and subordinates at every level.

Many American companies have commissioned organizational-climate studies of their operations; others have launched a variety of programs designed to improve their employees' "quality of work life." It remains to be seen whether all the activity will amount to mere puffery or whether it will result in serious attempts to reduce stress and humanize the work environment.

As the cases of Roger Berman and Roland Webster illustrate, the question of corporate responsibility for employee mental health is not simple. The cases depend in part on controversial legal and medical definitions of cause-and-effect in stress-related illness. They also raise questions about the kind of commitment a company makes in hiring an employee. Some companies are unwilling to accept any responsibility for employee mental health. Others recognize some limited responsibility but only as long as the employees continue to perform well. If mental or emotional problems begin to interfere with their work, the commitment often ends.

A more humane and, in the long run, perhaps more productive commitment might offer employees not only job security, but within reason, emotional security as well, particularly for those who have spent 20 years or more with the company. If an executive or a factory worker shows signs of emotional distress that—correctly or not—he or she attributes to the conditions of the job, a company that recognizes and accepts responsibility for that employee's mental health would try at least to alleviate the work-related source of the stress, or, as in many Japanese companies, shift the employee to a less stressful position. Tough-minded American businessmen may scoff and call that coddling. But if court decisions establish the employee's right to sue the employer for psychiatric injury by stress, assuming responsibility for employee mental health may become a matter of legal obligation rather than an optional policy of management.

Part III

BEHAVIOR WITHIN ORGANIZATIONS: GROUPS AND INTERPERSONAL INFLUENCES

In this part five articles examine groups and interpersonal influences within organizations. A group consists of two or more people interacting to accomplish goals. Organizations are in essence a set of interacting groups—formal and informal. When groups interact, there is potential for intra- and intergroup conflict. These realities are pointed out in this part.

Another portion of this part examines leadership—the influence process in action. Years of research, heated debate, and day-to-day practice has not clarified the notion of leadership. It is still quite controversial and very rich in research opportunities.

Alvin Zander in "The Study of Group Behavior during Four Decades" examines groups. He examines the history of research into group behavior. Zander traces group research prior to 1940, during the 1940s, during the 1950s, during the 1960s, and during the 1970s. He also makes his own general observations about the research.

In a much quoted and cited article, Irving L. Janis discusses "Groupthink." The dangers of thinking alike, going along with the group, and feeling too cozy with group members is interestingly presented. Janis relates examples of groupthink. One of the most insightful is his analysis of the Bay of Pigs plan adopted by the Kennedy in-group. The end products of such groupthinking are identified. He warns against groupthink especially in this area of atomic warheads, and urban problems. His warning seems to be right on target.

The next article is by George H. Labovitz and is entitled "Managing Conflict." He believes that managers can derive some positive benefits from conflict. Labovitz first explains why conflict exists. He then discusses different strategies for controlling conflict.

An article, "Managers and Leaders: Are They Different?" by Abraham Zaleznik, discusses the issue of whether managers and leaders are reasonably one and the same. The discussion focuses on the leader versus managerial personality concept. He presents comparisons on attitudes, on goals, conceptions of work, relations with others, and sense of self. He closes the article by presenting his view of whether organizations develop leaders.

The final article is entitled "Leadership Theory: Some Implications for Managers" by Chester A. Schriesheim, James M. Tolliver, and Orlando C. Behling. Three distinct phases of leadership thinking are identified—trait, behavioral, and situational. Each of these phases have resulted in theory and research insights. From these insights have evolved organizational and individual implications. Some of these implications are discussed.

The Study of Group Behavior during Four Decades*

ALVIN ZANDER

Without much warning about 40 years ago, students of human behavior developed an interest in how groups conduct their activities. This rise of attention among scholars was evident in the number and content of their publications, the creation of a communications network, and a zealous desire of some individuals in this network to improve ineffective groups before anyone knew how such improving could be done. Citizens were attracted to research on groups and some stated (extravagantly enough) that the products of this research would at last provide answers to tough problems in government and social relations.

During subsequent decades the quick growth of those early years settled down to a more measured pace and to a deeper perusal of particular topics, while scholars interested in training members of groups drew away, for the most part, from college campuses, or at least from researchers, and nurtured groups in natural settings and training laboratories. In this article we briefly review some of the main features in the history of research into group behavior, commenting on training activities only where these had an impact on empirical investigations.

PRIOR TO 1940 Before 1935 there had been little scientific effort to understand processes in groups. Research had been done on laughter in audiences and on the personality traits of designated leaders, but the only work close to current studies in group life were studies comparing how groups and individuals go about solving problems, a topic that remains of interest today. The dearth of earlier inquiries into group activities is not surprising when we recall that psychologists in the 30s devoted most of their attention to

* Reprinted by special permission from *The Journal of Applied Behavioral Science*, Volume 15, No. 3, pp. 272–82, copyright 1979, NTL Institute.

the study of physiology, motor skills, and cognitive processes of the individual. Social psychologists had hardly discovered their identity, and sociologists, for their part, were not yet collecting empirical data on groups.

In the last half of the 30s the time had come for attempts to explain events within organizations; several notable developments in research signaled this fact. Work on group structure and attraction between individual members [Moreno, 1934], the influence of group norms on members [Sherif, 1936], the impact of shared beliefs on the political attitudes of college students [Newcomb, 1943], and the effect that membership in a work group had upon the sentiments of factory workers [Roethlisberger & Dickson, 1939] revealed that aspects of collective behavior, previously of interest to social philosophers, could usefully be brought under scientific investigation.

The most influential research by far in the emerging study of group behavior was that of Lewin, Lippitt, and White [1939]. Their investigations of group climate, intergroup conflict, and styles of leadership (autocratic, democratic, and laissez-faire) made use, with important modifications, of the available techniques in experimental psychology, controlled observations of behavior, and methods of social group work. Their purpose was to expose some of the ways in which the behavior of leaders may differ and to discover how methods of leadership influence the properties of groups and the behavior of members. We should note that these investigations were not intended to make a contribution to the technology of group management per se. Rather, they sought to provide insight into the underlying dynamics of groups. The methods and results of the studies suggested that it might be feasible to construct a coherent body of knowledge about the nature of group life and eventually a general theory of groups. These studies had an originality and significance which produced a marked impact on the social sciences and professions. Almost immediately, associates of Lewin, and others, began research projects, most of them laboratory experiments, designed to contribute information relevant to a theory of group dynamics. The results of this work formed the core of a "critical mass" which eventually made this speciality distinctive and accepted.

Lewin's assumptions about the causes of human behavior were particularly suited to the study of group life, as he held that most of the variables determining behavior at a given time and place are extant in that setting. Past events and future ones were to be interpreted in terms of their current psychological representation. Lewin's emphasis on the forces and constraints arising in situations led to a concentration on the here-and-now in both research and training about group life. Because such notions were especially appropriate in the developing of theory, prediction, and experimentation, they helped to generate a special style of investigation.

DURING THE 1940s

As these investigations were getting under way, the United States entered World War II and little research on groups was accomplished for five years or so. In 1946, Lewin and a set of his former students founded the Research Center for Group Dynamics at the Massachusetts Institute of Technology, and in 1948 the Center moved to the University of Michigan after the untimely death of Lewin.

Through research done at this center, at half a dozen other centers with similar purposes in several countries, and at a number of campuses and government laboratories, knowledge about the social psychology of groups entered a period of active growth. Some of the topics studied most often in the 40s were: social pressures members place on one another within a group [Festinger, 1950], the direction and amount of communication among members [Bavelas, 1950], contrasts in the behavior of members in cooperative and competitive groups [Deutsch, 1949], and consequences of training community leaders [Lippitt, 1949], and the effects of social power among children [Lippitt, Polansky, Redl & Rosen, 1952].

The concepts and methods in this research were radical for their time and discipline. Thus, the scientists immersed in these efforts found it helpful to organize themselves informally to work toward a common end. Researchers distant from one another created a loose network, exchanged drafts of papers, and talked about their investigations in small meetings, conferences, and visits. The formation of this "invisible college" among students of groups was not unlike the voluntary associations, described by Griffith and Mullins [1972], that arise through the history of science whenever a strikingly new topic is taken up by members of a given discipline. Many of the early group scholars firmly believed that the output of their research would have a wide impact toward improving democratic methods, and the researchers consciously worked toward such ends. After World War II, it was more acceptable than it is now to claim that research in human behavior would have practical value for society.

Ordinary citizens gave considerable attention to this research, and the study of group processes received as much interest in the media of those days as have recombinant DNA, toxic chemicals, tranquilizers, or the effects of computers in more recent years. The reasons for the wide appeal of this research at that time merits detailed study someday. One can guess, however, that the attractiveness of the work arose in part because everyone was worried then about the fate of this country in World War II and about the future of democracy as a form of government. They were inclined, therefore, to welcome work by scientists who might increase our understanding of the dynamics of governing and might suggest ways of improving its procedures. Also, there was a widespread fear during the 40s, that dictatorships had developed irresistible methods for manipulating the minds of men. Perhaps we could learn how to oppose such pressures through research by students of groups. Not least was the wide interest, even delight, in the methods and results of experiments on small societies in the laboratory where it was shown that contrasting behavior of group members under contrasting circumstances could be predicted and explained. Citizens highly approved of scientists in physics and engineering during the 40s and 50s because these latter had helped in the winning of World War II.

Perhaps social scientists could be as useful in problems of group life if they were given proper encouragement and support. Accordingly, late in the decade, the Office of Naval Research created a unit to provide funds for research on group behavior regardless of the work's relevance to military conditions.

One other development in the 1940s is notable. In 1947 the National Training Laboratory for Group Development was organized by the Adult Education Division of the National Education Association in cooperation with the Research Center for Group Dynamics. This was a three-week workshop attended by professional persons from various walks of life who wished to improve their knowledge of groups and their abilities as members and managers. Because there was a limited supply of knowledge available for participants in this kind of laboratory, the teachers relied on having students learn from their experiences in small discussion groups. This procedure encouraged talk about the matters that excited them most and these turned out to be personal feelings, relations among members, differences in perceptions, and explanations for these differences. Such person-centered interaction, as we shall see, reduced regard for the study of groups. An account of these developments is offered in the book *Beyond Words* by Kurt Back [1972].

From the beginning, the founders of the National Training Laboratory had different ideas among them as to the purposes of the unit. Some of these objectives were: to teach group dynamics, to teach consultants how to facilitate change within an organization, to teach members "basic skills" of membership, to train participants in the teaching methods being employed at the laboratory, and to conduct research on behavior in groups. Because of these unlike views, the meetings of staff members when planning each laboratory were lively and stimulating, to say the least. There was no initial interest, we should emphasize, in encouraging personal growth, mental health, or sensitivity in interpersonal relations.

DURING THE 1950s

In the decade of the 50s, research in the social psychology of groups was highly innovative and the rate of publication more than doubled, according to Hare [1976]. Authors of chapters on group research in the *Annual Review of Psychology* published in 1951, 1953, 1954, and 1958 remarked that study of groups was the most lively and creative work in social psychology and provided a focus for the entire field.

The topics for investigation were those already mentioned, plus the flow of communication in groups when members have different degrees of connectedness among them, interpersonal power to influence, the sources of coalitions, and the nature and consequences of balanced relations within groups. Bales [1950] developed a method for observing and coding comments made by participants in small problem-solving groups. His treatment of these data, called interaction process analysis, revealed the kind of remarks (questions, suggestions, agreements, and the like) that were more likely to appear at each phase in a group's problem-solving effort. This work formed the basis of what sociologists came to call the study of small groups [Hare, Borgata & Bales, 1955]. It concentrated, however, on the acts and roles of individuals and paid little attention to the group as a unit.

The properties of groups, their origins and consequences, provided by this time a framework for the study of group dynamics; many of the findings of research concerned one or more of these properties, such as cohesiveness, goals, or leadership. A book summarizing results of research in group dynamics, arranged according to such headings, was published by Cartwright and Zander in 1953.

Even though one could now identify a coherent body of knowledge from the results of group research, there were "islands" of findings that did not fit together well and these separated results were not included in summaries of the field. The topics given most study, moreover, were not noticed most often by readers. Nelson and Kannenberg [1976] report a correlation of only $r = .12$ between the popularity of a topic among researchers in the 1950s and the interest accorded to it in subsequent articles. Additional government agencies began to provide financial aid for research on groups: the United States Public Health Service, the National Institute for Mental Health, parts of the Department of Defense, and (later on) the National Science Foundation. In addition, grants were not hard to obtain for promising projects from private foundations and industrial firms. It was a lively but not a well-organized time to be involved in the study of groups.

By the middle of this decade the National Training Laboratory in Group Development, which no longer had a formal relationship with the Research Center for Group Dynamics, dropped the words: "in Group Development" from its title and moved toward independence from the National Education Association. The NTL now encouraged laboratories in several parts of the country. Most prominent among these branches was one at the University of Los Angeles, run by students of personality theory, not social psychology. These teachers fostered an emphasis on personal growth and interpersonal relations, using the group as a setting for their teaching, not as a subject of instruction in itself. They placed more emphasis on personal feelings and problems than on cognitions or information —thus the term "sensitivity training" was an appropriate designation for their style of teaching.

Comparable developments were occurring at the original laboratory as the training began to emphasize self-awareness and personal improvement rather than understanding of group properties. Critics arose, especially among psychologists and professionals in mental health. They believed activities at training laboratories engendered stress of participants and that there was little evidence the activities had favorable effects on those who experienced them. Supporters of the training defended their programs by asserting that they were doing research and teaching about group behavior, not providing counseling for individuals. It had become evident, however, that a training laboratory was not a satisfactory place for conducting basic research, as the collecting of data often interfered with teaching activities and adequate experimental controls could seldom be developed in a training group.

DURING THE 1960s

By the 60s, the study of group behavior had become an accepted sub-discipline in departments of psychology and in places for the study of sociology, speech, social work, public health, education, and business. Technical articles in this specialty appeared somewhat less often than they did in the previous decade. The number of research publications dropped from perhaps 150 a year to 120, but I know of no accurate count of this frequency. In contrast, essays on the use of groups in education, therapy, and management increased in numbers. Many who had earlier been doing research on the social psychology of groups moved to other interests unrelated to group life, and all of the centers established for research on groups, except the one at Michigan, were gone by the middle of the decade. Sherif [1977] and Steiner [1974] assert that many social psychologists turned from the study of groups and other collective phenomena to the study of individuals during the 60s.

If this reduction of interest in groups occurred in fact, why did it happen? Several reasons may have played a part.

1. Research on groups is more difficult than research on individuals: When groups (compared to individuals) are the units of study, many more subjects are needed, they are harder to assemble in the required number at the proper time, the costs are higher, and the design, measurement, and analyses are more complicated and tricky.

2. Concepts about group life are often too clumsy to use, too austere to attract much interest, or too intricate to test with confidence.

3. Results of research on groups can be weak and unconvincing because it is hard to rule out noise and artifacts when measuring the varied behaviors in a group. Thus, many group researchers obtain small satisfaction from their efforts.

4. A researcher can get more help from current literature when studying individuals than when studying groups.

5. Funds for the support of social research began to be scarce late in the 60s and the study of groups did not compete well for these funds.

The fans of group dynamics dwindled in number during the 60s as their interests also moved, along with changes in social issues of the time, to topics where the study of groups was no longer as crucial. Some of the problems of group life during both the 60s and the 70s were not the kind, moreover, that stimulated theorizing about how groups effectively conduct their business. Unlike the 40s, much interesting group action was now intended to change conditions outside the group through demonstrations, disruptions, and other forms of confronting and militancy, rather than through the use of the democratic process. One cannot easily observe efforts to create social change, and thus research on such topics was done after the fact. As a result, sound theories have not been developed on these matters.

"Group watchers" may have noticed, furthermore, that results from research in group behavior had not lived up to the grand expectations held for them after World War II—the world had not been changed. Also, many of the best known results of group research emphasized the bad effects of groups on their members—a one-sided view that did not arouse enthusiasm for the study of group behavior. Accompanying this shift of interest among nonscientists was a gradual dissolution of the network that had been formed among like-minded scholars. The reduction of activist fervor within this network, however, was not a characteristic of this field alone. Griffith and Mullins [1972] observed that the most successful of informal associations among scientists lasted no longer than 10 to 15 years, usually because of low scientific vitality or low distinctiveness of the members' work and because fashions changed among supporters of research. These authors believed that a network must develop a coherent theory in order to last, and a coherence had not yet developed in the explanations of behavior in groups.

The fashionable topics for research on groups during these 10 years were conformity to group pressures, interpersonal relations between pairs of persons with mixed motives (e.g., the prisoner's dilemma), the "risky shift," and social facilitation. In 1967, Gerard and Miller remarked in the *Annual Review of Psychology* that most of the recent work on groups supported already familiar conclusions. In part, this was true.

DURING THE 1970s

In the 70s, the prime research topics were still familiar ones. Evidence for this can be seen in an account of group investigations during 1975, 1976, and 1977 that I prepared for the *Annual Review of Psychology* [1979]. The most frequently studied topics during the three years were social pressures in groups, the sources (not the consequences) of group cohesiveness, and cooperating versus competing groups. Less popular, but not less familiar, were leadership, group structure, and problem solving in groups. Polarization of beliefs among members, and other cognitive processes in groups, newly attracted interest from researchers, as did research on group size, crowding, and patterns of physical distance between participants. A good degree of activity, therefore, occurred in research, even though the number of agencies and the dollars to support the work had declined in the 70s to much less than in the early 60s. Social psychologists began to worry about the nature and direction of their field and subfields, including group behavior [Ring, 1967; Steiner, 1974; Elms, 1975; Silverman, 1977]. Finally, the use of groups for helping the "personal growth" of individuals became big business during the 70s, providing a fast service for anxious people who hoped to purchase comfort for themselves without investing in therapy.

SOME GENERAL OBSERVATIONS

Over the years, ever since research on groups came into its own, several features have typified its methods. Most investigations have been controlled experiments and a good proportion of these have used an instrument, experimental design, or procedure invented by someone else. Part of the reason for this dependence on established methods is that many graduate students, and their teachers too, cannot obtain funds for a program of studies, so they conduct isolated experiments that have a high probability of success.

Despite the preference for the experimental method, there have been surprisingly few full-blown theories in group dynamics. This says something about the difficulty in explaining collective events. No doubt many theories have been discarded because the results of research obstinately would not provide support for hypotheses developed in the theories; and revisions in these ideas to fit the actual findings fared no better in later tests. In other sciences and in other branches of psychology, scholars may refresh and adjust their supply of ideas outside the laboratory by observing phenomena that interest them. But group researchers seldom have collectives available for such observations and show little interest in them when they are available. Indeed, the phenomena they study may not resemble anything they can notice in a natural group. As a result, theories about groups are too often long on logic and short on researchability.

As is true in many other fields, earlier concepts in the social psychology of group life are gradually replaced by newer ideas, and these latter are stated a bit more precisely than the parent notions. To illustrate: Work on the impact of group decisions led to studies of social pressures in groups; demonstrations of leadership style moved into research on social power; research on the risky shift became work on the origin of polarized ideas in discussion; and investigations of intragroup competition developed into ways of resolving intergroup conflicts. Although we can easily find examples like those just cited, in which there has been movement toward greater specificity in concepts, research in group behavior still suffers from an absence of useful and well-stated primary notions. Examples of vaguely understood terms used in research are: role, group goal, group structure, status, de-individuation, leadership, socialization, and social environment. In the absence of adequate precision, ideas like these cannot be manipulated in a consistent fashion in the laboratory or measured validly in the conference room. Perhaps students of groups would benefit from a return to the days when scholars worried about how to construct useful concepts; but that idea is not yet ready for resurrection, I fear.

It seems likely that the soundness of knowledge increases as key ideas in a field are more neatly defined. When concepts become more valid and more commonly accepted, new results of research will more easily be integrated into a (growing) body of wisdom. As things now stand, researchers in group life are remarkably inventive in creating new terms for phenomena that already have a perfectly useful name, thus creating more semantic confusion than need be. A number of synonyms exist, for example, to denote each of a member's desire to remain in a group, the functions of leadership, the ends toward which groups strive, and the dimensions of group structure. Different terms, furthermore, are often used for the same definition, and a given scholar may ignore research done under a label unlike one he or she prefers even though the results of that research are quite relevant to his or her own interests. What may be worse is illustrated in a recent book where interpersonal power to influence is a primary theme. The author provides a definition of social power that is nowhere near the definition used in the studies of power she thoroughly summarizes. Thus, she brings data together to support a view that the studies do not support at all. Clearly, the slipperiness of concepts in group behavior can lead to a lack of precision in specifying them.

A relatively limited number of topics have been explored out of the number available for investigation. Some examples of questions that have had little study, considering their importance in the life of an organization, are: Why is it so difficult to expel a member from a group? Why do groups recruit certain persons rather than others? What are the reasons for secrecy as a routine practice in organizations? Why is a modern manager met by abrasive behavior from subordinates? Why do groups set difficult goals? How can members improve the efficiency of meetings? How do organizations respond to regulations that limit their actions? One can easily think of other subjects that warrant study: changes in the properties of groups over time, why members participate in a group, the sources of conflict between groups, the contrasting effects of centralization and decentralization in a group, the origins of a group's goals, the causes of productivity in a group, or the effects of the social environment on a group. In a recent volume I have discussed a number of these issues with a view toward stimulating research into them [Zander, 1977].

Why are ripe topics not picked for study? One reason, already implied, is that investigators are busy planning and conducting experiments on more familiar issues; in fact, a researcher seldom moves to matters that are vastly different from his or her former areas of interest. Another reason is that a problem may be widely recognized as a candidate for research but it is not an acceptable topic in the eyes of potential investigators, those who advise researchers, those who edit journals, or those who provide funds for research. The problem may be well known but set aside because there are no basic data on the matter, reliable measures cannot be made of the phenomena involved, the theoretical issues are not clearly stated, or the project is too costly in time, energy, and number of human subjects needed. Such obstacles turn researchers away from matters worthy of attention.

As is often said, it is true that nothing is so practical as a well-stated theory. Such a theory can explain the causes and effects of a given event in different settings. Through results of research, people discern how best to help themselves because they identify what conditions lead to what consequences, and why. The innovativeness of research in group dynamics has been on a plateau for a few years. It will not stay on that level long when new needs and means stimulate new developments among students of group behavior.

REFERENCES

Back, K. *Beyond words*. New York: Russell Sage Foundation, 1972.

Bales, R. F. *Interaction process analysis*. Cambridge, Mass.: Addison-Wesley Publishing, 1950.

Bavelas, A. Communication patterns in task-oriented groups. *Journal of Acoustical Society of America*, 1950, 22, 725–730.

Cartwright, D., & Zander, A. *Group dynamics, research and theory*. Evanston, Ill.: Row Peterson, 1953.

Deutsch, M. The effect of cooperation and competition upon group process. *Human Relations*, 1949, 2, 129–152 and 199–231.

Elms, A. C. The crisis of confidence in social psychology. *American Psychologist*, 1975, *30*, 967–976.

Festinger, L. Informal social communication. *Psychological Review*, 1950, *57*, 271–282.

Gerard, H., & Miller, N. Group dynamics. *Annual Review of Psychology*, 1967, 18, 287–332.

Griffith, B. C., & Mullins, N. C. Coherent social groups in scientific change. *Science*, 1972, 177, 959–964.

Hare, A. P., Borgatta, E. F., & Bales, R. F. *Small groups, studies in social interaction*. New York: Knopf, 1955.

Hare, A. P. *Handbook of small group research*. New York: Free Press, 1976.

Lewin, K., Lippitt, R., & White, R. Patterns of aggressive behavior in experimentally created "social climates." *Journal of Social Psychology*, 1939, *10*, 271–299.

Lippitt, R. *Training in community relations*. New York: Harper & Bros., 1949.

Lippitt, R., Polansky, N., Redl, F., & Rosen, S. The dynamics of power. *Human Relations*, 1952, *5*, 37–64.

Moreno, J. L. *Who shall survive*. Washington, D.C.: Nervous and Mental Diseases Publishing Company, 1934.

Nelson, C., & Kannenberg, P. Social psychology in a crisis. *Personality and Social Psychology Bulletin*, 1976, 2, 14–21.

Newcomb, T. *Personality and social change*. New York: Dryden, 1943.

Ring, K. Experimental social psychology: Some sober questions about some frivolous values. *Journal of Experimental Social Psychology*, 1967, *3*, 113–123.

Roethlisberger, F. J., & Dickson, W. J. *Management and the worker*. Cambridge, Mass.: Harvard University Press, 1939.

Sherif, M. *The psychology of social norms*. New York: Harper & Row, 1936.

Sherif, M. Crisis in social psychology: Some remarks towards breaking through the crisis. *Personality and Social Behavior Bulletin*, 1977, *3*, 368–382.

Silverman, I. Why social psychology fails. *Canadian Psychology Review*, 1977, *18*, 353–358.

Steiner, I. Whatever happened to the group in social psychology? *Journal of Experimental Social Psychology*, 1974, *10*, 93–108.

Zander, A. *Groups at work*. San Francisco: Jossey-Bass, 1977 .

Zander, A. The psychology of group processes. *Annual Review of Psychology*, 1979, *30*, 417–451.

Groupthink*

IRVING L. JANIS

"How could we have been so stupid?" President John F. Kennedy asked after he and a close group of advisers had blundered into the Bay of Pigs invasion. For the last two years I have been studying that question, as it applies not only to the Bay of Pigs decision makers but also to those who led the United States into such other major fiascos as the failure to be prepared for the attack on Pearl Harbor, the Korean War stalemate, and the escalation of the Vietnam War.

Stupidity certainly is not the explanation. The men who participated in making the Bay of Pigs decision, for instance, comprised one of the greatest arrays of intellectual talent in the history of American government—Dean Rusk, Robert McNamara, Douglas Dillon, Robert Kennedy, McGeorge Bundy, Arthur Schlesinger, Jr., Allen Dulles, and others.

It also seemed to me that explanations were incomplete if they concentrated only on disturbances in the behavior of each individual within a decision-making body: temporary emotional states of elation, fear, or anger that reduce a man's mental efficiency, for example, or chronic blind spots arising from a man's social prejudices or idiosyncratic biases.

I preferred to broaden the picture by looking at the fiascos from the standpoint of group dynamics as it has been explored over the past three decades, first by the great social psychologist Kurt Lewin and later in many experimental situations by myself and other behavioral scientists. My conclusion after poring over hundreds of relevant documents—historical reports about formal group meetings and informal conversatiins among the members—is that the groups that committed the fiascos were victims of what I call "groupthink."

"GROUPY"

In each case study, I was surprised to discover the extent to which each group displayed the typical phenomena of social conformity that are regu-

---

larly encountered in studies of group dynamics among ordinary citizens. For example, some of the phenomena appear to be completely in line with findings from social-psychological experiments showing that powerful social pressures are brought to bear by the members of a cohesive group whenever a dissident begins to voice his objections to a group consensus. Other phenomena are reminiscent of the shared illusions observed in encounter groups and friendship cliques when the members simultaneously reach a peak of "groupy" feelings.

Above all, there are numerous indications pointing to the development of group norms that bolster morale at the expense of critical thinking. One of the most common norms appears to be that of remaining loyal to the group by sticking with the policies to which the group has already committed itself, even when those policies are obviously working out badly and have unintended consequences that disturb the conscience of each member. This is one of the key characteristics of groupthink.

1984

I use the term *groupthink* as a quick and easy way to refer to the mode of thinking that persons engage in when *concurrence seeking* becomes so dominant in a cohesive in-group that it tends to override realistic appraisal of alternative courses of action. Groupthink is a term of the same order as the words in the newspeak vocabulary George Orwell used in his dismaying world of *1984*. In that context, groupthink takes on an invidious connotation. Exactly such connotation is intended, since the term refers to a deterioration in mental efficiency, reality testing, and moral judgments as a result of group pressures.

The symptoms of groupthink arise when the members of decision-making groups become motivated to avoid being too harsh in their judgments of their leaders' or their colleagues' ideas. They adopt a soft line of criticism, even in their own thinking. At their meeting, all the members are amiable and seek complete concurrence on every important issue, with no bickering or conflict to spoil the cozy "we-feeling" atmosphere.

KILL

Paradoxically, soft-headed groups are often hard-hearted when it comes to dealing with outgroups or enemies. They find it relatively easy to resort to dehumanizing solutions—they will readily authorize bombing attacks that kill large numbers of civilians in the name of the noble cause of persuading an unfriendly government to negotiate at the peace table. They are unlikely to pursue the more difficult and controversial issues that arise when alternatives to a harsh military solution come up for discussion. Nor are they inclined to raise ethical issues that carry the implication that *this fine group of ours, with its humanitarianism and its high-minded principles, might be capable of adopting a course of action that is inhumane and immoral.*

NORMS

There is evidence from a number of social-psychological studies that as the members of a group feel more accepted by the others, which is a central feature of increased group cohesiveness, they display less overt conformity to group norms. Thus we would expect that the more cohesive a group becomes, the less the members will feel constrained to censor what they say out of fear of being socially punished for antagonizing the leader or any of their fellow members.

In contrast, the groupthink type of conformity tends to increase as group cohesiveness increases. Groupthink involves nondeliberate suppression of critical thoughts as a result of internalization of the group's norms, which is quite different from deliberate suppression on the basis of external threats of social punishment. The more cohesive the group, the greater the inner compulsion on the part of each member to avoid creating disunity, which inclines him to believe in the soundness of whatever proposals are promoted by the leader or by a majority of the group's members.

In a cohesive group, the danger is not so much that each individual will fail to reveal his objections to what the others propose but that he will think the proposal is a good one, without attempting to carry out a careful, critical scrutiny of the pros and cons of the alternatives. When groupthink becomes dominant, there also is considerable suppression of deviant thoughts, but it takes the form of each person's deciding that his misgivings are not relevant and should be set aside, that the benefits of the doubt regarding any lingering uncertainties should be given to the group consensus.

STRESS

I do not mean to imply that all cohesive groups necessarily suffer from groupthink. All in-groups may have a mild tendency toward groupthink, displaying one or another of the symptoms from time to time, but it need not be so dominant as to influence the quality of the group's final decision. Neither do I mean to imply that there is anything necessarily inefficient or harmful about group decisions in general. On the contrary, a group whose members have properly defined roles, with traditions concerning the procedures to follow in pursuing a critical inquiry, probably is capable of making better decisions than any individual group member working alone.

The problem is that the advantages of having decisions made by groups are often lost because of powerful psychological pressures that arise when the members work closely together, share the same set of values and, above all, face a crisis situation that puts everyone under intense stress.

The main principle of groupthink, which I offer in the spirit of Parkinson's Law, is this: *The more amiability and esprit de corps there is among the members of a policy-making in-group, the greater the danger that independent critical thinking will be replaced by a groupthink, which is likely to result in irrational and dehumanizing actions directed against outgroups.*

SYMPTOMS   In my studies of high-level governmental decision makers, both civilian
and military, I have found eight main symptoms of groupthink.

    1. Invulnerability.   Most or all of the members of the in-group share
an *illusion* of invulnerability that provides for them some degree of reas-
surance about obvious dangers and leads them to become overoptimistic
and willing to take extraordinary risks. It also causes them to fail to respond
to clear warnings of danger.

    The Kennedy in-group, which uncritically accepted the Central Intelli-
gence Agency's disastrous Bay of Pigs plan, operated on the false assumption that they could keep secret the fact that the United States was
responsible for the invasion of Cuba. Even after news of the plan began to
leak out, their belief remained unshaken. They failed even to consider the
danger that awaited them, a worldwide revulsion against the United States.

    A similar attitude appeared among the members of President Lyndon
B. Johnson's in-group, the "Tuesday Cabinet," which kept escalating the
Vietnam War despite repeated setbacks and failures. "There was a belief,"
Bill Moyers commented after he resigned, "that if we indicated a willingness to use our power, they [the North Vietnamese] would get the message
and back away from an all-out confrontation. . . . There was a confidence—
it was never bragged about, it was just there—that when the chips were
really down, the other people would fold."

    A most poignant example of an illusion of invulnerability involves the
in-group around Admiral H. E. Kimmel, which failed to prepare for the
possibility of a Japanese attack on Pearl Harbor despite repeated warnings. Informed by his intelligence chief that radio contact with Japanese
aircraft carriers had been lost, Kimmel joked about it: "What, you don't
know where the carriers are? Do you mean to say that they could be
rounding Diamond Head (at Honolulu) and you wouldn't know it?" The
carriers were in fact moving full-steam toward Kimmel's command post
at the time. Laughing together about a danger signal, which labels it as a
purely laughing matter, is a characteristic manifestation of groupthink.

    2. Rationale.   As we see, victims of groupthink ignore warnings; they
also collectively construct rationalizations in order to discount warnings
and other forms of negative feedback that, taken seriously, might lead the
group members to reconsider their assumptions each time they recommit
themselves to past decisions. Why did the Johnson in-group avoid reconsidering its escalation policy when time and again the expectations on
which they based their decisions turned out to be wrong? James C. Thompson, Jr., a Harvard historian who spent five years as an observing participant in both the State Department and the White House, tells us that the
policy makers avoided critical discussion of their prior decisions and
continually invented new rationalizations so that they could sincerely
recommit themselves to defeating the North Vietnamese.

    In the fall of 1964, before the bombing of North Vietnam began, some
of the policy makers predicted that six weeks of air strikes would induce
the North Vietnamese to seek peace talks. When someone asked, "What if

they don't?" the answer was that another four weeks certainly would do the trick.

Later, after each setback, the in-group agreed that by investing just a bit more effort (by stepping up the bomb tonnage a bit, for instance), their course of action would prove to be right. *The Pentagon Papers* bear out these observations.

In *The Limits of Intervention,* Townsend Hoopes, who was acting Secretary of the Air Force under Johnson, says that Walt W. Rostow in particular showed a remarkable capacity for what has been called "instant rationalization." According to Hoopes, Rostow buttressed the group's optimism about being on the road to victory by culling selected scraps of evidence from news reports or, if necessary, by inventing "plausible" forecasts that had no basis in evidence at all.

Admiral Kimmel's group rationalized away their warnings, too. Right up to December 7, 1941, they convinced themselves that the Japanese would never dare attempt a full-scale surprise assault against Hawaii because Japan's leaders would realize that it would precipitate an all-out war which the United States would surely win. They made no attempt to look at the situation through the eyes of the Japanese leaders—another manifestation of groupthink.

3. Morality. Victims of groupthink believe unquestioningly in the inherent morality of their in-group; this belief inclines the members to ignore the ethical or moral consequences of their decisions.

Evidence that this symptom is at work usually is of a negative kind—the things that are left unsaid in group meetings. At least two influential persons had doubts about the morality of the Bay of Pigs adventure. One of them, Arthur Schlesinger, Jr., presented his strong objections in a memorandum to President Kennedy and Secretary of State Rusk but suppressed them when he attended meetings of the Kennedy team. The other, Senator J. William Fulbright, was not a member of the group, but the President invited him to express his misgivings in a speech to the policy makers. However, when Fulbright finished speaking the President moved on to other agenda items without asking for reactions of the group.

David Kraslow and Stuart H. Loory, in *The Secret Search for Peace in Vietnam,* report that during 1966 President Johnson's in-group was concerned primarily with selecting bomb targets in North Vietnam. They based their selections on four factors—the military advantage, the risk to American aircraft and pilots, the danger of forcing other countries into the fighting, and the danger of heavy civilian casualties. At their regular Tuesday luncheons, they weighed these factors the way school teachers grade examination papers, averaging them out. Though evidence on this point is scant, I suspect that the group's ritualistic adherence to a standardized procedure induced the members to feel morally justified in their destructive way of dealing with the Vietnamese people—after all, the danger of heavy civilian casualties from U.S. air strikes was taken into account on their checklists.

4. Stereotypes. Victims of groupthink hold stereotyped views of the leaders of enemy groups: They are so evil that genuine attempts at negotiating differences with them are unwarranted, or they are too weak or too stupid to deal effectively with whatever attempts the in-group makes to defeat their purposes, no matter how risky the attempts are.

Kennedy's groupthinkers believed that Premier Fidel Castro's air force was so ineffectual that obsolete B-26s could knock it out completely in a surprise attack before the invasion began. They also believed that Castro's army was so weak that a small Cuban-exile brigade could establish a well-protected beachhead at the Bay of Pigs. In addition, they believed that Castro was not smart enough to put down any possible internal uprisings in support of the exiles. They were wrong on all three assumptions. Though much of the blame was attributable to faulty intelligence, the point is that none of Kennedy's advisers even questioned the CIA planners about these assumptions.

The Johnson advisers' sloganistic thinking about "the Communist apparatus" that was "working all around the world" (as Dean Rusk put it) led them to overlook the powerful nationalistic strivings of the North Vietnamese government and its efforts to ward off Chinese domination. The crudest of all stereotypes used by Johnson's inner circle to justify their policies was the domino theory ("If we don't stop the Reds in South Vietnam, tomorrow they will be in Hawaii and next week they will be in San Francisco," Johnson once said). The group so firmly accepted this stereotype that it became almost impossible for any adviser to introduce a more sophisticated viewpoint.

In the documents on Pearl Harbor, it is clear to see that the Navy commanders stationed in Hawaii had a naive image of Japan as a midget that would not dare to strike a blow against a powerful giant.

5. Pressure. Victims of groupthink apply direct pressure to any individual who momentarily expresses doubts about any of the group's shared illusions or who questions the validity of the arguments supporting a policy alternative favored by the majority. This gambit reinforces the concurrence-seeking norm that loyal members are expected to maintin.

President Kennedy probably was more active than anyone else in raising skeptical questions during the Bay of Pigs meetings, and yet he seems to have encouraged the group's docile, uncritical acceptance of defective arguments in favor of the CIA's plan. At every meeting, he allowed the CIA representatives to dominate the discussion. He permitted them to give their immediate refutations in response to each tentative doubt that one of the others expressed, instead of asking whether anyone shared the doubt or wanted to pursue the implications of the new worrisome issue that had just been raised. And at the most crucial meeting, when he was calling on each member to give his vote for or against the plan, he did not call on Arthur Schlesinger, the one man there who was known by the President to have serious misgivings.

Historian Thompson informs us that whenever a member of Johnson's in-group began to express doubts, the group used subtle social pressures to "domesticate" him. To start with, the dissenter was made to feel at home, provided that he lived up to two restrictions: (1) that he did not voice his doubts to outsiders, which would play into the hands of the opposition; and (2) that he kept his criticisms within the bounds of acceptable deviation, which meant not challenging any of the fundamental assumptions that went into the group's prior commitments. One such "domesticated dissenter" was Bill Moyers. When Moyers arrived at a meeting, Thompson tells us, the President greeted him with, "Well, here comes Mr. Stop-the-Bombing."

6. Self-censorship. Victims of groupthink avoid deviating from what appears to be group consensus; they keep silent about their misgivings and even minimize to themselves the importance of their doubts.

As we have seen, Schlesinger was not all hesitant about presenting his strong objections to the Bay of Pigs plan in a memorandum to the President and the Secretary of State. But he became keenly aware of his tendency to suppress objections at the White House meetings. "In the months after the Bay of Pigs I bitterly reproached myself for having kept so silent during those crucial discussions in the cabinet room," Schlesinger writes in *A Thousand Days*. "I can only explain my failure to do more than raise a few timid questions by reporting that one's impulse to blow the whistle on this nonsense was simply undone by the circumstances of the discussion."

7. Unanimity. Victims of groupthink share an *illusion* of unanimity within the group concerning almost all judgments expressed by members who speak in favor of the majority view. This symptom results partly from the preceding one, whose effects are augmented by the false assumption that any individual who remains silent during any part of the discussion is in full accord with what the others are saying.

When a group of persons who respect each other's opinions arrives at a unanimous view, each member is likely to feel that the belief must be true. This reliance on consensual validation within the group tends to replace individual critical thinking and reality testing, unless there are clear-cut disagreements among the members. In contemplating a course of action such as the invasion of Cuba, it is painful for the members to confront disagreements within their group, particularly if it becomes apparent that there are widely divergent views about whether the preferred course of action is too risky to undertake at all. Such disagreements are likely to arouse anxieties about making a serious error. Once the sense of unanimity is shattered, the members no longer can feel complacently confident about the decision they are inclined to make. Each man must then face the annoying realization that there are troublesome uncertainties, and he must diligently seek out the best information he can get in order to decide for himself exactly how serious the risks might be. This is one of the unpleasant consequences of being in a group of hardheaded critical thinkers.

To avoid such an unpleasant state, the members often become inclined, without quite realizing it, to prevent latent disagreements from surfacing when they are about to initiate a risky course of action. The group leader and the members support each other in playing up the areas of convergence in their thinking at the expense of fully exploring divergencies that might reveal unsettled issues.

"Our meetings took place in a curious atmosphere of assumed consensus," Schlesinger writes. His additional comments clearly show that, curiously, the consensus was an illusion—an illusion that could be maintained only because the major participants did not reveal their own reasoning or discuss their idiosyncratic assumptions and vague reservations. Evidence from several sources makes it clear that even the three principals —President Kennedy, Rusk and McNamara—had widely differing assumptions about the invasion plan.

8. Mindguards.   Victims of groupthink sometimes appoint themselves as mindguards to protect the leader and fellow members from adverse information that might break the complacency they shared about the effectiveness and morality of past decisions. At a large birthday party for his wife, Attorney General Robert F. Kennedy, who had been constantly informed about the Cuban invasion plan, took Schlesinger aside and asked him why he was opposed. Kennedy listened coldly and said, "You may be right or you may be wrong, but the President has made his mind up. Don't push it any further. Now is the time for everyone to help him all they can."

Rusk also functioned as a highly effective mindguard by failing to transmit to the group the strong objections of three "outsiders" who had learned of the invasion plan—Undersecretary of State Chester Bowles, USIA Director Edward R. Murrow, and Rusk's intelligence chief, Roger Hilsman. Had Rusk done so, their warnings might have reinforced Schlesinger's memorandum and jolted some of Kennedy's in-group, if not the President himself, into reconsidering the decision.

PRODUCTS

When a group of executives frequently displays most or all of these interrelated symptoms, a detailed study of their deliberations is likely to reveal a number of immediate consequences. These consequences are, in effect, products of poor decision-making practices because they lead to inadequate solutions to the problems being dealt with.

First, the group limits its discussions to a few alternative courses of action (often only two) without an initial survey of all the alternatives that might be worthy of consideration.

Second, the group fails to reexamine the course of action initially preferred by the majority after they learn of risks and drawbacks they had not considered originally.

Third, the members spend little or no time discussing whether there are nonobvious gains they may have overlooked or ways of reducing the seemingly prohibitive costs that made rejected alternatives appear undesirable to them.

Fourth, members make little or no attempt to obtain information from experts within their own organizations who might be able to supply more precise estimates of potential losses and gains.

Fifth, members show positive interest in facts and opinions that support their preferred policy; they tend to ignore facts and opinions that do not.

Sixth, members spend little time deliberating about how the chosen policy might be hindered by bureaucratic inertia, sabotaged by political opponents, or temporarily derailed by common accidents. Consequently, they fail to work out contingency plans to cope with foreseeable setbacks that could endanger the overall success of their chosen course.

SUPPORT

The search for an explanation of why groupthink occurs had led me through a quagmire of complicated theoretical issues in the murky area of human motivation. My belief, based on recent social-psychological research, is that we can best understand the various symptoms of groupthink as a mutual effort among the group members to maintain self-esteem and emotional equanimity by providing social support to each other, especially at times when they share responsibility for making vital decisions.

Even when no important decision is pending, the typical administrator will begin to doubt the wisdom and morality of his past decisions each time he receives information about setbacks, particularly if the information is accompanied by negative feedback from prominent men who originally had been his supporters. It should not be surprising, therefore, to find that individual members strive to develop unanimity and esprit de corps that will help bolster each other's morale, to create an optimistic outlook about the success of pending decisions, and to reaffirm the positive value of past policies to which all of them are committed.

PRIDE

Shared illusions of invulnerability, for example, can reduce anxiety about taking risks. Rationalizations help members believe that the risks are really not so bad after all. The assumption of inherent morality helps the members to avoid feelings of shame or guilt. Negative stereotypes function as stress-reducing devices to enhance a sense of moral righteousness as well as pride in a lofty mission.

The mutual enhancement of self-esteem and morale may have functional value in enabling the members to maintain their capacity to take action, but it has maladaptive consequences insofar as concurrence-seeking tendencies interfere with critical, rational capacities and lead to serious errors of judgment.

While I have limited my study to decision-making bodies in government, groupthink symptoms appear in business, industry, and any other field where small, cohesive groups make the decisions. It is vital, then, for all sorts of people—and especially group leaders—to know what steps they can take to prevent groupthink.

REMEDIES
To counterpoint my case studies of the major fiascos, I have also investigated two highly successful group enterprises, the formulation of the Marshall Plan in the Truman Administration and the handling of the Cuban missile crisis by President Kennedy and his advisers. I have found it instructive to examine the steps Kennedy took to change his group's decision-making processes. These changes ensured that the mistakes made by his Bay of Pigs in-group were not repeated by the missile-crisis in-group, even though the membership of both groups was essentially the same.

The following recommendations for preventing groupthink incorporate many of the good practices I discovered to be characteristic of the Marshall Plan and missile-crisis groups:

1. The leader of a policy-forming group should assign the role of critical evaluator to each member, encouraging the group to give high priority to open airing of objections and doubts. This practice needs to be reinforced by the leader's acceptance of criticism of his own judgments in order to discourage members from soft-pedaling their disagreements and from allowing their striving for concurrence to inhibit criticism.

2. When the key members of a hierarchy assign a policy-planning mission to any group within their organization, they should adopt an impartial stance instead of stating preferences and expectations at the beginning. This will encourage open inquiry and impartial probing of a wide range of policy alternatives.

3. The organization routinely should set up several outside policy-planning and evaluation goups to work on the same policy question, each deliberating under a different leader. This can prevent the insulation of an in-group.

4. At intervals before the group reaches a final consensus, the leader should require each member to discuss the group's deliberations with associates in his own unit of the organization—assuming that those associates can be trusted to adhere to the same security regulations that govern the policy makers—and then to report back their reactions to the group.

5. The group should invite one or more outside experts to each meeting on a staggered basis and encourage the experts to challenge the views of the core members.

6. At every general meeting of the group, whenever the agenda calls for an evaluation of policy alternatives, at least one member should play devil's advocate, functioning as a good lawyeer in challenging the testimony of those who advocate the majority position.

7. Whenever the policy issue involves relations with a rival nation or organization, the group should devote a sizable block of time, perhaps an entire session, to a survey of all warning signals from the rivals and should write alternative scenarios on the rivals' intentions.

8. When the group is surveying policy alternatives for feasibility and effectiveness, it should from time to time divide into two or more sub-

groups to meet separately under different chairmen and then come back together to hammer out differences.

9. After reaching a preliminary consensus about what seems to be the best policy, the group should hold a "second-chance" meeting at which every member expresses as vividly as he can all his residual doubts and rethinks the entire issue before making a definitive choice.

HOW

These recommendations have their disadvantages. To encourage the open airing of objections, for instance, might lead to prolonged and costly debates when a rapidly growing crisis requires immediate solution. It also could cause rejection, depression, and anger. A leader's failure to set a norm might create cleavage between leader and members that could develop into a disruptive power struggle if the leader looks on the emerging consensus as anathema. Setting up outside evaluation groups might increase the risk of security leakage. Still, inventive executives who know their way around the organizational maze probably can figure out how to apply one or another of the prescriptions successfully without harmful side effects.

They also could benefit from the advice of outside experts in the administrative and behavioral sciences. Though these experts have much to offer, they have had few chances to work on policy-making machinery within large organizations. As matters now stand, executives innovate only when they need new procedures to avoid repeating serious errors that have deflated their self-images.

In this era of atomic warheads, urban disorganization, and ecocatastrophes, it seems to me that policy makers should collaborate with behavioral scientists and give top priority to preventing groupthink and its attendant fiascos.

Managing Conflict*

GEORGE H. LABOVITZ

Traditionally, management's handling of conflict has been based on the belief that conflict should be suppressed and eliminated; conflict was viewed as dysfunctional and time consuming. Over the years, however, management theorists and behavioral scientists have begun to recognize that in many instances conflict can be a sign of a healthy organization. The "productivity of the confrontation," in Richard Walton's phrase,[1] arises from the fact that conflict leads to change, change leads to adaptation, and adaptation leads to survival.

In *Managing Organizational Conflict,* Steven Robbins argues that more active discussion and conflict would have prevented the bankruptcy of the Penn Central Railroad, the Bay of Pigs invasion, and American involvement in Vietnam. For too long, Robbins points out, we have been operating under the influence of traditional philosophical teaching. Conflicts of any type or form are bad. The vast majority of us have been influenced at home, in school, and through the church to eliminate, suppress, and avoid conflict. We are uncomfortable in its presence. Abraham Maslow expressed this view vividly, describing our society as one in which there generally exists "a fear of conflict, of disagreement, of hostility, antagonism, enmity. There is much stress on getting along with other people even if you don't like them."[2]

It is difficult, therefore, for those who manage other people to accept the notion that anything other than peace and tranquility can be positive. Managers forget that some conflict is therapeutic; they seem to feel that any degree of conflict is too great. Instead of understanding that their chief responsibility is to achieve organizational goals, they fall into the trap of assuming that it is management's role to reduce tensions and promote

---

* Reprinted by permission of *Business Horizons*, June 1980, pp. 30–37.

[1] Richard Walton, *Interpersonal Peacemaking: Confrontations and Third Party Consultations* (Reading, Mass.: Addison-Wseley Publishing, 1969), p. 146.

[2] Abraham Maslow, *Eupsychian Movement* (Homewood, Ill.: Richard D. Irwin, Inc., 1965), p. 185, reprinted in Steven P. Robbins, *Managing Organizational Conflict* (Englewood Cliffs, N.J.: Prentice-Hall, 1974), pp. 17–18.

harmony and cooperation. But elimination of conflict in complex organizations is as undesirable as it is unrealistic.

WHY IS THERE CONFLICT?

Whenever human beings compete for scarce resources or share different goals and time perspectives, conflict is likely to exist. Two Harvard management theorists, Paul Lawrence and Jay Lorsch, have argued that the hallmark of complex organizations is their high degree of differentiation.[3] People in an organization do different kinds of work. Departments tend to differ in terms of goals, time orientation, formality of structure, and management styles. The greater the "differentiation" between departments, the greater the likelihood of conflict and the greater the need for mechanisms that will integrate those departments. Therefore, one source of conflict stems from the structure of an organization—the fact that complex institutions expect people who share different goals, time orientations, and management philosophies to integrate their efforts into a cohesive whole directed towards the accomplishment of organizational objectives.

Another source of conflict is communication distortion. Because of the complexity of modern institutions and their high degree of differentiation, communications between divisions as well as within divisions can easily become distorted. We all speak the language of our training and backgrounds. We suspect the motives of those who have goals different from our own. It is a well-known fact that human beings seek out people who are like themselves and tend to stereotype those who are different—especially if they are in competition with them.

Another and frequent source of conflict arises from interpersonal or behavioral factors. Differences between subordinates and supervisors in terms of role expectations, goals, and even personality characteristics are often sources of interpersonal conflict. In complex organizations, responsibilities are often defined through the organization chart and job descriptions; unfortunately, the job descriptions and departmental goals often let employees or customers slip through the cracks. When departments overlap and each must depend on the other to accomplish its objectives, jurisdiction is ambiguous and a high potential for conflict exists.

Allan Filley lists some characteristics of social relationships associated with various kinds or degrees of conflict.

Conflict of Interest. Conflict of interest exists where there is competition between the parties for scarce resources or one group gains at the expense of another, a common occurrence in the world made up of highly dependent and interdependent departments.

Communication Barriers. If parties are separated from each other physically, or by time—for example, day and night shifts—the possibility of misunderstanding and the opportunity for conflict are increased.

---

3 Paul Lawrence and Jay Lorsch, *Organization and Environment* (Homewood, Ill.: Richard D. Irwin, 1969), pp. 8–11.

Dependency.   The possibility of conflict will be greater where one party is dependent upon another for performance of tasks or for the provision of resources.

Degree of Association.   Conflict will be greater as the degree of participation in decision making and informal relations increases.

Need for Consensus.   Conflict will result if consensus is absolutely necessary in order to proceed.[4]

It is obvious that any effective management of conflict, one that is going to resolve conflict and move it in the direction of achieving organizational goals, must somehow deal with the structural, interpersonal, and communication factors as well as these social conditions associated with conflict. The *process* of managing conflict is therefore as important as the *product* of managing conflict.

WINNING AND LOSING

The literature on conflict management abounds with different techniques for controlling conflict situations. According to Filley, all of the techniques boil down to win-lose, lose-lose, or win-win methods.

Win-lose Methods

When a supervisor says, "You must do what I tell you because I am the boss," he or she is exercising the legitimate power bestowed by the organization. Win-lose methods, in which the supervisor inevitably wins and the employee inevitably loses, include the use of mental or physical power to bring about compliance. Other win-lose methods involve failing to respond to subordinates' suggestions for change. Majority rule is also a win-lose method, as is minority rule when the few are in control. For example, the supervisor of a work group says, "I think we have enough work to warrant a meeting here over the weekend. What do you think?" If there is no response, the supervisor can win by interpreting the silence as support for his or her position.

Lose-lose Methods

Lose-lose methods leave no one entirely happy. One lose-lose method is compromise which is based on the assumption that half a loaf is better than none. Another lose-lose strategy involves side payments—one party agrees to a solution in exchange for a favor from the other party later. Filley feels that organizations use side payments extensively and at great cost, paying individuals extra income to do disagreeable tasks. The result is that both sides are partial losers.

A third lose-lose strategy is submitting an issue to a neutral third party. When two department managers ask their common supervisor to decide an issue about which they disagree, or two parties in a labor dispute submit the issue to arbitration, both parties are usually disappointed. Arbitrators frequently resolve issues at some middle ground between the positions held

---

[4] Alan C. Filley, *Interpersonal Conflict Resolution* (Glenview, Ill.: Scott, Foresman, 1975), pp. 9–11.

by the disputants. Although each disputant gains something, the outcome is rarely satisfying to either side.

Filley lists several characteristics which win-lose and lose-lose methods of conflict resolution have in common:

> "There is a clear we-they distinction between the parties, rather than a we-versus-the-problem orientation."

> "Each party sees the issue only from its own point of view, rather than defining the problem in terms of mutual needs."

> "The emphasis is upon attainment of a solution, rather than upon a definition of goals, values, or motives that attainment of the solution will serve."

> "Conflicts are personalized, rather than being depersonalized by an objective focus on facts and issues."

> "The parties are conflict oriented and concentrate on the immediate disagreement, rather than relationship oriented and concerned with the long-term effect of their differences and how they are to be resolved."[5]

Win-win Methods

If conflict is to be turned into a positive force for organizational change, modern managers must adopt a point of view that is dramatically different from that held by managers in the past. The modern manager must:

> "Recognize the existence and usefulness of conflict.

> "Explicitly encourage opposition.

> "Define conflict management so as to stimulate as well as to resolve conflict.

> "Consider the management of conflict as a major responsibility on the part of all administrators."[6]

In contrast to win-lose and lose-lose strategies, win-win problem-solving strategies focus on ends or goals. Typically found under the heading of win-win strategies are problem solving and the establishment of superordinate goals. The problem-solving strategy involves identifying the sources of conflict and then presenting these as problems to be solved. A superordinate goal is one that is greater than the individual goals of the units of an organization, the end to which all departmental efforts are ultimately directed. Identifying superordinate goals reminds conflicting departments that, even though their particular goals are vitally important, they share a goal that cannot be attained without cooperation.

The heart of the win-win approach, therefore, is using participative management techniques in order to gain consensus and commitment to objectives. As Filley points out, when managers do so, what they are really saying to the parties involved is:

---

5 Ibid., p. 25.

6 Robbins, *Managing Organizational Conflict*, p. 13.

"I want a solution which achieves your goals and my goals and is acceptable to both of us.

"I will control the process by which we arrive at agreement but will not dictate the content. . . . I would like to find a solution in which you get what you want and I get what I want—that is, neither your solution nor my solution but a strategy which satisfies both of us."[7]

APPROACHES TO RESOLUTION

John B. Jones and J. Willard Pfeiffer specify five common ways of dealing with organizational conflict. Any one method will not apply to all situations or all personalities. The leader in a group must consider when to employ what style and with whom. If a leader has used one method successfully, he or she may use it to excess. Knowing alternative means of handling conflict gives managers a wider choice of actions to employ in any given situation and makes them better able to tailor the response to the situation.

Denial or Withdrawal

With this approach, a person attempts to get rid of conflict by denying that it exists. Usually, however, conflict does not go away; it grows to the point where it becomes all but unmanageable. But when the issue or the timing is not critical, denial may be the most productive way of dealing with conflict.

Suppression or Smoothing Over

"We run a happy ship here." "Nice people don't fight." A person using smoothing plays down differences and does not recognize the positive aspects of handling the conflict openly. Smoothing may, however, be employed appropriately when it is more important to preserve a relationship than to deal with an insignificant issue through conflict.

Forcing or Power

The source of the power may be vested in authority or position (including referral to "the system," higher supervision, and so on). Power may take the form of a majority (as in voting) or a persuasive minority. Power strategies, however, result in winners and losers, and the losers do not support a final decision in the same way that winners do. Future meetings of a group may be marred by a conscious or unconscious renewal of the struggle previously "settled" by the use of power. In some instances, however, especially where other forms of handling conflict are clearly inappropriate, power can be effective. Voting is used in national elections, for example, and laws apply equally to all.

Compromise or Negotiation

Although often regarded as a virtue in our culture, compromise has some serious drawbacks. Bargaining often causes both sides to assume an inflated position since they are aware that they are going to have to give a

---

[7] Filley, *Interpersonal Conflict Resolution*, pp. 27, 30.

little and want to buffer the loss. The compromise solution may be so watered down or weakened that it will not be effective. There is often little real commitment by any of the parties to a compromise solution. Yet there are times when compromise makes sense, such as when resources are limited or it is necessary to forestall a win-lose situation.

Confrontation or Integration

Lawrence and Lorsch examined the use of confrontation (win-win methods), forcing (resorting to authority or coercion), and smoothing (agreeing on an intellectual or nonthreatening level) in six organizations. They concluded that the two organizations with the highest performance used confrontation to a greater degree than the four other organizations and that the next two organizations (in order of performance) used confrontation more than the lowest two.[8] A study by Filley asked seventy-four managers to describe the way in which they and their immediate superiors dealt with conflict. Of the five types of conflict-resolution techniques identified, supervisors reported the best results in order of effectiveness, with confrontation, smoothing, compromise, forcing, withdrawal or noninvolvement.[9]

Confrontation does indeed seem to be the hallmark of both effective organizations and effective supervisors. In short, what the literature seems to be telling us is that confronting conflict situations, and using strategies that produce win-win results, is the key to managing conflict.

THE PROCESS OF RESOLUTION

For conflict to be effectively managed, the ends or goals of the parties involved must be identified and a mutually acceptable statement of those goals, or of the obstacles to those goals, must be formulated. In other words, parties may have different goals, but each party must accept the stated goals of the other and not consider the problem solved until the solution is acceptable to both parties. In order to achieve a mutually acceptable statement of problems or a definition of their sources, Filley's guidelines might be helpful.

"Conduct a Problem Analysis to Determine the Basic Issues. When parties enter into a potential conflict situation, it is not uncommon for them to have premature solutions to the stated objectives. . . . It is essential to find out the needs or desires of the parties by asking them to define specifically what they wish to accomplish with their proposed solutions or objectives.

"State the Problem as a Goal or as an Obstacle Rather Than as a Solution. Very often conflicts occur because individuals are solution-minded. For example, a labor union's demand for a union shop might be rejected by management for a variety of reasons. If, however, the union indicated that its demand was based on the problem of controlling its members when

---

8 Lawrence and Lorsche, *Organization and Environment,* p. 152.

9 Filley, *Interpersonal Conflict Resolution,* p. 31.

nonunion employes also benefit from union efforts but do not pay dues, then other solutions besides a union shop might be found.

"Identify the Obstacles to Attaining the Goal.   In some cases, the easiest way to identify problems is to clarify the obstacles in the way of the goal.

"Depersonalize the Problem.   Conflict management is greatly enhanced if the needs and objectives of the parties involved are described through some kind of impersonal format. Listing objectives on a flip chart or a blackboard helps shift attention away from the personalities to the problems themselves. For both parties, the problems, and not the opposing side, can then become the target.

"Separate the Process of Defining the Problem from the Search for Solutions and from the Evaluation of Alternatives.   Groups that are successful in achieving integrated solutions spend more time in problem definition than do groups that engage in solution methods. . . . The need to separate problem definition from solutions is particularly important when different individuals may engage in each of the two steps. The problem definition is always the necessary product of the interaction of the parties in a conflict situation, but solutions may be derived from sources other than the participants in the problem definition."[10]

MANAGEMENT AND MEDIATION

As the above guidelines clearly indicate, managers very often find themselves acting as mediators in a conflict situation between subordinates. Richard Walton focuses on steps that managers might take whenever they must assume the role of mediator:

Preliminary Interviewing.   The process of preliminary interviewing prior to a formal confrontation session is as important as the session iself. This stage is often described by practicing managers as "doing their hall work." One-to-one discussions with the contending parties provide each individual with the chance to present his or her perspective on the conflict. In addition, they give the manager the opportunity to develop insight into the source and nature of the problems that have led to the confrontation.

Structuring the Context.   Physical as well as social factors that provide the context for confrontation can be influenced by the manager/mediator. Walton calls particular attention to factors such as the neutrality of the turf, the formality of the setting, the time boundaries of the encounter, and the composition of meeting. The site for the confrontation—"my office or yours"—affects the balance of situational power. As a general rule, when two subordinates are in conflict, it is a good idea to bring them together in a neutral setting such as a conference room, another individual's office, or a luncheon meeting. The degree of formality of the setting should be appropriate to the type of work that needs to be accomplished.

Walton feels that managers should strive to make confrontation sessions both time bound and open ended. The parties should understand that they are meeting for a certain length of time, but more time can be made avail-

---

10 Ibid., pp. 109–12.

able in order to resolve their conflicts. Another benefit is that structuring time can have a synchronizing effect on the opposing parties. If they both know how much time is available for their work, they are more likely to reciprocate each others' moods.

Principals in the dispute can work on their relationship by meeting together, or inviting a third party, or calling together an even greater number of participants. Whatever method is chosen, however, the presence of a boss gives the parties incentive to confront their conflicts. Indeed, research indicates that when disputes cannot be settled directly by the principals involved, a meeting with their immediate supervisors is most likely to lead to successful conflict resolution.

Facilitate the Dialogue.   Managers are more effective in conflict resolution when they serve as facilitators rather than arbiters or judges. A third-party manager/mediator serves as the referee for the interaction process. His or her job is to initiate an agenda and keep the discussion on the central issues. Restating the issues from each participant's viewpoint is extremely valuable in facilitating discussion since redefinition often moves the process from a personal to a problem-centered orientation. The third-party manager also has a valuable role in eliciting reactions from and offering observations to the participants. The manager is often the only objective individual present at the meeting and can therefore serve to diagnose the sources of conflict and to prescribe other types of discussion methods between the parties.

Walton offers managers the following advice for setting a proper example for handling conflicts:

Encourage differences to emerge and confront them.

Be understanding rather than judgmental.

Clarify the nature of the issue.

Recognize and accept feelings.

Suggest a procedure for resolving differences.

Cope with threats to reasonable agreement.

Walton also points out that mediators need to synchronize. That is, they must judge when the parties are ready to confront each other and communicate. Premature confrontation may only promote escalation of a conflict, a fact well known to leaders who delay summit meetings until the potential for agreement is high. The essence of successful mediation lies in making the warring parties realize that they are dependent on each other and in finding an area of common agreement. This approach assumes that the issues to be resolved are objective and substantive and not merely a reflection of irrational behavior on the part of the contending parties. Therefore, the manager serves a vital role in establishing an objective and mutually agreeable definition of the problem.[11]

Complex organizations must move towards a more rational and open

---

11 Walton, *Interpersonal Peacemaking*, pp. 117–27.

handling of conflict. Human beings are always tempted to resort to a raw exercise of power to handle differences, but we can less afford such an approach now because the complexity of modern life is built upon interdependence and requires cooperation. It is increasingly important to find alternatives to force and make them work.

Since conflict can have either positive and negative consequences for an organization, effective management requires maintaining an optimal level of conflict and minimizing its undesirable consequences. Indeed, these two tasks of conflict management go hand in hand. By confronting disputes and providing a process that encourages handling them in a productive way, managers may help guarantee that the healthy aspects of conflict flourish in their organizations.

Managers and Leaders:
Are They Different?*

ABRAHAM ZALEZNIK

What is the ideal way to develop leadership? Every society provides its own answer to this question, and each, in groping for answers, defines its deepest concerns about the purposes, distributions, and use of power. Business has contributed its answer to the leadership question by evolving a new breed called the manager. Simultaneously, business has established a new power ethic that favors collective over individual leadership, the cult of the group over that of personality. While ensuring the competence, control, and the balance of power relations among groups with the potential for rivalry, managerial leadership unfortunately does not necessarily ensure imagination, creativity, or ethical behavior in guiding the destinies of corporate enterprises.

Leadership inevitably requires using power to influence the thoughts and actions of other people. Power in the hands of an individual entails human risks: first, the risk of equating power with the ability to get immediate results; second, the risk of ignoring the many different ways people can legitimately accumulate power; and third, the risk of losing self-control in the desire for power. The need to hedge these risks accounts in part for the development of collective leadership and the managerial ethic. Consequently, an inherent conservatism dominates the culture of large organizations. In *The Second American Revolution,* John D. Rockefeller III describes the conservatism of organizations:

> An organization is a system, with a logic of its own, and all the weight of tradition and inertia. The deck is stacked in favor of the tried and proven way of doing things and against the taking of risks and striking out in new directions.[1]

[1] John D. Rockefeller III, *The Second American Revolution* (New York: Harper & Row, 1973), p. 72.

Out of this conservatism and inertia organizations provide succession to power through the development of managers rather than individual leaders. And the irony of the managerial ethic is that it fosters a bureaucratic culture in business, supposedly the last bastion protecting us from the encroachments and controls of bureaucracy in government and education. Perhaps the risks associated with power in the hands of an individual may be necessary ones for business to take if organizations are to break free of their inertia and bureaucratic conservatism.

MANAGER VERSUS LEADER PERSONALITY

Theodore Levitt has described the essential features of a managerial culture with its emphasis on rationality and control:

> Management consists of the rational assessment of a situation and the systematic selection of goals and purposes (what is to be done?); the systematic development of strategies to achieve these goals; the marshalling of the required resources; the rational design, organization, direction, and control of the activities required to attain the selected purposes; and, finally, the motivating and rewarding of people to do the work.[2]

In other words, whether his or her energies are directed toward goals, resources, organization structures, or people, a manager is a problem solver. The manager asks himself, "What problems have to be solved, and what are the best ways to achieve results so that people will continue to contribute to this organization?" In this conception, leadership is a practical effort to direct affairs; and to fulfill his task, a manager requires that many people operate at different levels of status and responsibility. Our democratic society is, in fact, unique in having solved the problem of providing well-trained manager for business. The same solution stands ready to be applied to government, education, health care, and other institutions. It takes neither genius nor heroism to be a manager, but rather persistence, tough-mindedness, hard work, intelligence, analytical ability, and perhaps most important, tolerance and good will.

Another conception, however, attaches almost mystical beliefs to what leadership is and assumes that only great people are worthy of the drama of power and politics. Here, leadership is a psychodrama in which, as a precondition for control of a political structure, a lonely person must gain control of him or herself. Such an expectation of leadership contrasts sharply with the mundane, practical, and yet important conception that leadership is really managing work that other people do.

Two questions come to mind. Is this mystique of leadership merely a holdover from our collective childhood of dependency and our longing for good and heroic parents? Or, is there a basic truth lurking behind the need for leaders that no matter how competent managers are, their leadership

---

[2] Theodore Levitt, "Management and the Post Industrial Society," *The Public Interest,* Summer 1976, p. 73.

stagnates because of their limitations in visualizing purposes and generating value in work? Without this imaginative capacity and the ability to communicate, managers, driven by their narrow purposes, perpetuate group conflicts instead of reforming them into broader desires and goals.

If indeed problems demand greatness, then, judging by past performance, the selection and development of leaders leave a great deal to chance. There are no known ways to train "great" leaders. Furthermore, beyond what we leave to chance, there is a deeper issue in the relationship between the need for competent managers and the longing for great leaders.

What it takes to ensure the supply of people who will assume practical responsibility may inhibit the development of great leaders. Conversely, the presence of great leaders may undermine the development of managers who become very anxious in the relative disorder that leaders seem to generate. The antagonism in aim (to have many competent managers as well as great leaders) often remains obscure in stable and well-developed societies. But the antagonism surfaces during periods of stress and change, as it did in the Western countries during both the Great Depression and World War II. The tension also appears in the struggle for power between theorists and professional managers in revolutionary societies.

It is easy enough to dismiss the dilemma I pose (of training managers while we may need new leaders, or leaders at the expense of managers) by saying that the need is for people who can be *both* managers and leaders. The truth of the matter as I see it, however, is that just as a managerial culture is different from the entrepreneurial culture that develops when leaders appear in organizations, managers and leaders are very different kinds of people. They differ in motivation, personal history, and in how they think and act.

A technologically oriented and economically successful society tends to depreciate the need for great leaders. Such societies hold a deep and abiding faith in rational methods of solving problems, including problems of value, economics, and justice. Once rational methods of solving problems are broken down into elements, organized, and taught as skills, then society's faith in technique over personal qualities in leadership remains the guiding conception for a democratic society contemplating its leadership requirements. But there are times when tinkering and trial and error prove inadequate to the emerging problems of selecting goals, allocating resources, and distributing wealth and opportunity. During such times, the democratic society needs to find leaders who use themselves as the instruments of learning and acting, instead of managers who use their accumulation of collective experience to get where they are going.

The most impressive spokesman, as well as exemplar of the managerial viewpoint, was Alfred P. Sloan, Jr., who, along with Pierre du Pont, designed the modern corporate structure. Reflecting on what makes one management successful while another fails, Sloan suggested that "good management rests on a reconciliation of centralization, or 'decentralization with coordinated control.' "[3]

Sloan's conception of management, as well as his practice, developed by trial and error, and by the accumulation of experience. Sloan wrote:

> There is no hard and fast rule for sorting out the various responsibilities and the best way to assign them. The balance which is struck . . . varies according to what is being decided, the circumstances of the time, past experience, and the temperaments and skills of the executive involved.[4]

In other words, in much the same way that the inventors of the late 19th century tried, failed, and fitted until they hit on a product or method, managers who innovate in developing organizations are "tinkerers." They do not have a grand design or experience the intuitive flash of insight that, borrowing from modern science, we have come to call the "breakthrough."

Managers and leaders differ fundamentally in their world views. The dimensions for assessing these differences include managers' and leaders' orientations toward their goals, their work, their human relations, and themselves.

Attitudes toward Goals

Managers tend to adopt impersonal, if not passive, attitudes toward goals. Managerial goals arise out of necessities rather than desires and, therefore, are deeply embedded in the history and culture of the organization.

Frederic G. Donner, chairman and chief executive officer of General Motors from 1958 to 1967, expressed this impersonal and passive attitude toward goals in defining GM's position on product development:

> To meet the challenge of the marketplace, we must recognize changes in customer needs and desires far enough ahead to have the right products in the right places at the right time and in the right quantity.
>
> We must balance trends in preference against the many compromises that are necessary to make a final product that is both reliable and good looking, that performs well and that sells at a competitive price in the necessary volume. We must design, not just the cars we would like to build, but more importantly, the cars that our customers want to buy.[5]

Nowhere in this formulation of how a product comes into being is there a notion that consumer tastes and preferences arise in part as a result of what manufacturers do. In reality, through product design, advertising, and promotion, consumers learn to like what they then say they need. Few would argue that people who enjoy taking snapshots *need* a camera that also develops pictures. But in response to novelty, convenience, a shorter interval between acting (taking the snap) and gaining pleasure (seeing

---

[3] Alfred P. Sloan, Jr., *My Years with General Motors* (New York: Doubleday & Co., 1964), p. 429.

[4] Ibid., p. 429.

[5] Ibid., p. 440.

the shot), the Polaroid camera succeeded in the marketplace. But it is inconceivable that Edwin Land responded to impressions of consumer need. Instead, he translated a technology (polarization of light) into a product, which proliferated and stimulated consumers' desires.

The example of Polaroid and Land suggests how leaders think about goals. They are active instead of reactive, shaping ideas instead of responding to them. Leaders adopt a personal and active attitude toward goals. The influence a leader exerts in altering moods, evoking images and expectations, and in establishing specific desires and objectives determines the direction a business takes. The net result of this influence is to change the way people think about what is desirable, possible, and necessary.

Conceptions of Work

What do managers and leaders do? What is the nature of their respective work?

Leaders and managers differ in their conceptions. Managers tend to view work as an enabling process involving some combination of people and ideas interacting to establish strategies and make decisions. Managers help the process along by a range of skills, including calculating the interests in opposition, staging and timing the surfacing of controversial issues, and reducing tensions. In this enabling process, managers appear flexible in the use of tactics: They negotiate and bargain, on the one hand, and use rewards and punishments, and other forms of coercion, on the other. Machiavelli wrote for managers and not necessarily for leaders.

Alfred Sloan illustrated how this enabling process works in situations of conflict. The time was the early 1920s when the Ford Motor Company still dominated the automobile industry using, as did General Motors, the conventional water-cooled engine. With the full backing of Pierre du Pont, Charles Kettering dedicated himself to the design of an air-cooled engine, which, if successful, would have been a great technical and market coup for GM. Kettering believed in his product, but the manufacturing division heads at GM remained skeptical and later opposed the new design on two grounds: first, that it was technically unreliable, and second, that the corporation was putting all its eggs in one basket by investing in a new product instead of attending to the current marketing situation.

In the summer of 1923 after a series of false starts and after its decision to recall the copper-cooled Chevrolets from dealers and customers, GM management reorganized and finally scrapped the project. When it dawned on Kettering that the company had rejected the engine, he was deeply discouraged and wrote to Sloan that without the "organized resistance" against the project it would succeed and that unless the project were saved he would leave the company.

Alfred Sloan was all too aware of the fact that Kettering was unhappy and indeed intended to leave General Motors. Sloan was also aware of the fact that, while the manufacturing divisions strongly opposed the new engine, Pierre du Pont supported Kettering. Furthermore, Sloan had himself gone on record in a letter to Kettering less than two years earlier expressing full confidence in him. The problem Sloan now had was to make his decision stick, keep Kettering in the organization (he was much too valuable to lose), avoid alienating du Pont, and encourage the division heads to move speedily in developing product lines using conventional water-cooled engines.

The actions that Sloan took in the face of this conflict reveal much about how managers work. First, he tried to reassure Kettering by presenting the problem in a very ambiguous fashion, suggesting that he and the executive committee sided with Kettering but that it would not be practical to force the division to do what they were opposed to. He presented the problem as being a question of the people, not the product. Second, he proposed to reorganize around the problem by consolidating all functions in a new division that would be responsible for the design, production, and marketing of the new car. This solution, however, appeared as ambiguous as his efforts to placate and keep Kettering in General Motors. Sloan wrote: "My plan was to create an independent pilot operation under the sole jurisdiction of Mr. Kettering, a kind of copper-cooled-car division. Mr. Kettering would designate his own chief engineer and his production staff to solve the technical problems of manufacture."[6]

While Sloan did not discuss the practical value of this solution, which included saddling an inventor with management responsibility, he in effect used this plan to limit his conflict with Pierre du Pont.

In effect, the managerial solution that Sloan arranged and pressed for adoption limited the options available to others. The structural solution narrowed choices, even limiting emotional reactions to the point where the key people could do nothing but go along, and even allowed Sloan to say in his memorandum to du Pont, "We have discussed the matter with Mr. Kettering at some length this morning and he agrees with us absolutely on every point we made. He appears to receive the suggestion enthusiastically and has every confidence that it can be put across along these lines."[7]

Having placated people who opposed his views by developing a structural solution that appeared to give something but in reality only limited options, Sloan could then authorize the car division's general manager, with whom he basically agreed, to move quickly in designing water-cooled cars for the immediate market demand.

Years later Sloan wrote, evidently with tongue in cheek, "The copper-cooled car never came up again in a big way. It just died out, I don't know why."[8]

In order to get people to accept solutions to problems, managers need to coordinate and balance continually. Interestingly enough, this managerial work has much in common with what diplomats and mediators

---

6 Ibid., p. 91.

7 Ibid., p. 91.

8 Ibid., p. 93.

do, with Henry Kissinger apparently an outstanding practitioner. The manager aims at shifting balances of power toward solutions acceptable as a compromise among conflicting values.

What about leaders, what do they do? Where managers act to limit choices, leaders work in the opposite direction, to develop fresh approaches to long-standing problems and to open issues for new options. Stanley and Inge Hoffmann, the political scientists, liken the leader's work to that of the artist. But unlike most artists, the leader himself is an integral part of the aesthetic product. One cannot look at a leader's art without looking at the artist. On Charles de Gaulle as a political artist, they wrote: "And each of his major political acts, however tortuous the means or the details, has been whole, indivisible, and unmistakably his own, like an artistic act."[9]

The closest one can get to a product apart from the artist is the ideas that occupy, indeed at times obsess, the leader's mental life. To be effective, however, the leader needs to project his ideas into images that excite people and only then develop choices that give the projected images substance. Consequently, leaders create excitement in work.

John F. Kennedy's brief presidency shows both the strengths and weaknesses connected with the excitement leaders generate in their work. In his inaugural address he said, "Let every nation know, whether it wishes us well or ill, that we shall pay any price, bear any burden, meet any hardship, support any friend, oppose any foe, in order to assure the survival and the success of liberty."

This much-quoted statement forced people to react beyond immediate concerns and to identify with Kennedy and with important shared ideals. But upon closer scrutiny the statement must be seen as absurd because it promises a position which if in fact adopted, as in the Viet Nam War, could produce disastrous results. Yet unless expectations are aroused and mobilized, with all the dangers of frustration inherent in heightened desire, new thinking and new choice can never come to light.

Leaders work from high-risk positions, indeed often are temperamentally disposed to seek out risk and danger, especially where opportunity and reward appear high. From my observations, why one individual seeks risks while another approaches problems conservatively depends more on his or her personality and less on conscious choice. For some, especially those who become managers, the instinct for survival dominates their need for risk, and their ability to tolerate mundane, practical work assists their survival. The same cannot be said for leaders who sometimes react to mundane work as to an affliction.

Relations with Others   Managers prefer to work with people; they avoid solitary activity because it makes them anxious. Several years ago, I directed studies on the psychological aspects of career. The need to seek out others with whom to

---

9 Stanley and Inge Hoffmann, "The Will for Grandeur: de Gaulle as Political Artist," *Daedalus*, Summer 1968, p. 849.

work and collaborate seemed to stand out as important characteristics of managers. When asked, for example, to write imaginative stories in response to a picture showing a single figure (a boy contemplating a violin, or a man silhouetted in a state of reflection), managers populated their stories with people. The following is an example of a manager's imaginative story about the young boy contemplating a violin:

> Mom and Dad insisted that junior take music lessons so that someday he can become a concert musician. His instrument was ordered and had just arrived. Junior is weighing the alternatives of playing football with the other kids or playing with the squeak box. He can't understand how his parents could think a violin is better than a touchdown.
>
> After four months of practicing the violin, junior has had more than enough, Daddy is going out of his mind, and Mommy is willing to give in reluctantly to the men's wishes. Football season is now over, but a good third baseman will take the field next spring.[10]

This story illustrates two themes that clarify managerial attitudes toward human relations. The first, as I have suggested, is to seek out activity with other people (i.e., the football team), and the second is to maintain a low level of emotional involvement in these relationships. The low emotional involvement appears in the writer's use of conventional metaphors, even clichés, and in the depiction of the ready transformation of potential conflict into harmonious decisions. In this case, Junior, Mommy, and Daddy agree to give up the violin for manly sports.

These two themes may seem paradoxical, but their coexistence supports what a manager does, including reconciling differences, seeking compromises, and establishing a balance of power. A further idea demonstrated by how the manager wrote the story is that managers may lack empathy, or the capacity to sense intuitively the thoughts and feelings of others. To illustrate attempts to be empathic, here is another story written to the same stimulus picture by someone considered by his peers to be a leader:

> This little boy has the appearance of being a sincere artist, one who is deeply affected by the violin and has an intense desire to master the instrument.
>
> He seems to have just completed his normal practice session and appears to be somewhat crestfallen at his inability to produce the sounds which he is sure lie within the violin.
>
> He appears to be in the process of making a vow to himself to expend the necessary time and effort to play this instrument until he satisfies himself that he is able to bring forth the qualities of music which he feels within himself.
>
> With this type of determination and carry through, this boy became one of the great violinists of his day.[11]

Empathy is not simply a matter of paying attention to other people. It

---

10 Abraham Zaleznik, Gene W. Dalton, and Louis B. Barnes, *Orientation and Conflict in Career* (Boston: Division of Research, Harvard Business School, 1970), p. 316.
11 Ibid., p. 294.

is also the capacity to take in emotional signals and to make them mean something in a relationship with an individual. People who describe another person as "deeply affected" with "intense desire," as capable of feeling "crestfallen" and as one who can "vow to himself," would seem to have an inner perceptiveness that they can use in their relationships with others.

Managers relate to people according to the role they play in a sequence of events or in a decision-making *process,* while leaders, who are concerned with ideas, relate in more intuitive and empathic ways. The manager's orientation to people, as actors in a sequence of events, deflects his or her attention away from the substance of people's concerns and toward their roles in a process. The distinction is simply between a manager's attention to *how* things get done and a leader's to *what* the events and decisions mean to participants.

In recent years, managers have taken over from game theory the notion that decision-making events can be one of two types: the win-lose situation (or zero-sum game) or the win-win situation in which everybody in the action comes out ahead. As part of the process of reconciling differences among people and maintaining balances of power, managers strive to convert win-lose into win-win situations.

As an illustration, take the decision of how to allocate capital resources among operating divisions in a large, decentralized organization. On the face of it, the dollars available for distribution are limited at any given time. Presumably, therefore, the more one division gets, the less is available for other devisions.

Managers tend to view this situation (as it affects human relations) as a conversion issue: how to make what seems like a win-lose problem into a win-win problem. Several solutions to this situation come to mind. First, the manager focuses others' attention on procedure and not on substance. Here the actors become engrossed in the bigger problem of *how* to make decisions, not *what* decisions to make. Once committed to the bigger problems, the actors have to support the outcome since they were involved in formulating decision rules. Because the actors believe in the rules they formulated, they will accept present losses in the expectation that next time they will win.

Second, the manager communicates to his subordinates indirectly, using "signals" instead of "messages." A signal has a number of possible implicit positions in it while a message clearly states a position. Signals are inconclusive and subject to reinterpretation should people become upset and angry, while messages involve the direct consequence that some people will indeed not like what they hear. The nature of messages heightens emotional response, and, as I have indicated, emotionally makes managers anxious. With signals, the question of who wins and who loses often becomes obscured.

Third, the manager plays for time. Managers seem to recognize that with the passage of time and the delay of major decisions, compromises emerge that take the sting out of win-lose situations, and the original "game" will be superseded by additional ones. Therefore, compromises may mean that one wins and loses simultaneously, depending on which of the games one evaluates.

There are undoubtedly many other tactical moves managers use to change human situations from win-lose to win-win. But the point to be made is that such tactics focus on the decision-making process itself and interest managers rather than leaders. The interest in tactics involves costs as well as benefits, including making organizations fatter in bureaucratic and political intrigue and leaner in direct, hard activity and warm human relationships. Consequently, one often hears subordinates characterize managers as inscrutable, detached, and manipulative. These adjectives arise from the subordinates' perception that they are linked together in a process whose purpose, beyond simply making decisions, is to maintain a controlled as well as rational and equitable structure. These adjectives suggest that managers need order in the face of the potential chaos that many fear in human relationships.

In contrast, one often hears leaders referred to in adjectives rich in emotional content. Leaders attract strong feelings of identity and difference, or of love and hate. Human relations in leader-dominated structures often appear turbulent, intense, and at times even disorganized. Such an atmosphere intensifies individual motivation and often produces unanticipated outcomes. Does this intense motivation lead to innovation and high performance, or does it represent wasted energy?

Senses of Self

In *The Varieties of Religious Experience,* William James describes two basic personality types, "once-born" and "twice-born."[12] People of the former personality type are those for whom adjustments to life have been straightforward and whose lives have been more or less a peaceful flow from the moment of their births. The twice-borns, on the other hand, have not had an easy time of it. Their lives are marked by a continual struggle to attain some sense of order. Unlike the once-borns they cannot take things for granted. According to James, these personalities have equally different world views. For a once-born personality, the sense of self, as a guide to conduct and attitude, derives from a feeling of being at home and in harmony with one's environment. For a twice-born, the sense of self derives from a feeling of profound separateness.

A sense of belonging or of being separate has a practical significance for the kinds of investments managers and leaders make in their careers. Managers see themselves as conservators and regulators of an existing order of affairs with which they personally identify and from which they gain rewards. Perpetuating and strengthening existing institutions enhances a manager's sense of self-worth: He or she is performing in a role that harmonizes with the ideals of duty and responsibility. William James had this harmony in mind—this sense of self as flowing easily to and from the outer world—in defining a once-born personality. If one feels oneself

---

12 William James, *Varieties of Religious Experience* (New York: Mentor Books, 1958).

as a member of institutions, contributing to their well-being, then one fulfills a mission in life and feels rewarded for having measured up to ideals. This reward transcends material gains and answers the more fundamental desire for personal integrity which is achieved by identifying with existing institutions.

Leaders tend to be twice-born personalities, people who feel separate from their environment, including other people. They may work in organizations, but they never belong to them. Their sense of who they are does not depend upon memberships, work roles, or other social indicators of identity. What seems to follow from this idea about separateness is some theoretical basis for explaining why certain individuals search out opportunities for change. The methods to bring about change may be technological, political, or ideological, but the object is the same: to profoundly alter human, economic, and political relationships.

Sociologists refer to the preparation individuals undergo to perform in roles as the socialization process. Where individuals experience themselves as an integral part of the social structure (their self-esteem gains strength through participation and conformity), social standards exert powerful effects in maintaining the individual's personal sense of continuity, even beyond the early years in the family. The line of development from the family to schools, then to career is cumulative and reinforcing. When the line of development is not reinforcing because of significant disruptions in relationships or other problems experienced in the family or other social institutions, the individual turns inward and struggles to establish self-esteem, identity, and order. Here the psychological dynamics center on the experience with loss and the efforts at recovery.

In considering the development of leadership, we have to examine two different courses of life history: (1) development through socialization, which prepares the individual to guide institutions and to maintain the existing balance of social relations; and (2) development through personal mastery, which impels an individual to struggle for psychological and social change. Society produces its managerial talent through the first line of development, while through the second leaders emerge.

DEVELOPMENT OF LEADERSHIP

The development of every person begins in the family. Each person experiences the traumas associated with separating from his or her parents, as well as the pain that follows such frustration. In the same vein, all individuals face the difficulties of achieving self-regulation and self-control. But for some, perhaps a majority, the fortunes of childhood provide adequate gratifications and sufficient opportunities to find substitutes for rewards no longer available. Such individuals, the "once-borns," make moderate identifications with parents and find a harmony between what they expect and what they are able to realize from life.

But supposee the pains of separation are amplified by a combination of parental demands and the individual's needs to the degree that a sense of isolation, of being special, and of wariness disrupts the bonds that attach children to parents and other authority figures? Under such conditions, and given a special aptitude, the origins of which remain mysterious, the person becomes deeply involved in his or her inner world at the expense of interest in the outer world. For such a person, self-esteem no longer depends solely upon positive attachments and real rewards. A form of self-reliance takes hold along with expectations of performance and achievement, and perhaps even the desire to do great works.

Such self-perceptions can come to nothing if the individual's talents are negligible. Even with strong talents, there are no guarantees that achievement will follow, let alone that the end result will be for good rather than evil. Other factors enter into development. For one thing, leaders are like artists and other gifted people who often struggle with neuroses; their ability to function varies considerably even over the short run, and some potential leaders may lose the struggle altogether. Also, beyond early childhood, the patterns of development that affect managers and leaders involve the selective influence of particular people. Just as they appear flexible and evenly distributed in the types of talents available for development, managers form moderate and widely distributed attachments. Leaders, on the other hand, establish, and also break off, intensive one-to-one relationships.

It is a common observation that people with great talents are often only indifferent students. No one, for example, could have predicted Einstein's great achievements on the basis of his mediocre record in school. The reason for mediocrity is obviously not the absence of ability. It may result, instead, from self-absorption and the inability to pay attention to the ordinary tasks at hand. The only sure way an individual can interrupt reverie-like preoccupation and self-absorption is to form a deep attachment to a great teacher or other benevolent person who understands and has the ability to communicate with the gifted individual.

Whether gifted individuals find what they need in one-to-one relationships depends on the availability of sensitive and intuitive mentors who have a vocation in cultivating talent. Fortunately, when the generations do meet and the self-selections occur, we learn more about how to develop leaders and how talented people of different generations influence each other.

While apparently destined for a mediocre career, people who form important one-to-one relationships are able to accelerate and intensify their development through an apprenticeship. The background for such apprenticeships, or the psychological readiness of an individual to benefit from an intensive relationship, depends upon some experience in life that forces the individual to turn inward. A case example will make this point clearer. This example comes from the life of Dwight David Eisenhower and illustrates the transformation of a career from competent to outstanding.[13]

---

[13] The example is included in Abraham Zaleznik and Manfred F.R. Kets de Vries, *Power and the Corporate Mind* (Boston: Houghton Mifflin, 1975).

Dwight Eisenhower's early career in the Army foreshadowed very little about his future development. During World War I, while some of his West Point classmates were already experiencing the war first-hand in France, Eisenhower felt "embedded in the monotony and unsought safety of the Zone of the Interior . . . that was intolerable punishment."[14]

Shortly after World War I, Eisenhower, then a young officer somewhat pessimistic about his career chances, asked for a transfer to Panama to work under General Fox Connor, a senior officer whom Eisenhower admired. The army turned down Eisenhower's request. This setback was very much on Eisenhower's mind when Ikey, his first-born son, succumbed to influenza. By some sense of responsibility for its own, the army transferred Eisenhower to Panama, where he took up his duties under General Connor with the shadow of his lost son very much upon him.

In a relationship with the kind of father he would have wanted to be, Eisenhower reverted to being the son he lost. In this highly charged situation, Eisenhower began to learn from his mentor. General Connor offered, and Eisenhower gladly took, a magnificent tutorial on the military. The effects of this relationship on Eisenhower cannot be measured quantitatively, but in Eisenhower's own reflections and the unfolding of his career, one cannot overestimate its significance in the reintegration of a person shattered by grief.

As Eisenhower wrote later about Connor, "Life with General Connor was a sort of graduate school in military affairs and the humanities, leavened by a man who was experienced in his knowledge of men and their conduct. I can never adequately express my gratitude to this one gentleman. . . . In a lifetime of association with great and good men, he is the one more or less invisible figure to whom I owe an incalculable debt."[15]

Some time after his tour of duty with General Connor, Eisenhower's breakthrough occurred. He received orders to attend the Command and General Staff School at Fort Leavenworth, one of the most competitive schools in the army. It was a coveted appointment, and Eisenhower took advantage of the opportunity. Unlike his performance in high school and West point, his work at the Command School was excellent; he was graduated first in his class.

Psychological biographies of gifted people repeatedly demonstrate the important part a mentor plays in developing an individual. Andrew Carnegie owed much to his senior, Thomas A. Scott. As head of the Western Division of the Pennsylvania Railroad, Scott recognized talent and the desire to learn in the young telegrapher assigned to him. By giving Carnegie increasing responsibility and by providing him with the opportunity to learn through close personal observation, Scott added to Carnegie's self-confidence and sense of achievement. Because of his own personal strength

---

[14] Dwight D. Eisenhower, *At Ease: Stories I Tell to Friends* (New York: Doubleday, 1967), p. 136.

[15] Ibid., p. 187.

and achievement, Scott did not fear Carnegie's aggressiveness. Rather, he gave it full play in encouraging Carnegie's initiative.

Mentors take risks with people. They bet initially on talent they perceive in younger people. Mentors also risk emotional involvement in working closely with their juniors. The risks do not always pay off, but the willingness to take them appears crucial in developing leaders.

CAN ORGANIZATIONS DEVELOP LEADERS?

The examples I have given of how leaders develop suggest the importance of personal influence and the one-to-one relationship. For organizations to encourage consciously the development of leaders as compared with managers would mean developing one-to-one relationships between junior and senior executives and, more important, fostering a culture of individualism and possibly elitism. The elitism arises out of the desire to identify talent and other qualities suggestive of the ability to lead and not simply to manage.

The Jewel Companies, Inc., enjoy a reputation for developing talented people. The chairman and chief executive officer, Donald S. Perkins, is perhaps a good example of a person brought along through the mentor approach. Franklin J. Lunding, who was Perkins's mentor, expressed the philosophy of taking risks with young people this way.

> Young people today want in on the action. They don't want to sit around for six months trimming lettuce.[16]

This statement runs counter to the culture that attaches primary importance to slow progression based on experience and proved competence. It is a high-risk philosophy, one that requires time for the attachment between senior and junior people to grow and be meaningful and one that is bound to produce more failures than successes.

The elitism is an especially sensitive issue. At Jewel the MBA degree symbolized the elite. Lunding attracted Perkins to Jewel at a time when business school graduates had little interest in retailing in general and food distribution in particular. Yet the elitism seemed to pay off: not only did Perkins become the president at age 37, but also under the leadership of young executives recruited into Jewel with the promise of opportunity for growth and advancement, Jewel managed to diversify into discount and drug chains and still remain strong in food retailing. By assigning each recruit to a vice president who acted as sponsor, Jewel evidently tried to build a structure around the mentor approach to developing leaders. To counteract the elitism implied in such an approach, the company also introduced an "equalizer" in what Perkins described as "the first assistant philosophy." Perkins stated:

> Being a good first assistant means that each management person thinks of himself not as the order-giving, domineering boss, but as the first assist-

---

16 "Jewel Lets Young Men Make Mistakes," *Business Week,* January 17, 1970, p. 90.

ant to those who "report" to him in a more typical organizational sense. Thus we mentally turn our organizational charts upside-down and challenge ourselves to seek ways in which we can lead . . . by helping . . . by teaching . . . by listening . . . and by managing in the true democratic sense . . . that is, with the consent of the managed. Thus the satisfactions of leadership come from getting credit for doing and changing things ourselves.[17]

While this statement would seem to be more egalitarian than elitist, it does reinforce a youth-oriented culture since it defines the senior officer's job as primarily helping the junior person.

A myth about how people learn and develop that seems to have taken hold in the American culture also dominates thinking in business. The myth is that people learn best from their peers. Supposedly, the threat of evaluation and even humiliation recedes in peer relations because of the tendency for mutual identification and the social restraints on authoritarian behavior among equals. Peer training in organizations occurs in various forms. The use, for example, of task forces made up of peers from several interested occupational groups (sales, production, research, and finance) supposedly removes the restraints of authority on the individual's willingness to assert and exchange ideas. As a result, so the theory goes, people interact more freely, listen more objectively to criticism and other points of view, and finally, learn from this healthy interchange.

Another application of peer training exists in some large corporations, such as Philips, N.V., in Holland, where organization structure is built on the principle of joint responsibility of two peers, one representing the commercial end of the business and the other the technical. Formally, both hold equal responsibility for geographic operations or product groups, as the case may be. As a practical matter, it may turn out that one or the other of the peers dominates the management. Nevertheless, the main interaction is between two or more equals.

The principal question I would raise about such arrangements is whether they perpetuate the managerial orientation and preclude the formation of one-to-one relationships between senior people and potential leaders.

Aware of the possible stifling effects of peer relationships on aggressiveness and individual initiative, another company, much smaller than Philips, utilizes joint responsibility of peers for operating units, with one important difference. The chief executive of this company encourages competition and rivalry among peers, ultimately appointing the one who comes out on top for increased responsibility. These hybrid arrangements produce some unintended consequences that can be disastrous. There is no easy way to limit rivalry. Instead, it permeates all levels of the operation and opens the way for the formation of cliques in an atmosphere of intrigue.

A large, integrated oil company has accepted the importance of developing leaders through the direct influence of senior on junior execu-

---

17 "What Makes Jewel Shine So Bright," *Progressive Grocer*, September 1973, p. 76.

tives. One chairman and chief executive officer regularly selected one talented university graduate whom he appointed his special assistant, and with whom he would work closely for a year. At the end of the year, the junior executive would become available for assignment to one of the operating divisions, where he would be assigned to a responsible post rather than a training position. The mentor relationship had acquainted the junior executive firsthand with the use of power, and with the important antidotes to the power disease called *hubris*—performance and integrity.

Working in one-to-one relationships, where there is a formal and recognized difference in the power of the actors, takes a great deal of tolerance for emotional interchange. This interchange, inevitable in close working arrangements, probably accounts for the reluctance of many executives to become involved in such relationships. *Fortune* carried an interesting story on the departure of a key executive, John W. Hanley, from the top management of Procter & Gamble, for the chief executive officer position at Monsanto.[18] According to this account, the chief executive and chairman of P&G passed over Hanley for appointment to the presidency and named another executive vice president to this post instead.

The chairman evidently felt he could not work well with Hanley who, by his own acknowledgement, was aggressive, eager to experiment and change practices, and constantly challenged his superior. A chief executive officer naturally has the right to select people with whom he feels congenial. But I wonder whether a greater capacity on the part of senior officers to tolerate the competitive impulses and behavior of their subordinates might not be healthy for corporations. At least a greater tolerance for interchange would not favor the managerial team player at the expense of the individual who might become a leader.

I am constantly surprised at the frequency with which chief executives feel threatened by open challenges to their ideas, as though the source of their authority, rather than their specific ideas, were at issue. In one case a chief executive officer, who was troubled by the aggressiveness and sometimes outright rudeness of one of his talented vice presidents, used various indirect methods such as group meetings and hints from outside directors to avoid dealing with his subordinate. I advised the executive to deal head-on with what irritated him. I suggested that by direct face-to-face confrontation, both he and his subordinate would learn to validate the distinction between the authority to be preserved and the issues to be debated.

To confront is also to tolerate aggressive interchange and has the net effect of stripping away the veils of ambiguity and signaling so characteristic of managerial cultures, as well as encouraging the emotional relationship leaders need if they are to survive.

---

18 "Jack Hanley Got There by Selling Harder," *Fortune,* November 1976.

Leadership Theory: Some Implications for Managers*

CHESTER A. SCHRIESHEIM, JAMES M. TOLLIVER,
and ORLANDO C. BEHLING

In the past 70 years more than 3,000 leadership studies have been conducted and dozens of leadership models and theories have been proposed.[1] Yet, a practicing manager who reads this literature seeking an effective solution to supervisory problems will rapidly become disenchanted. Although we have access to an overwhelming volume of leadership theory and research, few guidelines exist which are of use to a practitioner. Nevertheless, interest in leadership—and in those qualities which separate a successful leader from an unsuccessful one—remains unabated. In almost any book dealing with management one will find some discussion of leadership. In any company library there are numerous volumes entitled "Increasing Leadership Effectiveness," "Successful Leadership," or "How to Lead." Typical management development programs conducted within work organizations and universities usually deal with some aspect of leadership. This intensity and duration of writing on the subject and the sums spent annually on leadership training indicate that practicing managers and academicians consider good leadership essential to organizational success.

What is meant by leadership, let alone *good* leadership? Many definitions have been proposed, and it seems that most are careful to separate management from leadership. This distinction sometimes becomes blurred in everyday conversations. The first term, *management,* includes those processes, both mental and physical, which result in other people executing prescribed formal duties for organizational goal attainment. It deals mainly with planning, organizing, and controlling the work of other people to

* From *MSU Business Topics,* Summer 1978, pp. 34–40. Reprinetd by permission of the publisher, Division of Research, Graduate School of Business Administration, Michigan State University.

[1] R. M. Stogill, *Handbook of Leadership* (New York: Free Press, 1974).

achieve organizational goals.[2] This definition usually includes those aspects of managers' jobs, such as monitoring and controlling resources, which are sometimes ignored in current conceptualizations of leadership. *Leadership,* on the other hand, is a more restricted type of managerial activity, focusing on the interpersonal interactions between a leader and one or more subordinates, with the purpose of increasing organizational effectiveness.[3] In this view, leadership is a social influence process in which the leader seeks the voluntary participation of subordinates in an effort to reach organizational objectives. The key idea highlighted by a number of authors is that the subordinate's participation is voluntary.[4] This implies that the leader has brought about some change in the way subordinates want to behave. Leadership, consequently, is not only a specific process (more so than management), but also is undoubtedly political in nature. The political aspect of leadership has been discussed elsewhere, so at this point it suffices to note that a major implication of leadership's political nature is that such attempts at wielding influence will not necessarily succeed.[5] In fact, other types of managerial tasks may have a stronger influence on organizational effectiveness than those interpersonal tasks usually labeled leadership.[6]

Despite this shortcoming, the examination of leadership as it relates to interpersonal interactions is still worthwhile simply because managers may, in many cases, have more control over how they and their subordinates behave than over nonhuman aspects of their jobs (such as the amount and types of resources they are given). In addition, some information does exist concerning which leadership tactics are of use under various conditions. For this information to be of greatest use, however, practicing managers should have some concept of the direction leadership research has taken. Thus, before attempting a provide guidelines for practitioners, we shall briefly review major approaches to the subject of leadership and point out their weaknesses and limitations.

BASIC APPROACHES TO LEADERSHIP

Thinking concerning leadership has moved through three distinct periods or phases.

The Trait Phase. Early approaches to leadership, from the pre-

---

[2] A. C. Filley, R. J. House, and Steven Kerr, *Managerial Process and Organizational Behavior,* 2d ed. (Glenview, Ill.: Scott, Foresman, 1976). See also R. C. Davis, *Industrial Organization and Management* (New York: Harper & Row, 1957).

[3] C. A. Gibb, "Leadership," in *The Handbook of Social Psychology,* ed. Gardner Lindzey and Elliot Aronson (Reading, Mass.: Addison-Wesley Publishing, 1969), vol. 4.

[4] See, for example, R. H. Hall, *Organizations: Structure and Process* (Englewood Cliffs, N.J.: Prentice-Hall, 1972).

[5] C. A. Schriesheim, J. M. Tolliver, and L. D. Dodge, "The Political Nature of the Leadership Process," unpublished paper, 1978.

[6] For examples of other types of managerial tasks which may have more of an impact on organizations, see J. P. Campbell, M. D. Dunnette, E. E. Lawler, and K. E. Weick, *Managerial Behavior, Performance, and Effectiveness* (New York: McGraw-Hill, 1970).

Christian era to the late 1940s, emphasized the examination of leader characteristics (such as age and degree of gregariousness) in an attempt to identify a set of universal characteristics which would allow a leader to be effective in all situations. At first a few traits seemed to be universally important for successful leaders, but subsequent research yielded inconsistent results concerning these traits; in addition, research investigating a large number of other traits (about 100) was generally discouraging. As a result of this accumulation of negative findings and of reviews of this evidence, such as that conducted by R. M. Stogdill, the tide of opinion about the importance of traits for leadership effectiveness began to change.[7] In the late 1940s, leadership researchers began to move away from trait research. Contemporary opinion holds the trait approach in considerable disrepute and views the likelihood of uncovering a set of universal leadership effectiveness traits as essentially impossible.

The Behavioral Phase.   With the fall of the trait approach, researchers considered alternative concepts, eventually settling on the examination of relationships between leader behaviors and subordinate satisfaction and performance.[8] During the height of the behavioral phase, dating roughly from the late 1940s to the early 1960s, several large research programs were conducted, including the Ohio State University leadership studies, a program of research which has received considerable publicity over the years.

The Ohio State studies started shortly after World War II and initially concentrated on leadership in military organizations. In one of these studies, a lengthy questionnaire was administered to B-52 bomber crews, and their answers were statistically analyzed to identify the common dimensions underlying the answers.[9] This analysis discovered two dimensions which seemed most important in summarizing the nature of the crews' perceptions about their airplane commanders' behavior toward them.

Consideration was the stronger of the two factors, and it involved leader behaviors indicative of friendship, mutual trust, respect, and warmth.

The second factor was Initiation of Structure, a concept involving leader behaviors indicating that the leader organizes and defines the relationship between self and subordinates.[10]

In subsequent studies using modified versions of the original questionnaire, Consideration and Structure were found to be prime dimensions of leader behavior in situations ranging from combat flights over Korea to assembly line work.[11] In addition, studies were undertaken at Ohio State

---

[7] R. M. Stogdill, "Personal Factors Associated with Leadership: A Survey of the Literature," *Journal of Psychology,* January 1948, pp. 35–71.

[8] T. O. Jacobs, *Leadership and Exchange in Formal Organizations* (Alexandria, Va.: Human Resources Research Organization, 1970).

[9] A. W. Halpin and B. J. Winer, "A Factorial Study of the Leader Behavior Descriptions," in *Leader Behavior: Its Description and Measurement,* ed. R. M. Stogdill and A. E. Coons (Columbus: Bureau of Business Research, The Ohio State University, 1957).

[10] Ibid., p. 42.

[11] Stogdill and Coons, *Leader Behavior.*

and elsewhere to compare the effects of these leader behaviors on subordinate performance and satisfaction. A high Consideration-high Structure leadership style was, in many cases, found to lead to high performance and satisfaction. However, in a number of studies dysfunctional consequences, such as high turnover and absenteeism, accompanied these positive outcomes. In yet other situations, different combinations of Consideration and Structure (for example, low Consideration-high Structure) were found to be more effective.[12]

Similar behaviors were identified and similar results obtained in a large number of studies, such as those conducted at the University of Michigan.[13] Although the display of highly Considerate-highly Structuring behavior was sometimes found to result in positive organizational outcomes, this was not true in all of the cases or even in most of them.[14] The research, therefore, clearly indicated that no single leadership style was universally effective, as the relationship of supervisory behavior to organizational performance and employee satisfaction changed from situation to situation. By the early 1960s this had become apparent to even the most ardent supporters of the behavioral approach, and the orientation of leadership researchers began to change toward a situational treatment.

The Situational Phase.   Current leadership research is almost entirely situational. This approach examines the interrelationships among leader and subordinate behaviors or characteristics and the situations in which the parties find themselves. This can clearly be seen in the work of researchers such as F. E. Fiedler, who outlined one of the first situational models.[15]

Fiedler claims that leaders are motivated primarily by satisfactions derived from interpersonal relations and task-goal accomplishment. Relationship-motivated leaders display task-oriented behaviors (such as Initiating Structure) in situations which are favorable for them to exert influence over their work group, and they display relationship-oriented behaviors (such as Consideration) in situations which are either moderately favorable or unfavorable. Task-motivated leaders display relationship-oriented behaviors in favorable situations and task-oriented behaviors in both moderately favorable and unfavorable situations. Fiedler's model specifies that relationship-motivated leaders will be more effective in situations which are moderately favorable for the leader to exert influence and that they will be less effective in favorable or unfavorable situations; the exact opposite is the case for task-motivated leaders. (They are most effective in favorable or unfavorable situations and least effective in mod-

12 Steven Kerr, C. A. Schriesheim, C. J. Murphy, and R. M. Stogdill, "Toward a Contingency Theory of Leadership Based upon the Consideration and Initiating Structure Literature," *Organizational Behavior and Human Performance*, August 1974, pp. 62–82.

13 See, for example, Daniel Katz, Nathan Maccoby, and Nancy Morse, *Productivity, Supervision and Morale in an Office Situation* (Ann Arbor: Survey Research Center, University of Michigan, 1951).

14 Kerr et al., "Contingency Theory."

15 See F. E. Fiedler, "Engineer the Job to Fit the Manager," *Harvard Business Review*, September–October 1965, pp. 115–22.

erately favorable ones.) According to Fiedler, the favorableness of the situation for the leader to exert influence over the work group is determined by (1) the quality of leader-group member relations (the warmer and friendlier, the more favorable the situation); (2) the structure of the tasks performed by the leader's subordinates (the more structured, the more favorable); and (3) the power of the leader (the more power, the more favorable the situation).[16]

A number of other authors propose similar types of interactions among the leader, the led, and the situation. We will not review all these other models, but the situational model of Victor Vroom and Phillip Yetton deserves mention.[17] Their model suggests the conditions under which the leader should share decision-making power. Five basic leadership styles are recommended. These range from unilateral decisions by the leader to situations in which the leader gives a great deal of decision power to subordinates and serves as a discussion coordinator who does not attempt to influence the group. Which style is recommended depends upon the leader's "yes" or "no" response to seven quality and acceptability questions which are asked sequentially. In those cases where more than a single style is suggested, the leader is expected to choose between recommendations on the basis of the amount of time to be invested. While this model, as is the case with most of the situational models, has not been fully tested, the literature supports the basic notion that a situational view is necessary to portray accurately the complexities of leadership processes.

ORGANIZATIONAL IMPLICATIONS

What does this discussion of leadership theory and research have to do with the practice of management?

Selection does not seem to be the primary answer to the organization's need to increase the pool of effective leaders. The results of the numerous trait studies summarized by Stogdill and others indicate that the search for universal personality characteristics of effective leaders is doomed.[18] This statement requires qualification, however. It should be recognized that the assertion concerns leadership effectiveness, which is only one aspect of managerial effectiveness. A manager may contribute to organizational effectiveness in many ways other than by being an effective leader. The role of selection in picking effective managers, as distinguished from effective leaders, consequently may be much greater. Furthermore, present disappointment with attempts at leader selection is derived from research which has sought to identify universal characteristics of effective leaders in all situations. Summaries such as Stogdill's demonstrate that leadership effectiveness is highly dependent upon the relationship between leader characteristics and the demands of particular situations, and thus universal

---

[16] F. E. Fiedler, *A Theory of Leadership Effectiveness* (New York: McGraw-Hill, 1967).

[17] V. H. Vroom and P. W. Yetton, *Leadership and Decision Making* (Pittsburgh, Pr.: University of Pittsburgh Press, 1973).

[18] R. M. Stogdill, "Personal Factors."

approaches will not work. Exploration of leader traits as they relate to performance in particular situations may reveal that careful selection has some potential. Unfortunately, given the many situational factors which appear to influence leadership effectiveness, it seems unlikely that selection procedures will be able to follow typical actuarial (statistical) selection procedures.[19] (It appears almost impossible to gather enough individuals in identical jobs to do this.) However, this does not preclude the use of clinical (judgmental) techniques for selection of leaders.

A further limitation on selection procedures as ways of increasing the pool of effective managers and/or leaders within organizations is the dynamic nature of managerial jobs and managers' careers. If, as research seems to indicate, leadership success is situation-specific, then the continual and inevitable shifts in the nature of a manager's assignment and his or her movement from one assignment to another may make the initial selection invalid.

Another implication is that existing forms of leadership training appear to be inappropriate, based on the evidence outlined here. There are two reasons for this. First, the majority of such training programs are based upon the assumption that there exists one best way to manage. Great emphasis usually is placed on an employee-centered (Considerate) approach or one which combines a concern for employees with a concern for high output (Initiating Structure). For example, the Managerial Grid and its associated Grid Organizational Development Program are popular approaches to management and organizational development.[20] Both are based on the premise that a managerial style which shows high concern for people and high concern for production is the soundest way to achieve excellence, and both attempt to develop this style of behavior on the part of all managers.[21] Rensis Likert's "System-Four" approach to managerial and organizational development, although different from the Grid approach, also assumes that one best way to manage exists (employee-centered leadership).[22] Clearly, these ideas are in conflict with the evidence and with contemporary opinion.

The other limitation of leadership training is that it seems ineffective in changing the behavior of participants. Leadership training aimed not directly at leadership behavior itself, but at providing diagnostic skills for the identification of the nature of the situation and the behaviors appropriate to it, appears to offer considerable potential for the improvement of leadership effectiveness. Obviously, however, additional research is needed

---

19 Kerr et al., "Contingency Theory."

20 R. R. Blake and J. S. Mouton, *The Managerial Grid* (Houston, Tex.: Gulf, 1964); and *Building a Dynamic Corporation through Grid Organizational Development* (Reading, Mass.: Addison-Wesley Publishing, 1969).

21 Ibid., p. 63.

22 Rensis Likert, *New Patterns of Management* (New York: McGraw-Hill, 1961); and *The Human Organization: Its Management and Value* (New York: McGraw-Hill, 1967).

to identify the dimensions of situations crucial to leadership performance and the styles effective under various circumstances.

Fiedler's suggestion that organizations engineer the job to fit the manager also has potential.[23] However, the idea is impractical, if not utopian. Application of this approach is limited because we have not identified the crucial dimensions of situations which affect leadership performance. Also, while the overall approach may offer theoretical advantages when leadership is treated in isolation, it ignores dysfunctional effects on other aspects of the organization's operations. Leadership effectiveness cannot be the only concern of administrators as they make decisions about job assignments. They must consider other aspects of the organization's operations which may conflict with their attempts to make good use of leadership talent. Some characteristics of the job, task, or organization simply may not be subject to change, at least in the short run. Thus, engineering the job to fit the manager may increase leadership effectiveness, but this approach seems risky, at least for the foreseeable future.

It should also be noted that it is not unusual for work organizations to use traits and trait descriptions in their evaluations of both leadership and managerial performance. A quick glance at a typical performance rating form usually reveals the presence of terms such as *personality* and *attitude* as factors for individual evaluation. Clearly, these terms represent a modern-day version of the traits investigated 30 years ago, and they may or may not be related to actual job performance, depending upon the specifics of the situation involved. Thus, some explicit rationale and, it is hoped, evidence that such traits do affect managerial performance should be provided before they are included in performance evaluations. Just feeling that they are important is not sufficient justification.

INDIVIDUAL IMPLICATIONS

The implications of our discussion of leadership theory and research for individual managers are intertwined with those for the total organization. The fact that leadership effectiveness does not depend on a single set of personal characteristics with which an individual is born or which the individual acquires at an early age should provide a sense of relief to many managers and potential managers. Success in leadership is not limited to an elite, but can be attained by almost any individual, assuming that the situation is proper and that the manager can adjust his or her behavior to fit the situation. The process leading to effective leadership, in other words, is not so much one of changing the characteristics of the individual as it is one of assuring that he or she is placed in an appropriate situation or of teaching the individual how to act to fit the situation.

Thus, a manager's effectiveness can be improved through the development of skills in analyzing the nature of organizational situations—both

---

23 Fiedler, "Engineer the Job."

task and political demands. Although it is difficult to provide guidelines, some recent research points to tentative prescriptions.[24]

Generally speaking, a high Consideration-high Structure style often works best. However, this approach cannot be used in all instances because dysfunctional consequences can result from such behaviors. For example, upper management sometimes gives highly considerate managers poor performance ratings, while in other instances high Structure has been related to employee dissatisfaction, grievances, and turnover. It sometimes will be necessary for a manager to choose between high Consideration and high Structure, and in these cases an individual's diagnostic ability becomes important.

If the diagnostician (manager) has little information, it is probably safe to exhibit high Consideration. Although it does not guarantee subordinate performance, its positive effects on frustration-instigated behavior—such as aggression—are probably enough to warrant its recommendation as a general style. However, in some situations Structure probably should be emphasized, although it may mean a decrease in subordinate perceptions of Consideration. Although the following is not an exhaustive list of these exceptions, it does include those which are known and appear important. The individual manager, from a careful analysis of the situation, must add any additional factors that can be identified.

Emergencies or High-Pressure Situations.   When the work involves physical danger, when time is limited, or when little tolerance for error exists, emphasis on Initiating Structure seems desirable. Research has demonstrated that subordinates often expect and prefer high Structure in such instances.

Situations in Which the Manager Is the Only Source of Information. When the leader is the only person knowledgeable about the task, subordinates often expect him or her to make specfic job assignments, set deadlines, and generally engage in structuring their behavior. This does not mean that the leader cannot be considerate if this is appropriate.

Subordinate Preferences.   There is limited evidence that some subordinates prefer high Structure and expect it, while others expect low Consideration and are suspicious of leaders who display high Consideration. Other preference patterns undoubtedly exist, and managers should attempt to tailor their behavior to each individual employee, as the situation dictates.

Preferences of Higher Management.   In some instances, higher management has definite preferences for certain leadership styles. Higher management sometimes prefers and expects high Structure and low Consideration, and rewards managers for displaying this behavioral style. The manager should be sensitive to the desires of superiors, in addition to those of subordinates. While it is not possible to specify how these expectations may be reconciled if they diverge, compromise or direct persuasion might

---

24 Kerr et al., "Contingency Theory."

be useful.[25] Once again, the success of these methods probably will depend both upon the situation and the manager's skill. This leads to the last point—adaptability.

Leader Ability to Adjust.   Some managers will be able to adjust their behavior to fit the situation. For others, attempts to modify behavior may look false and manipulative to subordinates. In these instances, the manager probably would be better off keeping the style with which he or she is most comfortable.

LIMITATIONS AND CONCLUSION

The situational approach avoids the major shortcomings of both the trait and behavioral approaches to leadership. However, the implicit assumption that hierarchical leadership is always important has recently come into question. Steven Kerr, for example, points out that many factors may limit the ability of a hierarchical superior to act as a leader for subordinates.[26] Factors such as technology (for example, the assembly line), training, clear job descriptions, and the like, may provide subordinates with enough guidance so that supervisor Structure may be unnecessary to ensure task performance. Also, jobs which are intrinsically satisfying may negate the need for supervisor Consideration, since Consideration is not needed to offset job dullness.

Another problem with the situational approach, and with leadership as a major emphasis in general, is that effective leadership may account for only 10 to 15 percent of the variability in unit performance.[27] While this percentage is certainly not trivial, it is clear that much of what affects performance in organizations is not accounted for by leadership. While studying and emphasizing leadership certainly has its merits, it could be argued that there is much to be gained by treating leadership effectiveness as but one component of managerial effectiveness. As an earlier publication emphasized:

> It is necessary to note that leadership is only one way in which the manager contributes to organizational effectiveness. The manager also performs duties which are *externally oriented* so far as his unit is concerned. For example, he may spend part of his time coordinating the work of his unit with other units. Similarly, not all of the manager's *internally oriented* activities can be labeled leadership acts. Some of them concern the physical and organizational conditions under which the work unit operates. For example, the manager spends part of his time obtaining resources (materials, equipment, manpower, and so on) necessary for unit operations. This is an es-

---

25 See Filley, House, and Kerr, *Managerial Process,* especially pp. 162–80; and George Strauss, "Tactics of Lateral Relations," in *Readings in Managerial Psychology,* ed. H. J. Leavitt and L. R. Pondy, 1st ed. (Chicago: University of Chicago Press, 1964), pp. 226–48.

26 Steven Kerr, "Substitutes for Leadership: Their Definition and Measurement," unpublished paper, 1978.

27 O. C. Behling and C. A. Schriesheim, *Organizational Behavior: Theory, Research and Application* (Boston: Allyn & Bacon, 1976).

sential internally oriented activity but hardly constitutes leadership. Clearly, the manager must perform a mix of internal and external activities if his unit is to perform well. Leadership is only one of the internal activities performed by managers.[28]

Thus, the manager should not overemphasize the importance of leadership activities, especially if this causes other functions to be neglected.

For managers to be effective as leaders, they must attempt to be astute politically and to tailor their behaviors, taking into account differences in subordinates, superiors, and situations. Leadership should be kept in perspective. Clearly, it is important, but it cannot be treated in isolation; the importance of leadership depends upon the situation, and the practicing manager must take this into account.

---

28 Ibid., p. 294.

Part IV

STRUCTURE WITHIN ORGANIZATIONS

The structure of an organization consists of relatively fixed relationships among jobs and groups of jobs. The formal structure is created by managerial decisions which (1) *define* jobs, (2) *group* jobs into departments, (3) *determine* size of groups reporting to a single manager, and (4) *delegate* authority to the manager. The resultant structure of jobs and authority determines to a considerable degree the behaviors of people who perform the jobs.

The decisions which managers must make in designing the structure relate to each of the four steps. The job definition subdecision must determine the extent to which jobs are highly specialized or highly generalized; the departmentalization subdecision determines the extent to which departments are highly homogeneous or highly heterogeneous; the size of the group must define whether a small or large number of subordinates reports to a manager; and the delegation subdecision must determine the extent to which authority is centralized or decentralized. If the range of alternatives for each of the four subdecisions is viewed as a continuum, then one can visualize an infinite variety of alternative organization structures.

Several general theories of organization structure appear in the literature. Important in this regard are the concepts of bureaucracy and System 4 organization. The bureaucratic theory argues that effective organization structures tend to be at one extreme of the continua—specialized jobs, homogeneous departments, narrow spans of managerial control, and centralized authority. System 4 organization proposes the opposite case—organizations characterized by generalized jobs, heterogeneous departments, wide spans, and decentralized authority. Contemporary theory is now advancing a situational, or contingency, point of view. According to situational theory, the most effective organization structure must be related to the situational factors, such as environmental demands and technological parameters.

Yet even with some generalized theory to guide the organizational design decision, management must still deal with specific problems of specialization, departmentalization, span of control, and delegation. Each of the six articles in this part discusses one or more of these problems. Moreover we shall see that these problems have their counterparts in academic departments and hospitals as well as in business firms.

The lead article in this section is "Should the Quality of Work Life Be Legislated?" by Edward E. Lawler III. It is his contention that, unless the government acts, work life will not improve within organizations. Lawler's article is presented in this part of the reader because it has implications for those in charge of structuring the organization and its jobs. Those at the top of the structure are asked by the author to come up with a public report on the quality of work life within the organization.

Locke takes exception to Lawler's position in an article entitled "The Case against Legislating the Quality of Work Life." Locke disagrees with Lawler's proposals and claims that they are based on wrong premises and faulty logic. Government should not initiate force against its own citizens. This is what Locke proposes will happen if Lawler's logic is followed.

J. Richard Hackman in "The Design of Work in the 1980s" discusses two routes to managing human resources. Route One involves fitting jobs to people, while Route Two is the approach of fitting people to jobs. Hackman in analyzing events and the environment believes that Route Two will predominate in the years to come. Thus, we can expect more work at fitting people to jobs. This is the way things have been for years and Hackman in a somewhat pessimistic tone believes things will remain like this in the 1980s.

Charles G. Burck in "How GM Turned Itself Around" talks about the remodeled management at GM. The story of GM's reactions to marketplace changes in terms of structural rearrangements is presented. There is a historical tracing of recent changes in the organization which presents an interesting picture of how reorganization which involves project centers occurred.

"Managing in a Matrix" by Harvey F. Kolodny informs us that matrix structures will require new managerial roles and behaviors. He discusses how matrix design is as much or more change in the behavior of the organization's members as it is a new structural design. Kolodny outlines the benefits of matrix design as well as the new behaviors that result.

Jay R. Galbraith in "Organization Design: An Information Processing View" presents a model. Organization design strategies are introduced and discussed. The author attempts to show why an organization must adopt one of the four strategies he discusses when faced with greater uncertainty.

Should the Quality of Work Life Be Legislated?*

EDWARD E. LAWLER III

Why would we want the government to legislate a better quality of work life? I believe that, unless the government acts, work life will not improve for many people. In many situations there is presently no clear motivation for organizations to provide employees with opportunities for personal growth and development, to see that employee needs are satisfied, or to eliminate those working conditions that contribute to mental illness, alcoholism, and drug abuse.

Little evidence exists to show that simply improving the quality of work will increase the profitability and economic soundness of most organizations. Given this situation, it is hardly surprising that many organizations are hesitant to undertake significant efforts to improve the quality of work life of their employees. Managers are held responsible for profitability; they cannot be expected to take actions which will endanger the economic soundness of their organization even though they might increase employee satisfaction. In my opinion, the only way this can be changed is by legislative action or by producing evidence that quality of work life improvement is good business from an economic point of view.

There are some situations in which improving the quality of work life may not, in fact, increase an organization's costs so as to put it at a competitive disadvantage. The research on job design, for example, suggests that job enrichment can, in some cases, reduce costs by bringing about higher quality products and lower turnover, while at the same time improving the quality of work life. In these situations there is economic pressure present toward improving the psychological quality of work life because it promises higher profit. These situations will probably correct themselves without government intervention, although the government

* Reprinted from the January 1976 issue of *Personnel Administrator*, 30 Park Drive, Berea, OH 44017.

could speed change by financing experimentation and information dissemination programs.

On the other hand, where the psychological quality of work life needs to be changed and increased costs are involved, the government may have to intervene to alter the economics of the situation, thus providing a strong motivation for change on the part of the organization in question. Despite the work that has gone into job enrichment, it is not clear how to enrich some assembly line jobs without increasing production costs. It is clear however, that in many of these situations enrichment would increase the quality of many people's lives. To change the situation so that organizations can act to improve these conditions without finding themselves at a competitive disadvantage, two types of government intervention are possible.

First, the government could charge organizations for the negative social outcomes they produce. For example, if because of a poor quality of work life a company had an unusually high rate of turnover, alcoholism, drug addiction, and mental illness among its employees, the government could increase its taxes proportionately. This is not dissimilar to present government practice in the area of unemployment insurance.

The second approach is to fine organizations not for the outcomes they produce (e.g., accidents, sick people) but for the practices in which they engage. In applying this approach to the area of the quality of work life, organizations could be fined or taxed on the basis of their management practices and policies and the nature of the jobs they have. For example, they might be taxed if they produce goods on an assembly line that had highly repetitive jobs. Such action could obviously serve to eliminate the economic advantage of producing goods on an assembly line.

It may seem far-fetched to envision the government taxing or fining an organization because it has a destructive human system that provides a poor quality of work life, but there are evidence and precedents available to suggest that these actions can and should happen. In the area of physical safety, for instance, there has been a long history of legislation regulating those organization practices and working conditions that can affect a person's physical health. Hours of work and equipment design are specified in considerable detail. Perhaps even more pertinent to problems of the psychological quality of work life, however, is the recent enactment of state and federal legislation controlling pollution.

A POSSIBLE PRECEDENT

Organizations that pollute the air, water, and soil are now subject to fines and, in some cases, shutdown. Since it costs industry more to manufacture many products in ways that will not pollute, any organization that tries to produce a product without polluting is at a competitive disadvantage in the market because pollution control equipment is expensive and adds to the company's costs. In a real sense, when goods are produced in a way that pollutes, their actual price tends to be too low because their full production costs are not charged to the customer. They are borne by society as a whole because it is the society which bears the cost of pollution (e.g., rivers to clean up, air that increases illness, and so on).

Using this logic, legislation that fines organizations for causing pollution is very much justified; it simply involves charging organizations in the name of the public for the cost of the pollution they are causing. It is also fair if this raises the price to the customer; he or she thus bears the full cost of the product rather than sharing it with people who do not buy and benefit from the item in question.

A parallel exists between the economics of pollution and the economics of providing a poor quality of work life for employees. Providing employees with dissatisfying, meaningless work lives is a form of pollution, the cost of which is borne by the society and the individual harmed rather than by the organizations responsible. This type of pollution leads to increased costs in such areas as mental illness, alcoholism, shorter life expectancy and less involvement in the community. These are expensive outcomes and ones that are paid for by the government and private funds that support unemployment insurance, welfare payments, hospitals, mental health centers and civic programs. Because these costs are absorbed by society, some goods are underpriced relative to their real costs; and just as with environmental pollution, a case can be made for government intervention designed to correct this situation.

All this talk about government action is very heady stuff and is indeed the kind of issue the people concerned with personnel should be debating. But before we go too far off into the stratosphere, we need to look at how well we can measure the quality of work life. Measures of it or the consequences of it are necessary if any of the legislative approaches mentioned so far are to work.

POSSIBLE MEASUREMENT APPROACHES

The behavioral science research that has been done on how people react to their work environments suggests the model shown in Figure 1. It shows that people's affective and attitudinal reactions to jobs are caused by a combination of the characteristics the person brings to the job and the characteristics of the job situation. These affective reactions in turn cause certain observable behavioral reactions which lead to organizational performance. This approach suggests three different kinds of measures: job and organizational conditions, affective reactions, and employee behavior. The problem is to determine which can and should be measured.

There are three characteristics desirable for any measure. First, the measure should be valid, in that it measures accurately all the important aspects of what needs to be measured. Secondly, it should have enough face validity so that it will be seen by all involved as a legitimate measure. Finally, it should be objective. This last point is important because objective measures are verifiable, can be audited by others, and are therefore less subject to distortion.

The importance of these characteristics (and especially of the last) varies

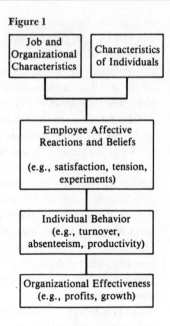

Figure 1

according to the purpose for which the information is to be used. It is always desirable to have objective measures, but in some instances it is less crucial. For example, it is often desirable to use self-report measures of the quality of work life and these are subjective. Despite their subjectivity, they do represent the most direct data available about the psychological state of an employee. Further, they allow us to account for individual differences better than do any of the other measures. The problem with measures of the working conditions to which individuals are exposed is that they cannot take into account individual differences in the way people respond to those conditions. This is not a serious problem when the issue is psychological.

Being exposed to extreme temperatures and noises of greater than 90 decibels is harmful to almost everyone; therefore, it makes sense to measure noise and temperature and to prohibit certain levels. It is not true, however, that repetitive assembly line jobs or authoritarian supervision are necessarily regarded as negative by all workers. Quite to the contrary, some see these factors as part of a high quality of work life. Others see them as very negative and as part of a low quality of work life.

Although self-reports of satisfaction do take into account individual differences, they are limited in their usefulness. They are satisfactory solutions only in those situations where there is little motivation present for the individual to report false data. In some instances the use for which the data are being gathered creates motivation for distortion as it probably would if government regulations were involved. In these cases, self-report measures would seem to be an unsatisfactory solution unless nonfakable measures are used and, at the moment, no such measures exist.

There have been some pioneering attempts in Europe to objectively define the conditions that are associated with the high quality of work life, but it is not clear that these efforts have been successful. One union in Germany, for example, has negotiated a contract that specifies the minimum repetitive cycle times for jobs. The assumption is that cycle time is a measure of job challenge and that, by requiring "long" cycle times, jobs will be made more satisfying. Cycle times have the advantage of being objectively measureable, but it is not clear that they are the best thing to focus on in order to assure that workers have satisfying jobs.

The governments of several countries have tried to increase the quality of work by requiring that organizations have workers on their boards of directors (e.g., West Germany) and that they have profit-sharing or joint ownership plans (e.g., Peru). Requiring administrative practices such as these makes some sense in that their presence or absence can be objectively measured. However, it remains to be established that these or similar practices will contribute to the quality of work life of most employees. Thus, as far as organizational conditions are concerned, we find ourselves in the position of being able to measure things that we are not sure contribute to a high quality of work life and not being able to specify or measure adequately what organizational conditions contribute to a high quality of work life.

One alternative to using the self-report and working condition measures mentioned earlier is to focus on the behavioral outcomes produced by working in an organization. Indicators such as turnover rates, absenteeism rates, mental illness rates, alcoholism rates, and community service rates can be measured and costed in terms of their economic impact on the community. This approach has the advantage of focusing on more "objective" outcomes. However, before the costing aspects can be operationalized, more work will have to be done to determine the actual values of these outcomes and the degree to which they can be linked to the work situation. This approach also has the disadvantage that it identifies bad conditions only after they have done their damage. Work situations that do not fit individuals produce dissatisfaction and a psychologically poor work environment. These, in turn, seem to produce social costs such as mental illness and alcoholism. Where possible, it is important to identify poor work environments before they produce serious negative outcomes.

PUBLIC REPORTING

It seems quite clear that none of the measures we have considered are sufficiently well developed to use as a basis for fining or regulating organizations. Does this mean there is nothing the government can do to improve the quality of work at this time? I don't think so. There are some things (in addition to sponsoring research) that the government can do. It can, as it has done with pollution, require organizations to prepare quality of work life statements when they build new plants and facilities. If nothing else, this would force organizations to think about how their way of designing and administering a plant is going to affect their employees' lives. Presently this is often considered only after an organization begins to have personnel problems (e.g., turnover, absenteeism, and strikes).

At the moment, companies are not required to inform stockholders about either the kind of life they provide for their employees or the kind of employee-organization relationship that exists. A case can be made for requiring organizations to furnish this kind of data. The quality of life a company affords can influence its financial success (turnover, absenteeism, and the like, are expensive); thus it would seem that investors should have the right to know what it is, so that they can make intelligent decisions. This is the logic that underlies the government requirement that organizations report on their economic conditions. But perhaps the most important effect of collecting and reporting these data would be to focus the attention of managers on the way the human resources in the organization are being managed. It has often been shown that managers attend to those things which are being measured. It should also help acquaint potential employees with the kind of work situation the organization offers; there is evidence that this kind of information can help people make better job choices. Disclosure of quality of work life data could result in bringing public and stockholder pressure to bear on those organizations that engage in deleterious practices; we might even see consumers boycotting those organizations that provide a poor quality of work life. Stockholders have recently demanded information from companies as to whether they discriminate against blacks and as to whether they pollute. It follows that before too long they may ask for information about the kind of life "their" company provides for its employees. They may even demand practices that will reduce profits in order to increase the quality of the life of the people who work in the company. This has already happened to a limited extent in some companies. For example, stockholders have demanded that American companies pay equal wages to blacks in South Africa, even though such payment is not required by law and could put the company at a financial disadvantage.

What kind of quality of life data should stockholders receive? Some have suggested that Human Resource Accounting (HRA) data should be provided and this might prove to be useful. (The R. G. Barry Corporation has been doing this for several years.) However, such data indicate only the worth of each individual employee and ignore the value of the total human organization.

As a first step, organizations could provide their stockholders with data on turnover, absenteeism, tardiness, accident, and grievance rates, as well as information on the rates of job-related physical and mental illness. Even though these measures may not be the kind that we would be willing to base fines and penalties on, they are sufficiently meaningful so that their release can be justified. Many of these measures can be costed so their financial impact could also be reported. They might be combined in a single "Quality of Life Index" that would provide some indication of what the consequences were of working for a particular company. If comparable data were collected from a number of companies, these could be reported in terms of the percentile standing of each company.

The difficult question to answer concerning any report to stockholders is whether it should include self-report data. This is information that investors should find very helpful since they are investing in the future of the company. However, if the employees are stockholders, they might be motivated to give invalid data. Since attitude data have never been gathered for distribution to stockholders, it is difficult to know how serious this problem would be. It is an area where some experimentation might be profitable.

The possibility of reporting to stockholders on the condition of the human aspects of organizations raises the question of who should prepare these reports. Just as with financial statements, it is not a job to be trusted to management; there simply would be too much pressure on them to give invalid data, since the reputation and value of the company are at stake. This suggests that people trained in behavioral science would be needed to audit the human system, just as accountants audit the financial system. They would have certain standard tests and procedures to use and they could eventually engage in direct observation of the management, leadership, and decision-making practices that take place. As in financial accounting, they would have to develop over time a standardized set of procedures and measures so that comparable data could be obtained from different firms. Presumably they, like accountants, would have the power to certify statements. Admittedly, considerable work needs to be done before it will be practical to begin doing certified human system audits, but that time will come sooner if the government requires this kind of reporting. At present there is little incentive for organizations to develop these measures. Like accounting measures, they can only be developed by a trial and error method that allows for refinements and the development of new principles.

It appears that some sort of government action is required to improve quality of work of many individuals. However, legislative action involving standards or fines does not seem appropriate because the needed measures do not exist. There is something the government can do. It is possible for the government to focus attention on the quality of work life in organizations by legislating that organizations publicly report on the quality of work they provide. This should result in efforts to develop better measures and to improve the quality of work life. The precedents for this action exist already in the financial reporting requirements: Considerable work needs to be done on measurement development, but now is the time to begin and government action is the stimulus that is needed.

The Case against Legislating the Quality of Work Life*

EDWIN A. LOCKE

In a recent article in this journal,[1] Edward E. Lawler proposed that companies be required to provide data on the "quality of work life" in their annual reports. He argued that this could be measured by means of "behavioral outcomes" such as employee turnover, absenteeism, alcoholism, drug addiction, and mental illness. To insure that these indices or the conditions which allegedly give rise to them do not deviate from "acceptable" levels, Lawler suggested that companies which exceed such levels could be taxed or fined proportionately by the government. The justification offered for these proposals was simply his belief that without legislation, "work life will not improve for many people."

This writer disagrees strongly with Lawler's proposals and will demonstrate that they are based on wrong premises and faulty logic.

First, an implicit premise of Lawler's position is that employees have a "right" to a satisfying job. Consider what this would actually mean. Job satisfaction results (with certain qualifications) when an employee gets what he wants from his job. Thus, if an employee has a "right" to job satisfaction, it means that other people must be forced to provide him with the kind of job he wants. This means that he has the "right," in effect, to enslave others. But what about the rights of these others, i.e., the people who must provide these jobs. What if they do not *want* to (or cannot) provide for all the wants of their employees? Why do those who want jobs, but cannot provide their own, have rights, while those with the knowledge and ability to create them have none? This is not only enslavement but the enslavement of the competent *because* they are competent.

Clearly there is a contradiction implied in the premise that there is a

---

* Reprinted from the May 1976 issue of *Personnel Administrator*, 30 Park Drive, Berea, OH 44017.

[1] Edward E. Lawler, "Should the Quality of Work Life Be Legislated?" *Personnel Administrator*, January 1976.

"right" to job satisfaction. Since there can be no right to violate a right, there can be no "right" to a satisfying job. Every person has the right to *pursue* his or her own happiness but does not have the right to force others to provide it, either on the job or off.

Second, Lawler's proposals assume that companies are the cause of the "behavioral outcomes" which he wants to eliminate, e.g., alcohol and drug addiction, mental illness, turnover.

There is not a single study in the literature which shows job dissatisfaction per se to be a cause of alcohol or drug addiction or mental illness. It is well known that these conditions involve profound cognitive disturbances (e.g., value conflicts, improper methods of mental functioning) which have nothing to do with the job the person holds (except to make the employee less effective). Furthermore, an employee accepts and retains his job by choice. No one forces him to accept a given job or to keep it, once accepted, forever. If an employee feels that his job is boring, frustrating, or stifling, or that the costs outweigh the benefits, he is free to quit and look for a better job.

It is true that many jobs are boring and repetitive, but these jobs are often highly paid (e.g., automobile assembly lines) which is why the employees chose them in the first place. Those who find them unbearable, despite the money, typically quit. Employees who choose to remain permanently on such jobs usually do so for one of two reasons: Either they are not capable of anything more complex and therefore are not overly dissatisfied, or they are not willing to use their minds to learn more advanced skills and therefore have no right to expect a better job or to force others to provide one. (Some people may also get "trapped" in such jobs through miscalculation or poor planning, but even this does not give these people the right to force others to pay for their errors.)

Behavioral outcomes such as turnover and absenteeism may be caused partly by company policies (pay, type of work, supervision, and the like) but only partly. Turnover, especially, is influenced by numerous other factors, including the state of the economy, technological developments in the industry, the nature of the local work force, the industry wage scale, government wage and unemployment policies, changes in demographic patterns, events in the employees' personal lives, and the values and attitudes the employees bring with them to the job. Thus, holding the company solely responsible for turnover (not to mention alcoholism and mental illness) is grossly unjust.

Furthermore, turnover is not necessarily unhealthy. It provides an escape valve for individuals who are not happy in a given company and allows them to look for a better situation elsewhere. The company also benefits by getting rid of disgruntled employees. Turnover is sometimes highest for the best (most able, most healthy, most ambitious) employees, because their high aspirations and great self-confidence make them difficult to satisfy.

If low turnover and absenteeism are to be taken as indicative of job satisfaction, then the slave labor camps of Soviet Russia (which also have low rates of alcoholism and drug abuse) should be taken as the epitome of a good environment. It is true that slave labor camps undermine mental health, but the fact that four out of Lawler's five criteria of job satisfaction are favorable to such an environment demonstrates the inadequacy of these criteria divorced from a wider context (e.g., what causes these outcomes, why, and so on).

Thirdly, Lawler's analogy between legislation regarding the work environment and antipollution legislation is invalid. Rational pollution laws differ in two fundamental respects from Lawler's proposed legislation concerning jobs. For one, rational pollution laws are designed to prohibit the *initiation* of force (in the form of pollutants) by one person against another. Such laws are valid because the victim is harmed against his will. Since no voluntary trade is involved, the victim's rights are violated. Secondly, rational pollution laws are *objective;* they prohibit an individual from taking actions which result in provable physical harm to other persons or their property based on objective standards. (Admittedly, all existing pollution laws are not rational by these criteria.)

In contrast, Lawler's proposals for legislation regarding the quality of work life are not designed to prohibit the initiation of force by a company against an employee. As noted above, a company can only offer an individual a job; it cannot force him to accept one. Rather than protecting the employee's rights, Lawler's proposals would violate those of company owners by denying their right to design jobs according to their own judgment. Further, Lawler provides no objective standards for defining a "healthy" work situation. In fact, he provides no standards at all except for certain arbitrarily chosen "behavioral outcomes" (e.g., alcoholism) which, for the reasons stated above, are totally inappropriate.

My fourth comment concerns Lawler's conclusions. After discussing at great length the need for government legislation to force improvements in the quality of work life, and the various alternative methods that could be used for measuring it, he suddenly acknowledges that behavioral outcome measures are not yet adequately developed to serve as a basis for fining or regulating companies. He then argues that companies nevertheless should be forced to provide this information in their annual reports, the most important benefit being that it would "focus the attention of managers on the way the human resources in the organization are being managed."

If it is in a manager's self-interest to develop and report such data, one wonders why Lawler does not believe they do it voluntarily. But then Lawler again switches focus and asserts (without evidence) that this information is needed by stockholders to evaluate companies.

At this point, the real motive for the proposed legislation emerges. Since corporate officers cannot be "trusted" to provide stockholders with accurate information on the quality of work life, "people trained in behavioral science would be needed to audit the human system, just as accountants audit the financial system." In the last analysis, Lawler's proposals seem to be nothing less than a technique for *enhancing the status and importance of social scientists through legislation* (i.e., force). Does this advocacy of force imply that Lawler believes social scientists cannot *persuade* businessmen of their importance? If so, could one reason be that they have not yet made a good case for themselves?

For all the reasons given above, I find Dr. Lawler's proposals dangerous and ill-advised. Job satisfaction and mental health are clearly desirable goals, but they cannot and should not be legislated. Health and happiness can only be achieved if an individual uses his mind properly. But no one can force a man to think; he must do it by choice. The proper role of government in this process is indirect; by protecting individuals from the initiation of force and fraud by others, it leaves each person free to think, to act on his judgment, and to enjoy the benefits of his actions. Dr. Lawler, however, advocates that the government reverse its proper role and initiate force against its own citizens. These arbitrary and capricious proposals pose a threat not only to the financial integrity of the corporations which produce our wealth, but to the individual liberty of all citizens.

The Design of Work in the 1980s*

J. RICHARD HACKMAN

Many observers are concerned these days about the quality of work life in organizations, about organizational productivity, and about possible changes in the work ethic of people in contemporary Western society. Indeed, there has been a clamor in the popular press of late that we are in the midst of a major "work ethic crisis" that has its roots in work that is designed more for robots than for mature, adult human beings. Even the very idea of work has taken on negative connotations for some commentators. Studs Terkel begins his book *Working*, in which the thoughts and feelings of workers from many occupations are reflected, as follows:

> This book, being about work, is, by its very nature, about violence—to the spirit as well as to the body. It is about ulcers as well as accidents, about shouting matches as well as fistfights, about nervous breakdowns as well as kicking the dog around. It is, above all (or beneath all), about daily humiliations. To survive the day is triumph enough for the walking wounded among the great many of us.

IS THERE A CRISIS? Those who perceive that we are in the midst of a crisis in the world of work tend to argue that no less than a revolution in the way productive work is done has occurred in the United States in this century. Organizations have steadily increased the use of technology and automation in attaining organizational objectives. Consistent with this trend (and with the dictates of the "scientific management" approach to work design, as

* Reprinted, by permission of the publisher, from *Organizational Dynamics*, Summer 1978, pp. 3–17. © 1978 by AMACOM, a division of American Management Associations. All rights reserved.

This essay was prepared for the Visiting Scholars Program of the College of Business Administration, University of Houston and was presented there in March 1977. It is based on research supported by the Organizational Effectiveness Research Program, Psychological Sciences Division, Office of Naval Research, under Contract N00014–75C–0269, NR 170–744. The comments and suggestions of numerous colleagues on an earlier draft are gratefully acknowledged.

espoused by F. W. Taylor at the turn of the century), work has become dramatically more specialized, simplified, standardized, and routinized. Moreover, organizations themselves have become larger in size and more bureaucratic in function. Partly as a consequence of the increase in organizational size, managerial and statistical controls are used more and more to direct and enforce the day-to-day activities of organization members.

The efficiencies of advanced technology, the economies of scale, and the benefits of increased managerial control have generated substantial increases in the productive efficiency of organizations and substantial economic benefits for both the owners of organizations and society as a whole. These economic benefits, in turn, have contributed to a general increase in the affluence, education, and personal level of aspiration of individuals in American society. As a result, people today want jobs that allow them to use their education, that provide "intrinsic" work satisfactions, and that meet their expectations that work should be personally meaningful. No longer will people accept routine and monotonous work as their legitimate lot in life.

According to this line of thinking, we have arrived at a point where the way most organizations function is in direct conflict with the talents and aspirations of the people who work in them. Such conflict manifests itself in increased personal alienation from work and in decreased organizational effectiveness. What worked for Taylor early in this century, it is argued, simply cannot work now because the people who populate organizations, especially well-educated younger workers, will not tolerate it.

Other observers hold a contrary view. Reports of worker discontent and demands for fulfilling work activities, they suggest, have been greatly exaggerated in the popular press and in behavioral science journals. The work ethic "crisis" may be more manufactured than real, they say, and probably represents a serious misapprehension of the actual needs and aspirations of people at work.

Considerable evidence can be marshaled in support of this contention. Perhaps most widely publicized is a project sponsored by the Ford Foundation to test how satisfied U.S. automobile workers would be working on highly "enriched" team assembly jobs in a Swedish automobile plant. Six Detroit auto workers were flown to Sweden and spent a month working as engine assemblers in a Saab plant. At the end of the month, five of the six workers reported that they preferred the traditional U.S. assembly line. As one put it: "If I've got to bust my ass to be meaningful, forget it; I'd rather be monotonous." Arthur Weinberg, a Cornell labor relations expert who accompanied the six workers to Sweden, summarized their negative reactions:

> They felt it was a deprivation of their freedom and it was a more burdensome task which required more effort which was more tedious and stressful. They preferred the freedom the assembly line allowed them, the ability to

think their own thoughts, to talk to other workers, sing or dance on the assembly line, which you can't do at Saab. There is a freedom allowed on the assembly line not possible in more complex work. The simplified task allows a different kind of freedom. The American workers generally reacted negatively to doing more than one task. They were not accustomed to it and they didn't like it.

Other studies support the results of this transatlantic experiment and cast doubt on the popular notion that people who work on routine and repetitive tasks invariably experience psychological and emotional distress as a consequence.[1] Perhaps most supportive of the "no crisis" view are the data reported by Robert P. Quinn, Graham L. Staines, and Margaret R. McCollough in a 1974 Department of Labor monograph titled *Job Satisfaction: Is There a Trend?* These researchers examined findings from national surveys of job satisfaction from 1958 to 1973 and found no decline in job satisfaction over the past two decades. The present level of employee satisfaction is, as it has been, quite high: Better than 80 percent of the work force consistently report being "satisfied" with their jobs.

The findings do show that younger workers are more dissatisfied with work than older workers. Yet younger workers also were more dissatisfied than their older colleagues 25 years ago, casting doubt on the hypothesis that contemporary young workers are at the cutting edge of a trend toward increasing job alienation and dissatisfaction. A crisis in job satisfaction? No. Data such as those summarized above suggest that the "crisis" may lie more in the minds of journalists and behavioral scientists than in the hearts of people who perform the work in contemporary organizations.

ARGUMENTS ON BOTH SIDES

Both the argument for and argument against a crisis in job satisfaction can be persuasive, and both sides of the question can be argued forcefully and with ample supportive data. How can we come to terms with this seeming conflict in the evidence as we attempt to generate some predictions about how work will be designed and managed in the 1980s? My own resolution of the issue takes the form of two complementary conclusions. Each of the conclusions strikes me as valid and as consistent with existing evidence about the state of work and workers in contemporary society. Yet, as will be seen, the conclusions provide quite different bases for decisions about how to proceed with the design of work in the decades to come.

Conclusion One: *Many individuals are presently underutilized and underchallenged at work.* It seems to me indisputable that numerous jobs have become increasingly simplified and routinized in the last several

---

[1] See, for example, George Strauss, "Is There a Blue-Collar Revolt against Work?" in *Work and the Quality of Life,* ed. James O'Toole (Boston: MIT Press, 1974), or Iradj Siassi, Guido Crocetti, and Herzl P. Spiro, "Loneliness and Dissatisfaction in a Blue Collar Population," *Archives of General Psychiatry* 30 (1974): 261–65.

decades, even as members of the U.S. work force have become better educated and more ambitious in their expectations about what life will hold
for them. The result is a poor fit between large numbers of people and
their work. These people, whom James O'Toole calls "the reserve army of
the underemployed," have more to offer their employers than those employers seek, and they have personal needs and aspirations that cannot be
satisfied by the work they do.

It also is indisputable that many people do *not* seek challenge and meaning in their work but instead aspire to a secure job and a level of income
that permits them to pursue personal interests and satisfactions off the job.
Do the underutilized and underchallenged workers comprise three-quarters
of the work force, or only one-quarter?

We cannot say for sure. What we can say—and this statement may be
much more important—is that for some unknown millions of people work
is neither a challenge nor a personally fulfilling part of life. And the
organizations that employ them are obtaining only a portion of the
contribution that these people could be making.

Conclusion Two: *People are much more adaptable than we often
assume.* When they must, people show an enormous capacity to adapt to
their environments. Through almost whatever happens to them, people
survive and make do: gradually going blind, winning the lottery, losing
one's home to fire or flood, gaining a spouse and children—or losing them.
The same is true for work. Some of us adjust to challenging, exciting jobs;
others of us to a pretty routine and dull state of affairs. But we adapt. Not
to do so would open us up to constant feelings of distress and dissatisfaction,
noxious states that we are well motivated to avoid.

This plasticity often goes unrecognized by those who argue loudly on
one or the other side of the "work ethic" debate. Part of the reason is that
it is very hard to see adaptation taking place, except when the environment
changes dramatically and suddenly. When change is gradual, as it is when
a young person adjusts to his or her job, it can be almost invisible. We tend,
in our studies of work and workers, to catch people after they have adapted
to their work situation or before they have done so rather than right in the
middle of the adaptation. It is tough to figure out what is happening (or
has happened) to a person at work if you look only once.

Precisely because we do adapt to our work environment, it is dangerous
to take at face value self-reports of how "satisfied" people are with their
work. Consider the case of Ralph Chattick, a 44-year-old worker in a metal
fabrication shop on the outskirts of a large midwestern city. Ralph (not his
real name) has worked in the same department of his company since grad-
uating from high school and is being interviewed about his job.

Are you satisfied with your work?
Yes, I guess so.
Would you keep working if you won a million dollars in the lottery?

Sure.

Why?

Well, you have to do something to fill the day, don't you? I don't know what I'd do if I didn't work.

Do you work hard on your job?

I do my job. You can ask them if I work hard enough.

It is important to you to do a good job?

Like I said, I do my job.

But is it important to you personally?

Look, I earn what I'm paid, okay? Some here don't, but I do. They pay me to cut metal, and I cut it. If they don't like the way I do it, they can tell me and I'll change. But it's their ball game, not mine.

Ralph is telling us that he is basically satisfied with his work. But how are we to interpret that? Take it at face value and conclude that he is a "satisfied worker"? No, there are some signs in this interview excerpt that all is not well with Ralph. Yet it also would be inappropriate to take a "yes" such as that provided by Ralph and routinely assume that he *really* isn't satisfied. Ralph is not lying to us. He *is* satisfied, as he understands what we are asking.

The phenomenon of job satisfaction becomes clearer, and the diagnostic task more difficult, when we put ourselves in Ralph's place and consider the alternatives he has in responding. In fact, things are not awful, which is part of the reason for responding affirmatively. Moreover, Ralph has made numerous small choices over the years (such as deciding not to change jobs or to quit work and attend school) that have increased his personal commitment to his job. To answer other than affirmatively would raise for Ralph the specter that perhaps these choices were poor ones, that in fact he has done a bad job in managing his career: "If I'm dissatisfied with this job, then what the hell have I been doing here all these years? Why haven't I done something about it?" That is an anxiety-arousing issue to face and one that most of us would prefer to ignore. So the easiest response, and one that represents Ralph's present feelings about his work situation fairly, is, "Sure, I guess I'm satisfied with my job."

Because, like Ralph, most people do adapt to their work, responses to questions about job satisfaction can be misleading, especially among people who have considerable tenure. For the same reason, self-reports of satisfaction or lack of satisfaction do not provide a sturdy enough basis on which to erect plans for organizational change—let alone national policy about quality of work life issues.

CHOICES FOR THE 1980s

The conclusions drawn above cast doubt on the usefulness of trying to decide whether or not we are now in the midst of a work ethic "crisis." They also highlight two quite different routes that can be taken as choices are made about how to design and manage work in the next decade and beyond. One route, which derives from the conclusion that many people are underultilized by the work they do, leads to increases in the level of challenge that is built into jobs and in the degree of control jobholders have in managing their own work. In effect, we would attempt to change jobs to make them better fits for the people who do them.

The other route derives from the second conclusion; namely, that people gradually adapt and adjust to almost any work situation, even one that initially seems to underutilize their talents greatly. This route leads to greater control of work procedures and closer monitoring of work outcomes by management to increase the productive efficiency of the work force. Technological and motivational devices would be used to attempt to change the behavior of people to fit the demands of well-engineered jobs. The expectation is that in a carefully designed work environment employees gradually will adjust to having little personal control of their work, and the efficiencies gained by using sophisticated managerial controls of work and workers will more than compensate for any temporary dissatisfaction the workers may experience.

Route One: Fitting Jobs to People

The core idea of Route One is to build increased challenge and autonomy into the work for the people who perform it. By creating job conditions that motivate employees *internally,* gains might be realized both in the productive effectiveness of the organization and in the personal satisfaction and well-being of the work force.

Specifically, the aspiration would be to design work so that employees experience the work as inherently meaningful, feel personal responsibility for the outcomes of the work, and receive, on a regular basis, trustworthy knowledge about the results of their work activities. Research by Greg Oldham and myself suggests that when all three of these conditions are met, most people are internally motivated to do a good job—that is, they get a positive internal "kick" when they do well, and feel bad when they do poorly. Such feelings provide an incentive for trying to perform well and, when performance is excellent, lead to feelings of satisfaction with the work and with one's self.

How might jobs be designed to create these conditions? Consider the assembly of a small electrical appliance, such as a toaster. Following traditional dictates of engineering efficiency, such devices usually are manufactured on some form of production line: One individual attaches the heating element to the chassis, another solders on the line cord, a third attaches the mechanical apparatus for handling the bread to be toasted, another inspects the assembled product, and so on.

An alternative design would be to make each employee, in effect, an autonomous toaster manufacturer. All necessary parts would be available at the employee's work station and he or she would be skilled in all aspects of toaster assembly, inspection, and repair. The employee would perform the entire assembly task, would inspect his or her own work, and then (when satisfied that the apparatus was in perfect working order) would place a sticker on the bottom of the toaster. The sticker would say something along these lines:

> This toaster was made by Andrew Whittier, an employee at the San Diego plant of General Toasters, Inc. I believe that it is in perfect condition and will give you years of reliable service. If, however, your toaster should malfunction in any way, please call me at my toll-free number, (800) 555–1217. We will see if we can clear up your problem over the telephone. If not, I will authorize you to send the toaster to me and I will either repair it or send you a replacement, under the terms of the limited warranty that I packed in the box with the toaster.

What would such a design achieve? Meaningful work? Yes, I'm making a useful household appliance all on my own. Personal responsibility for the work outcomes? Yes, I am personally accountable for the performance of any toaster I release for shipping; there is no one to blame but myself if I ship a bad product. Knowledge of results? Yes, in two ways. First, I do my own inspection and testing before shipping, which means I can self-correct any assembly problems. Second, I obtain direct and personal feedback from customers about any problems they have with my work (not to mention the embarrassment of having it announced on the shop loudspeaker that "Andy, you have another call on the 800 line . . . !").

Surely such a design would lead to a high internal motivation to perform effectively and, for able employees who value the internal rewards that can be obtained from doing a demanding job well, high satisfaction with the work. The quality of work should improve also. However, there might be some decrease in the *quantity* of work done by a given worker on a given day, as compared with the work done on the more technically efficient production line.

The hypothetical design for toaster manufacturing described above has much in common with many "job enrichment" experiments carried out in numerous organizations in the last decade. Although the changes made in such projects inevitably involve alterations, not just of the task itself, but of many aspects of the work organization, the focus clearly is on the work done by individual employees.

A different approach, but one that has many objectives in common with individual job enrichment, is to design work so that it is done by a more or less autonomous *group* of employees. Use of the work group as a design device requires simultaneous attention to the technical and social aspects of the work system, which often is advantageous. Indeed, the group may be the *only* feasible design alternative for creating a whole and meaningful piece of work in some cases. For example, the assembly of automobile transmission requires coordinated activity among several individuals because of the weight of the materials and the complexity of the assembly.

Probably the best-known application of group work design in a U.S. organization is in the Topeka pet-food plant of General Foods, where an entire new manufacturing organization was designed around the concept of the semiautonomous work group. Each work team at Topeka (consisting of seven to fourteen members) was given responsibility for a significant organizational task. In addition to doing the work required to complete the task, team members performed many activities traditionally reserved for management—such as coping with manufacturing problems, distributing individual tasks among team members, screening and selecting new team members, and participating in organizational decision making. Moreover, employees on each team were encouraged to broaden their skills on a continuous basis so that the employees and their teams would become able to handle even more responsibility for carrying out the work of the organization. Early reports from Topeka indicate that the innovative project has generated numerous beneficial outcomes, both for the organization and for the people who do the work.

Autonomous work teams and job-enrichment interventions have been used successfully in many organizations. Yet we still have much to learn about how to design, install, and diffuse such innovations most effectively—and about when they do (and do not) generate beneficial outcomes for people and for organizations.[2]

If we can find most of the answers during the next few years, the shape of work in the next decade could turn out to be quite different from what it is today. Assuming that we follow Route One and do so competently and successfully, here are some speculations about the design and management of work in the mid-1980s.

1. Responsibility for work will be pegged clearly at the organizational level at which the work is done. No longer will employees experience themselves as people who merely execute activities that "belong" to someone else (such as a line manager). Instead, they will feel, legitimately, that they are both responsible and accountable for the outcomes of their own work. Moreover, the resources and the information needed to carry out the work (including feedback about how well the work is getting done) will be provided directly to employees, without being filtered first through line and staff managers. As a result, we will see an increase in the personal motivation of employees to perform well and a concomitant increase in the quality of work being done.

2. Explicit consideration will be given to questions of employee motivation and satisfaction when new technologies and work practices are invented and engineered, on a par with the consideration now given to the employee's intellectual and motor capabilities. No longer will equipment and work systems be designed solely to optimize technological or engineering efficiency and motivational problems left in the laps of managers and personnel consultants after work systems are put in place.

Moreover, there will be no single "right answer" about how best to

---

[2] An informative summary and interpretation of what is known about the effects of Route One innovations (and what remains doubtful or ambiguous about their consequences) is provided by Raymond A. Katzell, David Yankelovich, and their colleagues in the monograph *Work, Productivity, and Job Satisfaction* (Psychological Corporation, 1975).

design work and work systems. Sometimes tasks will be arranged to be performed by individuals working more or less alone; other times they will be designed to be performed by interacting teams of employees. Choices among such design options will take into account the character of the work itself (such as any technological imperatives that may exist), the nature of the organization, and the needs, goals, and talents of the employees. In many cases work will be "individualized" to improve the fit between the characteristics of an employee and the tasks he or she performs. Standard managerial practices that apply equally well to all individuals in a work unit will no longer be appropriate. Instead, managers will have to become as adept at adjusting jobs to people as they now are at adjusting people to fit the demands and requirements of fixed jobs.

3.   Organizations will be leaner, with fewer hierarchical levels and fewer managerial and staff personnel whose jobs are primarily documentation, supervision, and inspection of work done by others. A new way of managing people at work will be needed, giving rise to new kinds of managerial problems. For example, to the extent that significant motivational gains are realized by enriched work in individualized organizations, managers will no longer have the problem of "how to get these lazy incompetents to put in a decent day's work." Instead, the more pressing problem may be what to do *next* to keep people challenged and interested in their work.

As people become accustomed to personal growth and learning at their work, what was once a challenge eventually becomes routine—and ever more challenge may be required to keep frustration and boredom from setting in. How to manage an organization so that growth opportunities are continuously available may become a difficult challenge—especially if, as predicted, the number of managerial slots into which employees can be promoted shrinks.

4.   Last, if the previous predictions are correct, eventually a good deal of pressure will be brought to bear on the broader political and economic system to find ways to make effective use of the human resources that are no longer needed to populate work organizations. Imagine that organizations eventually do become leaner and more effective and, at the same time, that the rate of growth of society as a whole is reduced to near zero. Under such circumstances, a number of people will be "free" for meaningful employment outside traditional private and public work organizations. To expand welfare services and compensate these people for not working would be inconsistent with the overall thrust of Route One toward meaningful, productive work. So would wholesale reductions of the workweek, unless useful "leisure" tasks could be created at the same time.

What, then, is to be done with the surplus of people and of time? Can we imagine groups of public philosophers, artists and poets, compensated by society for helping create an enriched intellectual and aesthetic environment for the populace? An interesting possibility, surely, but one that would require radical rethinking of public decision making about the goals of society and the way shared resources should be allocated to achieve those goals.

Route Two: Fitting People to Jobs

If we take Route Two, the idea is to design and engineer work for maximum economic and technological efficiency and then do whatever must be done to help people adapt and adjust in personally acceptable ways to their work experiences. No great flight of imagination is required to guess what work will be like in the 1980s if we follow Route Two; the sprouts of this approach are visible now. Work is designed and managed in a way that clearly subordinates the needs and goals of people to the demands and requirements of fixed jobs. External controls are employed to ensure that individuals do in fact behave appropriately on the job. These include close and directive supervision, financial incentives for correct performance, tasks that are engineered to minimize the possibility of human mistakes, and information and control systems that allow management to monitor the performance of the work system as closely and continuously as possible. And, throughout, productivity and efficiency tend to dominate quality and service as the primary criteria for assessing organizational performance.

If we continue down Route Two, what might we predict about the design and management of work in the 1980s? Here are my guesses.

1.   Technological and engineering considerations will dominate decision making about the design of jobs. Technology is becoming increasingly central to many work activities, and that trend will accelerate. Also, major advances will be achieved in techniques for engineering work systems to make them ever more efficient. Together, these developments will greatly boost the productivity of individual workers and, in many cases, result in tasks that are nearly "people proof" (that is, work that is arranged virtually to eliminate the possibility of error because of faulty judgment, lapses of attention, or misdirected motivation). Large numbers of relatively mindless tasks, including many kinds of inspection operations, will be automated out of existence. The change from person to machine will both increase efficiency and eliminate many problems that arise from human frailties, as suggested by B. M. Oliver in a 1977 essay in *Scientific American* on the future of automated instrumentation and control:

> Automatic test systems do not fudge the data or make mistakes in recording it or get tired or omit tests or do any of the dozens of troublesome things human beings are apt to do. Whatever tests the program specifies will be made regardless of the time of day or the day of the week; no front office pressure to ship goods by a certain date can compromise the computer's inspection.

Accompanying these technological advances will be a further increase in the capability of industrial psychologists to analyze and specify in advance the knowledge and skills that will enable a person to perform almost any task that can be designed satisfactorily. Sophisticated employee assessment and placement procedures will be used to select people and assign them to tasks, and only rarely will an individual be put into a job for which he or she is not fully qualified.

The result of all these developments will be a quantum improvement in the efficiency of most work systems, especially those that process physical materials or paper. And while employees will receive more pay for less work, they will also experience substantially less discretion and challenge in their work activities.

2.   Work performance and organizational productivity will be closely monitored and controlled by managers using highly sophisticated information systems. Integrated circuit microprocessors will provide the hardware needed to gather and summarize performance data for work processes that presently defy cost-efficient measurement. Software will be developed to provide managers with data about work performance and costs that are far more reliable, more valid, and more current than is possible with existing information systems. Managers increasingly will come to depend on these data for decision making and will use them to control production processes vigorously and continuously.

Because managerial control of work will increase substantially, responsibility for work outcomes will lie squarely in the laps of managers, and the gap between those who do the work and those who control it will grow. There will be accelerated movement toward a two-class society of people who work in organizations, with the challenge and intrinsic interest of managerial and professional jobs increasing even as the work of rank-and-file employees becomes more controlled and less involving.

3.   Desired on-the-job behavior will be elicited and maintained by extensive and sophisticated use of extrinsic rewards. Since (if my first prediction is correct) work in the 1980s will be engineered for clarity and simplicity, there will be little question about what each employee should (and should not) do on the job. Moreover (if my second prediction is correct), management will have data readily at hand to monitor the results of each employee's work on a more or less continuous basis. All that will be required, then, are devices to ensure that the person actually does what he or she is *supposed* to do.

Because many jobs will be routinized, standardized, and closely controlled by management, it is doubtful that employee motivation to perform appropriately can be created and maintained from intrinsic rewards (people working hard and effectively because they enjoy the tasks or because they obtain internal reinforcement from doing them well). So management will have to use extrinsic rewards (such as pay or supervisory praise) to motivate employees, providing such rewards for behavior that is in accord with the wishes of management.

In recent years the fine old principle of contingent rewards has been dressed up in the rather elaborate and worldly clothes of "behavior modification," as espoused by B. F. Skinner. Research evidence shows that in many circumstances contingent rewards do have a powerful effect on individual behavior. If we follow Route Two, I predict that behavior modification programs will be among the standard motivational techniques used in work organizations in the 1980s.

4. Most organizations will sponsor programs to aid employees in adapting to life at work under Route Two conditions, including systematic "attitude development" programs to foster high job satisfaction and organizational commitment. Sophisticated procedures for helping employees and their families deal with alcohol, drug abuse, and domestic problems also will be offered by many organizations. These latter programs will become much more prevalent (and necessary) than they are at present, I believe, because of some unintended spin-offs of the movement toward the productive efficiencies of Route Two.

Consider, for example, a person working in an organization in the mid-1970s whose work is undemanding, repetitive, and routine. It might be someone who matches checks and invoices and then clips them together to be processed by another employee. Imagine that we asked that individual the following question: "What happens to you, what are the outcomes, when you try to work especially hard and effectively on your job?" The answers are likely to be far from inspiring. Probably they will have more to do with headaches and feelings of robothood than with any sense of meaningful personal accomplishment from high on-the-job effort. Clearly, such perceived outcomes reveal a lack of any positive internal motivation to work hard and effectively.

Now let us transport that employee via time machine to the mid-1980s, and place him or her in a very similar job under full-fledged Route Two conditions. The work is just as routine and undemanding as it was before. The differences are that now there is greater management control over hour-by-hour operations, and valued external rewards are available—but the rewards are there only when the employee behaves in close accord with explicit management specifications. How will our hypothetical employee react to that state of affairs?

At first, he is likely to feel even more like a small cog in a large wheel than he did before. Before the new management controls were introduced he could get away with some personal games or fantasies on the job. Now that is much harder to do. Moreover, the problem is exacerbated, not relieved, by the addition of the performance-contingent rewards. The negative intrinsic outcomes of hard work in the 1970s are still felt—but they have been supplemented (not replaced) by a set of new and positive *extrinsic* outcomes. So the employee is faced with contingencies that specify, "The harder I work, the more negative I feel about myself and what I'm doing, the more likely I am to get tired and headachy on the job, *and* the more likely I am to get praise from my supervisor and significant financial bonuses."

The state of affairs is precisely what we might devise if we wished deliberately to drive someone insane—that is, having the work and its rewards arranged so that strong positive and strong negative outcomes are *simul-*

taneously contingent on the same behavior (in this case, working hard). Some of the problems of drug usage, alcoholism, and industrial sabotage that are found in work organizations appear to derive from this kind of no-win state of affairs. And if we move vigorously down Route Two, we can predict with some confidence that signs of employee "craziness" will increase.

Only a small proportion of the work force will exhibit severely mal-adaptive behaviors, however, even under full-fledged Route Two conditions. As suggested earlier, people have a good deal of resilience and usually can adjust and adapt to almost any work situation if given enough time and latitude to do so. So although we can predict that many people will suffer from tension and stress in adjusting to work in the 1980s and will find their aspirations for personal growth and development at work significantly dampened, we don't think that major overt problems will be observed with any frequency.

Yet because *any* "crazy" employee behavior is anathema to management (and clearly dysfunctional for organizational effectiveness), managers will attempt to head off such behaviors before they occur. When they do occur, management will deal with them as promptly and as helpfully as possible. So we should see in the 1980s a substantial elaboration of organizational programs to help people adapt in healthy ways to their work situations and to minimize the personal and organizational costs of maladaptive responses to the work. All will applaud such programs, because they will benefit both individual human beings and their employing organizations. Few will understand that the need for such programs came about, in large part, as a result of designing work and managing organizations according to the technological and motivational "efficiencies" of Route Two.

AT THE FORK IN THE ROAD

Which will it be in the 1980s—Route One or Route Two? There will be no occasion for making an explicit choice between the two. Instead, seemingly insignificant decisions about immediate questions such as how to design the next generation of a certain technology, how to motivate employees and increase their commitment to their present jobs, and how best to use the information technologies that are becoming available will determine what road we follow.

My view, based on the choices that are being made even now, is that we are moving with some vigor down Route Two. That direction, moreover, is unlikely to change in the years to come, for at least two reasons.

First, we know how to operate according to Route Two rules, and we're fumbling at best when we try to design a work unit in accord with Route One. Present theory about how to design enriched jobs and autonomous work groups is still primitive and is depressingly uninformative about how the properties of people, jobs, and organizational units *interact* in determining the consequences of a given innovative design for work. Also, we are only just beginning to develop procedures for assessing the economic costs and benefits of innovative work designs and for reconciling the dual criteria of efficiency and quality of work life in designing work systems.

Although it is not surprising, given the paucity of theory and research on work redesign, it is significant that no trained, competent cadre of managers and behavioral scientists primed to create innovative work systems in contemporary organizations exists. We do have a substantial and growing set of case studies describing successful work redesign projects, but little *systematic* knowledge about how to proceed with such work redesign activities has emerged from these studies. Moreover, there are very few instances in which even a highly successful program has been diffused throughout the larger organization in which it was developed—let alone from organization to organization—with the same success. Even the much-touted Topeka experiment has not had much of an impact on the broader General Foods organization, and it is now being viewed with a good deal of skepticism by some commentators (see, for example, "Stonewalling Plant Democracy," *Business Week,* March 28, 1977, pp. 78–82).

Second, even if we *did* know how to design and manage work according to Route One dictates, my guess is that we would decide not to do so. There are many reasons. One is that Route One solutions, if they are to prosper, require major changes in how organizations themselves are designed and managed; Route Two solutions fit nicely with traditional hierarchical organizational models and managerial practices. Another is that Route One depends heavily on behavioral science knowledge and techniques, whereas Route Two depends more on "hard" engineering technology and traditional economic models of organizational efficiency. If behavioral science has ever won out over an amalgam of engineering and economics, the case has not come to my attention. Also, the kinds of organizational changes made under Route One are likely to impoverish some managerial jobs, at least temporarily, in favor of enriched rank-and-file jobs. Route Two solutions enrich managerial jobs and make them more interesting. Given who makes the choices about how organizations are to be run, it doesn't seem to be much of a contest.

But perhaps most telling is the fact that Route Two is much more consistent with the behavioral styles and values of both employees and managers in contemporary organizations. Experienced employees know how to adapt and survive in relatively routine, unchallenging jobs. Would these people, most of whom are comfortable and secure in their work lives, leap at the chance for a wholly different kind of work experience? Some would, to be sure, especially some of the younger and more adventurous members of the work force; but I suspect that many would not. Learning how to function within a Route One organization would be a long and unpleasant process for a lot of people, and it is unclear how many would be willing to tolerate the upset and the anxiety of the change process long enough to gain a sense of what work in a Route One organization might have to offer.

Managers, too, have good reasons to be skeptical about Route One and its implications. The whole idea flies in the face of beliefs and values about people and organizations that have become very well learned and well accepted by managers of traditional organizations. Among those beliefs are that organizations are supposed to be run from the top down, not from the bottom up; that many employees have neither the competence nor the commitment to take real responsibility for carrying out the work of the organization on their own; that organizational effectiveness should be measured primarily, if not exclusively, in terms of the economic efficiency of the enterprise; and that more management control of employee behavior is better management.

Am I being too pessimistic? Perhaps. There are documented instances of employees and managers alike responding with enthusiasm to work redesign projects that had many of the trappings of the Route One approach. Yet it is troublesome to note that few of these experiments have persisted or diffused widely throughout the organizations in which they took place. Why? An optimistic view is that we do not have enough knowledge and skill yet to maintain and diffuse innovations in organizations, but that with additional research, we will soon be able to create the conditions necessary for Route One innovations to catch on and spread. The pessimistic view is that, without being fully aware of the fact, we have already progressed so far down Route Two that it may be nearly impossible to turn back.

As should be apparent from my remarks, I am in favor of the ideas and aspirations of Route One. But as may also be apparent, I suspect that the pessimistic outlook may have validity, that it may be too late to change directions, and that my description of Route Two will turn out to be a good characterization of what work will be like in the 1980s and beyond.

SELECTED BIBLIOGRAPHY

Two books frequently cited to make the case that there is a work ethic crisis are Studs Terkel's *Working* (Pantheon, 1974), in which workers' own thoughts and feelings about what they do are reported, and *Work in America* (MIT Press, 1973), the report of a special task force appointed by the secretary of health, education and welfare.

Contrary views are taken by Mitchell Fein in "The Real Needs and Goals of Blue Collar Workers" (*The Conference Board Record*, February 1972, pp. 26–33), and by William Gomberg in "Job Satisfaction: Sorting Out the Nonsense" (*AFL–CIO Federationist*, June 1973).

Several articles in the monograph *Improving Life at Work*, edited by J. Lloyd Suttle and myself (Goodyear, 1977), provide approaches to organizational change that are consistent with Route One guidelines. Included in the volume is a chapter on work design, in which I summarize the theory of individual job design developed by Greg Oldham and myself and describe the process by which changes in individual jobs are made. The classic work on individual job design has been done by Frederick Herzberg and is summarized in his new monograph, *The Managerial Choice* (Dow Jones–Irwin, 1976).

The well-known Topeka project, in which a new General Foods pet-food plant was designed using autonomous work groups as the basic organizational unit, is described in Richard Walton's "How to Counter Alienation in the Plant" (*Har-*

vard Business Review, November–December 1972, pp. 70–81). A recent analysis of that experiment is provided by Walton in "Work Innovations at Topeka: After Six Years" (*Journal of Applied Behavioral Science,* Summer 1977, pp. 422–33).

A review of the theory and application of behavior modification in organizations, which was suggested as a motivational technique central to Route Two approaches, is provided in Craig E. Schneier's "Behavior Modification in Management: A Review and Critique" (*Academy of Management Journal,* September 1974, pp. 528–48).

Problems in maintaining and diffusing Route One innovations are described and analyzed in Walton's "The Diffusion of New Work Structures: Explaining Why Success Didn't Take" (*Organizational Dynamics,* Winter 1975, pp. 3–22). Some ideas for attempting to reconcile Route One and Route Two approaches are provided by Tom Lupton in "Efficiency and the Quality of Worklife: The Technology of Reconciliation" (*Organizational Dynamics,* Autumn 1975, pp. 68–80). Last, the likely relationships among work, education, and the national economy in the future are thoughtfully probed in James O'Toole's recent book, *Work, Learning and the American Future* (Jossey–Bass, 1977).

How GM Turned Itself Around*

CHARLES G. BURCK

The perpetuation of leadership is sometimes more difficult than the attainment of that leadership in the first place. This is the greatest challenge to be met by the leader of an industry. It is a challenge to be met by the General Motors of the future.

—former Chairman Alfred P. Sloan, Jr.
My Years with General Motors (1963)

With giant corporations as with giant oil tankers, bigness confers advantages, but the ability to turn around easily is not one of them. Though General Motors does some things very well, one just doesn't expect it to be nimble. In so huge an organization, decision-making processes are inherently complex, and sheer mass generates a great deal of inertia. Four years ago, however, GM came up against the sort of challenge foreseen by Alfred Sloan. Though the company seemed ill prepared for change, it not only met the challenge but did so with a resounding success that surprised many observers of the U.S. auto industry.

The clearest evidence of GM's effective response to that challenge is the transformation of its product line to meet the demands of the marketplace —and the federal government—for better gas mileage. When the Arab oil embargo hit at the end of 1973, GM had the worst average gas mileage among U.S. automakers—a dismal 12 miles per gallon. As buyers turned away from gas-guzzlers in panic during the following year, GM's share of the U.S. new-car market slid to 42 percent, the lowest point since 1952 (not counting the strike of 1970). Just three years later, in the 1977-model year, the average mileage of GM cars, 17.8 mpg, was the *best* among the Big Three automakers. GM's big cars alone averaged 15 mpg, or 3 mpg better than the entire 1974 fleet. Largely as a result, the company's market share has rebounded to about 46 percent.

At the center of this product revolution was GM's downsizing strategy, which began last year with the big cars. GM gambled that it could redefine

* Reprinted by permission from *Fortune*, January 16, 1978, pp. 87–89, 92, 96, 100. © 1978 Time, Inc. All rights reserved.

the meaning of "big" in the American marketplace, from its traditional connotation of exterior bulk to a more functional, European-style definition based on interior space and driving quality. The gamble succeeded. In what proved to be a good year for big cars in general, GM's more than held their own against the conventional offerings of Ford and Chrysler.

The downsizing strategy is also the key to GM's hopes for the future. Despite the many difficulties and uncertainties of the auto market, General Motors is notably more confident than the other U.S. automakers of its ability to meet the government's tightening schedule of mileage laws for the years to come with cars that will still satisfy the American consumer. Says President Elliot M. Estes: "We're working on three or four scenarios for getting to 27.5 miles per gallon by 1985. It's a problem now of economics —how can we do it for the least cost?"

GM's headquarters are awash in self-assurance these days. There is more than a hint of that spirit in Chairman Thomas Aquinas Murphy's outspoken optimism about the economy, the automobile industry, and General Motors itself. Most remarkable is Murphy's unabashed determination to increase market share as much as possible—indeed, he has said on more than one occasion that he will not be satisfied "until we sell every car that's sold." That's an astonishing departure from the posture of earlier GM chief executives, who avoided *any* talk about expanding market share for fear of unleashing the hounds of antitrust.

Murphy explains his outspokenness by asking and then answering a rhetorical question.

> Should there be a limit to our return or our market penetration? I say no. The risks of the business today are as high as or higher than they've ever been, and the returns ought to be high. And if we're obeying the law, doing the best job of serving the customer, and discharging all the other responsibilities we have as a good employer and responsible citizen, then we've earned whatever we get.

Such spirit was nowhere to be found at GM four years ago. Nineteen seventy-four, in fact, seemed to confirm what many observers had been suspecting for some time—that GM was losing its capacity to lead the industry. Sloan, the man who established that leadership in the first place during the 1920s, had observed that "success may bring self-satisfaction . . . the spirit of venture is lost in the inertia of the mind against change," and it appeared in the early 1970s that his own company was fulfilling the prophecy.

Between 1962 and 1972, GM's market share drifted down from its all-time high of 51.9 percent to 44.2 percent. Most of the lost sales went to imports and did not greatly trouble GM. Following a strictly financial logic, the company concluded that it was sensible to stick with its traditional policies, which had earned it dominance of the highly profitable big-car market, rather than compete head-on in the less profitable small-car field.

For a while, events seemed to justify this reasoning. Measured in dollars, sales continued to rise. GM indisputably knew who the prime automobile customers were and how to make what they wanted.

But GM was slow to realize what besides efficiency made the imports so attractive: Agility and a certain sporty functionalism were increasingly appealing to a broader public than what GM understood as the economy market. There were executives at GM in 1970 who actually thought that—as one explained to a reporter—"there's something wrong with people who like small cars." GM's domestic and foreign competitors, knowing better, captured a lot of the growth while GM's chosen territory was contracting. Ford's market share during those years slipped only two percentage points to 24.3, while Chrysler's actually rose.

GM also seemed fundamentally out of touch with the outside world. Its size made it a natural target for antibusiness critics—especially the militant autophobes who held the auto industry responsible for everything from urban pollution to suburban sprawl. The company's reaction to its critics, as well as to the pollution and safety legislation pushed forth by the government, was defensive and even uncomprehending. Its labor relations presented a similarly sorry sight. The problems of the highly automated plant at Lordstown, Ohio, for example, which began building Vegas in 1971, became celebrated as a classic management failure to understand or communicate with employees.

Yet despite GM's insularity and self-preoccupation, managerial machinery was grinding along, resolutely if ponderously, in search of new directions. Sloan had, after all, set up a management system predicated upon change. But even important management decisions rarely show up visibly or dramatically on the outside. As Thomas Murphy says, "Drama in business lies mostly in doing well the job right before you."

New policies, moreover, like new cars, require lead times. Indeed, GM's top officers are not inclined to react with high emotion to the events of any given year, for the practical reason that in so massive an institution there is little they can do to affect the short run in any case. Experience has taught patience. They know, for example, that even a new division head cannot do much that will influence his division's results for a good 20 to 30 months. Asked about the process of change at GM, they invariably reply that it is "evolutionary, not revolutionary."

It is a characteristic of evolutionary processes, of course, that they are hard to perceive until after they have been going on for a while. GM's first response to those social-minded critics was aloof and almost brusque. But after handily turning aside their most flamboyant challenge—"Campaign GM" at the 1970 annual meeting—the company set up extensive machinery to bring new and critical thinking into its corporate planning process. It created a new public-policy committee, staffed entirely with outsiders, and the fresh viewpoints the committee brought to GM were listened to. The company also hired a number of important managers from outside—a radical departure from the tradition of near-exclusive reliance on internal management development. These people were assigned to key posts. For example, Stephen H. Fuller, who had been professor of business administration at Harvard Business School, was put in charge of the personnel administration and development staff. Ernest S. Starkman, from the school of engineering at the University of California, Berkeley, was made head of environmental activities.

The rapid turnaround of GM's product line over the past three years could not have been accomplished without a good deal of earlier thinking and planning. As far back as 1972, the board of directors created an ad hoc group called the energy task force, headed by David C. Collier, then GM's treasurer and now head of the Buick division. Collier's group included people from manufacturing, research, design, finance, and the economics staff, and it spent half a year on its research. "We came to three conclusions," said Collier. "First, that there was an energy problem. Second, the government had no particular plan to deal with it. Third, the energy problem would have a profound effect upon our business. We went to the board with those conclusions in March of 1973."

Collier's report made for a good deal of discussion throughout the company in the months following. "We were trying to get other people to think about it," says Richard C. Gerstenberg, who was then chairman of GM. Meantime, Collier's group was assigned to examine GM's product program, and when Collier reported back to the board again in October, the talk turned to what Gerstenberg refers to as "getting some downsizing in our cars."

The embargo, of course, intruded dramatically upon this rather studied planning process. But while no specific decisions had yet been made on the basis of Collier's report, the work of the task force had done much to create the right frame of mind at all levels of management. GM's board was able within two months to approve several specific proposals. Two were "crash" decisions for the 1976-model year. The Chevette would be built, using component designs from Opel and other overseas divisions, mainly Brazil; and so would the car that would become the Seville, under consideration for more than a year. And then, as Gerstenberg says, "the possible long-term program was to find a way to redesign all of our regular lines so we could get them all in a much more fuel-efficient area.

GM's product-policy committee had already decided, in April, to scale down the 1977 standard cars, but the reductions were to be modest, totaling about 400 pounds, and they were calculated to improve economy by only about one mile per gallon. By the end of 1973, however, mileage had suddenly become the overriding concern, and it was clear that practically the entire product line would eventually have to be redesigned. The biggest question, recalls Pete Estes, then executive vice president in charge of operations staffs, was where to begin. The committee's deliberations were intense, but not lengthy. The consensus that emerged, says Estes, was that "our business was family cars, so we had to start there. If we had started at the bottom, there would have been a gap for a year or so where the competition could have moved in."

The policy committee's new proposals went to the executive committee, which makes all of GM's major operational decisions (its members include the seven top officers). In December the executive committee instructed the company's engineers to come up with a plan for substantial reductions in the 1977 big cars and to start on the reductions for other body sizes in the years after.

Even as the product plans were being redrawn, GM was taking a broader look at itself—investigating how it had failed to deal with its problems and working up recommendations for change. Every summer, the executive committee undertakes what Gerstenberg calls "an inventory of people"—a review of the company's 6,000 or so top managers for possible promotion and replacement. In 1974, moreover, it was charged with picking successors to Gerstenberg and President Edward N. Cole, both of whom were retiring. In addition, the board asked the committee to take an inventory of GM's problems. Both inventories, in turn, were presented to the newly created organizations review committee, consisting mainly of the outside directors who serve on GM's bonus and salary committee. The job of this review committee was to analyze the problems and propose organizational solutions.

Many of those problems were in the process of being dealt with, of course—particularly in the transformation of the product line. But some of the most important were not so easily defined or specifically addressed. The process of running GM had grown considerably more compex since the 1950s. The business environment was still uncertain, and outside constraints had to be taken increasingly into account. The review committee wrestled with the implications of such matters during that summer; toward the end of its assignment it was augmented by Murphy, who had been nominated to replace Gerstenberg as chairman.

What the committee recommended, in September 1974, was a major reorganization at the top. That reorganization, says Murphy, "expanded importantly the top management group. Looking beyond where we were at the time, we designed it to bring new executives into a higher echelon." Complicated in its details, the reorganization upgraded the responsibilities of the executive vice presidents and added a fourth to the three already existing. The upgrading brought forward four relatively young men, all future prospects for the top, to serve on the board and the executive committee. Since the divisions now answer to top management through those executive vice presidents, the reorganization strengthened lines of authority and communication.

The reorganization also redefined and strengthened the jobs of the president and of the new vice chairman, Richard L. Terrell. Supervision of GM's eight operating staffs had previously been split between the president and the vice chairman; all were brought together under Terrell. That move freed the new president, Estes, to concentrate more fully on operations—and especially upon overseas operations, which were transferred to him from the vice chairman. Along with Ford and Chrysler, GM is planning a growing number of "world cars"—essentially similar models that can be built in the United States, Europe, or anywhere else. Though the first of those, the Chevette, was barely on the drawing boards for the United States that year, GM reasoned that overseas and domestic work could be more directly and effectively integrated if both divisions reported to Estes.

If the reorganization was a landmark event, it was in some ways less important than another change wrought in 1974—the adoption of the project center, a new concept in engineering management, devised to coordinate the efforts of the five automobile divisions. A GM project center, made up of engineers lent by the divisions, has no exact counterpart elsewhere in the auto industry—and perhaps in all of U.S. industry. NASA used the concept for the space program, and Terrell spotted it there when he was head of the nonautomotive divisions, one of which—Delco Electronics—was a NASA contractor. Sloan himself would have appreciated the concept, for it is right in line with the coordinated-decentralization approach to management.

GM adopted the project-center idea in order to meet the special demands created by the downsizing decision. Coordinating the development of a new body line among the various divisions is a complex undertaking even in normal times. To do what it wanted, the company would have to engineer its cars in a new way, using new design techniques and technologies, during a time when the margins for error and correction would be tighter than usual. Particularly under these circumstances, GM could no longer afford the old problem (by no means unique to GM) of what Estes calls "N-I-H, not invented here, a kind of disease engineers have." An engineer suffering from N-I-H resists new ideas that originate outside his bailiwick.

The project center is not a permanent group. Every time a major new effort is planned—a body changeover, say—a project center is formed, and it operates for the duration of the undertaking. Thus the A-body center, which shepherded this year's intermediates through development, ran from late 1975 until this past fall. The X-body center is now at work on next year's front-wheel-drive compacts. All project centers report to a board composed of the chief engineers of the automotive divisions.

Project centers work on parts and engineering problems common to all divisions, such as frames, electrical systems, steering gear, and brakes. Many of these are identical in every division; many others are what GM calls "common family parts"—e.g., shock absorbers—that are basically the same but are calibrated or adjusted to divisional specifications. The project center augments, but does not replace, GM's traditional "lead division" concept, in which one division is assigned primary responsibility for bringing some technical innovation into production.

The project center was probably GM's single most important managerial tool in carrying out that bold decision to downsize. It has eliminated a great deal of redundant effort and has speeded numerous new technologies into production. Its success, however, rests on the same delicate balance between the powers of persuasion and coercion that underlies GM's basic system of coordinated decentralization. "We become masters of diplomacy," says Edward Mertz, assistant chief engineer at Pontiac, who was manager of the now-disbanded A-body project center. "It's impossible to work closely on a design without influencing it somewhat. But the center can't force a common part on a division." Indeed, many of GM's engineers feel the project-center innovation has actually helped enhance the divisions' individuality, by freeing some of them to work on divisional projects.

The turnaround of the past few years has worked powerfully to lift GM's self-esteem and spirit. Spirit, of course, is a nebulous part of management, difficult to quantify. GM's state of mind has always been particularly hard to assess. Its elaborate management systems seem designed to function almost regardless of the people who work in them, and GM officers rarely waste much time telling outsiders how they feel about themselves or their company. They are practical men whose choose to be judged by results.

Indeed, the great defect of Sloan's landmark book as a management treatise was that it dealt exclusively with the practical aspects of professional management. As Peter Drucker pointed out in a critique of *My Years with General Motors,* "Something essential is lacking: people, ideas, and, above all, passion and compassion and a commitment to something more, and larger, than just the business." Sloan himself, Drucker was quick to observe, excelled at leading men and inspiring them and was a man of ideas and large commitment. But he did not talk about such matters, and it may well be that his paper legacy outlasted his personal legacy, contributing to the rather impersonal quality that has seemed to characterize GM's management during much of its recent history.

Nevertheless, there is an inescapable difference between the spirit at GM headquarters these days and what was observable a few years back. John DeLorean, who was one of GM's rising management stars, quit the company in 1973 complaining that it had "gotten to be totally insulated from the world." And Edward N. Cole retired from the presidency in 1974 with the gloomy remark that "the fun is gone . . . I wouldn't go into the automobile business again."

Today it is hard to find a top executive at GM who does not evidence enthusiasm for what he or the company is doing. The enthusiasm is most often expressed as excitement over the current "challenge" of the automobile business, and it is especially common among engineers. They agree that some of the fun may indeed have gone out of the business—as Mertz says, "You haven't got the same freedom; more of the targets are set in Washington." But meeting those targets has required a great deal of ingenuity and hard work, and the job has been enormously satisfying.

Indeed, the bottom line of change at GM is the company's state of mind—which today reflects a revivified sense of purpose and a much sharper understanding of the external world. As a practical example, it was difficult for engineers to muster much enthusiasm for their work on safety and emissions controls when the company was publicly condemning the requirements as onerous and ill conceived. GM has long since stopped complaining and has adopted a deliberately cooperative stance, in good part to restore its credibility and its battered public image. In doing so, it has transformed a major problem—the need for compliance with illogical and unfair policies—into a managerial and technical challenge.

More fundamentally, GM's entire approach to its business has changed. The company's downsizing plan was its first comprehensive new strategic attack upon the marketplace in many years. And it was shaped by a far better understanding of the market's changing nature than the strategies of the immediate past. The new top-management team that took over in 1974, moreover, was especially capable of making the new strategies work. To a degree rare among GM top managers over the years, Murphy, Estes, and Terrell are all confident, relaxed, and straightforward men, good at speaking and at listening, and broad in their vision and experience.

Indeed, a case can be made that GM has passed through one of the major turning points of its history. One authority who holds this view is Eugene E. Jennings, professor of management at Michigan State University, a consultant to top executives of numerous American corporations and a close observer of GM for more than 20 years. "In the late 1960s and early 1970s, GM was one of the most insular and inner-directed companies around," he says. "Now, more than any other company in the auto business, and more than most companies anywhere, it has moved up to a higher level of organizational effectiveness. It has learned how to be outer-directed and strategic—to use its head, rather than trying to use its clout." Jennings thinks those practical managers at GM don't fully realize as yet what they have accomplished—but he predicts that they will within a few years as they see the results accumulate.

There are tough years ahead for General Motors, unquestionably, as well as for the rest of the industry. The tug-of-war between emissions controls and fuel economy, for example, will intensify sharply under the proposed emissions standards for 1981. Publicly, GM is committed to good citizenship on the subject—the company has learned to its sorrow that credibility suffers badly when it complains about unreachable standards and then subsequently manages to meet them. But by any realistic measure, the 1981 standards are irrationally severe and, in terms of their costs, will levy enormous social disbenefits. People at GM do not talk much about the problem at present, but they may have to make the issue public at some point in the future.

The coming year, moreover, may challenge GM's downsizing strategy. The new GM intermediates are not the spectacular improvements over their predecessors that the standard cars were, and they face much stiffer competition. Ford's compact Fairmont and Zephyr, for example, are elegant designs, cleverly engineered, and are functionally comparable to the GM intermediates.

The costs of redoing the entire product line are enormous, of course. GM's R. and D. expenditures are running at an annual rate of well over $1 billion, which is equivalent to more than a third of 1976 net income ($2.9 billion, on revenues of $47 billion). By 1980, GM estimates, capital expenditures for the decade will have amounted to more than $25 billion, most of which will go to meet the demands of emissions, safety, and downsizing. And some tactical requirements are costly too. The company is selling Chevettes at a loss right now, for example—GM feels it must pay that price to establish itself more securely in the small end of the market.

Along with the problems, however, come opportunities. By downsizing the top of its line first, while competitors started from the bottom, GM has ended up with the standard-car market almost to itself for the next year or so. And that market is hardly the dinosaur preserve it may seem to be. Although all American cars are growing smaller, some will always be bigger than others. GM estimates that around 25 percent of the public will continue to want six-passenger cars into the foreseeable future.

Small cars, moreover, are turning out to be a great deal more profitable than the industry once believed them to be. Consumers at all but the rock-bottom level are evidently opting for as much automotive luxury as they can afford. As domestic automakers emerge from the struggle of meeting a concentration of expensive government demands, they can almost surely look to climbing rates of return. Those enormous capital outlays will be making a positive contribution too—they are hastening plant overhaul, providing opportunities for productivity gains and new operating efficiencies. Murphy sees no reason why GM's return on shareholders' equity should not climb back to the level of the mid-1960s—consistently above 20 percent.

Indeed, to GM's officers these days, the problems of the future look pretty pallid in comparison with those of the past few years. The system that Sloan built, with its capacity for change and evolution, has weathered a major crisis of adaptation and emerged stronger than ever. It is hard to imagine what might come along in the foreseeable future that could test General Motors more severely.

Managing in a Matrix*

HARVEY F. KOLODNY

Before its demise, for a lot of different reasons, the Applied Devices Center of Northern Electric was considered to be one of the most impressive examples of a comprehensive matrix organization. Conceived from the beginning as "The Factory of the Future," its design was based on the latest behavioral science concepts. As with so many who followed in its footsteps, the Applied Devices center wrestled daily with the difficulties of implementing its complex matrix design. Team management, specialists who reported to two or more bosses, decision making by consensus, elimination of or reductions in traditional hierarchical status devices—all demanded new behaviors from those who formed the central core of the matrix.

However, changes in behavior take time to learn. New cultures in old climates are always fragile. Other economic, marketing, and organizational woes set in before the learning was complete or the culture well established. Some eight years after it began, the Applied Devices Center was terminated. The complex processes associated with introducing the matrix design may have accelerated that unfortunate end. We will never really know. We just know that implementing a matrix organization design is tough.

Some organizations have managed to survive the difficulties. The TRW Systems Group initiated its matrix design as far back as 1959. Led by NASA, a large number of aerospace organizations followed suit soon after. Most are still going strong today. By the mid-1960s, matrix organization designs had been adopted by some of the largest domestic organizations, and towards the end of that decade "global matrix" structures were almost de rigueur for multinational companies. By the mid-seventies, usage of the matrix form had spread to government labs, hospitals and health agencies, professional firms, and a wide variety of service sector organizations.

Although the ranks of matrix adopters have swelled rapidly, there have also been some dissenters. The giant Dutch-based Philips has pulled back from matrix because of a concern for the negative impact of the design on

---

* Reprinted by permission of *Business Horizons,* March–April 1981, pp. 17–24.

entrepreneurship. And at the same time that the Chase Manhattan Bank has decided to embark on a matrix organization design, Citibank has chosen to withdraw from its elaborate matrix structure. In a recent issue of *Business Horizons,* one author has suggested that the complexity of matrix designs and the effects of that complexity on behavior, particularly strategic behavior, may be the root cause of some of those defections.[1]

Why do so many organizations continue to adopt a design that appears so difficult to manage even under the best of conditions? This article addresses this question and some of the relevant issues: namely, What are the benefits of matrix organization? What new behaviors are required? What are the difficulties of implementation? The answers to these questions suggest that interested managers must recognize the evolutionary process involved in implementing a matrix design. Managers must realize that ultimately matrix is as much or more a change in the behavior of the organization's members as it is a new structural design. Changes in behavior can take place only at a measured pace.

CONDITIONS FOR MATRIX

The question, "Why adopt a matrix organization design?" is best answered by examining some current concepts of the conditions that justify moving to a matrix. Recent research points to three such conditions:

Outside pressure for a dual focus;

A need to process large amounts of information simultaneously;

And, pressure for shared resources.[2]

The first condition, multiple orientation, recognizes that more than one orientation may be critical to managing an organization given its particular environment. A high technology manufacturing organization may have to maintain its scientific and technical knowledge or its manufacturing know-how at the state of the art while being equally responsive to changes in its market sector and product mix. An insurance company may have to respond simultaneously to product line competition (life, fire, marine, automobile) and to area differences (for example, urban versus rural, or west versus east). A human services department operating out of a central facility must continue to be effective in developing rehabilitation, corrections, social work, and psychological skills while it provides services to a variety of towns, villages, and "catchment" areas. Hence the matrix duality may be function-product, product-area, or function-area, as in each of these examples.

The second condition is a recognition of the increased amounts of information an organization must process when it tries to respond simultaneously to two critical subenvironments. The human services example is

---

[1] Thomas J. Peters, "Beyond the Matrix Organization," October 1979, pp. 15–27.

[2] Paul R. Lawrence, Harvey F. Kolodny, and Stanley M. Davis, "The Human Side of the Matrix," *Organizational Dynamics* 6, no. 1 (1979): 43–61.

an illustration. To provide effective services to a town, a "contact person," one of the interfaces between the town and the organization, must get to know all the local ways of getting help for the individuals being served. This includes knowing the local priest or minister, police, service clubs, community agencies, and business leaders if the problem is finding a job for a juvenile, qualified private homes if the problem is finding a room for a pensioner, or nursing homes if the client needs constant attention.

At the same time the contact person must know the resource capabilities of the organization: which doctors in the psychiatric group have shown a concern for teenagers in trouble; which social workers will take the time to acquire a sympathetic understanding for an older person who must be displaced from the home his or her family has lived in for generations.

With the social fabric in the town changing constantly, with new professionals coming in and out of the different functional groups, with new knowledge generated every day about problems of the young and the old, and with such knowledge showing up in all areas—rehabilitation, corrections, social work, and psychiatry—with a wide variety of contact persons with an even wider variety of clients, it is just not possible for the organization to develop and maintain an administrative system capable of matching all the different resources to all the sources of need. Nevertheless, the organization must develop the capacity to process all this information if its task of service is to be accomplished. Given this requirement, the justification for a matrix design continues to build.

Two illustrations will explore the concept of pressure for shared resources, the third condition that determines the need for a matrix organization design. In a typical industrial organization, product or business teams make up one side of the matrix (see Figure 1). At different stages in the life cycle of a product or business (product development, prototype testing, market testing, production tooling, marketing programs, product introduction, and so on) different resources are needed: design engineers, market research analysts, advertising experts, salespersons, and others.

Apart from the sequential demands, some resources may be required in quantities that are rarely large enough to justify their full-time application for even short periods (such as media experts, materials specialists, packaging consultants). Their justification for a place in the organization only comes about through shared usage. Where even sharing cannot provide that justification, product business team managers contract out for those services.

Another illustration is a government agency involved in the evaluation of many different projects. Such evaluation calls for the occasional expertise of a wide variety of specialists. To carry out its assessment of a particular project, the project leader may call on in-house economists, technical experts from a local university, and financial consultants from an international development agency. Budgetary constraints prevent the agency from hiring full-time resources as long as a continuously varying evaluation workload promises that the kinds of skills and talents needed will constantly

Figure 1
General Form of a Matrix Organization

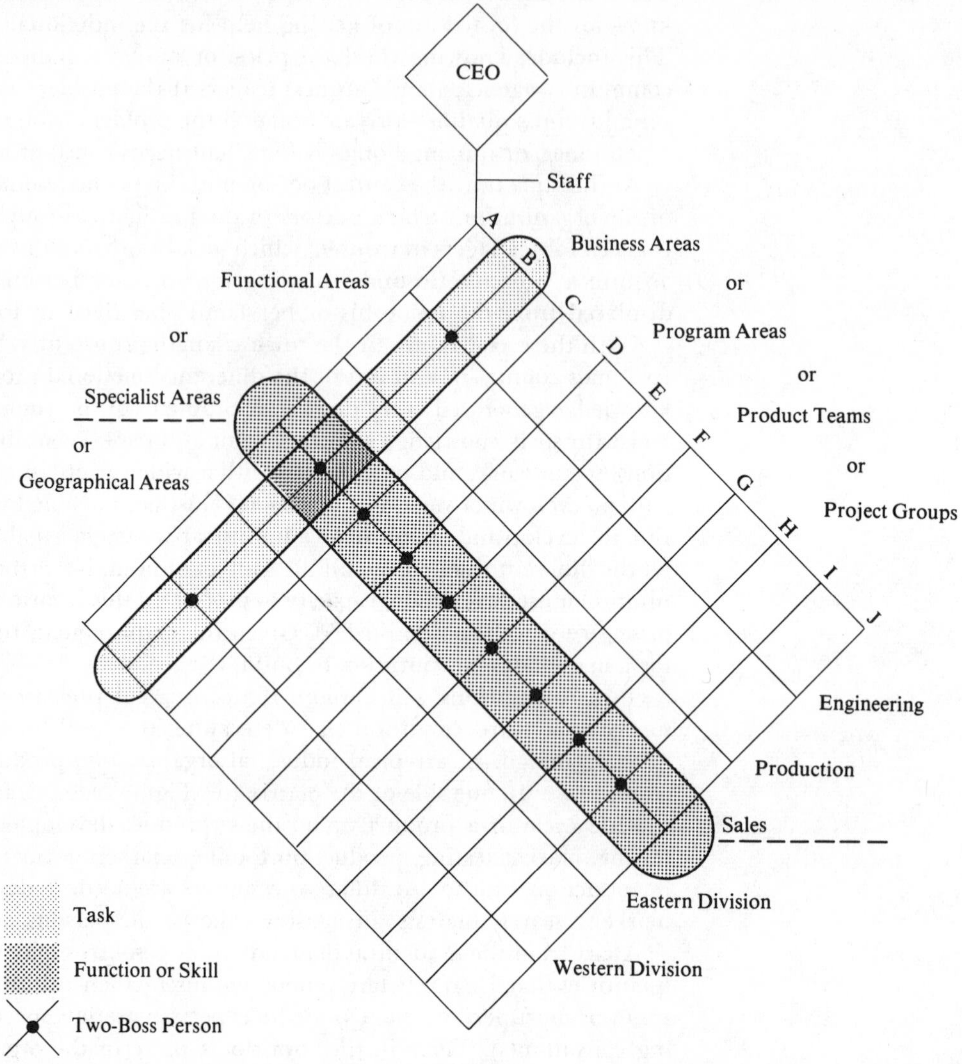

change. Sharing and contracting out for resources is the only way the agency can respond effectively to the variety in its project tasks and still stay within its budget constraints.

BENEFITS OF MATRIX

Some obvious benefits of matrix organization design flow directly from the conditions that drive organizations to adopt the form. The organization can respond simultaneously to sectors of the environment that are critical to its success. The external or environmental importance of one sector is not made secondary to the traditional arrangement (such as functional organization), since each side of the matrix has direct access to the chief executive officer and each is represented in the policy councils of the organization. There is a voice to speak directly for the importance of each of the environmental sectors, a voice that also serves as an identifiable point of contact for the constituents of that sector (customers, clients, suppliers, outside experts).

With a wide range of information to process, the organization can decentralize decision making to the level where the relevant knowledge to process that information properly and make the appropriate decision resides. This decentralization of responsibility to a particular manager provides the organization with confidence that individual "chunks" of the total organization are being managed and cared for.

While the business or product manager has the responsibility for a task, more often than not he or she has less than the required authority to carry it out. Resources are incomplete and must be shared, borrowed, or bargained for. Amongst themselves, product managers compete for capital funds and budget allocations. Functional managers negotiate for preferred people, the best facilities, and the newest equipment. Where their negotiated outcomes are unsatisfactory, they search outside the organization and its constituencies of outsiders (clients, suppliers); as a result, they transact heavily with that external world. The reality of their situations drives them into an extensive network of lateral communication—they have far more horizontal interactions than vertical contacts with their bosses. This is the way that matrix organization's capacity to process large amounts of information manifests itself.

With so much of the management decentralized, the upper level of the organization is not overloaded with operational decisions. The span of control of the CEO can be large because he or she is freed from day-to-day decisions. The CEO's information is good because it comes through fewer levels of hierarchy, fewer filters to absorb and distort relevant information about the markets, competitors, and changes in the relevant environmental sectors. Conversely, policy decisions are made in concert with those most in control of the relevant information, most capable of transmitting them with a minimum of distortion, and most responsible for making them happen.

The benefits from the third condition are clear. Resource utilization is efficient. With everyone double-counted, the matrix allows no place to hide. Key resources can be shared across several important programs or products at the same time. The organization can flexibly accommodate the different phases through which its products and programs pass. Information transfers easily from the program side to the functional through the shared personnel.

NEW BEHAVIORS IN THE MATRIX

Four particular roles are signficantly changed as an organization moves to a matrix design. The chief executive officer or person heading up the matrix organization (at the apex of the diamond in Figure 1) must learn to balance power between the dual orientations. The product or program managers become minigeneral managers and must learn the functions of general management. Most of all they must learn to stop being their own specialists. The functional managers must learn an entirely new style of behavior: proactive rather than reactive. Finally, the two-boss persons must learn to live with ambiguity.

The person at the apex of the matrix is the CEO if the entire organization is the unit under consideration. The matrix organization succeeds or fails according to how well that CEO understands how it works. A key element of that understanding is the importance of the appropriate balance of power.

Power must shift as the environment does. When economic times are tough, the power must swing to the product side. It is the product managers who have the short-term profit and loss orientation necessary for survival. When the environment is benevolent or generous, then it is the functions that must have the resources to advance the states-of-the-art in their specialties. During such economic times, the organization's competitors will also be investing in their functional areas. The organization cannot afford to lag too far behind if it is to maintain its competitive position. The functional competencies are, in the end, what the organization "is about"— in other words, what it brings to bear against the environment in order to give itself a justification for existing, for carving out a niche or domain in the larger society. Functional competence can occasionally be diminished when short-run survival is the issue; but in the long run it must be carefully guarded. Power balancing in the matrix is a matter of the *appropriate* balance for the particular situation.

To maintain the appropriate balance the CEO needs tools—organization mechanisms or support systems or processes—that can help to shift the emphasis when it needs to be shifted. However, it is not a single organizational issue that establishes an appropriate balance. It isn't even several. It is many. Understanding them and knowing how to manipulate them is what gives the CEO the ability to adjust the balance. Figure 2 illustrates a typical set of organizational issues (processes, systems, even concepts) that balance power in a product-function matrix structure. For the CEO who understands how to manipulate them, they are the levers for change.

Product or program managers (PMs) are usually chosen from the ranks of the particular functional area that is dominant for that organization. Hence, in engineering companies, engineers become PMs; in consumer marketing companies it is the marketers who get the job; in insurance companies it is actuaries, and in hospitals it is doctors. There are many reasons why: (1) PMs must be from the dominant specialty if they are to acquire credibility in the organization (where most of the power lies with the dominant function or functions); (2) they must be able to order the problems (but not necessarily solve them); (3) they can determine a good fit between the requirements of the subenvironment they face (e.g., market sector) and the resources or technical strengths the organization possesses;

Figure 2
The Balance of Power in a Matrix Organization

Function	Product/Project
	← *Gestalt Authority*
	Product managers are responsible for something whole which, no matter how small, is a type of perceived authority no functional manager obtains.
Sell Outside →|←	*Contract Outside*
The right to sell resources outside the organization, making the functional manager who does so also a product manager.	The right to buy/access resources outside the organization, even when same are available inside.
	← *Profit and Loss Responsibility*
	A measure of performance congruent with the way the organization itself is measured, suggesting high importance.
Control Over Technological Uncertainty →|←	*Control Over Market or Customer Uncertainty*
Control over important environmental uncertainties for the specialist areas gives off significant perceptions of power.	Control over important environmental uncertainties for the market segments of the different product lines gives off significant perceptions of power.
Nonsubstitutability (of unique resources) →←	*Rewards*
Control over the availability and development of resources not available elsewhere gives off significant real and perceived power.	Rewarding product managers more than functional managers and signaling same to the organizational shifts power to the product side.
People Management →|←	*Job Titles*
Hiring, firing, training, promoting, career trajectory decisions belong to the functional managers.	A fictitious perception of power accruing to the seemingly large group of similarly titled program managers, whose different goals rarely cause them to cooperate.
Reporting Level →|←	*Access to Leader*
Functional managers report directly to the CEO; a relationship obvious to the organization.	Product managers usually report to managers of product managers who serve as their functional bosses (of how to manage products and programs) while the CEO is their product boss and, as such, always provides them with direct access to himself or herself.
Career Evaluation →|←	*Performance Evaluation*
The functional managers exercise a powerful influence over the career trajectories of most people in the organization.	The product managers provide crucial inputs to the short-run appraisal of product/program people, particularly when such people are physically located with the product group.
Top Management Meetings →|←	*Control Over Budget*
Frequently (often weekly) operations meeting to manage the organization include the CEO and the first level functional managers, but usually not the product managers.	Product managers often have control over the budgeted dollars and negotiate with functional managers for needed resources.

and (4) the clients and subenvironments expect that it is just that type of person with whom they will interact.

Just because the PMs are so often drawn from the ranks of the dominant specialist function, there are problems created for that office. The PMs can be effective only if they *do not* become their own specialists—for example, their own project managers. It is hard for them not to want to do so. If they do, however, they will not tend to the particular external world they were

explicitly established to manage. In effect, they must become general management oriented. They must be wise enough in their knowledge of how
the dominant specialty works to put priorities on problems; but they must
be broad enough to see themselves in charge of a total program or product
line, not merely its specialist aspects.

Functional managers, long the repository of their particular skills within
their organizations, must stop functioning like librarians, that is, waiting
for people to come to them because they control the source of a particular
skill or knowledge or discipline for the organization. If PMs are truly to
manage their subenvironments, they need functional managers to take care
of their backside by managing the people and other internal aspects of the
product team. Functional managers are equipped to do so because they
normally have a long-run view of the organization. They should be able to
anticipate a product manager's functional needs.

However, this requires a *proactive* stance from functional managers.
Learning to say to PMs who are frequently much younger and have much
less seniority than the functional managers, "How can I help you?" is difficult for functional managers to learn to do. If they don't learn to do it,
however, the matrix often degenerates into acrimonious "we-they" squab-
bles as the product managers, overloaded with managing both internal and
external issues, fault the functions for not being sufficiently supportive. To
forestall this, functional managers must learn to go to the product managers. For some functional managers, this entails radically new behavior
and may take a long while to learn. The CEO must often intervene to keep
the peace while the new roles are being learned and understood. The personal stress can get quite high.

Last, but not least, in the list of those who must learn new behaviors are
the two-boss persons. For some, the ambiguity of the job is a reawakening,
an opportunity to flower and bloom, to carve out a role that fits better than
anything hierarchical organizations ever offered them. For others, it is a
disaster. It is not just a complex role that they cannot learn. It is more that
the clear career trajectory they once viewed has been suddenly truncated,
and just above the place where they are currently positioned. The dyadic
superior-subordinate behaviors of bureaucracies die hard. They take a
while to learn, and we have no idea how long they take to unlearn. Unfortunately, organizations often have less tolerance for the time that it takes
supervisors to learn to become "coordinators" in their new two-boss roles
than they do for the higher level functional managers who must learn to
become proactive. For some would-be two-boss persons, the coming of
matrix spells the end of a career.

Can people learn the needed new behaviors? Some can and can even do
so themselves. Others cannot. Even the retraining skills of many organizations are not adequate to help the second group. Many of them would be
better off continuing their careers in a more traditional form of organization.

The personnel implications of the preceding paragraph are frequently not as frightening as they at first appear. Not everyone need be involved in the new matrix behaviors. In a manufacturing organization, those actively involved in the dual functional orientations may be as few as 5 percent of the organization's members. They will comprise the product and functional managers and their next level of subordinates and not very many others. For the rest of the people, the organization will continue to function quite traditionally. For example, a two-boss person may be both a manufacturing manager for a program and a member of the functional manufacturing group. He or she may have several or several hundred subordinates reporting through a traditional hierarchical structure. The vast majority of those people might go on about their work quite oblivious to the existence of a matrix structure at the top.

Alternatively, if the matrix is in a professional organization, for example, a consulting firm where planners, architects, and engineers are shared across different projects, everyone, including the office secretaries, may feel the effects of the matrix design.

IMPLEMENTA-TION

For those who can learn the requisite new behaviors there is much to learn: conflict resolution, confrontation skills, negotiation skills, meeting management. Most organizations can work out the new needs. These issues are important to the individuals involved and they must be addressed. But they won't make or break the matrix. Because the anxieties of individuals are concerned, the organization must pay some attention to the two-boss roles; but it must pay much more attention to how the rest of the matrix works and not be seduced into believing that the "bottom cross-over points" are the dominant areas of concern. The two-boss roles will work out well if the CEO and the product and functional managers understand and carry out their required roles. They will never work out well if these high level roles are not well performed.

Getting started is difficult. If the organization has been a functional one, where do the product bosses come from? If they are capable but low level younger managers, will it take too long before they can swing the balance of power even a little bit away from the entrenched positions of strong functional managers? If the new product managers come from the ranks of the senior functional managers, will they be capable of acquiring a general management orientation? How long can the organization operate with the confusion of whether the ex-functional managers are exercising the new roles appropriately and of whether subordinate managers are able to cast off their deference to the historic roles these managers held? If the new product managers come from outside, will it be too much to expect them to both gain credibility and make a possibly unpopular structural change work?

Starting up is indeed difficult. It is best if everyone is clear in their understanding that it is going to be a very different way of working. If the organization has had considerable lateral communication and has begun to be familiar with interpersonal methods of information processing, the transition should come easier. (As an aside, if the organization hasn't had a lot of such experience, there is a real question about whether it is an environment that truly demands a matrix design.) There must be mechanisms to allow people to raise their concerns (1) about how the matrix works, and (2) what impact it might have on their individual jobs.

There are stages toward the development of an effective matrix organization design.[3] The process demands a significant amount of behavioral, structural, and cultural change and will necessarily take a long time. It will be costly. The organization that chooses to adopt a matrix design had first better be certain it cannot possibly manage its tasks in a simpler way before embarking on a matrix journey.

---

[3] See Harvey F. Kolodny, "Evolution to a Matrix Organization," *Academy of Management Review* 4, no. 4 (1979): 543–53.

Organization Design:
An Information Processing View*

JAY R. GALBRAITH

THE INFORMATION PROCESSING MODEL

A basic proposition is that the greater the uncertainty of the task, the greater the amount of information that has to be processed between decision makers during the execution of the task. If the task is well understood prior to performing it, much of the activity can be preplanned. If it is not understood, then during the actual task execution more knowledge is acquired which leads to changes in resource allocations, schedules, and priorities. All these changes require information processing *during* task performance. Therefore *the greater the task uncertainty, the greater the amount of information that must be processed among decision makers during task execution in order to achieve a given level of performance.* The basic effect of uncertainty is to limit the ability of the organization to preplan or to make decisions about activities in advance of their execution. Therefore it is hypothesized that the observed variations in organizational forms are variations in the strategies of organizations to (1) increase their ability to preplan, (2) increase their flexibility to adapt to their inability to preplan, or (3) to decrease the level of performance required for continued viability. Which strategy is chosen depends on the relative costs of the strategies. The function of the framework is to identify these strategies and their costs.

THE MECHANISTIC MODEL

This framework is best developed by keeping in mind a hypothetical organization. Assume it is large and employs a number of specialist groups and resources in providing the output. After the task has been divided into specialist subtasks, the problem is to integrate the subtasks around the

* Reprinted from "Organizational Design: An Information Processing View," by Jay R. Galbraith, *Interfaces* 4, no. 3 (May 1974): 28–36, published by the Institute of Management Sciences.

completion of the global task. This is the problem of organization design. The behaviors that occur in one subtask cannot be judged as good or bad per se. The behaviors are more effective or ineffective depending upon the behaviors of the other subtask performers. There is a design problem because the executors of the behaviors cannot communicate with all the roles with whom they are interdependent. Therefore the design problem is to create mechanisms that permit coordinated action across large numbers of interdependent roles. Each of these mechanisms, however, has a limited range over which it is effective at handling the information requirements necessary to coordinate the interdependent roles. As the amount of uncertainty increases, and therefore information processing increases, the organization must adopt integrating mechanisms which increase its information processing capabilities.

1. Coordination by Rules or Programs

For routine predictable tasks March and Simon have identified the use of rules or programs to coordinate behavior between interdependent subtasks (March and Simon, 1958, chap. 6). To the extent that job related situations can be predicted in advance, and behaviors specified for these situations, programs allow an interdependent set of activities to be performed without the need for interunit communication. Each role occupant simply executes the behavior which is appropriate for the task related situation with which he is faced.

2. Hierarchy

As the organization faces greater uncertainty its participants face situations for which they have no rules. At this point the hierarchy is employed on an exception basis. The recurring job situations are programmed with rules while infrequent situations are referred to that level in the hierarchy where a global perspective exists for all affected subunits. However, the hierarchy also has a limited range. As uncertainty increases the number of exceptions increases until the hierarchy becomes overloaded.

3. Coordination by Targets or Goals

As the uncertainty of the organization's task increases, coordination increasingly takes place by specifying outputs, goals, or targets (March and Simon, 1958, p. 145). Instead of specifying specific behaviors to be enacted, the organization undertakes processes to set goals to be achieved and the employees select the behaviors which lead to goal accomplishment. Planning reduces the amount of information processing in the hierarchy by increasing the amount of discretion exercised at lower levels. Like the use of rules, planning achieves integrated action and also eliminates the need for continuous communication among interdependent subunits as long as task performance stays within the planned task specifications, budget limits and within targeted completion dates. If it does not, the hierarchy is again employed on an exception basis.

The ability of an organization to coordinate interdependent tasks depends on its ability to compute meaningful subgoals to guide subunit action. When uncertainty increases because of introducing new products, entering new markets, or employing new technologies these subgoals are incorrect. The result is more exceptions, more information processing, and an overloaded hierarchy.

DESIGN
STRATEGIES

The ability of an organization to successfully utilize coordination by goal setting, hierarchy, and rules depends on the combination of the frequency of exceptions and the capacity of the hierarchy to handle them. As the task uncertainty increases, the organization must again take organization design action. It can proceed in either of two general ways. First, it can act in two ways to reduce the amount of information that is processed. And second, the organization can act in two ways to increase its capacity to handle more information. The two methods for reducing the need for information and the two methods for increasing processing capacity are shown schematically in Figure 1. The effect of all these actions is to reduce

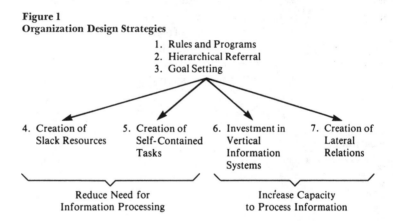

Figure 1
Organization Design Strategies

1. Rules and Programs
2. Hierarchical Referral
3. Goal Setting

4. Creation of Slack Resources
5. Creation of Self-Contained Tasks
6. Investment in Vertical Information Systems
7. Creation of Lateral Relations

Reduce Need for Information Processing

Increase Capacity to Process Information

the number of exceptional cases referred upward into the organization through hierarchical channels. The assumption is that the critical limiting factor of an organizational form is its ability to handle the nonroutine, consequential events that cannot be anticipated and planned for in advance. The nonprogrammed events place the greatest communication load on the organization.

1. Creation of
Slack Resources

As the number of exceptions begin to overload the hierarchy, one response is to increase the planning targets so that fewer exceptions occur. For example, completion dates can be extended until the number of exceptions that occur are within the existing information processing capacity of the organization. This has been the practice in solving job shop scheduling problems (Pounds, 1963). Job shops quote delivery times that are long enough to keep the scheduling problem within the computational and information processing limits of the organization. Since every job shop has the same problem standard lead times evolve in the industry. Similarly, budget targets could be raised, buffer inventories employed, and so on. The greater the uncertainty, the greater the magnitude of the inventory, lead time or budget needed to reduce an overload.

All of these examples have a similar effect. They represent the use of slack resources to reduce the amount of interdependence between subunits (March and Simon, 1958, Cyert and March, 1963). This keeps the required amount of information within the capacity of the organization to process it. Information processing is reduced because an exception is less likely to occur and reduced interdependence means that fewer factors need to be considered simultaneously when an exception does occur.

The strategy of using slack resources has its costs. Relaxing budget targets has the obvious cost of requiring more budget. Increasing the time to completion date has the effect of delaying the customer. Inventories require the investment of capital funds which could be used elsewhere. Reduction of design optimization reduces the performance of the article being designed. Whether slack resources are used to reduce information or not depends on the relative cost of the other alternatives.

The design choices are: (1) among which factors to change (lead time, overtime, machine utilization, and the like) to create the slack, and (2) by what amount should the factor be changed. Many operations research models are useful in choosing factors and amounts. The time-cost trade-off problem in project networks is a good example.

2. Creation of Self-Contained Tasks

The second method of reducing the amount of information processed is to change the subtask groupings from resource (input) based to output based categories and give each group the resources it needs to supply the output. For example, the functional organization could be changed to product groups. Each group would have its own product engineers, process engineers, fabricating and assembly operations, and marketing activities. In other situations, groups can be created around product lines, geographical areas, projects, client groups, markets, and so on, each of which would contain the input resources necessary for creation of the output.

The strategy of self-containment shifts the basis of the authority structure from one based on input, resource skill, or occupational categories to one based on output or geographical categories. The shift reduces the amount of information processing through several mechanisms. First, it reduces the amount of output diversity faced by a single collection of resources. For example, a professional organization with multiple skill specialties providing service to three different client groups must schedule the use of these specialties across three demands for their services and determine priorities when conflicts occur. But, if the organization changed to three groups, one for each client category, each with its own full complement of specialties, the schedule conflicts across client groups disappear and there is no need to process information to determine priorities.

The second source of information reduction occurs through a reduced division of labor. The functional or resource specialized structure pools the demand for skills across all output categories. In the example above each client generates approximately one third of the demand for each skill. Since the division of labor is limited by the extent of the market, the division of labor must decrease as the demand decreases. In the professional organization, each client group may have generated a need for one third of a computer programmer. The functional organization would have hired one programmer and shared him across the groups. In the self-contained structure there is insufficient demand in each group for a programmer so the professionals must do their own programming. Specialization is reduced but there is no problem of scheduling the programmer's time across the three possible uses for it.

The cost of the self-containment strategy is the loss of resource specialization. In the example, the organization forgoes the benefit of specialist in computer programming. If there is physical equipment, there is a loss of economies of scale. The professional organization would require three machines in the self-contained form but only a large time-shared machine in the functional form. But those resources which have large economies of scale or for which specialization is necessary may remain centralized. Thus, it is the degree of self-containment that is the variable. The greater the degree of uncertainty, other things equal, the greater the degree of self-containment.

The design choices are the basis for the self-contained structure and the number of resources to be contained in the groups. No groups are completely self-contained or they would not be part of the same organization. But one product divisionalized firm may have 8 of 15 functions in the division while another may have 12 of 15 in the division. Usually accounting, finance, and legal services are centralized and shared. Those functions which have economies of scale, require specialization or are necessary for control remain centralized and not part of the self-contained group.

The first two strategies reduced the amount of information by lower performance standards and creating small autonomous groups to provide the output. Information is reduced because an exception is less likely to occur and fewer factors need to be considered when an exception does occur. The next two strategies accept the performance standards and division of labor as given and adapt the organization so as to process the new information which is created during task performance.

3. Investment in Vertical Information Systems

The organization can invest in mechanisms which allow it to process information acquired during task performance without overloading the hierarchical communication channels. The investment occurs according to the following logic. After the organization has created its plan or set of targets for inventories, labor utilization, budgets, and schedules, unanticipated events occur which generate exceptions requiring adjustments to the original plan. At some point when the number of exceptions becomes substantial, it is preferable to generate a new plan rather than make incremental changes with each exception. The issue is then how frequently should plans be revised—yearly, quarterly, or monthly? The greater the frequency of replanning the greater the resources, such as clerks, computer time, input-output devices, and the like, required to process information about relevant factors.

The cost of information processing resources can be minimized if the language is formalized. Formalization of a decision-making language simply means that more information is transmitted with the same number of symbols. It is assumed that information processing resources are consumed in proportion to the number of symbols transmitted. The accounting system is an example of a formalized language.

Providing more information, more often, may simply overload the decision maker. Investment may be required to increase the capacity of the decision maker by employing computers, various man-machine combinations, assistants-to, and so on. The cost of this strategy is the cost of the information processing resources consumed in transmitting and processing data.

The design variables of this strategy are the decision frequency, the degree of formalization of language, and the type of decision mechanism which will make the choice. This strategy is usually operationalized by creating redundant information channels which transmit data from the point of origination upward in the hierarchy where the point of decision rests. If data is formalized and quantifiable, this strategy is effective. If the relevant data are qualitative and ambiguous, then it may prove easier to bring the decision down to where the information exists.

4. Creation of Lateral Relationships

The best strategy is to employ selectively joint decision processes which cut across lines of authority. This strategy moves the level of decision making down in the organization to where the information exists but does so without reorganizing around self-contained groups. There are several types of lateral decision processes. Some processes are usually referred to as the informal organization. However, these informal processes do not always arise spontaneously out of the needs of the task. This is particularly true in multinational organizations in which participants are separated by physical barriers, language differences, and cultural differences. Under these circumstances lateral processes need to be designed. The lateral processes evolve as follows with increases in uncertainty.

4.1. Direct Contact.   Between managers who share a problem. If a problem arises on the shop floor, the foreman can simply call the design engineer, and they can jointly agree upon a solution. From an information processing view, the joint decision prevents an upward referral and unloads the hierarchy.

4.2. Liaison Roles.   When the volume of contacts between any two departments grows, it becomes economical to set up a specialized role to handle this communication. Liaison men are typical examples of specialized roles designed to facilitate communication between two interdependent departments and to bypass the long lines of communcation involved in upward referral, Liaison roles arise at lower and middle levels of management.

4.3.   Task Forces.   Direct contact and liaison roles, like the integration mechanisms before them, have a limited range of usefulness. They work when two managers or functions are involved. When problems arise involving seven or eight departments, the decision-making capacity of direct contacts is exceeded. Then these problems must be referred upward. For uncertain, interdependent tasks such situations arise frequently. Task forces are a form of horizontal contact which is designed for problems of multiple departments.

The task force is made up of representatives from each of the affected departments. Some are full-time members, others may be part-time. The task force is a temporary group. It exists only as long as the problem remains. When a solution is reached, each participant returns to his normal tasks.

To the extent that they are successful, task forces remove problems from higher levels of the hierarchy. The decisions are made at lower levels in the organization. In order to guarantee integration, a group problem-solving approach is taken. Each affected subunit contributes a member and therefore provides the information necessary to judge the impact on all units.

4.4.   Teams.   The next extension is to incorporate the group decision process into the permanent decision processes. That is, as certain decisions consistently arise, the task forces become permanent. These groups are labeled teams. There are many design issues concerned in team decision making such as at what level do they operate, who participates, and so on (Galbraith, 1973, chaps. 6 and 7). One design decision is particularly critical. This is the choice of leadership. Sometimes a problem exists largely in one department so that the department manager is the leader. Sometimes the leadership passes from one manager to another. As a new product moves to the market place, the leader of the new product team is first the technical manager followed by the production and then the marketing manager. The result is that, if the team cannot reach a consensus decision and the leader decides, the goals of the leader are consistent with the goals of the organization for the decision in question. But quite often obvious leaders cannot be found. Another mechanism must be introduced.

4.5.   Integrating Roles.   The leadership issue is solved by creating a new role—an integrating role (Lawrence and Lorsch, 1967, chap. 3). These roles carry the labels of product managers, program managers, project managers, unit managers (hospitals), materials managers, and the like. After the role is created, the design problem is to create enough power in the role to influence the decision process. These roles have power even when no one reports directly to them. They have some power because they report to the general manager. But if they are selected so as to be unbiased with respect to the groups they integrate and to have technical competence, they have expert power. They collect information and equalize power differences due to preferential access to knowledge and information. The power equalization increases trust and the quality of the joint decision process. But power equalization occurs only if the integrating role is staffed with someone who can exercise expert power in the form of persuasion and informal influences rather than exert the power of rank or authority.

4.6. Managerial Linking Roles. As tasks become more uncertain, it is more difficult to exercise expert power. The role must get more power of the formal authority type in order to be effective at coordinating the joint decisions which occur at lower levels of the organization. This position power changes the nature of the role which for lack of a better name is labeled a managerial linking role. It is not like the integrating role because it possesses formal position power but is different from line managerial roles in that participants do not report to the linking manager. The power is added by the following successive changes:

a. The integrator receives approval power of budgets formulated in the departments to be integrated.

b. The planning and budgeting process starts with the integrator making his initiation in budgeting legitimate.

c. Linking manager receives the budget for the area of responsibility and buys resources from the specialist groups.

These mechanisms permit the manager to exercise influence even though no one works directly for him. The role is concerned with integration but exercises power through the formal power of the position. If this power is insufficient to integrate the subtasks and creation of self-contained groups is not feasible, there is one last step.

4.7. Matrix Organization. The last step is to create the dual authority relationship and the matrix organization (Galbraith, 1971). At some point in the organization some roles have two superiors. The design issue is to select the locus of these roles. The result is a balance of power between the managerial linking roles and the normal line organization roles. Figure 2 depicts the pure matrix design.

The work of Lawrence and Lorsch is highly consistent with the assertions concerning lateral relations (Lawrence and Lorsch, 1967, Lorsch and Lawrence, 1968). They compared the types of lateral relations undertaken by the most successful firm in three different industries. Their data are summarized in Table 1. The plastics firm has the greatest rate of new product introduction (uncertainty) and the greatest utilization of lateral processes. The container firm was also very successful but utilized only standard practices because its information processing task is much less formidable. Thus, the greater the uncertainty the lower the level of decision making and the integration is maintained by lateral relations.

Table 1 points out the cost of using lateral relations. The plastics firm

Figure 2
A Pure Matrix Organization

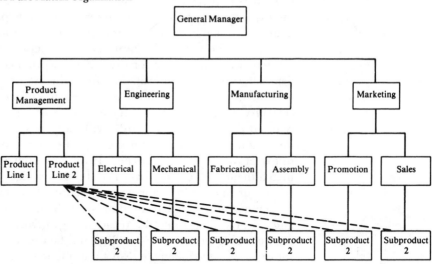

---- ⸗ Technical authority over product
——— ⸗ Formal authority over product (in product
organization, these relationships may be reversed)

Table 1

	Plastics	*Food*	*Container*
Percent new products in last ten years	35%	20%	0%
Integrating devices	Rules	Rules	Rules
	Hierarchy	Hierarchy	Hierarchy
	Planning	Planning	Planning
	Direct contact	Direct contact	Direct contact
	Teams at 3 levels	Task forces	
	Integrating department	Integrators	
Percent integrators/managers	22%	17%	0%

Source: Adopted from Lawrence and Lorsch, 1967, pp. 86–138 and Lorsch and Lawrence, 1968.

has 22 percent of its managers in integration roles. Thus, the greater the use of lateral relations the greater the managerial intensity. This cost must be balanced against the cost of slack resources, self-contained groups, and information systems.

CHOICE OF STRATEGY   Each of the four strategies has been briefly presented. The organization can follow one or some combination of several if it chooses. It will choose that strategy which has the least cost in its environmental context. (For an example, see Galbraith, 1970.) However, what may be lost in all of the explanations is that the four strategies are hypothesized to be an exhaustive set of alternatives. That is, if the organization is faced with greater uncertainty due to technological change, higher performance standards due to increased competition, or diversifies its product line to reduce dependence, the amount of information processing is increased. *The organization must adopt at least one of the four strategies when faced with greater uncertainty.* If it does not consciously choose one of the four, then the first, reduced performance standards, will happen automatically. The task information requirements and the capacity of the organization to process information are always matched. If the organization does not consciously match them, reduced performance through budget and schedule overruns will occur in order to bring about equality. Thus the organization should be planned and designed simultaneously with the planning of the strategy and resource allocations. But if the strategy involves introducing new products, entering new markets, and so on, then some provision for increased information must be made. Not to decide is to decide, and it is to decide upon slack resources as the strategy to remove hierarchical overload.

There is probably a fifth strategy which is not articulated here. Instead of changing the organization in response to task uncertainty, the organization can operate on its environment to reduce uncertainty. The organization through strategic decisions, long-term contracts, coalitions, and the like, can control its environment. But these maneuvers have costs also. They should be compared with costs of the four design strategies presented above.

SUMMARY

The purpose of this paper has been to explain why task uncertainty is related to organizational form. In so doing the cognitive limits theory of Herbert Simon was the guiding influence. As the consequences of cognitive limits were traced through the framework, various organization design strategies were articulated. The framework provides a basis for integrating organizational interventions, such as information systems and group problem solving, which have been treated separately before.

BIBLIOGRAPHY

Cyert, Richard, and James March. *The Behavioral Theory of the Firm*. Englewood Cliffs, N.J.: Prentice-Hall, 1963.

Galbraith, Jay. "Environmental and Technological Determinants of Organization Design: A Case Study." In *Studies in Organization Design*, edited by Lawrence and Lorsch. Homewood, Ill.: Richard D. Irwin, 1970.

Galbraith, Jay. "Designing Matrix Organizations." *Business Horizons*, February 1971, pp. 29–40.

Galbraith, Jay. *Organization Design*. Reading, Mass.: Addison-Wesley Publishing, 1973.

Lawrence, Paul, and Jay Lorsch. *Organization and Environment*. Boston: Division of Research, Harvard Business School, 1967.

Lorsch, Jay, and Paul Lawrence. "Environmental Factors and Organization Integration." Paper read at the Annual Meeting of the American Sociological Association, August 27, 1967, Boston, Mass.

Match, James, and Herbert Simon. *Organizations*. New York: John Wiley & Sons, 1958.

Pounds, William. "The Scheduling Environment." In *Industrial Scheduling*, edited by Muth and Thompson. Englewood Cliffs, N.J.: Prentice-Hall, Inc., 1963.

Simon, Herbert. *Models of Man*. New York: John Wiley & Sons, 1957.

Part V

PROCESSES WITHIN ORGANIZATIONS

This part of the book contains articles related to fundamental processes which are vital to the effective functioning of every organization: communicating, decision making, evaluation, and career development. The flow of the preceding sections leads logically to a discussion of organizational processes. People behave as individuals and as members of groups within an organization structure and communicate for many reasons, one of which is to make decisions. The evaluation and reward processes of any organization rely upon communication and require that decisions be made. In fact, some of the most important purposes of an organization structure are to evaluate, reward, and to facilitate the processes of communication and decision making.

It would be extremely difficult to find an aspect of a manager's job that does not involve communication. Serious problems arise when directives are misunderstood, when casual kidding leads to anger, or when informal remarks by a manager are distorted. Each of these is a result of a breakdown somewhere in the process of communication.

An article on this topic, "Communication Revisited" by Jay Hall, begins by stating that 74 percent of the managers sampled in a cross-cultural study reported communication breakdown as the single greatest barrier to organizational effectiveness. Hall notes that communication problems cited by people are not communication problems as such, but rather symptoms of difficulties at more fundamental levels of organizational life. He believes that the problems of communication in organizations are the feelings people have about where or with whom they work and that the quality of relationships in an organization greatly influence the effectiveness of communication. He then sets out to review what he believes is the critical factor underlying the quality of relationships in organizations: the interpersonal style of the parties to a relationship.

John E. Baird, Jr., and Gretchen K. Wieting in "Nonverbal Communication Can Be a Motivational Tool" discuss the powerful impact of nonverbal communication. The authors discuss postures, gestures, the environment, facial expressions, eye behavior, and vocalics. They believe that managers can learn to control nonverbal behaviors on their own and with training.

The next article discusses hunches and is by Roy Rowan. It is entitled "Those Business Hunches Are More Than Blind Faith." "I feel," "intuition," and "hunches" are what Rowan discusses in the article. Some executives make decisions and solve problems using hunches and not computer logic or specific guidelines. Rowan discusses examples of "hunches" which proved to be success stories. The occasional hunch may be healthy and good policy for executives. As Rowan would state, this is only a hunch.

Craig Schneier and Richard W. Beatty discuss performance appraisal in their article entitled "Integrating Behaviorally-Based and Effectiveness-Based Appraisal Methods." First, the authors discuss job performance. Second, they introduce their view of performance appraisal. Third, they compare a number of rating formats—global, trait, behavior, and effectiveness. Various sources of problems in the appraisal process are shown in a model. Included are problems of judgment, raters, criteria, policy, legislation and inflexibility.

The final article in Part V is "Thinking Clearly about Career Choices" by Irving Janis and Dan Wheeler. Avoiding career mistakes is a concern of the authors. They illustrate two risky career scenarios. A manager's balance sheet to help make decisions is presented to readers. Finally, Janis and Wheeler discuss stress inoculation as a method to make better quality decisions.

Communication Revisited*

JAY HALL

High on the diagnostic checklist of corporate health is communication; and the prognosis is less than encouraging. In a recent cross-cultural study,[1] roughly 74 percent of the managers sampled from companies in Japan, Great Britain, and the United States cited communication breakdown as the single greatest barrier to corporate excellence.

Just what constitutes a problem of communication is not easily agreed upon. Some theorists approach the issue from the vantage point of information bits comprising a message; others speak in terms of organizational roles and positions of centrality or peripherality; still others emphasize the directional flows of corporate data. The result is that more and more people are communicating about communication, while the achievement of clarity, understanding, commitment, and creativity—the goals of communication— becomes more and more limited.

More often than not, the communication dilemmas cited by people are not communication problems at all. They are instead *symptoms* of difficulties at more basic and fundamental levels of corporate life. From a dynamic standpoint, problems of communication in organizations frequently reflect dysfunctions at the level of *corporate climate*. The feelings people have about where or with whom they work—feelings of impotence, distrust, resentment, insecurity, social inconsequence, and all the other very human emotions—not only define the climate which prevails but the manner in which communications will be managed. R. R. Blake and Jane S. Mouton[2] have commented upon an oddity of organizational life: When management is effective and relationships are sound, problems of communication tend not to occur. It is only when relationships among members of the organization are unsound and fraught with unarticulated tensions that one

---

[1] R. R. Blake and Jane S. Mouton, *Corporate Excellence through Grid Organization Development* (Houston, Tex.: Gulf Publishing, 1968), p. 4.

[2] Ibid., pp. 3–5.

hears complaints of communication breakdown. Thus, the quality of relationships in an organization may dictate to a great extent the level of communication effectiveness achieved.

INTERPERSONAL STYLES AND THE QUALITY OF RELATIONSHIPS

The critical factor underlying relationship quality in organizations is in need of review. Reduced to its lowest common denominator, the most significant determinant of the quality of relationships is the interpersonal style of the parties to a relationship. The learned, characteristic, and apparently preferred manner in which individuals relate to others in the building of relationships—the manner in which they monitor, control, filter, divert, give, and seek the information germane to a given relationship—will dictate over time the quality of relationships which exist among people, the emotional climate which will characterize their interactions, and whether or not there will be problems of communication. In the final analysis, individuals are the human links in the corporate network, and the styles they employ interpersonally are the ultimate determinants of what information goes where and whether it will be distortion-free or masked by interpersonal constraints.

The concept of interpersonal style is not an easy one to define; yet, if it is to serve as the central mechanism underlying the quality of relationships, the nature of corporate climate, managerial effectiveness, and the level of corporate excellence attainable, it is worthy of analysis. Fortunately, Joseph Luft[3] and Harry Ingham—two behavioral scientists with special interests in interpersonal and group processes—have developed a model of social interaction which affords a way of thinking about interpersonal functioning, while handling much of the data encountered in everyday living. The Johari Window, as their model is called, identifies several interpersonal styles, their salient features and consequences, and suggests a basis for interpreting the significance of style for the quality of relationships. An overview of the Johari model should help to sharpen the perception of interpersonal practices among managers and lend credence to the contention of Blake and Mouton that there are few communication problems as such, only unsound relationships. At the same time, a normative statement regarding effective interpersonal functioning and, by extension, the foundations of corporate excellence may be found in the model as well. Finally, the major tenets of the model are testable under practical conditions, and the latter portion of this discussion will be devoted to research on the managerial profile in interpersonal encounters. The author has taken a number of interpretive liberties with the basic provisions of the Johari Awareness model. While it is anticipated that none of these violate the integrity of the model as originally described by Luft, it should be emphasized that many of the inferences and conclusions discussed are those of the author, and Dr. Luft should not

---

3 Joseph Luft, *Of Human Interaction* (Palo Alto, Calif.: National Press Books, 1969), passim.

be held accountable for any lapses of logic or misapplications of the model in this paper.

THE JOHARI WINDOW: A GRAPHIC MODEL OF INTERPERSONAL PROCESSES

As treated here, the Johari Window is essentially an information processing model; interpersonal style and individual effectiveness are assessed in terms of information processing tendencies and the performance consequences thought to be associated with such practices. The model employs a four-cell figure as its format and reflects the interaction of two interpersonal sources of information—Self and Others—and the behavioral processes required for utilizing that information. The model, depicted in Figure 1, may be thought of as representing the various kinds of data avail-

Figure 1
The Johari Window: A Model of Interpersonal Processes

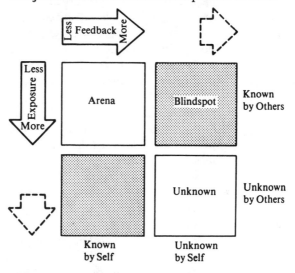

able for use in the establishment of interpersonal relationships. The squared field, in effect, represents a personal space. This in turn is partitioned into four regions, with each representing a particular combination or mix of relevant information and having special significance for the quality of relationships. To appreciate fully the implications that each informational region has for interpersonal effectiveness, one must consider not only the size and shape of each region but also the reasons for its presence in the interpersonal space. In an attempt to "personalize" the model, it is helpful to think of oneself as the *Self* in the relationship for, as will be seen presently, it is what the Self does interpersonally that has the most direct impact on the quality of resulting relationships. In organizational terms, it is how the management-Self behaves that is critical to the quality of corporate relationships.

Figure 1 reveals that the two informational sources, Self and Others, have information which is pertinent to the relationship, and at the same time, each lacks information that is equally germane. Thus, there is relevant and necessary information which is *Known by the Self, Unknown by the Self, Known by Others,* and *Unknown by Others.* The Self/Other combinations of known and unknown information make up the four regions within the interpersonal space and, again, characterize the various types and qualities of relationships possible within the Johari framework.

Region I, for example, constitutes that portion of the total interpersonal space which is devoted to mutually held information. This Known-by-Self-Known-by-Others facet of the interpersonal space is thought to be the part of the relationship which, because of its shared data characteristics and implied likelihood of mutual understanding, controls interpersonal productivity. That is, the working assumption is that productivity and interpersonal effectiveness are directly related to the amount of mutually held information in a relationship. Therefore, the larger Region I becomes, the more rewarding, effective, and productive the relationship. As the informational context for interpersonal functioning, Region I is called the "Arena."

Region II, using the double classification approach just described, is that portion of the interpersonal space which holds information Known-by-Others but Unknown-by-Self. Thus, this array of data constitutes an interpersonal handicap for the Self, since one can hardly understand the behaviors, decisions, or potentials of others if he doesn't have the data upon which these are based. Others have the advantage of knowing their own reactions, feelings, perceptions, and the like while the Self is unaware of these. Region II, an area of hidden unperceived information, is called the "Blindspot." The Blindspot is, of course, a limiting factor with respect to the size of Region I and may be thought of, therefore, as inhibiting interpersonal effectiveness.

Region III may also be considered to inhibit interpersonal effectiveness, but it is due to an imbalance of information which would seem to favor the Self; as the portion of the relationship which is characterized by information Known-by-Self but Unknown-by-Others, Region III constitutes a protective feature of the relationship for the Self. Data which one perceives as potentially prejudicial to the relationship or which he keeps to himself out of fear, desire for power, or whatever, make up the "Façade." This protective front, in turn, serves a defensive function for the Self. The question is not one of whether a Façade is necessary but rather how much Façade is required realistically; this raises the question of how much conscious defensiveness can be tolerated before the Arena becomes too inhibited and interpersonal effectiveness begins to diminish.

Finally, Region IV constitutes that portion of the relationship which is devoted to material neither known by the self nor by other parties to the relationship. The information in this Unknown by-Self–Unknown-by-Others area is thought to reflect psychodynamic data, hidden potential, unconscious idiosyncrasies, and the data-base of creativity. Thus, Region IV is the "Unknown" area which may become known as interpersonal effectiveness increases.

Summarily, it should be said that the information within all regions can be of any type—feeling data, factual information, assumptions, task skill data, and prejudices—which are relevant to the relationship at hand. Irrelevant data are not the focus of the Johari Window concept: just those pieces of information which have a bearing on the quality and productivity of the relationship should be considered as appropriate targets for the information processing practices prescribed by the model. At the same time, it should be borne in mind that the individuals involved in a relationship, particularly the Self, control what and how information will be processed. Because of this implicit personal control aspect, the model should be viewed as an open system which is *dynamic* and amenable to change as personal decisions regarding interpersonal functioning change.

BASIC INTERPERSONAL PROCESSES: EXPOSURE AND FEEDBACK

The dynamic character of the model is critical; for it is the movement capability of the horizontal and vertical lines which partition the interpersonal space into regions which gives individuals control over what their relationships will become. The Self can significantly influence the size of his Arena in relating to others by the behavioral processes he employs in establishing relationships. To the extent that one takes the steps necessary to apprise others of relevant information which he has and they do not, he is enlarging his Arena in a downward direction. Within the framework of the model, this enlargement occurs in concert with a reduction of one's Façade. Thus, if one behaves in a nondefensive, trusting, and possibly risk-taking manner with others, he may be thought of as contributing to increased mutual awareness and shareing of data. The process one employs toward this end has been called the "Exposure" process. It entails the open and candid disclosure of one's feelings, factual knowledge, wild guesses, and the like in a conscious attempt to share. Frothy, intentionally untrue, diversionary sharing does not constitute exposure; and as personal experience will attest, it does nothing to help mutual understanding. The Exposure process is under the direct control of the Self and may be used as a mechanism for building trust and for legitimizing mutual exposures.

The need for mutual exposures becomes apparent when one considers the behavioral process required for enlarging the Arena laterally. As a behavior designed to gain reduction in one's Blindspot, the Feedback process entails an active solicitation by the Self of the information he feels others might have which he does not. The active, initiative-taking aspect of this solicitation behavior should be stressed, for again the Self takes the primary role in setting interpersonal norms and in legitimizing certain acts within the relationship. Since the extent to which the Self will actually receive the Feedback he solicits is contingent upon the willingness of others to expose their data, the need for a climate of mutual exposures becomes apparent. Control by the Self of the success of his Feedback-seeking behaviors is less direct therefore than in the case of self-exposure. He will achieve a reduction of his Blindspot only with the cooperation of others; and his own prior willingness to deal openly and candidly may well dictate what level of cooperative and trusting behavior will prevail on the part of other parties to the relationship.

Thus, one can theoretically establish interpersonal relationships characterized by mutual understanding and increased effectiveness (by a dominant Arena) if he will engage in exposing and feedback soliciting behaviors to an optimal degree. This places the determination of productivity and amount of interpersonal reward—and the quality of relationships—directly in the hands of the Self. In theory, this amounts to an issue of interpersonal competence; in practice, it amounts to the conscious and sensitive management of interpersonal processes.

INTERPERSONAL STYLES AND MANAGERIAL IMPACTS

While one can theoretically employ Exposure and Feedback processes not only to a great but to a similar degree as well, individuals typically fail to achieve such an optimal practice. Indeed, they usually display a significant preference for one or the other of the two processes and tend to overuse one while neglecting the other. This tendency promotes a state of imbalance in interpersonal relationships which, in turn, creates disruptive tensions capable of retarding productivity. Figure 2 presents several commonly used approaches to the employment of Exposure and Feedback

Figure 2
Interpersonal Styles as Functions of Exposure and Feedback Solicitation

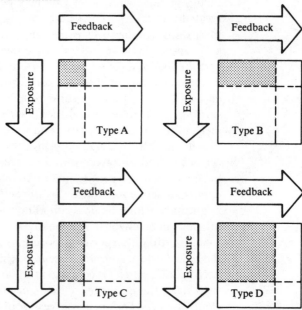

processes. Each of these may be thought of as reflecting a basic inter-personal style—that is fairly consistent and preferred ways of behaving interpersonally. As might be expected, each style has associated with it some fairly predictable consequences.

Type A

This interpersonal style reflects a minimal use of both Exposure and Feedback processes; it is a fairly impersonal approach to interpersonal relationships. The Unknown region dominates under this style; and unrealized potential, untapped creativity, and personal psychodynamics prevail as the salient influences. Such a style would seem to indicate withdrawal and an aversion to risk-taking on the part of its user; interpersonal anxiety and safety-seeking are likely to be prime sources of personal motivation. Persons who characteristically use this style appear to be detached, mechanical, and uncommunicative. They may often be found in bureaucratic, highly structured organizations of some type where it is possible, and perhaps profitable, to avoid personal disclosure or involvement. People using this style are likely to be reacted to with more than average hostility, since other parties to the relationship will tend to interpret the lack of Exposure and Feedback solicitation largely according to their own needs and how this interpersonal lack affects need fulfillment.

Subordinates whose manager employs such a style, for example, will often feel that this behavior is consciously aimed at frustrating them in their work. The person in need of support and encouragement will often view a Type A manager as aloof, cold, and indifferent. Another individual in need of firm directions and plenty of order in his work may view the same manager as indecisive and administratively impotent. Yet another person requiring freedom and opportunities to be innovative may see the Type A interpersonal style as hopelessly tradition-bound and as symptomatic of fear and an overriding need for security. The use of Type A behaviors on a large scale in an organization reveals something about the climate and fundamental health of that organization. In many respects, interpersonal relationships founded on Type A uses of exposure and feedback constitute the kind of organizational ennui about which Chris Argyris[4] has written so eloquently. Such practices are, in his opinion, likely to be learned ways of behaving under oppressive policies of the sort which encourage people to act in a submissive and dependent fashion. Organizationally, of course, the result is lack of communication and a loss of human potentials; the Unknown becomes the dominant feature of corporate relationships, and the implications for organizational creativity and growth are obvious.

Type B

Under this approach, there is also an aversion to Exposure, but aversion is coupled with a desire for relationships not found in Type A. Thus, Feedback is the only process left in promoting relationships and it is much

---

[4] C. Argyris, *Interpersonal Competence and Organizational Effectiveness* (Homewood, Ill.: Dorsey, 1962), passim.

overused. An aversion to the use of Exposure may typically be interpreted as a sign of basic mistrust of self and others, and it is therefore not surprising that the Façade is the dominant feature of relationships resulting from neglected Exposure coupled with overused Feedback. The style appears to be a probing, supportive interpersonal ploy, and once the Façade becomes apparent, it is likely to result in a reciprocal withdrawal of trust by other parties. This may promote feelings of suspicion on the part of others; such feelings may lead to the manager being treated as a rather superficial person without real substance or as a devious sort with many hidden agenda.

Preference for this interpersonal style among managers seems to be of two types. Some managers committed to a quasi-permissive management may employ Type B behaviors in an attempt to avoid appearing directive. Such an approach results in the manager's personal resources never being fully revealed or his opinions being expressed. In contrast—but subject to many of the same inadequacies—is the use of Type B behaviors in an attempt to gain or maintain one's personal power in relationships. Many managers build a façade to maintain personal control and an outward appearance of confidence. As the Johari model would suggest, however, persons who employ such practices tend to become isolated from their subordinates and colleagues alike. Lack of trust predominates and consolidation of power and promotion of an image of confidence may be the least likely results of Type B use in organizations. Very likely, the seeds of distrust and conditions for covert competitiveness—with all the implications for organizational teamwork—will follow from widespread use of Type B interpersonal practices.

Type C

Based on an overuse of Exposure to the neglect of Feedback, this interpersonal style may reflect ego-striving and/or distrust of others' competence. The person who uses this style usually feels quite confident of his own opinions and is likely to value compliance from others. The fact that he is often unaware of his impact or of the potential of others' contributions is reflected in the dominant Blindspot which results from this style. Others are likely to feel disenfranchised by one who uses this style; they often feel that he has little use for their contributions or concern for their feelings. As a result, this style often triggers feelings of hostility, insecurity, and resentment on the part of others. Frequently, others will learn to perpetuate the manager's Blindspot by withholding important information or giving only selected feedback: as such, this is a reflection of the passive-aggressiveness and unarticulated hostility which this style can cause. Labor-management relations frequently reflect such Blindspot dynamics.

The Type C interpersonal style is probably what has prompted so much interest in "listening" programs around the country. As the Johari model makes apparent, however, the Type C overuse of Exposure and neglect of Feedback is just one of several interpersonal tendencies that may disrupt communications. While hierarchical organizational structure or centrality in communication nets and the like may certainly facilitate the use of individual Type C behaviors, so can fear of failure, authoritarianism, need for control, and overconfidence in one's own opinions; such traits vary from person to person and limit the utility of communication panaceas. Managers who rely on this style often do so to demonstrate competence; many corporate cultures require that the manager be *the* planner, director, and controller, and many managers behave accordingly to protect their corporate images. Many others are simply trying to be helpful in a paternalistic kind of way; others are, of course, purely dictatorial. Whatever the reason, those who employ the Type C style have one thing in common: Their relationships will be dominated by Blindspots and they are destined for surprise whenever people get enough and decide to force Feedback on them, solicited or not.

Type D

Balanced Exposure and Feedback processes are used to a great extent in this style; candor, openness, and a sensitivity to others' needs to participate are the salient features of the style. The Arena is the dominant characteristic, and productivity increases. In initial stages, this style may promote some defensiveness on the part of others who are not familiar with honest and trusting relationships; but perseverance will tend to promote a norm of reciprocal candor over time in which creative potential can be realized.

Among managers, Type D practices constitute an ideal state from the standpoint of organizational effectiveness. Healthy and creative climates result from its widespread use, and the conditions for growth and corporate excellence may be created through the use of constructive Exposure and Feedback exchanges. Type D practices do not give license to "clobber," as some detractors might claim; and for optimal results, the data explored should be germane to the relationships and problems at hand, rather than random intimacies designed to overcome self-consciousness. Trust is slowly built, and managers who experiment with Type D processes should be prepared to be patient and flexible in their relationships. Some managers, as they tentatively try out Type D strategies, encounter reluctance and distrust on the part of others, with the result that they frequently give up too soon, assuming that the style doesn't work. The reluctance of others should be assessed against the backdrop of previous management practices and the level of prior trust which characterizes the culture. Other managers may try candor only to discover that they have opened a Pandora's box from which a barrage of hostility and complaints emerges. The temptation of the naive manager is to put the lid back on quickly; but the more enlightened manager knows that when communications are opened up after having been closed for a long time, the most emotionally laden issues—ones which have been the greatest source of frustration, anger, or fear—will be the first to be discussed. If management can resist cutting the dialogue short, the diatribe will run its course as the emotion underlying it is drained off, and exchanges will become more problem-centered and future-oriented. Management intent will have been tested and found worthy of trust, and creative unrestrained interchanges will occur. Organizations built on such practices are those headed for corporate climates and re-source utilization of the type necessary for true corporate excellence. The manager's interpersonal style may well be the catalyst for this reaction to occur.

Summarily, the Johari Window model of interpersonal processes sug-gests that much more is needed to understand communication in an organi-zation than information about its structure or one's position in a network. People make very critical decisions about what information will be processed, irrespective of structural and network considerations. People bring with them to organizational settings propensities for behaving in certain ways interpersonally. They prefer certain interpersonal styles, sharpened and honed by corporate cultures, which significantly influence—if not dictate entirely—the flow of information in organizations. As such, individuals and their preferred styles of relating one to another amount to the synapses in the corporate network which control and coordinate the human system. Central to an understanding of communication in organi-zations, therefore, in an appreciation of the complexities of those human interfaces which comprise organizations. The work of Luft and Ingham, when brought to bear on management practices and corporate cultures, may lend much needed insight into the constraints unique to organizational life which either hinder or facilitate the processing of corporate data.

RESEARCH ON THE MANAGERIAL PROFILE: THE PERSONAL RELATIONS SURVEY

As treated here, one of the major tenets of the Johari Window model is that one's use of Exposure and Feedback soliciting processes is a matter of personal decision. Whether consciously or unconsciously, when one em-ploys either process or fails to do so, he has decided that such practices somehow serve the goals he has set for himself. Rationales for particular behavior are likely to be as varied as the goals people seek; they may be in the best sense of honest intent or they may simply represent evasive logic or systems of self-deception. The *purposeful* nature of interpersonal styles remains nevertheless. A manager's style of relating to other members of the organization is never simply a collection of random, unconsidered acts. Whether he realizes it or not, or admits it or denies it, his interpersonal style *has purpose* and is thought to serve either a personal or interpersonal goal in his relationships.

Because of the element of decision and purposeful intent inherent in one's interpersonal style, the individual's inclination to employ Exposure and Feedback processes may be assessed. That is, his decision to engage in open and candid behaviors or actively to seek out the information that others are thought to have may be sampled, and his Exposure and Feed-back tendencies thus measured. Measurements obtained may be used in determining the manager's or the organization's Johari Window con-figuration and the particular array of interpersonal predictions which underlie it. Thus, the Luft-Ingham model not only provides a way of con-ceptualizing what is going on interpersonally, but it affords a rationale for actually assessing practices which may, in turn, be coordinated to practical climate and cultural issues.

Hall and Williams have designed a paper-and-pencil instrument for use with managers which reveals their preferences for Exposure and Feedback in their relationships with subordinates, colleagues, and superiors. The *Personnel Relations Survey*,[5] as the instrument is entitled, has been used extensively by industry as a training aid for providing personal feedback of a type which "personalizes" otherwise didactic theory sessions on the Johari, on one hand, and as a catalyst to evaluation and critique of ongoing relationships, on the other hand. In addition to its essentially training oriented use, however, the *Personnel Relations Survey* has been a basic research tool for assessing current practices among managers. The results obtained from two pieces of research are of particular interest from the standpoint of their implications for corporate climates and managerial styles.

Authority
Relationships and
Interpersonal Style
Preferences

Using the *Personnel Relations Survey,* data were collected from 1,000 managers. These managers represent a cross section of those found in organizations today; levels of management ranging from company president to just above first-line supervisor were sampled from all over the United States. Major manufacturers and petroleum and food producers contributed to the research, as well as major airline, state and federal governmental agencies, and nonprofit service organizations.

Since the *Personnel Relations Survey* addresses the manner in which Exposure and Feedback processes are employed in one's relationships with his subordinates, colleagues, and superiors, the data from the 1,000 managers sampled reveal some patterns which prevail in organizations in terms of downward, horizontal, and upward communications. In addition, the shifting and changing of interpersonal tactics as one moves from one authority relationship to another is noteworthy from the standpoint of power dynamics underlying organizational life. A summary of the average tendencies obtained from managers is presented graphically in Figure 3.

Of perhaps the greatest significance for organizational climates is the finding regarding the typical manager's use of Exposure. As Figure 3 indicates, one's tendency to deal openly and candidly with others is directly influenced by the amount of power he possesses relative to other parties to the relationship. Moving from relationships with subordinates in which the manager obviously enjoys greater formal authority, through colleague relationships characterized by equal authority positions, to relationships with superiors in which the manager is least powerful, the plots of Exposure use steadily decline. Indeed, a straight linear relationship is suggested between amount of authority possessed by the average manager and his use of candor in relationships.

---

5 J. Hall and Martha S. Williams, *Personnel Relations Survey* (Conroe, Tex.: Teleometrics International, 1967).

Figure 3
Score Plots on Exposure and Feedback for the "Average" Manager
from a Sample of 1,000 Managers in the United States

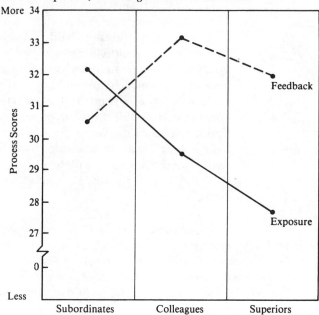

While there are obvious exceptions to this depiction, the average managerial profile on Exposure reveals the most commonly found practices in organizations which, when taken diagnostically, suggest that the average manager in today's organizations has a number of "hang-ups" around authority issues which seriously curtail his interpersonal effectiveness. Consistent with other findings from communication research, these data point to power differences among parties to relationships as a major disruptive influence on the flow of information in organizations. A more accurate interpretation, however, seems to be that it is not power differences as such which impede communication, but the way people *feel* about these differences and begin to monitor, filter, and control their contributions in response to their own feelings and apprehensions.

Implications for overall corporate climate may become more obvious when the data from the Exposure process are considered with those reflecting the average manager's reliance on Feedback acquisition. As Figure 3 reveals, Feedback solicitation proceeds differently. As might be expected, there is less use of the Feedback process in relationships with subordinates than there is of the Exposure process. This variation on the Type C interpersonal style, reflecting an overuse of Exposure to some neglect of Feedback, very likely contributes to subordinate feelings of resentment, lack of social worth, and frustration. These feelings—which are certain to manifest themselves in the *quality* of subordinate performance if not in production quantity—will likely remain as hidden facets of corporate climate, for a major feature of downward communication revealed in Figure 3 is that of managerial Blindspot.

Relationships at the colleague level appear to be of a different sort with a set of dynamics all their own. As reference to the score plots in Figure 3 will show, the typical manager reports a significant preference for Feedback seeking behaviors over Exposure in his relationships with his fellow managers. A quick interpretation of the data obtained would be that, at the colleague level, everyone is seeking information but very few are willing to expose any. These findings may bear on a unique feature of organizational life—one which has serious implications for climate among corporate peers. Most research on power and authority relationships suggests that there is the greatest openness and trust among people under conditions of equal power. Since colleague relationships might best be considered to reflect equal if not shared distributions of power, maximum openness coupled with maximum solicitation of others' information might be expected to characterize relationships among management coworkers. The fact that a fairly pure Type B interpersonal style prevails suggests noise in the system. The dominant Façade which results from reported practices with colleagues signifies a lack of trust of the sort which could seriously limit the success of collaborative or cooperative ventures among colleagues. The climate implications of mistrust are obvious, and the present data may shed some light on teamwork difficulties as well as problems of horizontal communication so often encountered during interdepartmental or intergroup contacts.

Interviews with a number of managers revealed that their tendencies to become closed in encounters with colleagues could be traced to a competitive ethic which prevailed in their organizations. The fact was a simple one: "You don't confide in your 'buddies' because they are bucking for the same job you are! Any worthwhile information you've got, you keep to yourself until a time when it might come in handy." To the extent that this climate prevails in organizations, it is to be expected that more effort goes in façade building and maintenance than is expended on the projects at hand where colleague relationships are concerned.

Superiors are the targets of practices yielding the smallest, and therefore least productive, Arena of the three relationships assessed in the survey. The average manager reports a significant reluctance to deal openly and candidly with his superior while favoring the Feedback process as his major interpersonal gambit; even the use of Feedback, however, is subdued relative to that employed with colleagues. The view from on high in organizations is very likely colored by the interpersonal styles addressed to them; and based on the data obtained, it would not be surprising if many members of top management felt that lower level management was submissive, in need of direction, and had few creative suggestions of their own. Quite aside from the obvious effect such an expectation might have on performance reviews, a characteristic reaction to the essentially Type B style directed at superiors is, on their part, to invoke Type C behaviors. Thus, the data obtained call attention to what may be the seeds of a self-reinforcing cycle of authority-obedience-authority. The long-range consequences of such a cycle, in terms of relationship quality and interpersonal style, has been found to be corporatewide adoption of Type A behaviors which serve to depersonalize work and diminish an organization's human resources.

Thus, based on the present research at least, a number of interpersonal practices seem to characterize organizational life which limit not only the effectiveness of communication within, but the attainment of realistic levels of corporate excellence without. As you will see, which style will prevail very much depends upon the individual manager.

Interpersonal
Practices and
Managerial Styles

In commenting upon the first of their two major concerns in programs of organization development, Blake and Mouton[6] have stated: "The underlying causes of communication difficulties are to be found in the character of supervision. . . . The solution to the problem of communication is for men to manage by achieving production and excellence through sound utilization of people." To the extent that management style is an important ingredient in the communication process, a second piece of research employing the Johari Window and Managerial Grid models in tandem may be of some interest to those concerned with corporate excellence.

Of the 1,000 managers sampled in the *Personnel Relations Survey,* 384 also completed a second instrument, the *Styles of Management Inventory,*[7] based on the Managerial Grid (a two-dimensional model of management sytles).[8] Five "anchor" styles are identified relative to one's concern for production vis-à-vis people, and these are expressed in grid notation as follows: 9,9 reflects a high production concern coupled with high people concern; 5,5 reflects a moderate concern for each; 9,1 denotes high production coupled with low people concerns, while 1,9 denotes the opposite orientation; 1,1 reflects a minimal concern for both dimensions. In an attempt to discover the significance of one's interpersonal practices for his overall approach to management, the 40 individuals scoring highest on each style of management were selected for an analysis of their interpersonal styles. Thus, 200 managers—40 each who were identified as having dominant managerial styles of either 9,9; 5,5; 9,1; 1,9; or 1,1— were studied relative to their tendencies to employ Exposure and Feedback processes in relationships with their subordinates. The research question addressed was: How do individuals who prefer a given managerial style differ in terms of their interpersonal orientations from other individuals preferring other managerial approaches?

The data were subjected to a discriminant function analysis, and statis-

---

[6] Blake and Mouton, *Corporate Excellence,* p. 5.

[7] J. Hall, J. B. Harvey, and Martha S. Williams, *Styles of Management Inventory* (Conroe, Tex.: Teleometrics International, 1963).

[8] R. R. Blake and Jane S. Mouton, *The Managerial Grid* (Houston, Tex.: Gulf Publishing, 1964), *passim.*

ticially significant differences were revealed in terms of the manner in which managers employing a given dominant managerial style also employed the Exposure and Feedback processes. The results of the research findings are presented graphically in Figure 4. As the bar graph of Exposure and Feedback scores reveals those managers identified by a dominant

Figure 4
A Comparison of Exposure and Feedback Use among Managers with Different Dominant Managerial Styles

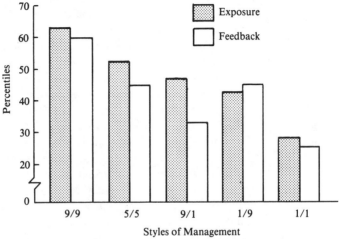

management style of 9,9 displayed the strongest tendencies to employ both Exposure and Feedback in their relationships with subordinates. In addition, the Arena which would result from a Johari plotting of their scores would be in a fairly good state of balance, reflecting about as much use of one process as of the other. The data suggest that the 9,9 style of management—typically described as one which achieves effective production through the sound utilization of people—also entails the sound utilization of personal resources in establishing relationships. The Type D interpersonal style which seems to be associated with the 9,9 management style is fully consistent with the open and unobstructed communication which Blake and Mouton view as essential to the creative resolution of differences and sound relationships.

The 5,5 style of management appears, from the standpoint of Exposure and Feedback employment, to be a truncated version of the 9,9 approach. While the reported scores for both processes hover around the 50th percentile, there is a noteworthy preference for Exposure over Feedback. Although a Johari plotting of these scores might also approach a Type D profile, the Arena is less balanced and accounts for only 25 percent of the data available for use in a relationship. Again, such an interpersonal style seems consistent with a managerial approach based on expediency and a search for the middle ground.

As might be expected, the 9,1 managers in the study displayed a marked preference for Exposure over Feedback in their relationships with subordinates. This suggests that managers who are maximally concerned with production issues also are given to an overuse of Exposure—albeit not maximum Exposure—and this is very likely to maintain personal control. In general, a Type C interpersonal style seems to underlie the 9,1 approach to management; and it is important that such managerial practices may be sustained by enlarged Blindspots.

Considering the opposing dominant concerns of the 1,9 manager as compared to the 9,1, it is not too surprising to find that the major interpersonal process of these managers is Feedback solicitation. As with the 9,1 style, the resulting Arena for 1,9 managers is not balanced; but the resulting tension likely stems from less than desired Exposure, leading to relationships in which the managerial Façade is the dominant feature. The Type B interpersonal style may be said to characterize the 1,9 approach to management, with its attendant effects on corporate climate.

Finally, the use of Exposure and Feedback processes reported by those managers identified as dominantly 1,1 is minimal. A mechanical impersonal approach to interpersonal relationships which is consistent with the low profile approach to management depicted under 1,1 is suggested. The Unknown region apparently dominates relationships, and hidden potential and untapped resources prevail. The consequences of such practices for the quality of relationships, climates, and communication effectiveness have already been described in the discussion of Type A interpersonal behaviors.

In summary, it appears that one's interpersonal style is a critical ingredient in his approach to management. While the uses of Exposure and Feedback reported by managers identified according to management style seem to be quite consistent with what one might expect, it is worthy to mention that the test items comprising the *Personnel Relations Survey* have very little, if anything, to do with production versus people concerns. Rather, one's willingness to engage in risk-taking disclosures of feelings, impressions, and observations coupled with his sensitivity to others' participative needs and a felt responsibility to help them become involved via Feedback solicitation were assessed. The fact that such purposive behaviors coincide with one's treatment of more specific context-bound issues like production and people would seem to raise the question: Which comes first, interpersonal or managerial style? The question is researchable, and management practices and information flow might both be enhanced by the results obtained.

CORPORATE CLIMATE AND PERSONAL DECISION
The major thesis of this article has been that interpersonal styles are at the core of a number of corporate dilemmas: Communication breakdowns, emotional climates, the quality of relationships, and even managerial practices have been linked to some fairly simple dynamics between people. The

fact that the dynamics are simple should not be taken to mean that their management is easy—far from it. But, at the same time, the fact that individuals can and do change their interpersonal style—and thereby set in motion a whole chain of events with corporate significance—should be emphasized. A mere description of one's interpersonal practices has only limited utility, if that is as far as it goes. The value of the Johari Window model lies not so much with its utility for assessing what is but, rather, in its inherent statement of what might be.

Although most people select their interpersonal styles as a *reaction* to what they anticipate from other parties, the key to effective relationships lies in "pro-action"; each manager can be a norm setter in his relationships if he will but honestly review his own interpersonal goals and undertake the risks necessary to their attainment. Organizations can criticize their policies—both formal and unwritten—in search for provisions which serve to punish candor and reward evasiveness while equating solicitation of data from others with personal weakness. In short, the culture of an organization and the personal and corporate philosophies which underlie it may be thought of as little more than a *decision product* of the human system. The quality of this decision will directly reflect the quality of the relationships existing among those who fashion it.

If the model and its derivations make sense, then corporate relationships and managerial practices based on candor and trust, openness and spontaneity, and optimal utilization of interpersonal resources are available options to every member of an organizational family. As we have seen, power distributions among people may adversely influence their interpersonal choices. Management styles apparently constrain individuals, but the choice is still there. Type A practices require breaking away from the corporate womb into which one has retreated; personal experiments with greater Exposure and Feedback, however anxiety-producing, may be found in the long-run to be their own greatest reward. For the manager locked into Type B behaviors, the task is more simple; he already solicits Feedback to an excellent degree. Needed is enough additional trust in others—whether genuine or forced—to allow a few experiences with Exposure. Others may be found to be less fragile or reactionary than one imagined. Learning to listen is but part of the task confronting managers inclined toward Type C styles; they must learn to seek out and encourage the exposures of others. This new attention to the Feedback process should not be at the expense of Exposure, however. Revamping Type C does not mean adopting Type B. These are all forms of low-risk high-potential-yield personal experiments. Whether they will ever be undertaken and their effects on corporate excellence determined depends upon the individual; the matter is one of personal decision.

Nonverbal Communication Can Be a Motivational Tool*

JOHN G. BAIRD, JR., and GRETCHEN K. WIETING

Of the issues which have haunted managers ever since people began forming organizations, none has been more persistent than the question, "How do I motivate my employees?" For years, motivation was thought to be a trait possessed in varying degrees by everyone. Recently, however, theorists have come to the realization that much of motivation is external to the individual. As Hill concludes, motivation "is not so much a personal characteristic as it is a product of the interaction between an executive and an individual staff member."[1] Still, such interaction is closely related to employee characteristics. Hill points out that "nothing is as important in individual productive functioning as self-esteem," and adds that "no influence is as great in the development of a person's self-esteem as the feeling that someone whom he respects believes in him."[2] Superior-subordinate communication therefore serves both to influence a subordinate's personal characteristics and to establish his or her level of motivation.

The impact of communication is dramatically illustrated by the "Pygmalion effect," whereby the expectations of a manager influence the performance of subordinates. Berlew and Hall, for example, found that the relative success of 49 AT&T employees depended largely on the company's expectations of them.[3] Rosenthal and Jacobsen observed the same effect in educational settings, and since the 1968 publication of their *Pygmalion in the Classroom,* nearly 100 studies have obtained findings supporting their

* Reprinted by permission of *Personnel Journal,* September 1979, pp. 607–10, Costa Mesa, California. Copyright 1979, all rights reserved.

[1] Norman Hill, "Staff Members Do Better When You Set High Standards." *Association Management,* February 1977, pp. 75–77.

[2] Ibid.

[3] David E. Berlew and Douglas T. Hall, "Some Determinants of Early Managerial Success," Alfred P. Sloan School of Management Organization Research Program #81–64 (Cambridge: Massachusetts Institute of Technology, 1964), pp. 13–14.

conclusions.[4] All of these studies underscore the importance of communication—particularly nonverbal communication. Livingston, for example, claims that "what seems to be critical in the communication of expectations is not what the boss says, so much as the way he behaves."[5] "The nonverbal communication which accompanies your verbal communication," McSweeney adds, "will very likely project the message that you are expecting the workers to live up to their potential."[6] Similarly, Hill argues that "expectations are communicated in a variety of ways besides verbal messages."[7] Through their nonverbal behavior, then, managers motivate—or demotivate—their employees.

Despite recent interest in nonverbal communication, the relationship between managers' nonverbal cues and employees' motivation has not been explored. Many authors have discussed the interpretation of nonverbal cues, and a few have considered the effective use of nonverbal communication, but none have examined specifically the use of cues to transmit high expectations.[8] Indeed, Livingston implies that such an examination would be fruitless: "If a manager believes the subordinate will perform poorly, it is virtually impossible for him to mask his expectations, because the message is communicated unintentionally, without conscious action on his part."[9] We contend, however, that managers can "mask" their expectations—that if they understand the role of nonverbal cues in transmitting expectations, they can consciously use those cues to motivate their employees.

CONTENT AND RELATIONSHIP

According to Watzlawick, Beavin, and Jackson, communication has two levels: "content," or the words one person transmits to another, and "relationship," or the nonverbal cues which accompany those words.[10] They use the term *relationship* because nonverbal behaviors serve chiefly to define the relationship between the interactants by indicating how the spoken words are to be interpreted. Argyle provides more specific information, claiming that nonverbal communication serves to express one's emotions, convey interpersonal attitudes, present one's personality, and regulate

---

4 Robert Rosenthal and Lenore Jacobsen. *Pygmalion in the Classroom* (New York: Holt, Rinehart & Winston, 1968).

5 J. Sterling Livingston, "Pygmalion in Management," *Harvard Business Review*, January–February 1969, p. 84.

6 John P. McSweeney, "Pygmalion in the Plant," *Personnel Journal*, August 1977, pp. 380–81.

7 Norman Hill, "Staff Members Do Better," p. 75.

8 See, for example: Ed Roseman, "People Reading: The Art of Recognizing Hidden Messages," *Product Marketing*, June 1977, pp. 36–39; Richard W. Brunson, Sr., "Perceptual Skills in the Corporate Jungle," *Personnel Journal*, January 1972, pp. 50–53; D. M. Ehat and M. Schnapper, "What Your Employees' Nonverbal Cues Are Telling You," *Administrative Management*, August 1974, pp. 64–66; "Listen with Your Eyes," *Industry Week*, July 16, 1973, pp. 37–39; Julius Fast, *Body Language* (New York: M. Evans, 1970).

9 Livingston, "Pygmalion in Management," pp. 81–84.

10 Paul Watzlawick, J. H. Beavin, and Don Jackson, *Pragmatics of Human Communication* (New York: W. W. Norton, 1967).

the interaction.[11] To determine which nonverbal behaviors ought to be displayed by managers, then, we must determine the sorts of superior-subordinate relationships which seem most desirable and then identify the cues which, by conveying certain emotions and attitudes, contribute to the development of such relationships.

Livingston supplies several characteristics of good superior-subordinate relationships.[12] In this opinion, subordinates are more likely to be productive if they feel that the supervisor views them with confidence, respect, and concern. McSweeney adds yet another factor: "Having the worker perceive you as a capable authority in your work is valuable, but your projections to the workers that you share a commonness with them is even more important."[13] Hill similarly argues that managers should reward initiative, correct mistakes, ask for input, share feelings, and be open-minded in their relations with subordinates.[14] Therefore, desirable nonverbal cues are those which express warmth, respect, concern, equality, and a willingness to listen; while undesirable behaviors are those which show coolness, superiority, disinterest, and disrespect. With this knowledge, we can begin to isolate the specific nonverbal behaviors which managers should strive to exhibit or avoid.

EFFECTS OF NONVERBAL CUES

In his summary of research in nonverbal communication, Knapp discusses several categories of nonverbal cues, including the environment, proxemics, postures, gestures, facial expressions, eye behavior, and vocalics.[15] Each of these categories plays an important role in superior-subordinate communication; consequently, we will examine each category in turn.

The Environment. The first category considers the setting in which communication occurs, including time elements, room color, temperature, lighting, attractiveness of the surroundings, furniture arrangement, and so on. Three environmental factors particularly relevant here are time, arrangement, and attractiveness, for all three communicate subtle messages to the people present in the setting.

Expectations and attitudes toward a specific employee are shown in three temporally related issues: how long he or she must wait to see the supervisor, how much time the supervisor devotes to the conference, and how frequently the supervisor communicates with the employee. If a supervisor keeps an employee waiting a long time (probably more than ten minutes), devotes only a short time to the meeting when a longer conference

---

11 Michael Argyle, *Bodily Communication* (New York: International Universities Press, 1975).

12 Livingston, "Pygmalion in Management," pp. 81–84.

13 McSweeney, "Pygmalion in the Plant," p. 380.

14 Hill, "Staff Members Do Better," p. 76.

15 Mark Knapp, *Nonverbal Communication in Human Interaction,* 2d ed. (New York: Holt, Rinehart & Winston, 1978).

is appropriate, and meets only occasionally with the employee, then the supervisor is communicating a negative, disrespectful attitude toward that individual. Conversely, if the supervisor sees the employee immediately, devotes adequate time to the meeting, and confers with the employee frequently, he or she demonstrates esteem for that person.

Furniture arrangement also has an impact on superior-subordinate relationships, serving to establish a cold, formal, authoritative environment or a warmer, informal, cooperative setting. Michael Korda, publishing house executive and author, describes how placement of a desk and chairs in an office can influence the atmosphere of a meeting.[16] Korda cites three specific basic office arrangements, each creating a different sort of climate. In the first, dominance is minimized and warmth maximized. The visitor sits next to the desk, making him or her virtually equal to the occupant and forcing the latter to assume a relatively uncomfortable position in order to talk face to face. Arrangement number two is more powerful and less warm; the occupant sits regally behind the desk, which serves as a barrier. But the third arrangement is the least warm of all. The visitor is sitting back to the wall, occupying minimal space, while the occupant has the remainder of the office in which to move about. This, coupled with the interposed desk, makes the situation the most domineering possible. But Korda points out one final extreme instance of furniture and power. One executive not only arranged his desk as in the third example, but also placed it on a platform so that he could look down at his visitors, and gave the visitors an extremely soft chair so that they sank up to their chins when they sat down. Peering over one's knees at an executive sitting behind a desk on a platform would almost certainly make anyone feel rather submissive.

Finally, there is some evidence that environmental attractiveness has an influence on interaction. Maslow and Mintz[17] and Mintz[18] asked subjects to evaluate a series of photographs while working in three different settings: an ugly room, an average room, and a beautiful room. Comparisons of the ratings given in these settings showed that people felt more positively toward the faces in the photographs when working in the beautiful room than when in the ugly room. In addition, the subjects reported changes in their emotional states. In the ugly room, they describe their experience as irritating, tiring, dull and generally unpleasant, while in the beautiful room they reported feeling comfortable, pleasant, and eager to continue the activity. Apparently, then, one's feelings about an environment extend to the people encountered there.

Consideration of environmental factors is thus important to establishing

---

[16] Michael Korda, *Power: How to Get It, How to Use It* (New York: Random House, 1975), pp. 194–97.

[17] A. H. Maslow and N. L. Mintz, "Effects of Esthetic Surroundings: I. Initial Effects of Three Esthetic Conditions upon Perceiving 'Energy' and 'Well-being' in Faces," *Journal of Psychology* 41, no. 3 (1956): 247–54.

[18] N. L. Mintz, "Effects of Esthetic Surroundings: II. Prolonged and Repeated Experience in a 'Beautiful' and 'Ugly' Room," *Journal of Psychology* 41, no. 4 (1956): 459–66.

desirable super-subordinate relationships. Employees should not be kept waiting, should be given adequate time, and should be met with relatively frequently. Employers should seek to establish an informal, cooperative atmosphere by interposing little or no furniture between themselves and their employees. The surroundings of the conversation, finally, should be as pleasant and attractive as possible to promote positive interaction.

Proxemics.   Proxemics involves the placement of one's body relative to the placement of someone else—their physical proximity. A number of studies have noted a relationship between people's physical distance and the sorts of attitudes each infers the other to hold. Patterson cites research indicating that people located in relatively close proximity are seen as warmer, friendlier, and more understanding than people located further away.[19] Moreover, Mehrabian found that status differences are emphasized by physical distance and minimized by greater closeness.[20] Indeed, after reviewing research on proximity, Mehrabian concluded that "the findings of a large number of studies corroborate one another and indicate that communicator-addressee distance is correlated with the degree of negative attitude communicated to and inferred by the addressee."[21] Thus, assuming a position close to the employee seems to convey a variety of positive attitudes.

Postures.   General bodily movements also have a message value. In studies of bodily posture, Mehrabian found a close relationship between posture and liking for the other person.[22] When confronting someone they intensely dislike, women particularly tend to be very indirect in their direction of face, looking away from the other person as much as possible. If they like the other person, they vary their direction of face, sometimes looking squarely at that person and sometimes looking away, while when dealing with a total stranger, they tend to look directly at that person. Similar although less consistent results were obtained for males. Mehrabian also found that openness of the arms or legs serves as an indicator of liking as people maintain open positions when meeting those they like, but establish closed postures (arms folded and legs crossed) when speaking with people they dislike. Lastly, a forward lean seems to indicate liking for the other, while a backward lean seems to convey negative feelings. A manager's postures thus tell much about his or her feelings toward others.

Gestures.   Studies of gestures or specific bodily movements have found those behaviors to convey rather specific information. Research summarized by Bonoma and Felder indicates that positive attitudes toward another person are shown by frequent gesticulation, while dislike or disinterest

19 M. Patterson, "Spatial Factors in Social Interaction," *Human Factors* 2, no. 3 (1968): 351–61.

20 Albert Mehrabian, "Significance of Posture and Position in the Communication of Attitude and Status Relationships," *Psychological Bulletin* 71 (1969): 363.

21 Ibid.

22 Albert Mehrabian, "Inference of Attitude from the Posture, Orientation and Distance of a Communicator," *Journal of Consulting and Clinical Psychology* 32, no. 2 (1968): 296–308.

usually produces few gestures.[23] However, the types of gestures displayed are also important. Random fidgeting, such as drumming the fingers or twiddling the thumbs, is a set of gestural activities which convey extremely negative attitudes. Similarly, aggressive gestures with clenched fists and menacing postures convey hostile feelings while frequent use of relaxed, open-palm gestures toward the other person typically conveys positive attitudes.

A specific sort of gesture is touch, something used rather infrequently in American society. Yet there are indications that this element of communication may be extremely important. Bardeen compared reactions to three situations: communication by words only, communication by sight only and communication by touch.[24] He found that reactions to the first two were largely negative. The talk-only setting was rated distant, artificial, formal, insensitive, and noncommunicative, while the visual-only situation was termed artificial, childish, comical, cold, and arrogant. But the touch-only situation was rated trustful, sensitive, natural, mature, serious, and warm. It would seem, then, that this element of nonverbal interaction, important in other cultures but neglected in our own, could do much to improve relations with other people.

Head/Face/Eye Behaviors.   Perhaps the clearest indication of interpersonal attitudes comes from the combined actions of the communicator's head, face, and eyes. Head nods are signs of positive feelings, and as Matarazzo et al. demonstrated, they have a significant impact on the recipients' behavior.[25] Similarly, head shakes indicate negative attitudes. But head behaviors can be even more subtle. Lowering the head and peering, perhaps over glasses, at the other person is, according to Levy, the nonverbal equivalent of "you're putting me on."[26] Sheridan observes that cocking the head slightly to one side may indicate rejection or suspicion.[27] Indeed, progressively lifting the head backward while the other person speaks also indicates doubt or disbelief. Thus, a variety of head cues convey information to the recipient.

Facial expressions also indicate communicator attitudes. Rosenfeld noted that people seeking approval seem to smile more frequently, and Mehrabian and Williams observed that people trying to persuade others also show an increase in facial activity.[28] In research of another sort, Ekman

---

23 Thomas V. Bonoma and Leonard C. Felder, "Nonverbal Communication in Marketing: Toward a Communicational Analysis," *Journal of Marketing Research*, May 1977, pp. 169–180.

24 J. P. Bardeen, "Interpersonal Perception through the Tactile, Verbal, and Visual Modes" (Paper presented at the convention of the International Communication Association, Phoenix, 1971).

25 John Matarazzo et al., "Interviewer Influence of Durations of Interviewee Speech," *Journal of Verbal Learning and Verbal Behavior* 1, no. 4 (1963): 451–58.

26 Robert Levy, "Through a Glass, Darkly," *Dun's Review*, February 1976, pp. 77–78.

27 John H. Sheridan, "Are You a Victim of Nonverbal 'Vibes'?" *Industry Week,* July 10, 1978, pp. 36–42.

28 H. Rosenfeld, "Instrumental Affiliative Functions of Facial and Gestural Expressions," *Journal of Personality and Social Psychology* 4, no. 1 (1966): 65–72; Albert Mehra-

divided the face into three regions and attempted to determine which regions best express certain emotions.[29] He found that happiness is shown most by the lower face and eyes; sadness is seen primarily in the eyes; surprise is indicated by the eyes and lower face; anger is shown in the lower face, brows, and forehead; and fear is shown most clearly in the eyes. While facial expressions are relatively difficult to control, they nevertheless clearly mirror a manager's intentions and emotional state.

Studies of eye contact in human communication have identified the situations in which one seeks or avoids eye contact with others. Generally, one will seek eye contact with others when wanting to communicate with them, when physically distant from them, when friendly toward them, when feeling extremely hostile toward them (as when two bitter enemies try to stare each other down), or when wanting feedback from them. Conversely, a person will avoid eye contact if he or she wishes to avoid communication, is physically close to the other person, dislikes the other, is trying to deceive, or is disinterested. Given the positiveness of eye contact, one should find that it improves communication—and indeed it does. Exline and Eldridge found that messages accompanied by eye contact are more favorably interpreted by observers than are messages sent without eye contact.[30] Therefore, if a manager maintains eye contact with subordinates, communication with them probably will be significantly improved.

Vocalics.   The aspects of the voice, such as pitch, volume, quality, and rate, which accompany the spoken words comprise this final category. Apparently, people make two sorts of judgments about others on the basis of vocal cues. First, as Addington discovered, one judges personality characteristics on the basis of voice.[31] Second, and perhaps more important, Davitz discovered that judgments of emotion are also perceived in vocal cues.[32] Affection, for instance, seems to be indicated by low pitch, softness, slow rate, regular rhythm, and slurred enunciation. Anger is best perceived when the source speaks loudly, at a fast rate, in a high pitch, with irregular inflection, and clipped enunciation. Boredom is indicated by moderate volume, pitch, and rate, and a monotone inflection; joy by loud volume, high pitch, fast rate, upward inflection, and regular rhythm; and sadness by soft volume, slow rate, low pitch, downward inflection, and slurred enunciation. While specific individuals may differ in the ways in which they

bian and M. Williams, "Nonverbal Concomitants of Perceived and Intended Persuasiveness," *Journal of Personality and Social Psychology* 13, no. 1 (1969): 37–58.

29 Paul Ekman, "Differential Communication of Affect by Head and Body Cues," *Journal of Personality and Social Psychology* 2, no. 4 (1965): 726–35.

30 Robert V. Exline and Carl Eldridge, "Effects of Two Patterns of a Speaker's Visual Behavior upon the Perception of the Authenticity of His Verbal Message" (Paper presented to the Eastern Psychological Association, Boston, 1967).

31 David W. Addington, "The Effect of Vocal Variations on Ratings of Source Credibility," *Speech Monographs* 38, no. 2 (1971): 242–47.

32 J. R. Davitz and L. Davitz, "Nonverbal Vocal Communication of Feeling," *Journal of Communication* 11, no. 1 (1961): 81–86.

express these emotions, for the most part these patterns seem to reflect the vocalic behaviors typifying particular emotions. Through the careful use of vocal cues, supervisors can convey positive attitudes and, if necessary, mask negative ones toward their subordinates.

At this juncture, three conclusions seem abundantly clear:

1. Supervisors motivate or demotivate subordinates by communicating high or low expectations to them.

2. Much of that communication is accomplished nonverbally, so that environmental, physical, and vocal cues convey information to the employee.

3. By carefully using these nonverbal factors, supervisors can deliberately eliminate low-expectation cues and substitute behavior indicating high expectations.

One question remains: Can managers actually learn to control something as subtle as nonverbal communication? We believe they can, both alone and with training. On their own, they can make a conscious effort to observe the nonverbal behaviors of others and note their own responses to those cues. Moreover, they can engage in some "role playing," trying to convey the positive attitudes discussed above and observing the recipients' responses as a gauge of their success. Role playing according to prestructured exercises with feedback provided by a qualified trainer may speed learning, as might the opportunity to view one's efforts with video-tape playbacks. Still other methods have been used successfully by Argyle, Ekman, and Friesen, and others.[33] Certainly, managers can learn skills in communicating nonverbally.

Granting the desirability and practicality of using these nonverbal behaviors, one still might ask, "Is it ethical to convey cues which are contrary to one's true feelings?" That is, should a manager feign high expectations when, in fact, they are low? Our response is two-fold. First, there are situations in which the "polite lie" benefits everyone. The person who, upon leaving an incredibly dull party, thanks the host for a "wonderful evening" illustrates the point. Typically, the supervisor who transmits high expectations, whether true or not, will have a more productive, happy employee as a consequence. Second, by changing behaviors, a supervisor may also change his or her own attitudes. Evidence exists that people infer their attitudes from their personal behaviors.[34] Thus, a manager who exhibits high expectation cues may actually develop higher expectations of employees. The self-fulfilling prophecy will then become doubly effective.

---

[33] Michael Argyle, *Social Interaction* (New York: Atherton, 1969); Paul Ekman and William Friesen, *Unmasking the Face* (Englewood Cliffs, N.J.: Prentice-Hall, 1975); also see J. W. Pfeiffer and J. E. Jones, *A Handbook of Structured Experiences for Human Relations Training* (Iowa City, Iowa: University Associates, 1969–1970), vol. 1, pp. 109–11, vol. 2, pp. 102–104; M. Wiemann and M. Knapp, *Instructor's Guide to Nonverbal Communication in Human Interaction* (New York: Holt, Rinehart & Winston, 1978).

[34] Joseph DeVito, *The Psychology of Speech and Language* (New York: Random House, 1970), pp. 238–52.

Those Business Hunches Are More Than Blind Faith*

ROY ROWAN

The feasibility study is a beauty. The cost analysis looks right on the money. Even the sales projections, sometimes a little pie-in-the-sky, seem pretty solid. All the ingredients needed for a sound decision say "Go!" Yet this nagging voice from a mysterious echo chamber deep inside his brain keeps repeating "No!"

"Let's hold off on this one," announces the CEO to his astonished subordinates. "We've got enough on our plates for now."

Lame excuses like that cannot disguise the fact that most of the chief executives who control the destinies of the biggest corporations are often guided by ill-defined gut feelings. The intuitive boss, of course, is a recurring figure in American business. J. P. Morgan (who was known to visit fortune-tellers) and Cornelius Vanderbilt (who consulted clairvoyants and believed in ghosts) took enormous pride in their enormously profitable hunches. So did their legendary contemporaries, without seeking the counsel of mediums. Even today, when the empirical world of business is practically paved over with M.B.A.'s who can figure the risk-reward ratio of any decision at the drop of a computer key, the old-fashioned hunch continues to be a managerial tool.

WHEN BIOLOGY FEEDS BACK

Society's current addiction to psychic advice is hardly what executives mean when they admit to following hunches. Biofeedback, for example, has proved helpful in the healing process, but most businessmen—and not businessmen only—would consider it just short of sorcery.

Yet a handful of scientists and academicians have come up with measurable proof that subconscious elements play a role in the decision-making process. They are convinced that heeding a strong hunch may be a wise move, and even see a correlation between the boss's precognitive ability and his company's profitability. In any case, they point out that it isn't realistic for executives to rely solely on logic to cope with the complexities of modern business.

Broach these thoughts to a board chairman or president, and you had better watch your language. To begin with, *hunch* is an odious word to the professional manager. It's a stock market plunger's term, rife with imprecision and unpredictability. *Psychic* and *precognitive* are just as bad, since they smack of the occult. Self-proclaimed psychics pop up all over the place, insisting they can bend metal, project photographic images, or remove diseased organs by using nothing more than intense mental concentration. The business leader understandably shrinks from the thought of being associated with such kooks.

But suggest to this same executive that he might indeed possess certain intuitive powers, which could be of real assistance in generating ideas, choosing alternative courses of action, and picking people, and you'll elicit some interested responses:

"The chief executive officer is not supposed to say, 'I feel.' He's supposed to say, 'I know,' " asserts David Mahoney, chairman of Norten Simon. "So we deify the word instinct by calling it judgment. But any attempt to deny instinct is to deny identity. It's the most current thing. It's me—in everything from picking a wife to picking a company for acquisition."

"Intuition helps you read between the lines," says John Fetzer, owner of the Detroit Tigers and chairman of Fetzer Broadcasting Company. "Or walk through an office, and intuition tells you if things are going well." A staunch believer in mind over matter, Fetzer explains that he would never suggest to star pitcher Mark Fidrych that he stop talking aloud to the baseball and telling it where to go.

"In a business that depends entirely on people and not machinery," says Robert Bernstein, chairman of Random House, "only intuition can protect you against the most dangerous individual of all—the articulate incompetent. That's what frightens me about business schools. They train their students to sound wonderful. But it's necessary to find out if there's judgment behind the language."

"Physics is all hunches and intuition," admits Herman Kahn, a trained physicist-turned-futurist and now director of the Hudson Institute. "My research is a combination of intuition and judgment. I don't know where it comes from. The mind simply puts things together."

Precisely how the mind puts things together has never been adequately charted. If only we knew how the human brain constantly delves into the subconscious to retrieve buried fragments of knowledge and experience, which it then instantaneously fuses with all the new information, we might better be able to define the hunch and assess its reliability.

ARE YOU FORTUNE'S DARLING?

Nevertheless, we do know certain characteristics of the hunch. It concerns relationships, involves simultaneous perception of a whole system, and can draw a conclusion (not necessarily correct) without proceeding through logical intermediary steps. As Max Gunther points out in *The Luck Factor:* "The facts on which the hunch is based are stored and processed on some level of awareness just below the conscious level. This is why the hunch comes with that peculiar feeling of almost-but-not-quite knowing." But Gunther, an author of books on human relations, also warns against disregarding those "odd little hunches that are trying to tell you what you don't want to hear. Never assume you are fortune's darling." Failure to maintain some degree of pessimism, he claims, is to be in a state of peril.

There are other caveats that the wily manager should heed: Never confuse hope with a hunch, and never regard a hunch as a substitute for first acquiring all known data (laziness usually produces lousy hunches). However, since management itself is an inexact science—frequently defined as the "art of making decisions with insufficient information"—even the most deliberate CEO may be forced to act prematurely on an inner impression.

Possibly, then, it is in matters of timing that the business hunch is most critical, as Robert P. Jensen, chairman of General Cable Corporation, will testify. Last year, sensing the need for his company to diversify, he found himself faced with five major decisions that involved $300 million in sell-offs and acquisitions. "On each decision," says Jensen, "the mathematical analysis only got me to the point where my intuition had to take over"—as was the case with the $106-million cash purchase of Automation Industries. General Cable's strategic-planning department had come up with a purchase price based on Automation's future sales. "It's not that the numbers weren't accurate," Jensen recalls. "But were the underlying assumptions correct?"

An engineer not given to precipitate decisions, he calls "patience" crucial to the intuitive process. "It's easy to step in and say I have a feeling we ought to do this or that. But then you haven't let your managers weigh in with their feelings first." At the same time, he warns that the perfectionist who keeps waiting for new information never gets anything done. "Intuition is picking the right moment for making your move," adds Jensen, who spent three years as a tight end for the Baltimore Colts.

REVELING IN "CALCULATED CHAOS"

There is, in fact, considerable evidence that the wholly analytical creature pictured at the corporate pinnacle is so much folklore. That, anyway, is the view of Professor Henry Mintzberg of the McGill University Faculty of Management, who has been dissecting and writing about the executive animal for a dozen years.

According to Mintzberg, the CEO pays lips service to systematic long-range planning, elaborate tables of organization, and reliance on computers and esoteric quantitative techniques (more folklore). In reality he's a "holistic, intuitive thinker who revels in a climate of calculated chaos." Mintzberg portrays the CEO as working at an unrelenting pace, jumping from topic to topic, disposing of items in ten minutes or less, and "constantly relying on hunches to cope with problems far too complex for rational analysis."

No criticism intended. The puckish 39-year-old professor has immense admiration for the CEO's innate sense of direction, which he claims is much more reliable than that of the analytical consultant who is forever devising inflexible guidance systems for unmapped business terrain. "After all," says Mintzberg, "the intuitive Eskimo crosses the ice cap without a compass." The intuitive executive, he explains, solves problems in four interrelated stages set forth in Gestalt psychology: preparation ("creativity favors the prepared mind"), incubation ("letting the subconscious do the work"), illumination ("waking up in the middle of the night and shouting, 'Eureka, I've got it!' "), and verification ("then working it all out linearly").

In performing all of his tasks, the CEO—as students of intuitive decision making have noted—must know how to read a lot more than words. He assimilates gestures and moods and thrives on head-to-head encounters with both colleagues and competitors. His own language suggests this hunger for sensory information. He wants to get the "big picture," the "feel of a situation," and "hot gossip" and "cold facts."

This ability to absorb all manner of information stems from the fact that chief executives seem to be "right-brain dominated." It was long known that the right hemisphere of the brain controls the left side of the body—and vice versa. Only recently, however, was it discovered that the two sides of the brain seem to specialize in different activities. The left appears to handle the logical, linear, verbal functions. The right takes care of the emotional, intuitive, spatial functions. Therefore, as in baseball, a savvy board of directors might pick an intuitive right-brained CEO to pitch for the company.

To confirm this application of the right-brain, left-brain theory to business, Robert Doktor, a University of Hawaii business school professor, wired up a number of CEOs to an electroencephalograph to find out which hemisphere they relied on most. The right hemispheres won hands (or should it be heads?) down.

It was only a question of time before word of the right-brained boss would leak out and somebody would develop a market for the "soft information"—gossip, clues, insights, and other intangibles—on which the intuitive mind feeds. Infer-mation, as the Williams Inference Service of New York calls itself, now sells educated hunches ("disciplined intuition" is the term it uses) to companies such as Travelers and IU International.

"Lead time is the most valuable thing a corporation can have," claims Bennett Goodspeed, marketing chief for Williams. "Yet by the time the numbers are in on any new trend, the change is obvious to everyone." Williams combs hundreds of trade and technical journals for early, isolated clues that, when connected, may convey an "unintended message." But, as Goodspeed laments, corporations resist change. He points out that of six vacuum-tube manufacturers only one had the foresight to switch to transistors.

A MASQUERADE OF MEMORIES

In today's unpredictable environment, it's hard to tell whether even the "best" hunches will work. A CEO may come up with an ingenious concept that he can't sell—leaving him feeling as if he's suspended on a limb after the tree has fallen. Aware that universities were concerned about the "social content of their investments," Howard Stein, chairman of Dreyfus Corporation, launched a special mutual fund in 1972 composed only of companies that strictly complied with environmental safeguards and fair-employment practices. "Ironically, this Third Century Fund has outperformed most others," reports Stein, "but the colleges called it a 'do-good attempt' and stuck to traditional investments."

In addition, William F. May, chairman of American Can Company, warns that "you have to be alert not to let bad memories masquerade as intuition." He cites his company's experience with the two-quart milk container, which failed miserably when it was first introduced in 1934. The company revived the idea in 1955 in the belief that its time had come. "Our executives turned it down," says May ruefully. Today, American Can's competitors have two-quart containers in every dairy case.

One area where the hunch player has repeatedly scored is in figuring out the fickle American appetite. Confronted in 1960 with what his lawyer called a bad deal—$2.7 million for the McDonald name—Ray Kroc says: "I closed my office door, cussed up and down, threw things out of the window, called my lawyer back, and said: 'Take It!' I felt in my funny bone it was a sure thing." Last year, systemwide sales of Kroc's hamburger chain exceeded $4.5 billion.

PRECOGNITION AND PROFITS

This ability to decipher the telltale signs of the future puts an enormous premium on what the parapsychologists (ESP specialists) call "precognition." Almost two decades of testing executives have uncovered a close link between a CEO's precognitive and profit-making abilities. In research conducted at the New Jersey Institute of Technology, engineer John Mihalasky and parapsychologist E. Douglas Dean found that more than 80 percent of CEOs who had doubled their company's profits within a five-year period proved to have above-average precognitive powers. (The executives had to predict a 100-digit number that would be randomly selected by a computer anywhere from two hours to two years later.)

Mihalasky visualizes precognition as a flow of information particles moving forward and backward in time. He uses the stock market crash of 1929 to illustrate his point. For "precognitive" investors, there was strong evidence that it was coming and that there would be violent repercussions afterward.

"If something goes beyond the logic that we understand," cautions Mihalasky, "we say forget it." In any case, "the biggest roadblock to intuitive decision making is not having the guts to follow a good hunch." Although Mihalasky admits that the world is full of "psi-hitters" and "psi-missers," he offers certain recommendations for inducing intuition: (1)

Concentrate on what is unique. (2) Be aware of the gaps in your knowledge. (3) Make connections between diverse factors. (4) Avoid becoming overloaded with information.

While executives may hide the importance of the hunch, nonbusiness leaders are not so reluctant to acknowledge their indebtedness to it. Helen Gurley Brown confides that she uses "secret personal knowledge" in editing *Cosmopolitan*. "When I read a manuscript, even if it's not well written, only intuition can say this is truth, readers will like it. Or intuition may tell me that a piece by a Pulitzer prizewinner is a phony."

Dr. Jonas Salk, discoverer of the polio vaccine, says: "Intuition is something we don't understand the biology of yet. But it is always with excitement that I wake up in the morning wondering what my intuition will toss up to me like gifts from the sea. I work with it and rely upon it. It's my partner." After tedious experiments seeking ways to immunize against polio, Salk made an intuitive leap to the correct vaccine. R. Buckminster Fuller, creator of the geodesic dome, says: "I call intuition cosmic fishing. You feel a nibble, then you've got to hook the fish." Too many people, he claims, get a hunch, then light up a cigarette and forget about it.

Artists, certainly, always assumed that creativity doesn't spring from a deductive assault on a problem. Yet there are instances where a melding of the intuitive and deductive helped them produce magnificent results. From Leonardo da Vinci's pen came detailed drawings of the first flying machine. Both Robert Fulton, inventor of the steamboat, and Samuel Morse, inventor of the telegraph, started out life as artists. But intuition led them elsewhere.

Today, it is an explorer back from outer space, Edgar Mitchell, who has turned into intuition's most fervent evangelist—and almost a mystic as well. A doctor of science from M.I.T., Navy captain, and the sixth man on the moon, he believes that "man's potential knowledge is more than the product of his five senses."

Following that journey, Mitchell founded the Institute of Noetic Sciences (Greek for *intuitive knowing*) in California, and not long ago became a director of two computer-software companies—Information Science in West Palm Beach and Forecast Systems in Provo, Utah. In all three endeavors, his aim is to help his fellow man—especially the businessman—develop intuitive decision-making powers to the point where, as he says, "they can control the scientific beast."

EXPLORING INNER SPACE

In preparing for a lunar flight, Mitchell explains, "we spent 10 percent of our time studying plans for the mission, and 90 percent of our time learning how to react intuitively to all the 'what if's.' " At Forecast Systems, Mitchell and his associates use this same approach to help clients identify potential problem areas. They interview managers, foremen, and workers to uncover their fears about all the things that might go wrong. "With a computer printout of the resulting 'fault tree' in front of him, a CEO can almost smell those failures before they occur," says Mitchell, explaining "failure analysis," a space-age spinoff.

However methodical even scientific Mitchell and other researchers may be, the explanations of intuition and its powers remain elusive. All of the parts, added up, fall short of making a sum called the hunch. But the businessman like David Mahoney or Ray Kroc who has relied on an occasional hunch to solve an important business problem cares less about analyzing the phenomenon than seeing the results. Often, these can be spectacular.

In the future it will probably be sparks thrown off by minds trained in still newer disciplines which produce the best hunches. Not that this amorphous, intuitive power will be any more measurable then. Of course, that is simply a hunch.

Integrating Behaviorally-Based and Effectiveness-Based Appraisal Methods*

CRAIG ERIC SCHNEIER and RICHARD W. BEATTY

Most organizations are dissatisfied with their performance appraisal (PA) process, particularly for administrative/managerial positions. They have concerns about its objectivity, its relevance, and its validity. In many cases the complaint is that the appraisal system simply does not work! In a three-part series on this topic which begins with this article, we take a good, hard look at appraisal. First the objectives and legal requirements for appraisal systems are discussed and potential problem sources are identified. Appraisal is seen as a process involving key decisions and having important consequences. PA is not simply a form or a rating scale, but an integral managerial tool which can improve performance of individuals and units.

In the second article, the advantages of behaviorally-based and effectiveness-based systems are noted. A detailed procedure is given for developing Behaviorally-Anchored Rating Scales (BARS), a job-related practical and valid system. In the third article BARS are combined with Management by Objectives (MBO) to form a behaviorally-based/effectiveness-based system which is truly integrated. A large organization's success with such a system is described and a diagnostic procedure for identifying performance problems is detailed.

> You could always tell how you were doing by the way the (pitching) coach said good morning. If he said, "Well, now, good morning Jimsie boy," that meant you'd won your last two or three games and were in the starting rotation. If he nodded his head to you and said, "Jimbo, how are you doin', how are you doin'?" you were still in the starting rotation, but your record probably wasn't much over .500. If he just said, "Mornin'," that meant you were on your way down, that you'd probably lost four out of five and it was doubtful if you would be getting any more starts. If he simply looked at you and gave a solemn nod, that meant you might get some mop-up relief

---

* Reprinted from the July 1979 issue of *Personnel Administrator*, 30 Park Drive, Berea, OH 44017.

work, or you might not, but you definitely weren't starting anymore and would never get into a close game again. And if he looked past you, over your shoulder as if you didn't exist, it was all over and you might as well pack your bag because you could be traded or sent down at any moment.[1]

The appraisal of human performance in organizations is vital, yet problematic. Herbert Meyer was recently led to remark, "of all the uncertainties that have kept executives from sleeping peacefully at night, probably none are quite so unsettling as those related to the difficulty of figuring out their boss's real opinion of them."[2]

Performance appraisal (PA) is required for it forms the rationale for key decisions regarding promotion, wage and salary administration, and selection for training programs. However, despite noteworthy advances in scaling techniques to reduce such psychometric errors as leniency, many organizations still feel their appraisal systems are ineffective[3] and still have problems removing subjectivity and bias of raters. They have given up the search for perfect form, hoping to develop any acceptable one.

WHAT IS JOB PERFORMANCE?

Much of the activity observed on a job results in an evaluation of the *performance* of a person, team, unit, or an entire organization. In order to understand how such evaluations are made, the distinction between the following three terms is essential: behavior, performance, and effectiveness (see also Figure 1).[4]

Behavior is simply what people do on a job—their activity. Writing reports, holding meetings, analyzing documents and conversing with others are possible behaviors exhibited on the job. Effective behavior is a function of the interaction between ability *and* effort—the behavior initiated to put one's ability to use. *Performance* is the term used for the evaluation of these behaviors as to their desirability or efficacy on the job. For example, writing reports in a specific style is evaluated as desirable performance. The report writing is evaluated according to a set of standards, or *criteria,* used by the evaluator. Certain behaviors or groups of behaviors are evaluated as good performance, others as fair performance and still others as unacceptable performance. Performance is the evaluated behavior and is what is measured in appraisal systems.

Effectiveness refers to the outcomes or results of various degrees of performance at the individual, unit, or organizational level. Did the behaviors which produced an excellent report actually result in a desired organiza-

[1] Bill Bouton in M. W. McCall and D. L. DeVries, *Appraisal in Context* (Greensboro, N.C.: Center for Creative Leadership, 1977).

[2] H. E. Meyer, "The Science of Telling Executives How They're Doing," *Fortune,* January 1974, p. 102.

[3] Bureau of National Affairs, *Management of Performance Appraisal Systems* (Washington, D.C.: BNA, 1974).

[4] See also J. P. Campbell, et al., *Managerial Behavior, Performance, and Effectiveness* (New York: McGraw-Hill, 1970).

Figure 1
What Is Job Performance?

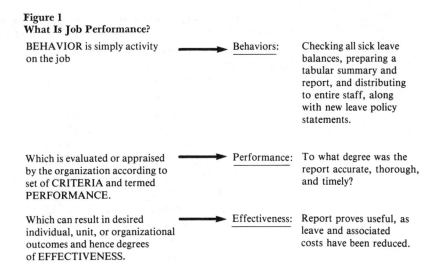

BEHAVIOR is simply activity on the job ———▶ Behaviors: Checking all sick leave balances, preparing a tabular summary and report, and distributing to entire staff, along with new leave policy statements.

Which is evaluated or appraised by the organization according to set of CRITERIA and termed PERFORMANCE. ———▶ Performance: To what degree was the report accurate, thorough, and timely?

Which can result in desired individual, unit, or organizational outcomes and hence degrees of EFFECTIVENESS. ———▶ Effectiveness: Report proves useful, as leave and associated costs have been reduced.

tional outcome, such as more efficient spending or the development of more relevant programs? Did holding a meeting with appropriate persons actually result in a more effective plan?

A key aspect of judgment in the appraisal setting thus involves drawing cause-and-effect inferences between behaviors and effectiveness. For example, if a rater observes that profit in a unit has gone down (i.e., the unit has become less effective), he or she must draw a conclusion concerning whether behaviors exhibited by management or others responsible were inappropriate or whether other factors may have caused the decline, such as a drop in demand for the product. As will be discussed in subsequent sections, Management by Objectives (MBO) appraisal systems, designed to measure outcomes or effectiveness, are deficient if they are unable to identify and measure the effectiveness of the behaviors which produced (or failed to produce) the outcomes.

WHAT IS PERFORMANCE APPRAISAL?

Performance appraisal or evaluation is the *process of identifying, measuring, and developing human performance* in organizations. An effective appraisal system must not only *accurately measure current performance levels,* but also contain mechanisms for *reinforcing strengths, identifying deficiencies,* and feeding such information back to ratees in order that they may *improve future performance.* This second, developmental aspect of appraisal is as important as the measurement aspect.

As noted in the preceding section, the term *performance* itself denotes judgment—behavior which has been evaluated. Performance appraisal is thus the process of *observing* and *identifying, measuring* and *developing* human behavior in the organization. These activities are described as follows:

Observation and *identification* refers to the process of viewing or scrutinizing job behaviors. It consists of choosing what job behaviors to look at among all that are emitted by a ratee, as well as how often to observe them. The choices inherent in this process add subjectivity to appraisal.

Measurement refers to ascertaining the extent, degree, level, and so on of a behavior. After raters choose what information to examine, they compare this information about ratee behavior against a set of organizational or personal expectations for each job. The degree to which observed behavior meets or exceeds the expectations determines its desirability, or the level of performance it reflects, such as excellent or satisfactory.

Development refers to performance improvement over time. An appraisal system must contain mechanisms to communicate the expectations and measurement process to persons being appraised, motivate them to remove any deficiencies uncovered, and reinforce them to build on strengths in order to improve future performance.

When PA is considered in terms of its utility to an organizaton, several operational PA objectives seem critical. These include (1) the ability to provide adequate feedback to employees to improve subsequent performance, (2) the identification of employee training needs, (3) the identification of criteria used to allocate organizational rewards, (4) the validation of selection techniques to meet Equal Employment Opportunity (EEO) requirements and (5) the identification of promotable employees from internal labor supplies (see Figure 2). In order to accomplish these objectives, the PA system must, of course, be an accurate measure of performance.

A PA's adequacy to *provide feedback and improve performance* requires that it possess the following characteristics: be unambiguous and clearly specify the job-rated performance expected, use behavioral terminology, set behavioral targets for ratees to work toward, and use a problem-solving focus which culminates in a specific plan for performance improvement. If PAs are to identify training needs, the format must specify ratee deficiencies in behavioral terms, include all relevant job dimensions, and identify environmental deterrents to desired performance levels.

PAs are also used in the *allocation of organizational rewards* such as merit pay and punishments, such as disciplinary actions. Effective reward allocation may require a valid PA which ranks employees according to a quantifiable scoring system. Sufficient variance in scores is essential to differentiate across performers. In allocating rewards, PAs must have credibility with employees. The same PA format must also be used for disciplinary action, which may range from warnings to termination. Thus, the documentation required for such decisions must also be facilitated by the PA format. With the recent passage of Civil Service Reform Act and its provisions tying performance to merit pay and bonuses, the importance of PAs in the public sector has been greatly heightened.

PAs must be designed to facilitate the *validation of selection* techniques. This process requires, in general terms and at a minimum, measures of employee output or job-rated dimensions that tap the behavioral domain

Figure 2
Objectives of Performance Appraisal Systems

1 Feedback Development Requires:	2 Assessing Training Needs Requires:	3 Identifying Promotion Potential Requires:	4 Rewards Allocation Requires:	5 Validation of Selection Techniques Requires:	6 Measurement Accuracy Requires:
Specifying behavioral terminology on the format.	Specifying deficiencies in behavioral terms.	Job-related criteria	Ability to rank order ratees or results in quantifiable, performance scores.	Job relatedness and a comprehensive list of dimensions tapping the behavioral domain of the job.	Reducing rater responses set errors (e.g., leniency, restriction of range, halo).
Setting behavioral targets for ratees to work toward.	Rating on all relevant job dimensions.	Job dimensions dealing with ability to assume increasingly difficult assignments built into the form.	Facilitating a variance or spread of scores to discriminate between good, bad, fair, etc. ratees.	Systematic job analysis to derive criteria.	Agreeing with other performance measures not on the format (e.g., direct indices such as salary, number of promotions.)
Job-related, problem-solving performance review which ends with a plan for performance improvement.	Identifying motivation/ attitude and environmental conditions as causes of inadequate performance.	Ability to rank ratees comparatively.	Measuring contributions to organization/ department objectives.	Assessing interrater reliability.	Reliability across multiple raters.
Reducing ambiguity/ anxiety of ratees regarding job performance required and expected by raters/ organization.		Measuring of contribution to organization/ department objectives.	Accuracy and credibility with employees.	Professional, objective administration of format.	Flexibility to reflect changes in job or environment.
		Assessing of ratee's career aspirations and long-range goals.		Continual observation of ratee performance by raters.	Job-related criteria
					Commitment of raters to observe ratee performance frequently and complete format seriously.

of the job obtained through systematic job analysis, the facilitation of interrater reliability measures, professional and objective administration of the PA, and continual rater observation of ratee performance.[5]

The *identification of promotion potential* requires that job-related PAs have several dimensions in the incumbent's job, the same, or similar to, the job to which the incumbent may be promoted. This indicates the incumbent's ability to assume increasingly difficult assignments. The PA must also rank ratees comparatively, measure the contribution to departmental objectives, and perhaps capture a ratee's career aspirations and long-term goals.

---

[5] See "Uniform Guidelines on Employee Selection Procedures," *Federal Register*, December 30, 1977; D. B. Schneier, "The Impact of EEO Legislation on Performance APPRAISAL," *Personnel* 55 no. 4 (1978): 24–34.

The final but perhaps most important PA objective is its accuracy in measuring performance. In some ways, it could be conceived as essential for meeting the PA objectives mentioned above. The issues of concern here would include PA formats which minimize rater response set errors (e.g., leniency, restriction of range, halo), those which agree with other measures of performance using alternative formats (e.g., direct indices such as salary or number of promotions), those which obtain reliability across raters, those which have the flexibility to reflect changes in the job environment and those possessing credibility with raters such that they complete the format seriously.

Thus, there are several criteria which PAs should meet to be fully operational. But which types of formats—those which measure worker behavior or those which measure the outcomes of that behavior—are more effective? No simple answer is available, but the utility of various types of behavior-based and effective-based formats can best be ascertained by comparing them against the PA objectives identified above.

COMPARISON OF FORMATS

Global Ratings. The first PA format alternative is a unidimensional, global rating which uses a rater's overall estimate of performance without distinguishing between critical job elements or dimensions. There are numerous problems in the use of unidimensional formats, and when compared to the six PA objectives described above, they generally fall far short (see Figure 3). Unidimensional PA formats are also questionable as measures of performance (i.e. criteria) from a legal standpoint because they are not based on job analysis and thus are not job-rated.

Trait-Based Scales. There are numerous multidimensional (or graphic) approaches to measuring performance. They are more useful than global scales because they recognize that job performance consists of separate dimensions, or job elements. The first of these is the familiar trait-based scale using dimensions such as loyalty, dependability, and so on. Other dimensions traditionally found on these formats are cooperation, initiative,

Figure 3
Generalized Evaluation of PA Formats Compared to PA Objectives

Objective / Format	Feedback/ Development	Assessing Training Needs	Identification of Promotion Potential	Reward Allocation	Selection System Validation	Measurement Accuracy
Global	Poor	Poor	Poor to fair	Poor	Poor	Poor
Trait-based	Poor	Poor	Poor to fair	Poor to fair	Poor to fair	Poor to fair
Behavior-based (if behaviorally anchored)	Very good to excellent	Very good	Very good	Very good	Very good to excellent	Good
Effectiveness-based	Fair to good	Fair to good	Fair to good	Very good to excellent	Fair to good	Very good to excellent

and self-confidence. There are problems in the use of trait-based scales centering around potential ambiguity and subjectivity. That is, specifically what is meant by "lack of cooperation"? Thus, many trait-based scales are generally evaluated as only poor to fair relative to PA objectives. Further, and perhaps most important, trait-based scales are typically not sufficiently job-related or based on a thorough job analysis. Thus an organization's vulnerability to Equal Employment Opportunity (EEO) litigation is not alleviated.

Behavior-Based Scales.   A significant step beyond global and trait-based formats are behaviorally based scales. These are based upon a job analysis and attempt to determine what an employee actually *does* at work. A behavior-based scale provides specific feedback to employees because it is based on the activities required of the job. It captures specific information across employees for reward allocation and about each employee specifically in the assessment of training needs because it identifies the activities (dimensions) in which an employee may be deficient. For promotion potential, a dimension-based scale can certainly be useful because it may specify the kinds of behaviors incumbents are to demonstrate in their present jobs. Performance on these dimensions can then be compared to the dimensions required in the next job level (for which the employee is a promotion candidate). Behavior-based scales are often seen as more accurate than the previous two PA formats because of their job-relatedness and specificity. Thus we can expect less rater error and higher interrater agreement (and/ or reliability). Finally, because dimension-based scales can meet the legal requirements for criterion measures, these certainly can be an improvement for the validation of selection procedures.

The major drawback with dimension-based scales is that although they provide specification of the particular activities of an employee, the scale points are of limited use if they are only numerically and/or adjective-anchored. They provide little specific feedback on what behaviors led to the particular rating given, even though the area of performance deficiency has been identified. Thus, a dimension-based PA may be deficient in assessing an employee's specific behaviors within job dimensions since only adjective or numerical anchors are used.

Behavioral expectation scales or *behaviorally-anchored rating scales (BARS)* are also dimensional scales.[6] The scale points are behavioral statements illustrating various degrees of performance, not merely adjectives or numbers. Thus, BARS are far more specific in terms of identifying employee behavior relative to performance on a specific job dimension. These are also more sophisticated than dimensions-based formats and require more time to develop.

Behavior-based scales seem to provide excellent feedback to employees

---

[6] The development and utility of BARS is the subject of Part II of this series of three articles. See also C. E. Schneier and R. W. Beatty, *Personnel Administration Today* (Reading, Mass.: Addison-Wesley Publishing, 1978) and S. J. Carroll and C. E. Schneier, *Performance Appraisal* (Goodyear Publishing, forthcoming).

in specifying not only what activities employees are to engage in, but also the behaviors a rater perceives that a ratee has demonstrated during the performance period. In fact, performance improvement has been demonstrated through the use of behavior-based systems.[7]

Effectiveness-Based Systems. Another multidimensional system is results, or effectiveness, based scaling. Effectiveness-based scales attempt to provide "objective" indicators for levels of performance and are, of course, typically called Management by Objectives (MBO) systems.[8] Although it is a multidimensional approach in that there are often many objectives which are to be accomplished, effectiveness-based scaling is unique in that what it provides is a measure of an employee's *contribution,* not an employee's *activities or behaviors.*

Ratees evaluated with effectiveness-based scaling are being evaluated not on what they *do* but what they *produce;* not on how they spend their time, but what they contribute. This is an important difference and a major shortcoming of the previously discussed PA approaches. Obviously, it is difficult to develop specific indicators of employee contribution, but it can be done for many jobs. It is accomplished with more ease in lower level jobs and entry-level jobs within an organization than in higher level jobs.

Thus, effectiveness-based scales offer something that is critical and often overlooked in the assessment of performance appraisals. MBO systems are often used to measure unit productivity to which a manager presumably makes a contribution.

WHAT ARE THE CAUSES OF PROBLEMS?

Regardless of what format is used, problems can deter PA system effectiveness. The cause of the ineffectiveness of any particular PA system is a function of many variables, acting singly or in groups, which characterize the job, organizational setting, and users. However, most often specific causes are located within the following broad problem categories: human judgment, raters, criteria and formats, organization policy, legal requirements, and Equal Employment Opportunity (EEO) legislation and inflexibility. Each of these six broad categories contains several possible sources of PA problems (see Figure 4), discussed briefly below.

Problems in a PA system ultimately can only be judged as to their degree of severity and dysfunctional consequences in light of the original objectives developed for each system. For example, a PA system may sacrifice some degree of applicability across job-type (and would, possibly have higher developmental costs) in order to have a greater amount and specificity of information about performance available to a certain group of ratees. Hence, it may have greater ability to pinpoint performance deficiencies

---

[7] R. W. Beatty, C. E. Schneier, and J. R. Beatty, "An Empirical Investigation of Perceptions of Ratee Behavior Frequency and Ratee Behavior Change Using Behavioral Expectation Scales (BES)," *Personnel Psychology* 30 (1977): 647–58.

[8] See S. J. Carroll and H. Tosi, *Management by Objective* (New York: Macmillan, 1973).

Figure 4
Sources of Problems in Appraisal Systems

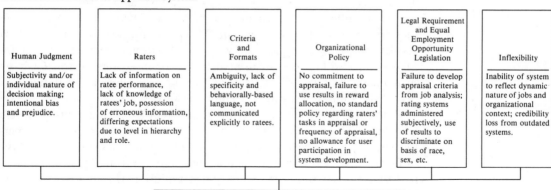

Human Judgment	Raters	Criteria and Formats	Organizational Policy	Legal Requirement and Equal Employment Opportunity Legislation	Inflexibility
Subjectivity and/or individual nature of decision making; intentional bias and prejudice.	Lack of information on ratee performance, lack of knowledge of ratees' job, possession of erroneous information, differing expectations due to level in hierarchy and role.	Ambiguity, lack of specificity and behaviorally-based language, not communicated explicitly to ratees.	No commitment to appraisal, failure to use results in reward allocation, no standard policy regarding raters' tasks in appraisal or frequency of appraisal, no allowance for user participation in system development.	Failure to develop appraisal criteria from job analysis; rating systems administered subjectively, use of results to discriminate on basis of race, sex, etc.	Inability of system to reflect dynamic nature of jobs and organizational context; credibility loss from outdated systems.

CREDIBILITY AND EFFECTIVENESS OF APPRAISAL SYSTEMS

and thus reduce costs of unnecessary training programs. If the objectives of a PA system are predetermined and prioritized, the system can be designed to make such trade-offs rationally and at minimal cost. Further, after PA design and implementation, problems diagnosed can be judged as to seriousness and corrective action planned in light of objectives. This relationship between PA objectives and both the design and revision of PA systems, while considering various PA problems, is emphasized in the discussion to follow.

Problem No. 1: Human Judgment. A fundamental source of problems in PA is the *subjectivity and individuality* which accompanies the human judgment process. Individual differences among people influence their attitudes, values, perceptions, behavior, and judgment, a fact as true in the PA setting as it is in all others. Intelligence, cognitive style, amount of education, age, sex, and self-esteem are but a few of the individual level characteristics which have been found to influence the making of judgments of others. The expectations raters' supervisors hold for them, as well as a rater's own level of job performance and competence, have also been found to effect ratings.[9]

All of these factors, however, act in an implicit manner. They reflect "honest" or legitimate differences in personality, background, or ability between participants in PA which influence their perception—their view of reality—and thus perceptions of the behavior of ratees. While these individual differences typically do not result in deliberate attempts to bias or prejudice ratings, their result on PA (e.g., inaccuracies) is similar.

Besides these *un*intentional PA errors resulting from individual differences, are those overt, deliberate attempts to distort PAs based upon per-

9 See e.g., C. E. Schneier, "The Psychometric Characteristics and Operational Utility of Behavioral Expectation Scales (BES): A Cognitive Reinterpretation," *Journal of Applied Psychology* 62 (1977): 541–48.

sonal prejudices and biases against others of a certain religion, national origin, race, sex, age, political ideology, and the like. The result can be the setting of different performance standards for two people performing the same job or the distorting of PA results upward or downward to correspond to one's prejudices. Even when performance criteria are quantifiable and visible, figures can be distorted or interpreted erroneously by such judgmental factors as perceived amount of effort or initiative and hence intentional bias can still enter the process.

Problem No. 2: Raters.   PA problems stem from conscientious raters who possess *inadequate and/or erroneous information* about ratee performance. Many supervisors, due to their own job duties which may physically separate them from their subordinate ratees, are able to observe ratee performance too infrequently to judge typical performance accurately. Many must thus "sample" performance over a long period. But nonrepresentative sampling or allowing a typical positive or negative performance occurring during their infrequent observation periods to bias their judgments of performance over the entire period can lead to inaccurate appraisals.

In addition, members of each hierarchical level within an organization may view a ratee's performance from a different vantage point or hold differing expectations for desired performance based upon their roles.[10] Thus a ratee's supervisor may be in an excellent position to judge the ratee's technical competence, but not his or her ability to interact effectively with others. Peer raters may possess the best information regarding a ratee's interpersonal effectiveness. Supervisors of ratees, as critics and evaluators of their subordinates, typically judge performance more harshly than do job incumbents themselves.

Problem No. 3: Criteria and PA Formats.   The identification of specific, consistent performance criteria are the first objective of a PA system, as discussed earlier. The easiest way to assure that a ratee's performance can be evaluated based upon only the whim of a rater is of course to keep the criteria ambiguous and/or secret, to change them capriciously, or never to develop them at all! As discussed above, each type of appraisal format has advantages and disadvantages relative to this issue of defining the criteria against which to base evaluations. The overall objective, of course, is to develop a format which identifies and defines the criteria in explicit, concrete terms.

Problem No. 4: Organizational Policy.   Problems in PA systems arise from the relationship between organizational policies regarding performance, promotion, merit raises, and other decisions and the uses for which PA results are intended. If these types of decisions are actually to be made on the basis of performance, rather than on the basis of seniority or other criteria, results of a PA obviously assume a great deal of importance. Here

---

10 See C. E. Schneier and R. W. Beatty, "The Influence of Role Prescriptions on the Performance Appraisal Process," *Academy of Management Journal* 21 (1978): 129–34.

problems arise when PA formats are ambiguous, criteria are not communicated to raters and ratees and/or if each of several degrees of performance (e.g., good, fair, and so on) do not have observable, behavioral referents.

For example, if a supervisor (rater) is given the authority to set merit raises for a group of subordinates (ratees) and the PA format which is used to measure performance is of the global type involving overall ranking, the supervisor can easily feel trapped. Of course, the supervisor might have a definite and accurate overall impression as to the relative performance of his or her ratees and can easily discriminate between the excellent and average performers. But if the top performers are given merit raises and the others are not, the supervisor needs a rationale for this action to give to those who were denied the merit raise. The global PA format provides little help since it does not specify and define the exact criteria used in PA or the different levels of performance within each criteria. To develop a formal, written rationale for each rating may not only be seen as too bothersome for many raters but they may find it difficult to articulate the exact criteria to ratees. The result is often that either extreme leniency is used on many ratings or that all ratees are rated about the same and hence each receives a smaller merit raise. Thus, expediency rather than discriminability between good and poor performers characterizes the PA system and its credibility is destroyed.

Problem No. 5: Legal Requirements and Equal Employment Opportunity (EEO) Legislation. The risk of precipitating charges of discrimination as a result of policy decisions based upon PA results is now itself a serious cause of problems in PA systems. The ramification of subjective, unsubstantiated PAs can be devastating to an organization. Recently, through several pieces of legislation, court decisions, and guidelines of various federal agencies, the issue of discrimination in employment as a result of PAs has become more visible and spelled out in more detail than ever before.[11]

Organizations must present PA forms and any instructions given to raters as part of the evidence for the validity of such selection techniques as employment tests. Thus, the use of, for example, an application blank, would be judged acceptable in certain situations only if answers to particular items on the blank were found to correlate highly with the probability of future job "success" of workers in the job. Job "success" is demonstrated typically by results of a PA system. The PA system is thus open to scrutiny by the courts and must therefore be thorough and as bias-free as possible.

Violation of civil rights legislation can also come from the use of PAs *directly* in promotion decisions. The following excerpts from discussions

---

11 See W. H. Holley and H. S. Feild, "Performance Appraisal and the Law," *Labor Law Journal,* July 1975, pp. 423–29; "Uniform Guidelines on Employee Selection Procedures," *Federal Register,* December 30, 1977; Schneier, "Impact of EEO Legislation APPRAISAL."

of recent court cases involving PAs illustrate the potential consequences of an inadequate system:

> The court found the following as a basis for discrimination: Recommendations by foremen were based on standards which were vague and subjective and were made without written instructions concerning qualifications necessary for promotion . . . one company was required to offer training programs to upgrade personnel, to provide foremen with written instructions delineating objective criteria. . . . The other company was ordered to post announcements of preforemen training classes, to post notices of qualifications required for salaried positions. . . .
>
> Using performance ratings for determining personnel layoffs was found to be in violation of Title VII of the Civil Rights Act when an employer failed to validate the appraisal methods according to EEOC guidelines. The evaluations were judged invalid because they were based on subjective observations (two of three evaluators did not observe the employee on a daily basis), evaluations were not administered and scored under controlled and standardized conditions. . . . The courts ordered the company to reinstate the employees with nominal back pay and required the company not to use performance ratings until they had been validated.[12]

Problem No. 6: Inflexibility.   The final cause of problems in PA systems is the dynamic nature of jobs and job performance and the static nature of any written PA document typically developed several months before it is to be used. As job responsibilities, duties, requirements and job environments change over time, a PA format may become obsolete before it is even used! Further, as worker's performance levels change over time, perhaps due to training and experience, the standards set in PA formats may be too low, geared only for newer workers. Even the same jobs within classes are not identical.

One solution is, of course, to develop new PA formats continually as all of the above factors change and to develop separate PA formats for each and every position. But this solution is an economic impossibility. A solution often used by organizations is to develop a few broad categories of formats—perhaps one format for operating-level workers, one for clerical workers, one for technical workers, and one for managers. A reasonable solution? Yes, provided raters are knowledgeable, competent, use identical standards, observe performance equally, are generally bias-free, and are provided with specific, detailed criteria. But in the all too often instances when the "ideal" rater is unavailable, PA formats applicable across job types may lead to subjectivity and possibly to litigation for discrimination.

The view of PA systems presented above is, admittedly, problematic. Yet it is a realistic one as many organizations find their appraisal system to be the source of continual problems. As discussed, no system is capable of alleviating all appraisal problems completely. Yet there are a few things which can be done to enhance a system's effectiveness.

---

12 Holley and Feild, "Performance Appraisal and the Law," pp. 427–28.

The first way to improve appraisal systems is to recognize that the appraisal process entails far more than measurement and the use of a form. It also includes observation and identification of performance, as well as development of performance. As discussed, PA systems have several objectives. They must be developed in light of both the trade-offs between these objectives and the potential problem sources in appraisal.

The second mechanism for improved appraisal is to integrate the best aspects of the various formats. Behavior-based systems, such as Behaviorally-Anchored Rating Scales (BARS), specify criteria in very concrete terms to improve accuracy, provide detailed feedback to ratees, and help comply with legal requirements due to the job-relatedness of criteria. Effectiveness-based systems, such as Management by Objectives (MBO) are very popular due to their ability to measure and quantify results, redirect effort to important tasks and allow for ratee participation in goal setting. The next article in this series demonstrates how and why BARS and MBO can be integrated to derive the benefits from both systems. The developmental procedure for BARS is explained and the samples of all required forms are included. The last article in the series describes the final integrated system and explains its operation through an actual case study.

Thinking Clearly about Career Choices*

IRVING JANIS and DAN WHEELER

"Years ago I made a bad mistake, and now I'm paying for it: I'm trapped in this job."

"I should have found out how this firm was run before taking their offer. I had other good prospects at the time."

"They led me down the garden path, and I was damn fool enough to be taken in."

When 81 middle-level executives of a large industrial organization were interviewed for a study of career satisfaction several years ago, a sizable number said they were disgusted with their jobs. In confidence, they complained about petty rules and dull routines that interfered with getting their work done, obstacles to being promoted, long hours that were ruining their home lives, and the disruptions caused by repeated reorganizations. Listening carefully to their complaints, the investigators also heard something else: the men's regrets at their own miscalculations when they first decided to come to work for the company. A few (like those quoted above) candidly admitted that they should have found out much more about what it would really be like to work there before accepting the job.

We have heard comparable complaints from lawyers, physicians, public administrators, and technical specialists. Why do so many intelligent, well-educated people make poor career choices they sooner or later regret? Why do so many fail to correct their mistakes, despite opportunities to reshape their careers?

When people confront a complex problem of trying to satisfy many different objectives and foresee the consequences of various alternatives, they often come up against the limitations of their mental capabilities. Misjudgments also stem from pressures to conform and other social constraints. Above all, the stress of making crucial choices, with serious consequences that one might later regret, sometimes itself impairs critical judgment.

---

* Reprinted from *Psychology Today Magazine,* May 1978, pp. 66–68, 70, 75–76, 121–22. Copyright © 1978 Ziff-Davis Publishing Company.

Psychological studies suggest that most people tend to short-circuit the essential stages of search and appraisal when they become aware of possible undesirable consequences of their choices. Even the most mature and the best educated can deceive themselves into believing they have complete information after brief contact with a so-called expert and perhaps a few informal discussions with friends.

Whenever a decision entails serious, lifelong consequences, it pays to use sound decision-making procedures. People *can* make sound decisions, and new psychological theories and findings can help them. Some of the approaches we will discuss can be carried out on one's own. Others may require the help of a career counselor or personal adviser. Even people who are highly experienced at making decisions can benefit from a bit of guidance if they are choosing a career, changing jobs, moving to a different city, or whatever.

Consider the following dilemma: You are offered an excellent position in a large organization that is much better than any alternative offer. It will make more use of your training and skills and offers better pay, better working conditions, and greater opportunities for advancement. But the organization is having some financial difficulties that sooner or later could require drastic budget cuts, which could result in the elimination of a large number of jobs, including the one you are being offered. For a decision of this kind, there are *two* risky scenarios to worry about: one is dramatic and obvious, while the other is more subtle and might not receive as much attention as it deserves.

Scenario 1.   Recognizing a unique opportunity, you decide to accept the offer. You work hard, you are successful, and you are rapidly promoted, just as you had been led to expect. But after a few years, your worst fears come true. You are laid off, along with hundreds of others, and you suddenly find you are unable to find an acceptable opening in your field in a tight job market. This is what actually happened to thousands of professional engineers and executives when the aerospace industry underwent cutbacks during the early 1970s. And something similar is happening right now to thousands of men and women who have just obtained their Ph.D. degrees and are trying to get jobs in college teaching.

Scenario 2.   Recognizing the risks posed by Scenario 1, you decide to play it safe by refusing the offer. Instead, you accept an inferior position, with less opportunity for career development, in a financially untroubled organization that everyone says will be going strong long after you reach retirement age. But suppose Scenario 1 does not materialize and you regret the sacrifice you made for the sake of job security? Your work in the safe organization turns out to be no better than could be expected—dull, routine, very little opportunity to make use of your skills or develop your potentialities, and no real hope of promotion. As the years go by, you learn that people in your occupation who took jobs in the more attractive company are comparatively well satisfied with the most talented ones are being rapidly promoted. In short, you have to live not only with a blighted career, but also with the realization that you have failed to grasp your one great career opportunity.

Though the different consequences of such decisions may seem quite obvious, many people overlook some of the risks that could lead to unpleasant outcomes. Sometimes they are simply unwilling to think about such painful things. In the case described above, the most attractive alternative required the calculated risk of a relatively sudden, dramatic disaster, whereas the calculated risk for not choosing that alternative was a long, drawn-out tragedy that could be just as bad or worse. Our choices are often structured in just that way.

What is the advantage of working out these gloomy scenarios? If we don't, we may not know what kind of information we need on the possible consequencies of our choices. If we ignore the threat of a drastic budget cut, for instance, we're not likely to seek inside information that will enable us to estimate the likelihood that such a cut will occur. Even if no such information can be obtained, there are advantages to becoming keenly aware of all the things that can go wrong after a decision is made. We can then keep our losses to a minimum by making *contingency plans.*

Studies of occupational choices by economist Eli Ginzberg and others indicate that many people never make a deliberate decision at all. They move from one job to another in haphazard fashion, accepting any new offer that seems better than their current position, without systematically, weighing the pros and cons. Even people who are in skilled occupations sometimes find themselves slipping into a career they might not want by taking one small step after another. A person hears about an opportunity to obtain specialized training that sounds as if it could be useful, signs up for it, and then accepts the first job that comes along that makes some use of that training.

Conflict over a career decision usually begins when a man or woman is confronted by some challenging new information. Such a "challenge" may take the form of an opportunity or a threat, an offer of another job that has many attractive features, perhaps, or a report that his or her company may go out of business. Only when people believe that the risks involved in the decision are serious—and that they can find a satisfactory solution—do they actively and thoroughly examine the alternatives. In their recent book, *Decision Making,* Irving Janis and Leon Mann identify serious flaws in the way many people make decisions and four coping patterns.

Complacency.   People who ignore challenging information about the choices they must make are demonstrating complacency. A typical challenge that people who work in large organizations sometimes choose to ignore is the threat of losing their status and some of their special prerogatives as a result of a reorganization. When complacency is the dominant pattern, people do not believe the risks are serious. They take the attitude that it won't happen, or, even if it does, "It won't affect me."

Complacency also occurs when the challenging information is accepted and the person acknowledges there are risks in continuing with what he's doing—but sees no risks in choosing a new course of action. This type of complacency is shown by men and woman who immediately accept an offer of what appears to be a better job with more opportunity for advancement without spending any time or effort to find out what they might be letting themselves in for.

Of course, complacency is entirely appropriate for many decisions, especially when nothing much is at stake. It is justified whenever there are no serious risks from failing to make the best choice among alternatives or when there is no reason to believe dire warnings of disaster.

Defensive avoidance. When people confronted with a decision believe there is a danger but don't believe that they can find an acceptable solution, they are engaging in what we call defensive avoidance. They may be upset on one level but manage to remain calm by resorting to wishful thinking, which enables them to deny the seriousness of the threat. The specific patterns of denial can vary considerably. Sometimes it is much like the reaction of people who ignore danger signals from their bodies. For example, there are many who do not do anything about swellings, even though they know such symptoms could be cancer. They try not to think about their symptoms, and they stay away from their physicians and others who could tell them what the symptoms may mean.

Middle-level executives may be reacting in essentially the same defensive way when they fail to think about the implications of a series of minor complaints about their work from superiors. Policy makers engage in defensive avoidance when they are intent on developing rationalizations for a particular course of action—without examining alternative courses. Some political writers argue that this was the flaw of "the best and the brightest" who were making policy in Washington during the Vietnam war. The most common strategies of defensive avoidance are (1) rationalization ("It can't happen to me"), (2) procrastination ("Nothing needs to be done about it now. I can take care of it later"), and (3) buck-passing ("I am not the one who needs to do something about it; let George do it").

People engaging in defensive avoidance often appear outwardly calm. They are even able to hide the stress from their own awareness. Only when people are forced to deal with some aspect of the threatening situation does the anxiety appear.

Hypervigilance. When people are faced with an immediate threat and believe that there is not enough time to find a solution, they may become hypervigilant. In its most extreme form, hypervigilance is referred to as panic. When hypervigilance is the dominant pattern, people search frantically for a way out of the dilemma and seize upon hastily contrived solutions. They are likely to overlook the full range of consequences of their choice—as well as other viable alternatives. People who are in a panic or near-panic state sometimes show signs of cognitive constriction, such as a reduction in immediate memory span and simplistic thinking. Fortunately, panic is not a very common response.

When a man or woman realizes that the deadline for accepting an offer is approaching and is keenly aware of the risks and consequences of the choices, he or she may display all the symptoms of acute emotional stress. Such a person is likely to fail to make effective use of the limited time available and to choose on the basis of grossly inadequate search and appraisal. Similarly, when people are heavily in debt and lose their jobs, they may get into near-panic states in their attempts to find another one immediately. In their excited state, they may accept the first offer that comes along, but they may also fail to notice subtle signs of trouble ahead that they would normally take seriously.

Vigilance.   Vigilant decision making occurs when anyone faced with a crucial choice believes that (1) the threat is serious, (2) they can find a solution, and (3) there is enough time. When these conditions are met, people conduct an effective search for alternatives and carefully evaluate those alternatives.

Further, they evaluate the information in a relatively *unbiased* way. They also work out contingency plans in case one or another of the risks materializes. In contrast, those who display complacency, defensive avoidance, or hypervigilance are unprepared for even minor setbacks. They develop strong feelings of regret and are much less likely to stick to their decision, even though changing may be quite costly in terms of time, money, and reputation.

Several procedures have been developed to encourage the vigilant coping pattern. They are most applicable at the point that a person is approaching an irrevocable commitment but has not yet started to carry out the decision. One of these is the balance-sheet procedure, an exercise that requires a person to answer questions about potential risks as well as gains that he or she had not previously contemplated. The procedure involves classifying the expected consequences for each alternative course of action into four main categories: (1) utilitarian gains or losses for self, (2) utilitarian gains or losses for significant others, (3) self-approval or -disapproval, and (4) approval or disapproval from significant others. The decision maker fills out for each alternative a balance-sheet grid, which describes the positive anticipations and negative anticipations expected from each of the four categories.

One executive who filled out such a balance sheet was thinking about whether to leave his position as a production manager in a large manufacturing plant (see Figure 1). He listed a number of "negative anticipations," from long hours and constant time pressures to "stupid" demands made by the top managers, to his own irritability at home as a consequence of job problems. Nevertheless, this man decided to stay where he was. Why? Because of the weight he gave to the positive entries in the nonutilitarian categories—his pride in his role as leader of a competent team, his sense of welcome responsibility for their high morale, his warm, friendly relationship with the others whom he did not want to let down by leaving. He felt that his friendship with his immediate superior was especially rewarding and that together the two of them could save their team from the negli-

Figure 1
A Manager's Balance Sheet

	Positive Anticipations	*Negative Anticipations*
Tangible gains and losses for self	1. Satisfactory pay. 2. Plenty of opportunities to use my skills and competencies. 3. For the present, my status in the organization is okay (but it won't be for long if I am not promoted in the next year).	1. Long hours. 2. Constant time pressures—deadlines too short. 3. Unpleasant paper work. 4. Poor prospects for advancement to a higher level position. 5. Repeated reorganizations make my work chaotic. 6. Constant disruption from higher turnover of other executives I deal with.
Tangible gains and losses for others	1. Adequate income for family. 2. Wife and children get special privileges because of my position in the firm.	1. Not enough time free to spend with my family. 2. Wife often has to put up with my irritability when I come home after bad days at work.
Self-approval or self-disapproval	1. This position allows me to make full use of my potentialities. 2. Proud of my achievements. 3. Proud of the competent team I have shaped up. 4. Sense of meaningful accomplishment when I see the products for which we are responsible.	1. Sometimes feel I'm a fool to continue putting up with the unreasonable deadlines and other stupid demands made by the top managers.
Social approval or disapproval	1. Approval of men on my team, who look up to me as their leader and who are good friends. 2. Approval of my superior who is a friend and wants me to stay.	1. Very slight skeptical reaction of my wife—she asks me if I might be better off in a different firm. 2. A friend in another firm who has been wanting to wangle something for me will be disappointed.

The grid lays out the pros and cons of one alternative facing a production manager at a large manufacturing plant who is contemplating a job change: whether or not to remain in his present position. Balance sheets would be filled out for all other alternatives as well—for example, whether to seek a lateral transfer within the company. The information comes from Irving Janis and Leon Mann, *Decision Making*.

gence and stupidity of the firm's top managers. All the negative aspects of the job did, however, affect this executive's contingency plans: He was determined to find a position in another firm if the men in his unit were scattered in a planned reorganization.

Studies with Yale College seniors suggest that the balance sheet is a feasible way of stimulating people to become aware of major gaps in their information about decisions. In *Decision Making*, Janis and Mann illustrate with the following example how this procedure can be something quite different from a coldly intellectual exercise:

One senior who originally was planning to go to a graduate business school for training to become an executive in his father's Wall Street firm was surprised at first when he discovered that the cells in the balance-sheet grid pertaining to self-approval or -disapproval were almost completely empty.

After looking over the standard list of items to be considered in those categories, he was stimulated to write down several ways in which his career as a
broker would fail to meet his ethical ideals or satisfy his desire to help improve the quality of life for people in his community. As he thought about
these neglected considerations, he became worried and depressed. Then,
while filling out the cells of the balance-sheet grid for his second choice—
going to law school—he began to brighten up a bit. Eventually he became
glowingly enthusiastic when he hit upon the notion that instead of becoming a Wall Street lawyer he might better meet his objectives by being trained
for a career in a legal aid clinic or in public-interest law. Finally, his mood
became more sober, but with some residual elation, as he conscientiously
listed the serious drawbacks (parental disapproval, relatively low income,
poor prospects for travel abroad, and so on) of the new career plan he had
conceived. Afterward he thanked the interviewer for making him realize
he had been on the wrong track and for helping him arrive at his new career
plan, which, in fact, he had worked out entirely by himself in response to the
open-ended nature of the balance-sheet procedure.

What works for Yale seniors may not, of course, work for other kinds of
people. However, three large field experiments have shown that it can work
with other populations as well. The tests were done on high-school seniors
trying to decide where to go to college and two groups of adults deciding
whether or not to diet and attend an early-morning exercise class for health
reasons. Those who were asked to fill out balance sheets in making their
choices were more likely to adhere to their decision and had fewer regrets
afterward than those who did not use the balance sheets.

Why is it beneficial to go through the laborious procedure of filling out a
balance sheet? First of all, as in the case of contrasting outcome scenarios,
such a procedure counteracts complacency and promotes vigilance. Second,
it makes the decision maker realize the need for contingency plans—figuring out what to do if one or another of the unfavorable consequences listed
in the minus columns were to materialize. Third, it helps one to make a
more comprehensive appraisal of the alternatives. By seeing all the entries,
the decision maker can start thinking about possible trade-offs, concentrate
on the major differences among alternatives, and think about the degrees of
importance of crucial pros and cons.

Another procedure designed to promote vigilance is stress inoculation,
which is appropriate shortly after a decision is made but before it is carried
out. Under this approach, a person is given vivid descriptions of what it
will be like to experience the expected negative consequences of the chosen
course. Such a method not only makes him or her more aware of the prob-
able difficulties and losses to be expected, but also promotes a certain
amount of inner preparation that reduces the likelihood that the person
will feel helpless and demoralized if temporary or long-range setbacks
occur. We would expect stress-inoculation procedures to be effective for
any decision that entails severe short-term losses before substantial long-
term gains are attained. The decision to become a lawyer or a physician,
for example, entails many long years of training and apprenticeship before

attaining professional status and the rewards that go with it. Irving Janis's studies of surgery patients tend to confirm the benefits of stress inoculation. Patients who received information about the unpleasant consequences of their operations were less likely to overreact emotionally to setbacks and adversities after making their decisions (although the data are correlational —that is, other possible explanations for the patients' improved attitudes are not ruled out). Supporting evidence was subsequently obtained by other investigators in controlled field experiments with hospitalized patients.

Does the same sort of thing happen when a person is choosing a job or making plans to retire? The answer is yes. Evidence from a dozen or so field experiments shows that stress inoculation can dampen postdecisional stress and minimize the tendency to reverse the decision when setbacks are encountered. A number of studies indicate that new employees who are given realistic preparatory information when offered the job, or immediately after they accept it, are more likely to stay with the organization.

Where can people go to obtain stress inoculation when they are about to start a new job or make some other important life decision? If they try to do it on their own, they should seek as much information as possible about the job, preferably from someone who knows the inside story and can give a vivid account of what is in store for them, along with some realistic reassurances that counteract feelings of helplessness and hopelessness. It may be very difficult to find a good informant. In such a case, a professional counselor can be helpful if he or she is trained as a decision counselor.

The term *decision counseling* refers to the collaboration of a consultant and client in diagnosing and improving the quality of the person's decisions. This type of counseling can be quite nondirective: The counselor refrains from giving advice about which course of action is best. Instead, he tries to help clients make the fullest possible use of their own resources and reach decisions consistent with their own values. The counselor may be somewhat directive, however, in suggesting where to go for pertinent information, how to take account of knowledge about alternative courses of action, how to find out if deadlines are real or can be negotiated, what risks might require preparing contingency plans, and the like.

Although there are, as yet, few people who specialize in decision counseling, all these methods may be employed by psychotherapists, career counselors, social workers, and other clinicians who deal with people at a time when they are making important personal decisions. The proposed interventions, which usually require only one or two hours of counseling, obviously cannot be expected to transform persons with neurotic disorders who have chronic difficulties in arriving at decisions. Such persons require therapy far beyond the scope of decision counseling. But for people who occasionally display the defective coping patterns that are in everyone's repertoire, a session or two with a skilled counselor might bring about a marked improvement in the quality of the clients' decisions.

For example, if the client appears to be in a state of acute conflict and is losing hope of finding a good solution, the counselor can try to prevent defensive avoidance. He can start by asking whether there are relatives, friends, or acquaintances who know something about the problem who might convey new perspectives. When a counselor senses that a client's rational capabilities are blocked by wishful thinking or rationalizations, he may try to stimulate a full exploration of the pros and cons by asking him to develop a balance sheet. But this alone may not be enough.

With a new type of role-playing technique, called outcome psychodrama, the counselor can attempt to counteract defensive avoidance and stimulate vigilance. The client is asked to participate in a scenario that requires him to project himself into the future and to improvise a vivid retrospective account of what has happened as a consequence of choosing one or another alternative. The procedure is repeated as many times as necessary to explore the potential risks and consequences of each choice. The counselor refrains from mentioning any specific consequences, leaving it up to the client's imagination to improvise the specific losses (or gains) that might result.

Outcome psychodrama was first used by Janis with clients who came to a family-service clinic with serious marital problems and were undecided about a divorce. Since the technique appeared to be helpful to them, Janis also tried it with male seniors at Yale who were deciding what to do after graduation. Each student was given a framework for constructing psychodramatic scenarios for each of his leading alternatives. He was told to imagine that it was a year after graduation, that things were going "very badly—worse than you thought they would," and that he was having a heart-to-heart talk with a close friend. A supplementary psychodrama was also tried out for favorable-outcome scenarios.

In most cases, new considerations emerged during the unfavorable-outcome psychodrama that affected the students' evaluation of the alternatives. Some of them were so impressed they changed their preferences. One senior, for example, came up with a number of negative outcomes when he played the role of a lawyer, his first choice of career, going through a post-decisional crisis. He felt the work involved "dull routines," the "stifling of all creativity," and a variety of ethical problems. As a result, he announced that he was inclined to pursue his second choice, a teaching career.

So far only a small amount of research has been done on the effectiveness of outcome psychodrama. What we have learned from recent research suggests it could have a detrimental effect in the early stages of decision making: If the experience is an intense one, the client may lose hope of finding an adequate solution to his dilemma. It may be quite beneficial, however, in the later stages, especially if a person is about to make a drastic change without having worked out contingency plans. Counselors who try the outcome-psychodrama procedure should obviously use it with caution, and perhaps only in the later stages of decision making.

While some interventions are not uniformly successful, there is impressive evidence that new self-help procedures and decision counseling, based on the theoretical model of coping patterns, are effective in many cases.

There is good reason to be optimistic about the prospects of improving the quality of decisions that profoundly affect our lives. By helping people arrive at an accurate blueprint not only of the favorable and unfavorable consequences of what they decide, but also of the resources at their disposal, the decision counselor can help them build self-confidence, avoid biases and mental blocks, and develop realistic expectations of the future.

DEVELOPING ORGANIZATIONAL EFFECTIVENESS

The process by which managers sense and respond to the necessity for change has been the focus of much research and practical attention in recent years. If managers were able to design and to perfect social and technical organizations, and if the scientific, market, and technical environments were stable and predictable, there would be less pressure for change. But such is not the case. In fact the statement that "we live in the midst of constant change" has become a well-worn cliché despite its relevance. Of course, the need for change affects organizations differently; those which operate in relatively certain environments need to be less concerned with change than those which operate in less certain environments. But even managers in relatively certain environments must continually combat the problems of complacency.

The literature which deals with the process of organizational change cannot be conveniently classified because of the yet unsettled nature of this aspect of organizational behavior. We have various conceptualizations and theories whose meanings and interpretations are subject to considerable disagreement. The current trend is to use the term *"organizational development"* (OD) to refer to the process of preparing for and managing change.

Organizational development as we will use the term refers to (1) a planned, systematic program initiated by an organization's management, (2) with the aim of making the organization more effective, (3) through the use of a variety of methods designed to change environmental behavior, and (4) based upon the assumption that organizational effectiveness is enhanced to the extent that the program facilitates the integration of individual and organizational objectives. These four statements capture the essence of OD. It is admittedly broader than some experts would like, since it permits the inclusion of methods other than sensitivity training. Our view is consistent with others who note the trend toward a more "eclectic approach" utilizing a number of methods depending upon the situation.

It is apparent that OD is oriented toward problem solving where the underlying problem is defined in terms of actual or potential organizational ineffectiveness. As such we can cast OD in the managerial language of problem-solving:

1.   What is the problem? (diagnosis)
2.   What are the alternatives? (methods)
3.   How should the method be implemented? (implementation)
4.   Did it work? (evaluation)

Three articles in this section deal with development, change, and the world in which managers must understand behavior, structure, and processes. First, W. Warner Burke in "Organization Development and Bureaucracy in the 1980s" discusses what is being practiced in the field by OD practitioners. His discussion focuses on bureaucracies and OD cures. Burke cites examples such as General Motors, NASA, and AT&T. He also proposes what OD consultants can do for bureaucracies. His discussion covers group interventions, participative management, and reward systems.

The second article is entitled "Selecting an Intervention for Organization Change" by William G. Dyer. The article attempts to show how a change agent and/or manager determines what actions to take following a diagnosis. The possibility of taking different action steps is highlighted through an examination of the famous William F. Whyte restaurant study. After this discussion Dyer presents his criteria for intervention selection. They are (1) root cause, (2) time frame, (3) financial resources, (4) client support, (5) change agent skill, and (6) energy level. He also presents a matrix of interventions which focuses on two dimensions—the unit of focus and the location of the intervention.

Peter Drucker's interesting article entitled "Behind Japan's Success" clearly shows that the world has changed. Drucker believes that a driving force behind Japan's economic success has been the ability to manage complex organizations in the modern world. Japan has been able to respond to the needs of a pluralist society better than any other nation. There is nothing magical about this success unless one believes that adapting to change requires some kind of mystical approach. While the first two articles in this part by Burke and Dyer deal with organizations, Drucker's concluding article focuses on societal/national mechanisms and processes of change.

Organizational Development and Bureaucracy in the 1980s*

W. WARNER BURKE

Even though organization development may:

a.   Represent nothing more than a convenient rubric for a conglomeration of activities (Kahn, 1974).
b.   Suffer from problems of diffusion of success (Walton, 1975).
c.   Now be confused with or merely serve as another name for quality of working life.
d.   Be considered a taboo term in certain organizations (better to say "human resource development").
e.   Disappear by being absorbed into other organizational functions such as "human resource management" (Tichy, 1978).
f.   Never have a comprehensive theoretical base.

the field is alive and well. The OD network numbers more than 2,000 members, the OD division of the American Society for Training and Development has even more, and the OD division of the Academy of Management has approximately 1,000 members. There is overlapping membership among these three primary OD groups, but it is reasonable if not conservative to assume that the number of people in the United States who call themselves OD practitioners or OD consultants is near 5,000. The total number of OD practitioners outside the United States is probably smaller than this estimate of 5,000, but the number is increasing especially in Western Europe and Japan.

The number of organization development courses in universities and books on the subject continues to increase, and the job market is as active as ever. At this writing I know of a dozen positions to be filled in the greater New York City area alone—and the employing organizations are using the

* Reproduced by special permission from the *Journal of Applied Behavioral Science* (1980), pp. 423–37. Copyright 1980 by NTL Institute Publications.

OD label for these openings. OD practitioners still come from a variety of backgrounds—not just psychology, sociology, and education—but they presently have more opportunity for training in the applied behavioral sciences, at least at universities, than was the case a decade ago.

Though diverse in background and wide-ranging in skills and competencies, OD practioners have choice since the job market remains healthy. And even though external consultants in OD have more autonomy than their internal counterparts, the latter nevertheless have more freedom of action, as a rule, than many other groups inside organizations. Internal practitioners do have restrictions, however. For example, they rarely consult with the top management group of the total organization (a limitation that may be appropriate), or get involved with top management succession planning or corporate planning in general. But if they feel too restricted by their employing organization, they can strike out on their own—I continue to be amazed at the number who choose to take this step and actually "make it"—or, of course with the job market continuing to be healthy, join another organization.

Although there has not been a substantial increase in new methods and techniques in recent years, people in the field remain quite busy, and they continue to have more choice in their careers than many other groups.

OD IN BUREAUCRACIES

Organization development practitioners in bureaucracies, however, have not had an easy time of it. Earlier there was optimism (Bennis, 1967; Slater and Bennis, 1964). Bennis (1966) went so far as to predict "the coming death of bureaucracy." He gave it another 25 years or so. Bennis believed that bureaucracy was vulnerable because of:

1. Rapid and unexpected change—a bureaucracy could not cope with the accelerated pace of change.

2. Growth in size—with growth organizations becoming more complex and not as amenable to the bureaucratic simplicities of division of labor, hierarchy, standardization, roles, procedures, and so forth for effectively coping with their environments.

3. More diverse and highly specialized competence is now required—with increases in size and complexity, organizations require greater and different specializations whereas bureaucracy demands standardization, common policy and procedures, routine, and well-defined jobs.

4. A change in managerial behavior—rather than the impersonality in human relations characteristic of bureaucracies, a new philosophy is emerging which is based on changing concepts of:

   a. The human being—more complex with recognized needs.

   b. Power—collaboration and reason being more highly valued than coercion and threat.

   c. Organizational values—based more on humanistic and democratic ideals than the depersonalized, mechanistic value system of bureaucracy.

Others shared much of these same beliefs especially with respect to changes in values (e.g., Tannenbaum & Davis, 1969).

Then there was pessimism (Bennis, 1970). As a result of his experience as an academic administrator (a bureaucratic situation if there ever was one), Bennis came to the view that, human nature being what it is, bureaucracies were not amenable to the kinds of changes in organizational life that he had previously predicted. He reluctantly declared that people as a rule are more concerned with: (a) power and personal gain than with openness and love, (b) clarity of organization than with ambiguity, and (c) self-interests than with the good of the organization or public interest. No doubt many readers of Bennis's change in attitude commented, "I could have told you so."

Later came pragmatism (Perrow, 1977; Schein & Greiner, 1977). Perrow has paradoxically argued that the efficient bureaucracy can centralize in order to decentralize. His ideas are not as far-fetched as this statement may sound. In fact, his argument is based primarily on the accepted and valid principle of management in any organization—delegation. Schein and Greiner have addressed more directly the applicability of organization development (OD) to bureaucracies. They pointed out that the basic ideology of OD is that organizations in response to their changing environments should become more organic systems and therefore more capable of responding to rapid change. Organic systems were characterized by Schein and Greiner as having structures such as matrix or project rather than functional designs and as having open communications, interdependence among groups, considerable trust, joint problem solving, and employees who take risks. Schein and Greiner (1977, p. 49) did not believe that many of these kinds of organizations exist:

> Despite OD's preoccupation with organic practices, we contend . . . that the millennium of organic organizations is not on the horizon, which in turn causes us to question the relevance of the present OD movement for the great bulk of business and public organizations. The preponderance of evidence, by contrast, shows that bureaucratic structures are still the dominant organizational form, either for an entire firm or for product groups.

They assumed that different organizational structures develop unique and inherent behavioral problems and that "behavioral diseases" emerging from bureaucracies differ from those which emanate from organic structures. Accordingly, they argued for a contingency model of OD and proposed a "fine tuning" approach in dealing with bureaucracies. By fine tuning Schein and Greiner meant using OD techniques as a way of sharpening "the operations of an organization" and freeing it from "dysfunctional behaviors" (p. 53). For bureaucracies, then, OD consultants should not attempt to bring about significant change but rather work to improve or fine tune the operations of the system.

Schein and Greiner were specific in their recommendations for fine tuning bureaucracies. They used two criteria for the selection of OD techniques for fine tuning: that the quality of working life will be enhanced as a result, but the situations bounded by the environmental and technological realities of the organization will not be the prime focus of change. They went on to specify four "behavioral diseases" of bureaucracies and to suggest certain OD techniques as potential cures. The four diseases are:

1. *Functional myopia and suboptimization*—results from high division of labor and individuals' allegiance to their specialty.
2. *Vertical lock-in and incompetency*—promotions stay within a single function, emphasis on rank, and seniority.
3. *Top-down information flow and problem insensitivity*—authority, problem solving, plans, and objectives are defined at the top.
4. *Routine jobs and dissatisfaction*—results from bureaucratic need for economies of scale and labor being considered a variable cost.

Table 1 is a summary of Schein and Greiner's behavioral diseases in bureaucracies, the associated behavioral symptoms, and the cures from OD

Table 1
A Summary of "Behavioral Diseases" of Bureaucracies, Their Symptoms and OD Cures—from Schein and Greiner (1977)

Critical Behavioral Diseases of Bureaucracies	Behavioral Symptoms	OD Cures for Fine Tuning
Functional myopia and suboptimization	Interdepartmental conflict Lack of planning coordination Lack of adequate communication across functions	Team building for top management groups Off-site meeting of top two or three levels of management for participative planning and budgeting session Limited structural intervention designed to facilitate goal integration, e.g., senior coordination group Job rotation of high potential managers
Vertical lock-in and incompetency	Frustration Boredom Technical knowledge valued more than managerial ability	Assessment center Job posting Manpower information system Career counseling Management training
Top-down information flow and problem insensitivity	Lack of innovation Minor problems become major by the time they reach top management	Develop "shadow" structure Reflective (Greiner) Collateral (Zand) Parallel (Carlson) Junior board of middle managers Ombudsman
Routine jobs and dissatisfaction	Absenteeism Boredom First-line superivsors feel caught between workers' problems and management's pressure for production	Job enrichment Job rotation Vary work schedules Flexi-time Supervisory training Scanlon plan Salary instead of hourly wages Employee stock ownership plans

for purposes of fine tuning the operations of the system.

Schein and Greiner's final recommendations were that OD consultants:

Adopt a more positive and accepting attitude toward bureaucratic organizations.

Acquire a more thorough knowledge of bureaucratic operations.

Adopt a more conceptual and realistic orientation for understanding bureaucratic behavior.

Develop a more versatile range of OD techniques that apply to bureaucracies.

Where is OD today vis-à-vis bureaucracies, and what about the next decade? The remainder of this paper is an attempt to respond to these questions.

CURRENT OD IN BUREAUCRACIES

It is difficult to know precisely, but from what is known, it seems reasonable to generalize that very little OD is being practiced today in bureaucracies whether they be in the private or public sector. To the extent that OD is practiced in bureaucracies, it is much as Schein and Greiner described: Techniques are used to respond to system ills. But this use of OD techniques is really not organization development. If we subscribe to Beckhard's (1969) definition (no doubt the most popular one), what is practiced in bureaucracies is not "systemwide, planned change managed from the top." And if one chooses my definition—i.e., change in the organization's culture (Burke, 1971)—then the actual practice of OD in bureaucracies may be even more limited.

There is at least one exception to the above generalization. If we can agree that General Motors Corporation is a bureaucracy, then OD in such a system, now under a new name, QWL, is in place (Carlson, 1978). Carlson (in press) now sees organization development as a part of GM's quality of working life effort; an integral part but subsumed under its QWL umbrella nevertheless. In any case, GM's practice of QWL does appear to be a systemwide change effort primarily because:

a. Its effects are regularly surveyed and fed back among a wide range of employees.

b. Managers' performances are partially assessed and rewarded as a function of how well their units rate on these surveys of the employees' (including management) perceived feelings regarding their quality of work life.

c. These QWL efforts are strongly supported by the UAW.

I know of no other such examples from private industry, and I know of none at all in the public sector. The U.S. Army is active with its organizational effectiveness (OE) program, and perhaps in time this entire segment of the Department of Defense may be affected. But for now the OE consultation, while proving to be helpful, is rather limited in scope and impact.

Robert Golembiewski is one of the more experienced consultants in the field of OD with bureaucracies, especially in the public sector. He tends to be optimistic about such consultation and has even provided 19 guidelines for consulting effectively with bureaucracies (Golembiewski, 1978). To the extent that he has been successful as a consultant, he may be an exception to my remarks about the absence of OD in the public sector. Most OD consultants find working with bureaucracies, especially public ones, to be difficult at best (Goodstein, 1978). And there are enough failures on record (Bennis, 1977; Crockett, 1977; Glaser, 1977; Goodstein & Boyer, 1972) to give one pause.

Apparently, most OD consultants have either become more pragmatic and realistic or they have given up when it comes to working with large bureaucratic organizations. Tichy (1978) has found that both internal and external consultants in OD has: (a) become rather doubtful about the possibilities of their consultation having any significant impact toward systemwide change, and (b) come to recognize that what they espouse regarding organizational change and what they actually practice as consultants differ rather dramatically. Tichy's sample was quite small—11 external and 17 internal consultants—and generalizing to all OD consultants is obviously inappropriate. Tichy's sample included, however, OD consultants experienced in the field (some for 15 or more years), and therefore these results should not be ignored.

So, whether present OD consultation with bureaucracies can be characterized as pragmatic and realistic or as tinkering with the system and fundamentally changing nothing depends on how you choose to define organization development. Is OD a process of helping the client organization to adapt and cope with its environment and internal work force more effectively or is it a process of bringing about some fundamental changes in the organization's culture—i.e., its way of doing things? Is it single-loop learning or double-loop (Argyris & Schön, 1978)?

Although there is a question of definition here, there is a deeper concern than merely attempting to redefine OD. As far as I am concerned, the definitions we have are adequate. Some of my preferred definitions, in addition to my own, include those by Beckhard (1969), Golembiewski (1979), Hornstein, Bunker, and Hornstein (1971), Margulies and Raia (1978), and Weisbord (1978). Thus, I am not calling for a conference to define or redefine OD.

The deeper concern to which I wish to draw attention is not merely a matter of whether OD techniques are used in organizations. They are. Moreover, it seems that more and more people are calling themselves OD consultants. The fundamental question concerns what these people are accomplishing: Is planned organizational change resulting from their efforts or not? I believe the answer is that very little or no fundamental change is occurring in bureaucratic organizations.

In spite of heavy criticism especially from the humanistic perspective (e.g., Argyris, 1964, 1973; Bennis, 1966; Emery, 1974; Singer & Wooten, 1976), bureaucracy as a form of organization persists. I think this persistence will increase during the 1980s, assuredly for the first half of the decade. A number of facts support this prediction. Perhaps the most important one comes from economics. Inflation is obviously persistent and large organizations (and small ones) are searching for ways to economize. Managers are being rewarded not only for the amount of gross income they can show, but also for how much cost savings they can demonstrate as well. A concurrent and natural inclination is to centralize. It is generally believed —and there is supportive evidence—that centralization will help to cut costs. When duplication (often a consequence of decentralization) can be eliminated, significant savings will frequently be realized. Three examples should support the prediction if increased bureaucracy.

General Motors, paragon of the huge but decentralized organization, has recently centralized its purchasing function. Formerly, the purchasing function was located in each division, and gradually each corporate unit has transferred its purchasing operations to corporate headquarters. Considerable conflict between corporate and the divisions had to be managed for these transfers to occur, but the "numbers" were clear—with the greater volume of purchasing power, significant cost savings could be realized.

At AT&T, a corporation consisting of relatively autonomous operating companies and similarly autonomous supporting units (e.g., Western Electric), more centralization is under consideration. Billions of dollars are spent annually on training and education. Each of these relatively autonomous units has its own training function—and so does AT&T corporate. People in the system who know agree that there is considerable duplication of effort. It therefore seems clear that centralizing at least more of training would save money. A kind of OD consultation, incidentally, is being used to help with this decision-making process.

The National Aeronautics and Space Administration has become more centralized in recent years. In the days of the Apollo mission, NASA centers competed for the same project. With less money available today, more centralization of decision making assures that costly competition does not occur.

Typically, centralization breeds bigger bureaucracy. Standardization may save, but more people and functions have to conform to the same rules. As one manager at AT&T put it, "Managing is not as much fun as it used to be. Everything has to go upward through one layer of committees after another, just to make sure we are going to do it 'the right way.' "

In summary, today OD in bureaucracies can be characterized at best as fine tuning the system. Although OD techniques are used, fundamental changes in large organizations rarely occur. Changes in General Motors, in spite of some centralization and potential increase in bureaucratization, seems to be occurring. But other examples are hard to find. Furthermore, since centralization will probably be on the increase, dismantling the bureaucratic structure of large organizations is not in the offing.

WHAT'S AN OD CONSULTANT TO DO?

If my analysis of the situation is correct, we must ask. "What is an OD consultant to do?" Continuing to fine tune and tinker with the system is one obvious choice for organizational consultants. This option allows OD consultants to provide help to client organizations, and consultants may realize satisfaction as a result. I am not opposed to this option. I have exercised it myself and will probably continue to do so. In fact, I enjoy helping, but I also worry.

The source of my uneasiness grows from Hart and Scott's (1975) discussion of the "organization imperative." They make the obvious but very substantive case that our society has gradually shifted from an individual value base to an organizational one. To oversimplify their point a bit—you can do anything without an organization. Specifically, they state that our cultural values have shifted in the following ways:

From individuality to obedience.

From the indispensability of the unique individual to dispensability.

From community to specialization.

From spontaneity to self-conscious planning.

From voluntarism to an organizational paternalism.

In helping organizations to "renew, improve, and become more effective," we OD consultants may be doing nothing more than responding to and facilitating, the organizational imperative. The client is the system, right? Golembiewski (1979) puts it this way:

> However noble the professed goals underlying OD interventions, some danger—or perhaps an absolute inevitability—exists that those values will be perverted by the inexorable demands of the organizational system (p. 155).

Referring to Walton and Warwick (1973), Golembiewski goes on to state that:

> OD interventions may be tolerated only when they basically serve to stabilize the system, as in "cooling out" those members who develop antagonistic feelings toward some system. Human needs will be responded to, in this view of the world, only (or mostly) when they happen to coincide with the organizational imperative (1979, p. 115).

These remarks may spell out the consequences of the first option: tinkering with existing bureaucracies. They also suggest a second option for OD consultants: They may quit. Some have and are now managers, trainers and educators, personnel specialists, academicians, entrepreneurs, and real estate agents. But for many a commitment to changing organizations continues, and dropping out is not the preferred option.

The third option, albeit the most difficult one, is to try to do OD—to attempt to change the system itself, especially its culture, to stem the tide of the organizational imperative at least to the point where the individual is not sacrificed. I honestly cannot say that with my accumulated knowledge of and experience in organization development, I know how to stem this tide and eliminate the inhumane aspects of bureaucracy. At the risk of sounding like Don Quixote or perhaps Sisyphus, I will nevertheless make three recommendations. These recommendations are somewhat strategic and in any case emphasize particular interventions. Strategically, I am recommending certain OD interventions aimed toward the decentralization of power. These interventions already have precedence, so we are dealing with a matter of emphasis.

1. **Group Interventions.** These interventions are critical because: (*a*) they are based on the key strengths of OD knowledge: group dynamics and process consultation, and (*b*) because the organizational work group is one, if not the only, primary linkage between the individual employee and the organization. In other words, more may be done for the individual via his or her work group than through any other medium or organizational juncture. Two kinds of group interventions hold promise for dealing with bureaucracies: autonomous (or semiautonomous) work groups and the so-called quality control (QC) circles.

Based on Bion's (1961) theory concerning authority issues in small groups and its application in sociotechnical systems (Emery & Trist, 1960, Rice, 1958), "autonomous" or "self-managing" work groups are designed to alleviate problems associated with supervisor-subordinate relationships by encouraging group members to: (*a*) share leadership functions among themselves rather than depend on a formal leader (i.e., supervisor), and (*b*) work collaboratively. The work of these groups is designed to include whole tasks, skill variety among group members, worker discretion regarding methods, schedules and division of labor, and pay and feedback on performance based on the group as a whole (Hackman & Oldham, 1980).

> The attributes are intended to provide the work group with the task boundary, autonomy, and feedback necessary to control variances from goal achievement within the unit rather than external to it. This self-regulating capacity is hypothesized to lead to greater productivity and worker satisfaction (Cummings, 1978, p. 625).

And there is evidence to support that hypothesis (Cummings & Molloy, 1977).

My purpose here is to point out that supervisory functions change significantly as a result of this kind of intervention. If indeed a first-line supervisor is needed at all, his or her job would not be "the exercise of power over individuals, but the coordination of the group's legitimate requirements to do its job with the resources and objectives of the organization" (Emery, 1974, p. 12). Supervisors become managers rather than "the person in the middle."

It is interesting to learn that even though quality control circles (quality circles or simply QC groups as they are frequently called) were developed in Japan, the technical foundation for such groups—e.g., statistical methodology for determining quality control—was provided by Americans, W. Edwards Deming and Joseph Juran, who lectured in Japan during the early 1950s (Gregerman, 1979). QC groups are problem-solving groups composed of volunteer workers who meet periodically—typically once a week—to discuss work problems, especially those concerned with quality. These discussions are usually chaired by a supervisor but are participative in nature. That is, solutions to work problems proposed by the groups are then implemented via the regular managerial and operational process. QC groups are becoming popular in the United States. For example, with only 15 circle groups in operation, the Lockheed Corporation has documented savings of more than a quarter million dollars over a two-year period. Moreover, 97% of those who participated in the QC circles showed a strong preference for continuing the program (Yager, 1979). The Buick division of General Motors has been active with QC groups as well.

As an intervention, quality control circles facilitate the solving of problems at the level where most of the information can be found and simultaneously decentralize some of the power in the organization. The effectiveness of autonomous work groups and quality circles is generally improved via the more traditional forms of OD work—team building and process consultation.

2. Participative Management.   More research and evidence is accumulating to support OD consultants' authoritatively advocating this approach to management (Burke, 1979). Also, Ackoff's (1974) circular organization, in which every manager has a board, clearly demonstrates the possibility of having a certain amount of democracy within a hierarchical system. I believe we are in a stronger position now to advocate with supportive data that, in general, a participative approach to management will certainly be more fruitful than a unilateral one and probably more effective than even a consultative approach. I am using the term "authoritatively" in the same sense that Argyris (1971) has suggested: OD consultation can at times take the form of recommending certain directions for change. The authority of the recommendation is based on sound research and theory from the behavioral sciences. I believe we now have a sound case.

3. Reward Systems.   It is a fact that people will tend to do in the future what they have been rewarded for doing in the past, and behavior in organizations is no exception to the rule. In addition to interventions that decentralize power, OD consultants should look to changes in reward systems as ways of changing an organization's culture. Inherent within these latter interventions should be processes for providing employees with choice (Argyris, 1970). Lawler (1977) has summarized much of what is known about the pros and cons of certain rewards in organizations, especially those that are classified as extrinsic. Along with this summary, Lawler provides an explanation of some of the newer alternatives in rewards for organizational members. These include job posting, cafeteria-style fringe benefits, pay based on skill evaluation rather than job evaluation, all salary as opposed to salary and hourly paid, lump sum increases instead of monthly or biweekly increases, and the Scanlon Plan, an older innovation that is now receiving renewed attention. Many of these newer aspects of reward systems provide more choice for individuals and thereby place more control in their hands rather than management's. Lawler also points out the merits of openness in organizations rather than secrecy with respect to pay and compensation and participation by employees in the decision-making process regarding changes in the reward system.

CONCLUSION FOR THE 80s

Bureaucracies will remain, at least for the foreseeable future. We should also keep in perspective the fact that bureaucracies have been around for quite some time—much longer than organization development. To assume that OD can affect bureaucracy is to believe that all or most OD consultants are Davids facing Goliath. The analogy is about right for age and size comparisons but not for level of skill and quality of instrument. And since we are not as skillful as David, we should not rely on only one instrument anyway. Just to work with groups particularly at the "shop floor" is to intervene at the micro-level and is therefore limited. I have recommended the above three interventions for emphasis and as a priority, but at the same time I view them as a minimum and as supplementary—not as the only ones.

OD consultants should continue fine tuning, keeping in mind the risk of furthering the organizational imperative, but they should also attempt to change bureaucracy in some fundamental ways. OD is one way that is still worth pursuing.

REFERENCES

Ackoff, R. L. *Redesigning the future.* New York: Wiley, 1974.

Argyris, C. T-groups for organizational effectiveness. *Harvard Business Review,* 1964, *42,* 60–74.

Argyris, C. *Intervention theory and method.* Reading, Mass.: Addison-Wesley Publishing, 1970.

Argyris, C. *Management and organizational development.* New York: McGraw-Hill, 1971.

Argyris, C. *On organizations of the future.* Beverly Hills, Calif.: Sage Publications, 1973.

Argyris, C., & Schön, D. A. *Organizational learning: A theory of action perspective.* Reading, Mass.: Addison-Wesley Publishing, 1978.

Beckhard, R. *Organization development—strategies and models.* Cambridge, Mass.: Addison-Wesley Publishing, 1969.

Bennis, W. G. The coming death of bureaucracy. *Think,* 1966, November–December, 30–35.

Bennis, W. G. Organizations of the future. *Personnel Administration,* 1967, September–October, 6–19.

Bennis, W. G. A funny thing happened on the way to the future. *American Psychologist*, 1970, *25*, 595–608.

Bennis, W. G. Bureaucracy and social change: An anatomy of a training failure. In P. H. Mirvis & D. N. Berg (Eds.), *Failures in organization development and change*. New York: John Wiley & Sons, 1977, pp. 191–215.

Bion, W. F. *Experiences in groups*. New York: Basic Books, 1961.

Burke, W. W. A comparison of management development and organization development. *Journal of Applied Behavioral Science*, 1971, *7*, 569–579.

Burke, W. W. Leaders and their development. *Group and Organization Studies*, 1979, *4*(3), 273–280.

Carlson, H. C. GM's quality of work life efforts . . . an interview. *Personnel*, 1978, July–August, 11–23.

Carlson, H. C. Improving the quality of work life. In P. Mali (Ed.), *Management handbook*. New York: John Wiley & Sons (in press).

Crockett, W. J. Introducing change to a government agency. In P. H. Mirvis & D. N. Berg (Eds.), *Failures in organization development and change*. New York: John Wiley & Sons, 1977, pp. 111–147.

Cummings, T. G. Self-regulating work groups. A sociotechnical synthesis. *The Academy of Management Review*, 1978, *3*(3), 625–634.

Cummings, T. G., & Molloy, E. S. *Improving productivity and the quality of work life*. New York: Praeger Publishers, 1977.

Emery, F. E. Bureaucacy and beyond. *Organizational Dynamics*, 1974, *2*(3), 2–13.

Emery, F. E., & Trist, E. L. Sociotechnical systems. In C. W. Churchman & M. Verhulst (Eds.), *Management sciences: Models and techniques, Vol. 2*. London: Pergamon Press, 1960.

Glaser, E. M. Facilitation of knowledge utilization by institutions for child development. *Journal of Applied Behavioral Science*, 1977, *13*, 89–109.

Golembiewski, R. T. Managing the tension between OD principles and political dynamics. In W. W. Burke (Ed.), *The cutting edge: Current theory and practice in organization development*. La Jolla, Calif.: University Associates, 1978, pp. 27–46.

Golembiewski, R. T. *Approaches to planned change. Part I: Orienting perspectives and micro-level interventions*. New York: Marcel-Dekker, 1979.

Goodstein, L. D. Organization development in bureaucracies: Some caveats and cautions. In W. W. Burke (Ed.), *The cutting edge: Current theory and practice in organization development*. La Jolla, Calif.: University Associates, 1978, pp. 47–59.

Goodstein, L. D., & Boyer, R. K. Crisis intervention in a muncipal agency: A conceptual case analysis. *Journal of Applied Behavioral Science*, 1972, *8*, 318–340.

Gregerman, I. B. Introduction to quality circles: An approach to participative problem solving. *Industrial Management*, 1979, September–October, 21–26.

Hackman, J. R., & Oldham, G. R. *Work redesign*. Reading, Mass.: Addison-Wesley Publishing, 1980.

Hart, D. K., & Scott, W. G. The organizational imperative. *Administration & Society*, 1975, *7*(3), 259–284.

Hornstein, H. A., Bunker, B. B., & Hornstein, M. G. Some conceptual issues in individual- and group-oriented strategies of intervention into organizations. *Journal of Applied Behavioral Science,* 1971, *7,* 557–568.

Kahn, R. I. Organization development: Some problems and proposals. *Journal of Applied Behavioral Science,* 1974, *10,* 485–502.

Lawler, E. E. III. Reward systems. In J. R. Hackman & J. L. Suttle (Eds.), *Improving life at work.* Santa Monica, Calif.: Goodyear Publishing Company, 1977, pp. 163–226.

Margulies, N., & Raia, A. P. *Conceptual foundations of organizational development.* New York: McGraw-Hill, 1978.

Perrow, C. The bureaucratic paradox: The efficient organization centralizes in order to decentralize. *Organizational Dynamics,* 1977, *5*(4), 3–14.

Rice, A. K. *Productivity and social organization: The Ahmedabad experiments.* London. Tavistock Publications, 1958.

Schein, V. E., & Greiner, L. E. Can organization development be fine tuned to bureaucracies? *Organizational Dynamics,* 1977, *5*(3), 48–61.

Singer, E. A., & Wooton, L. M. The triumph and failure of Albert Speer's administrative genius. *Journal of Applied Behavioral Science.* 1976, *12,* 79–103.

Slater, P., & Bennis, W. G. Democracy is inevitable. *Harvard Business Review,* 1964, *42,* 51–59.

Tannenbaum, R., & Davis, S. A. Values, man, and organizations. *Industrial Management Review,* 1969, *10*(2), 67–83.

Tichy, N. M. Demise, absorption or renewal for the future of organization development. In W. W. Burke (Ed.), *The cutting edge: Current theory and practice in organization development.* La Jolla, Calif.: University Associates, 1978, pp. 70–88.

Walton, R. E. The diffusion of new work structures: Explaining why success didn't take. *Organizational Dynamics,* 1975, *3*(3), 2–22.

Walton, R. E., & Warwick, D. P. The ethics of organization development. *Journal of Applied Behavioral Science,* 1973, *9,* 681–698.

Weisbord, M. R. Input- versus output-focused organizations: Notes on a contingency theory of practice. In W. W. Burke (Ed.), *The cutting edge: Current theory and practice in organization development.* La Jolla, Calif.: University Associates, 1978, pp. 13–26.

Yager, E. Examining the quality control circle. *Personnel Journal,* 1979, October, 682–684, 708.

Selecting an Intervention for Organizational Change*

WILLIAM G. DYER

In the field of organizational development, it is almost self-evident that an intervention or change action comes after a period of data gathering and/or analysis of the organization. There often is a kind of underlying assumption that, if a good organizational diagnosis is done, the activity needed to improve the situation is obvious. Such is rarely the case. Given any particular set of organizational problems and conditions, a variety of actions probably could be taken. How does the change agent and/or manager determine what actions to take following the diagnosis. This article is an attempt to deal with this question.

The Need for Good Diagnosis. Without belaboring the point, it has been said over and over again that an effective intervention depends on a good diagnosis. The best intervention selection process possible will undoubtedly be unsuccessful if the diagnosis is faulty. Jerry Harvey describes the disconcerting experience of a consultant doing team building in a New England paper mill. The diagnosis indicated that productivity was down, morale was low, conflicts were apparent between individuals and units. In light of this information, team building was selected as the appropriate change action. The change agent worked with skill, but little improvement was noticed. One day a visiting engineer listened to the main mill machinery and commented, "It sounds like your major drive shaft is out of line." Following this lead, the drive shaft was examined, found to be faulty, and replaced. Productivity immediately jumped, accompanied by feelings of satisfaction and improved morale. Conflicts dropped. Someone then asked the intriguing question, "Why did we do all of that team building when what was needed was a new drive shaft?"

This incident points out two important considerations for change agents. First, if the diagnosis has not included all relevant factors, it is

---

* Reproduced by special permission from the April 1981 *Training and Development Journal.* Copyright 1981 by the American Society for Training and Development, Inc.

impossible to even think about an appropriate range of interventions. Second, this case makes it seem as though there is exactly one precise action that will solve or cope with the problem. This may be true in the case of a fault in the technical system, but often it is not feasible for other types of conditions that emerge in the social system, the administrative system, or the external environment system. Often there are alternative actions that make sense and could have positive results.

MULTIPLE INTERVENTION POSSIBILITIES

When one examines an organization that has evidence of a "problem" or a condition that requires alteration, there are usually several different ways of approaching the analysis and the possible interventions. Let me use a famous early case as an example.[1]

William Foote Whyte was asked to consult with a restaurant with a problem. The immediate condition of concern was the loss of waitress performance during rush times of the day, leaving the job and spending time in the restroom upset and crying. An examination of the situation led to the following analysis: Waitresses were caught between customers and chef.

Upon receiving the order, the waitress would hand the order slip directly to the chef, often with requests for immediate action or special service. The chef began to bristle with resentment as several waitresses gave him orders, and he began to exert slow-down controls on the waitresses. Waitresses began to try to placate customers and put more pressure on the chef to meet the needs of the customer. The chef was the ultimate factor in the output of food, and he was able to withhold service from certain waitresses. When customers got upset with the slow service and reprimanded the waitresses, some waitresses would become so frustrated and upset, they would have to leave the job for a period of time.

Whyte's analysis of the situation is interesting. He saw this as a problem in the work-flow system, for in his view the "system" required lower-status personnel (waitresses) to initiate work for a higher-status person (the chef). Whyte concluded that any system so designed would result in negative reactions from the higher status person. Based on this analysis, Whyte created an intervention to alter the work-flow system and to terminate the interface between waitresses and chef. He had a wall constructed blocking off direct contact between the two parties. A rotating spindle was located in the wall so waitresses could clip their orders on a spindle, getting information to the chef without direct interaction. The chef could now organize his work without pressure from waitresses. Should waitresses have a complaint, they were now to go to the assistant manager, who would talk with the chef, thus preserving an appropriate line of authority.

Reading this case makes it seem as though there is one diagnosis and one appropriate intervention. The intervention does meet the major prag-

---

[1] W. F. Whyte, *Men at Work* (Homewood, Ill.: Dorsey Press, 1961), pp. 125–35.

matic requirement for determining the appropriateness of the intervention —namely, the problem situation is improved as a result of the action.

However, another person looking at the same organizational dynamics might have come up with a different diagnosis—or even the same diagnosis —and developed a much different action intervention which also might have been equally effective. For example:

1. **Waitress-Chef Interaction.** Some might see in this case a major problem in the interaction between two parties and could have interpreted this as a classic case of people applying pressures to control others' behavior with resulting hostile responses. It is possible that if waitresses and chef could have met together in a typical "team-building" format they could have worked through a set of agreements about pressure situations, unacceptable demands, and a priority method agreeable to all which would have resulted in a smoother flow of work, thereby keeping the work-flow system intact. This intervention would have required a great deal more time and skillful interpersonal problem solving to work through a solution.

2. **Distribution of Rewards.** It is possible that some might see this situation as one where the rewards of one party (tips to waitresses) are in jeopardy because of the control of another party (the chef). In situations like this a successful solution has been to work out a tip-sharing procedure approved by all parties so the chef feels a stake in cooperating with waitresses for direct financial benefit.

3. **Inadequate Resources.** Again another possible diagnosis might be (depending on the data gathered) that the problem is one of inadequate resources—either not enough help for the chef or not enough equipment to handle the press of rush orders. If this were in fact the case, the frustrated chef trying to handle too much work with too few resources could be venting his frustration on the waitresses. The problem then is not the interface between these two parties—the points of conflict are only symptoms of a deficiency located elsewhere. Constructing a spindle would eliminate the open, observable conflict but not the frustration or the slow service, because the problem is located elsewhere.

Obviously, the solution to such a situation is to increase the resource base—or reduce the flow of orders, a solution most restaurants are reluctant to employ.

4. **"Personality" Conflicts.** A more simplistic analysis—with some concrete support from Whyte's data—is that some chefs are "ornery" and some waitresses "too sensitive." This results in a personality clash as ornery chefs are very disruptive to sensitive waitresses. Whyte did find some chefs who were more belligerent, especially when working with females. He also saw that certain dependent, inexperienced waitresses had difficulty in dealing with aggressive chefs.

If one were to accept this diagnosis, then a set of actions might include better selection of waitresses, assuming the chef's position was fixed. If more experienced waitresses, who could handle pressure and difficult chefs, were hired, the situation might maintain its stability. It might also be possible to think of replacing the chef, but turnover of personnel as a plan of action usually has some disruptive consequences. It is also possible to think of asking "ornery" chefs or overly sensitive waitresses to engage in some type of counseling, therapy, or individually focused workshop.

5. Reducing Waitress-Customer Pressure.   Still another possible diagnosis-action sequence could be centered not on the waitress-chef interaction but the customer-waitress interface. It could be that customers are putting unreasonable pressure for rush service on the waitress, and her most obvious response is to pass the pressure on to the chef. In such a situation, it may be possible to reduce this pressure by:

a.   Having a set menus that eliminates special orders.

b.   Putting a notice by certain items that additional time would be required.

c.   Having a salad bar to speed up direct service.

d.   Having only experienced waitresses work during rush hours, using only those waitresses who can cope with customer pressure.

Again, let me make the following point: For each of the five alternative courses of action, the presenting problem is exactly the same; namely, waitresses are leaving the job during rush hours, upset and weeping. To determine what course of action would be most effective, it is critical that data be gathered about the causal factors. How do you get such data? Unfortunately, the simple answer "ask the people" may not always give sufficient insight (although this is always a good place to start). Waitresses and chefs may only be aware of pressures and responses without complete awareness as to the cause of either.

In a previous article,[2] it was pointed out that, in one case, workers saw a problem as being a function of ineffective management while managers were sure the difficulty rested in lazy, uncooperative workers. A deeper analysis showed a more root cause to be a work system that overloaded both management and workers with such heavy schedules they took their frustrations out on each other.

This analysis suggests that organizational problems often are complex, that any problem might have a diversity of possible causes, and there may not be any one intervention that would be *the* right action to take. How does one determine what intervention to select that would lead to the most fruitful results? Following are some criteria that may be used.

CRITERIA FOR INTERVENTION SELECTION

1. "Root" Cause.   While in my experience organizational problems are usually complex and are multiply determined, if there is a root factor like a faulty drive shaft, every effort should be made to trace it down.

The selection question is, "Does this intervention deal with the basic causal factors so far as we have been able to ascertain them?"

2 W. G. Dyer, "When Is a Problem a Problem," *The Personnel Administrator*, June 1978.

2. Time frame. In selecting an intervention, there needs to be a determination as to the length of time it would take to initiate and complete the action. Once I was dealing with an organization where the immediate problem for management was pressure to unionize professional workers. Management did not want to unionize and wanted to know why this pressure occurred after a long history with no concern for union membership. The data indicated that the most underlying factor was a continuing restrictive management style that bred resentment in new, younger professionals who did not accept the old traditions of management that were deemed appropriate by older workers.

Given this diagnosis, one of the suggestions for change was to begin a program of management training for the group of supervisors and managers who were handling these professionals. Since a union vote was imminent (within four to six months), it was felt there was not enough time to plan, implement, and see the consequences of a really well-considered management training program.

A more direct kind of intervention was planned to deal more directly with worker discontent, working out agreements between workers and managers more consistent with the intervention around role negotiations described by Harrison.[3]

I have also been party to proposed actions that were seen by key management people as being too hasty. They felt people needed more time to think about the proposed action, to consolidate support, and increase the amount of agreement. Since organization change is still more of an art form than a science, it takes some judgment to determine if a delay is an avoidance strategy or a legitimate request.

The selection question is, "How soon should the intervention begin and when should it be completed to have optimum impact?"

3. Financial Resources. It is one thing to design an intervention in the abstract; it is quite another matter to plan against real budgeting constraints. The ideal intervention might be to have a top-flight external consultant working closely with the top management team over the next year and a half. This intervention may not be feasible by either the time constraint requirement given the time available by the top management group or the finance resource requirement. A top consultant working 20 to 30 days a year could easily cost between $30,000 to $50,000. This may not be possible given the budgets of some organizations.

Again, some managers may use budget constraints as a way of avoiding action. Some conditions may demand the organization make a real commitment to change by investing some considerable amount of resource to the effort. The unwillingness to expend monies may be symptomatic of a problem in some systems. But for other units, financial limitations may be

---

3 R. Harrison, "Role Negotiations" in *The Social Technology of Organization Development,* ed. by W. Burke and H. Hornstein (Washington, D.C.: NTL Learning Resources, 1971).

real and the change agent must then plan within those limits. It is also possible that budget considerations are too restrictive and the change agent would be well advised to tell the client honestly that it would be better not to start a program at all than to do something that would not be appropriate or would be too limited in scope or impact.

The intervention question is: "How much financial resource is needed and available to finance a suitable plan of action?"

4. Client Support.   The graveyard of interventions is filled with creative change programs that were not supported by management and/or other members of the client system who were affected by the intervention and who had to support the action to insure the success of implementation.

One of my early recollections of change agentry was trying to get units in a larger paper products company to deal with survey feedback data they did not understand or want to use. It seemed so easy to get agreement to gather data and feed the results back to working units. Everyone agreed to gather the data and to share it with relevant persons, but agreements began to dissipate when the hard data emerged that pinpointed real problems between real people.

Questions critical to identifying client support are: "Does the client realistically understand the nature of the intervention and what it means to those who will be involved?" and, "Knowing the process and potential impact, will involved parties support the change program?"

5. Change Agent Skill.   It is entirely possible that there could be an elegant intervention available but no one in the critical change agent positions with appropriate skills to implement the action. There seems to be good evidence that one factor in change failure is the effect of change agents trying actions they are not prepared to handle.

In an excellent article summarizing effective and ineffective organizational development programs, Franklin[4] points out that in successful change programs, the internal change agents had better skills than those people handling nonsuccessful programs. Successful change agents had more change agent training prior to the organization development effort and had better "assessment-prescriptive" skills—particularly the ability to identify problems, select appropriate interventions, and then sequence the intervention so problems got solved.

Franklin also observed that in unsuccessful OD efforts it was more likely that the internal change agent had more change agent training just prior to the OD effort coming out of a background in Personnel. This suggests the possibility that change agents, wanting to try out their new knowledge, plunge into activities for which neither they nor their clients are prepared.

6. Energy Level.   This dimension can be described as amount of enthusiasm, commitment, and motivation to engage in the change effort. One possible intervention may grab the interest of the client system and capture

---

4 J. Franklin, "Characteristics of Successful and Unsuccessful Organization Development," *Journal of Applied Behavioral Science* 12, no. 4 (1976).

the motivational set to begin work. This may be the deciding factor in selecting one intervention over another if other important factors appear to be equal.

TYPES OF INTERVENTIONS

Figure 1 presents a matrix of possible interventions. According to this schema, the intervention can be selected from two dimensions—the unit

Figure 1
A Matrix of Interventions

	SOCIAL SYSTEM	TECHNICAL SYSTEM	ADMINISTRATIVE SYSTEM	EXTERNAL SYSTEM
INDIVIDUAL	Counseling-Coaching	Technical Training	Individual MBO	Client Interview
TEAM OR UNIT	Team Building	Job Enrichment	Unit Goal Setting	Open System Mapping
INTER-GROUP	Intergroup Development	Work Flow Planning	Scheduling Review	Joint Client Planning
TOTAL ORGANIZATION	Confrontation Meeting	Work Re-Design	Analysis of Pay System	Survey—Feedback of Client Reactions

of focus, from individual to total organization, and the location of the intervention, either internal systems (social, technical, or administrative) or the external environment.

Since interventions result from an analysis of the organization and analysis derives from some type of data that have been collected, it is important that the different aspects of both the internal and external worlds be systematically reviewed in the data-gathering phase. Too often data are gathered by change agents who have a particular intervention bias, and it is not surprising that the data turn out to support the need for the intervention of their expertise.

One of the great contributions of the OD field has been the creation of a wide range of interventions into the social system. Earlier, the industrial engineering and operations research movements had emphasized changes in the technical system or the administrative system. The training of change agents in the 1960s and 1970s emphasized the social system components, and many change agents trained during that period are almost complete strangers to technical and administrative aspects of organizations. As a result, they do what they know.

OD efforts have often not been successful, not because of a lack of soundness of the overall idea of organization development, but due to the limited data and the inappropriate selection of interventions. This orientation strongly suggests the advisability of a team of experts or personnel in the several areas of organizations designing the data-gathering process, participating in the analysis, and agreeing on the appropriateness of the action strategy.

INDIVIDUAL VERSUS SYSTEM INTERVENTIONS

If the constraints described earlier concerning time and available resources are important factors in intervention selection, it seems critical to look at the selection of interventions at the individual versus the larger organization or system level. To focus on the alteration of individual behavior or performance is usually a costly and time-consuming direction to produce change.

At one university, a program was initiated to look at the reduction of the amount of cheating among students. The reasons for cheating distinctly uncovered the need for students to get grades to meet expectations of parents or peers or to appear well in competitive comparisons for jobs or graduate schools. There were also some pressures to cheat from peers because "everyone does it." How do you devise an action plan to reduce cheating?

One method is to identify each student who cheats and then engage in an individual counseling program with each. This is a long, laborious process. A different intervention at the group level might be more efficient. This would require some type of group counseling, establishing new norms for peer group behavior.

Other possibilities include altering the physical administration of exams; e.g., different exams for alternate students, monitoring, spaced seating, and so on. Still another approach considered was to change the whole policy and program about testing and grading. If grades in the ordinary sense were eliminated, there would be no need for cheating; or if it were possible to shift to an individual oral examination, then cheating possibilities would be seriously reduced.

To alter the seating or monitoring systems is fairly easy to introduce with little change in existing organization processes for evaluation and grading. The need for cheating is still there, and such changes could be expected to lead to more innovation on the part of students to try to "beat the system." To change the overall administrative policy about grades and grading would, undoubtedly, reduce cheating most directly; but getting a change of policy of that magnitude may not be feasible given the realities of university policies and administration.

Still this issue about intervention selection is important. Generally, interventions at the individual level will take more time and resources than making appropriate adjustments in larger aspects of the total system. However, it is often the case that programs centered on altering individual behavior are easier to "sell" to administrators. This results in starting change programs at the individual change level that produces poor overall results. Some individuals may change, but the system factors connected with the problem remained unchanged.

SYSTEM REACTIONS TO LOCALIZED INTERVENTIONS

Another significant issue in the selection of an intervention centers on the reaction of others in the larger system to an intervention in another part of the system. In another classic case (Hovey and Beard) change was introduced in a toy assembly line. The target of change was the paint unit —one part of the total assembly line. Since this was the bottleneck in production, a development program was begun with the paint crew.

After much negotiation and resistance from others in the organization, the paint crew was allowed to make a major change in the technical system. The intervention called for a switch that controlled the speed of the conveyor belt that brought the toys through the paint shop. This switch allowed the paint crew to control their speed of work during the day. From the perspective of the paint crew, the technical intervention was a smashing success. Production jumped markedly and morale was high.

Unfortunately, the "spread effect" was not so positive. The other units on either side of the paint crew were now under pressure to increase their productivity to meet the standards of the revitalized paint group. These other units felt pressured and resentful. The intervention was selected without a thoughtful concern about the spread effects on other aspects of the organization as a result of the intervention. Some interventions can be correctly anticipated to have localized impact with little or no spread to other parts of the system. Other interventions could probably be accurately predicted as to spread consequences if the intervention were, in fact, successful while other interventions may be quite unpredictable.

The important issue for the change agent is to build the anticipated spread effect into the intervention selection process. Some interventions might reasonably be rejected because of anticipated negative spread impacts, while it could also conceivably be the case that an intervention might be rejected because it does not have enough spread potential.

Spread effects can occur through both the formal and informal systems. You cannot create change in a vacuum. People will talk. It seems wisest to anticipate spread effects and get all possible people who might be impacted involved in at least understanding the change action and giving their support *before* the change effort begins.

INTERVENTION REINFORCEMENT

A significant factor in achieving positive results from an intervention is the reinforcement of the intervention from other parts of the system. Most OD people who have been involved in training have experienced the unhappy situation where the learnings of an apparently successful training program were not applied in any significant sense on the job.

The evidence shows that behaviors emphasized in the training program may not be accepted and supported by co-workers in the social system nor acknowledged and rewarded in the pay-advancement part of the administrative system. A person would have to be an absolute idealist, a fool, or a dunce to persist in behaviors that are not accepted or rewarded elsewhere in the organization. Too often interventions are planned and implemented without carefully building into the change plan the reinforcers that will be needed from other parts of the system to sustain and support the new actions.

Many organizations will get excited about team building, job enrichment, or MBO and will begin the new activity. However, as the regular processes of the organization move along, it often becomes apparent to the manager engaging in the team-building activity that his efforts are not acknowledged or rewarded. His boss does not ask him about the team-building effort, and the success or failure of this activity is not reflected in his raises or promotions. My experience with team building has been that managers will engage in this activity with greater commitment if they feel supported and rewarded generally by others in the organization.

CONSTRAINTS AND COMMITMENTS

I trust that the argument of this article is clear: OD is not a science in the sense that clear, precise actions are neatly available for every organizational problem situation. In its current state, OD must represent, rather than precise science, intelligent analysis and selection. If both the change agent and the client are aware of the range of possible actions that are available for a particular problem, they may be able to make choices that will make sense in terms of the constraints present and will have the commitment of those who must participate in the intervention.

Behind Japan's Success*

PETER F. DRUCKER

"I am more afraid of the Japanese than I am of the Russians," a young lawyer said to me recently. "To be sure, the Russians are out to conquer the world. But their unity is imposed from the top and is unlikely to survive a challenge. The Japanese too are out to conquer us, but their unity comes from within. They act as one superconglomerate"—a conglomerate Westerners often call "Japan, Inc."

To the Japanese, however, Japan, Inc., is a joke and not a very funny one. They see only cracks and not, as the foreigner does, a monolith. What they experience in their daily lives are tensions, pressures, conflicts, and not unity. They see intense, if not cutthroat, competition both among the major banks and among the major industrial groups. And the Japanese are themselves involved every day in the bitter factional infighting that characterizes their institutions: The unremitting guerilla warfare that each ministry wages against all other ministries and the factional bickering that animates the political parties, the Cabinet, the universities, and individual businesses.

Perhaps most important, where the foreigner sees close cooperation between government and business, the Japanese often see only government attempts to meddle and dictate. "We pull at the same rope," the chief executive officer of one big company remarked, "but we pull in opposite directions."

The Japanese government is not always successful in making industries work together in the national interest. Despite 20 years of continual pressure, the supposedly all-powerful Ministry of International Trade and Industry (MITI) has simply not been able to get the major computer manufacturers to pool their efforts—something that the governments of Germany, France, and Britain have all accomplished.

---

* Source: *Harvard Business Review*, January–February 1981, pp. 83–90. Reprinted with permission. Copyright 1981 by the President and Fellows of Harvard College; all rights reserved.

One foreigner after another extols Japan's harmonious industrial relations, but the Japanese public curses the frequent wildcat strikes on the government-owned national railways. Only where the labor unions are exceedingly weak—that is, in the private sector—are labor relations harmonious. As Japanese labor leaders point out somewhat acidly, Western companies without unions (IBM, for example) tend to have the same kind of equable labor relations as do Japanese companies. In the public sector, where unions are strong (a legacy of the U.S. occupation after World War II), there is no sign of this fabled harmony.

Still, the Japanese have achieved the necessary consensus to participate effectively in the world economy. Contrary to popular belief in the miracle of Japan, Inc., the competitive success of Japanese industry is not the result of some uniformity of thought and action. It is the result of something far more interesting—habits of political behavior that use the diversity in Japanese national life to produce effective economic action.

TAKE COMPETITIVENESS SERIOUSLY

One of these habits is to consider thoroughly a proposed policy's impact on the productivity of Japanese industry, on Japan's competitive strength in the world market, and on Japan's balance of payments and trade. This has become almost second nature for Japanese policy makers in the ministries, in the Diet, and in business as well as for analysts and critics in the popular newspapers and university economics departments.

Unlike the Americans, for example, the Japanese are far too conscious of their dependence on imports for energy, raw materials, and food ever to shrug off the rest of the world or to push it out of their field of vision altogether. These broad considerations do not always carry the day—but again, unlike the Americans—every interested party in Japan takes them seriously.

The Automobile Industry

MITI has, since around 1960, steadily opposed expansion of the Japanese automobile industry because, in large part, it views the private automobile as a self-indulgence and as the opening wedge of a consumer society, which it finds abhorrent. In addition, it has maintained, at least it did in the early years, considerable skepticism about the ability of untried Japanese manufacturers to compete against the likes of GM, Ford, Fiat, and Volkswagen. It has also been quite fearful that a large automobile market in Japan would provoke irresistible demands to open Japan to foreign imports, the one thing it has been determined to prevent.

But MITI has also believed, quite sincerely, that expansion of the automobile industry would have an adverse, indeed a deleterious, effect on Japan's balance of trade, on her ability to earn her way in the world economy, and on her productivity generally. The more successful the Japanese automobile industry, MITI has argued, the worse the economic impact on Japan. The automobile, it has pointed out, requires the two raw materials that are in shortest supply in Japan: petroleum and iron ore. It also requires the diversion of scarce resources, both food-growing land and capital, to highways and highway construction. Instead of an automobile industry, what MITI has wanted is massive investment to upgrade the railroads' freight-handling capacity.

There are plenty of diehards left, and not only at MITI, who still maintain that letting the Japanese automobile industry expand was a serious mistake. Even with record sales to North America and Western Europe, the industry's export earnings, they argue, are only a fraction of what the automobile costs Japan in foreign exchange for petroleum and iron ore imports. A small part of the sums spent on highways would have given the Japanese railroads the freight-carrying capacity that the country still lacks, for the enormous amounts spent on roads have not been enough to build an adequate highway system. Trucks clog the roads; port cities are overcrowded; and air pollution is increasing.

MITI lost its fight against the automobile. It was defeated in part by the automobile industry, which forged ahead despite MITI's disapproval, and in part by the infatuation of "Nabe-san," the Japanese "man in the street," with the motor car—despite its high costs, despite the lack of places to park, and despite the traffic jams about which no one complains louder than Nabe-san sitting in the driver's seat. But at least—and this is the point— the automobile's impact on Japan's productivity, competitive position, and balance of trade was rigorously considered. Even the automobile company executives who fought MITI the hardest admit openly that it was the ministry's duty to make sure that these considerations were taken seriously, no matter how eager they might have been to proceed with production or how devoted Nabe-san might have been to his automobile.

PUT NATIONAL INTEREST FIRST

Estimating the impact of various policy alternatives on Japan's competitive position in the world economy is only one of the habits of behavior expected of Japanese leaders. They are also expected to start out with the question "What is good for the country?" rather than the question "What is good for us, our institution, our members, and our constituents?"

The Basis of Leadership

In no other country are interest groups as well organized as in Japan, with its endless array of economic federations, industry associations, professional societies, trade groups, special interest clubs, and guilds. Each of these groups lobbies brazenly, openly using its voting power and money to advance its own selfish ends in ways that would make a Tammany boss blush. Yet if it wants to be listened to and to have influence on the policy-making process, every group must start out in its deliberations by considering the national interest, not its own concerns.

No group is expected to be completely unselfish or to advocate policies that might cost it money, power, or votes; Japan's Confucian tradition distrusts self-sacrifice as unnatural. Each group is, however, expected to fit its self-interest into a framework of national needs, national goals, national aspirations, and national values. Sometimes this expectation produces blatant hypocrisy, as when Japanese physicians claim that the only thought behind their successful demand for near-total exemption from taxes is concern for the nation's health. Still, the physicians pay at least lip service to the rule that demands that the question "What is the national interest?" be asked first.

By failing to do even that and, instead, asserting that what is good for labor is ipso facto good for the country, Japanese unions have largely forfeited political influence and public acceptance, despite their impressive numbers. Conversely, a substantial proportion of Japan's business leaders has for 100 years subscribed to the rule that the national interest comes first, a rule first formulated by the 19th-century entrepreneur, banker, and business philosopher Eiichi Shibusawa (1840–1931). As a result, business management is respectfully listened to whenever it discusses economic and social policies, even by the two fifths of the Japanese population who faithfully vote for avowedly Marxist or stridently antibusiness parties and candidates.

The demand that Japanese leadership groups—especially Japan's business leaders—take responsibility for thinking through the policies that the national interest requires forces them to lead. It forces them to take the initiative and to formulate, propound, and advocate national policies *before* they become issues. Indeed, it forces them to define what the proper issues are.

The Western Approach

In the West, particularly in the United States, the conventional economic interests are expected to be preoccupied with their own concerns, their own needs and wants. As a rule, they are rarely prepared to act in a manner of general rather than factional interest. They can only react. They cannot lead; they can only oppose what someone else proposes. Whenever a legitimate matter of general concern comes up, someone within the group is bound to see it as a threat; another will oppose doing anything at all; and a third will drag his feet.

In Japan, new proposals are also likely to run into opposition within particular interest groups, but the special concerns of their members are held in abeyance until the national interest has been thought through. In the West, these special concerns are the focus of policy debate; in Japan, they are peripheral. The Western approach can lead to inaction or to doing "another study"—until someone from the outside proposes a law or a regulation that can then be fought as "unacceptable." But this is only rearguard action and damage containment. Inevitably, it leaves the definition of issues to others, even though, as the Japanese see clearly, to define issues is the first duty of a leader.

The Japanese do not, of course, always discharge this responsibility successfully. Both the bureaucracy and the business leaders of Japan were totally unprepared for the explosion of environmental issues 10 years ago, an explosion for which they had had plenty of warning. Today they still prefer to ignore the challenge posed by the movement of women into professional and managerial jobs—a movement that is gathering momentum and is grounded in irreversible demographics.

For the most part, however, the Japanese have been successful in defining critical issues. In contrast, U.S. leaders spoke of lowering the mandatory retirement age at the very moment when the growing power of older Americans made first California and then the U.S. Congress enact laws postponing retirement or prohibiting mandatory retirement altogether. Business leaders in Japan anticipated the issue, faced the high costs involved, and without any prompting from external constituencies raised the mandatory retirement age. "It's what the country needs" was the explanation they gave.

The Western "self-interest first" approach worked reasonably well as long as national policy could effectively be formed through adversary proceedings that balanced the conflicting demands of large, well-established interest blocs. But since politics in the industrial West is currently fragmented and since the balance of national power has all too often come to rest in the hands of small groups of single-cause zealots, this traditional approach is clearly no longer adequate. Perhaps the Japanese model, under which both leaders and special interests derive their legitimacy from their stewardship of the national interest, might better serve the unavoidable pluralism of modern industrial society.[1]

KNOW HOW TO SIT

In addition to taking competitiveness seriously and balancing local interests for the general good, the leaders of Japanese business have a duty, or so Shibusawa taught them, to understand the views, behavior, assumptions, expectations, and values of all other major groups in their society. At the same time, the leader feel they have an equal duty to make their own views, behavior, assumptions, expectations, and values known and understood. This does not require public relations in the Western sense but rather private relations—relations made not by speeches, pronouncements, and press releases but by the continual interaction of responsible men in policy-making positions.

Irving Shapiro, chairman and CEO of E.I. du Pont de Nemours, the world's largest chemical company, was widely quoted in the U.S. press last year for having pointed out that he now had to devote four fifths of his time to "relations" with policy makers in the Congress and the Washington bureaucracy and could only spend one fifth to manage his company. The only thing that would have surprised a Japanese CEO in a business of comparable importance is the one fifth Shapiro has available to run his company.

[1] For more discussion of this, see my recent book, *Managing in Turbulent Times* (New York: Harper & Row, 1980), especially "Business Enterprise as a Political Institution," p. 205, and "Managing in a Political Environment," p. 216.

Very few CEOs of large Japanese companies have *any* time available for managing their companies. All their time is spent on relations, even the time spent on internal company business. They keep control of things by giving careful attention to personnel decisions in the upper ranks and by requiring meticulous financial and planning reports. But they do not "manage"—that is left to lower levels.

The top people spend their time sitting, sipping cups of green tea, listening, asking a few questions, then sitting some more, sipping more cups of green tea, listening, asking a few more questions. They sit with the people from their own industries, with suppliers, with the trading company people, with the managers of subsidiaries. They sit with top people from other companies in their groups—as, for instance, in the famous five-hour luncheons in which the presidents of all companies in the Mitsubishi group come together once a week. They sit with people from the banks, with senior bureaucrats from the various ministries, with people from their own companies in after-hours parties in Ginza bars. They sit on half a dozen committees in half a dozen economic and industry federations. They sit and sit and sit.

In all these sittings they do not necessarily discuss business, surely not their own business. Indeed, to a Westerner their conversation at times appears quite pointless. It ranges far afield, or so it seems, moving from issues of economic policy to personal concerns, from the other fellow's questions and problems to the topics of the day, from expectations for the future to reappraisals of the past.

Their aim, of course, is not to solve anything but to establish mutual understanding. When there is a problem, one knows where to go. One knows what the other person and his institution expect, what they can and will do, and what they cannot or will not do. When either crisis or opportunity arrives, these immobile sitters are able to act with amazing speed, decisiveness, and at times ruthlessness, for the purpose of all this sitting is not to produce mutual liking, agreement, or trust. It is to produce an understanding of why one does not like another, does not agree, does not trust.

SEEK NO FINAL VICTORIES

The last of these habits of Japanese economic behavior is to base human interactions not solely on adversarial relations but also on common interest and mutual trust.

Yet, adversarial relations in Japan have historically been fiercer, more violent, less forgiving, and less compassionate than in the West. Neither "love thine enemy" nor "turn the other cheek" is to be found in any of Japan's creeds. Even nature is violent in Japan, a country of typhoons, volcanoes, and earthquakes.

Where the Westerner sees no need for feuding or recrimination—as, for instance, when in times past a painter or an artist parted company with his teacher and established his own style or school—Japanese convention dictates that relations be antagonistic or at least be made to appear so. This tradition extends today to divorce, which has reached epidemic, almost Californian, proportions, especially among young, educated couples. An "amicable" divorce is apparently not considered proper. It must be made to look adversarial even if the two people part by mutual consent and on reasonably good terms.

But all these are situations in which a relationship is to be dissolved permanently. However, when people or parties must live together, let alone when they must work together, the Japanese make sure that their relationships have at their core a mutuality of interest. Then, whatever conflict or disagreement exists can be subsumed in the positive bond of broadly shared concerns.

One of the main, though rarely voiced, reasons that the Japanese automobile companies have been reluctant to build plants in the United States is their bafflement at management-union relations in the American automobile industry. They simply cannot understand them. "Our unions fight management," a young Toyota engineer, an avowed leftist and socialist with strong prounion leanings, recently told me. "But yours fight the company. How can they not know that, for anything to be good for the company's employees, it has to be good for the company? Where this is not taken for granted—and it's completely obvious to every one of us—no Japanese could be a manager; but no Japanese could be an employee or a subordinate, either."

One usually does not have to live or work closely with a competitor; hence, competition tends to be ruthless between companies in the same field and between groups of companies—for example, between Sony and Panasonic or between Mitsui Bank and Fuji Bank. But whenever there has to be a continuing relationship with an opponent, the Japanese tend to seek common ground. And it is here that asking the questions to which all those endless sittings are largely devoted begins to pay handsome dividends.

Great care is taken by all parties that there be no damage done to common interests. Great care is also taken that there be no final victory over the individuals or groups with whom one has to live and work. The Japanese know that to win such a war is to lose the peace. Whenever groups in Japan have to live together, both sides will be more concerned with making their conflict mutually productive than with winning in any absolute sense. Yet these same people will go all out for total victory against an opponent with whom they do not share common interests and who therefore can be destroyed.

IDEALS AND REALITIES

These four habits, or rules, of competitive success—taking competitiveness seriously, considering the national interest first, making external relationships important, and not seeking final victory over opponents with whom one still has to live—are, of course, ideals and precepts. They are normative rather than descriptive of universal practice. Every Japanese can point to dozens of cases in which the rules have been broken or disregarded with impunity. Not every Japanese necessarily accepts them as being right.

Some of Japan's most successful entrepreneurs and companies—Honda, for instance, or Matsushita as well as Panasonic or Sony—have shown scant respect for some of the rules. These leaders do not give a great deal of time or attention to outside relationships, nor do they much care whether they are accepted into "the club." They do not automatcially agree that putting the national interest first in one's thinking is the responsibility of the business leader. They have even, on occasion, been quite willing to inflict crushing defeats on opponents with whom they have still had to live and work.

There is also a good deal of criticism within Japan, especially within business circles, of some of the rules, and there is grave doubt whether they are still fully appropriate to Japan's needs. Can top management, some leaders ask, devote practically all its time to outside relationships without losing touch with the swiftly changing realities of economics, markets, and technologies? Others grumble that efforts to find common ground with other groups, with government in particular, have led to spineless appeasement and bureaucratic arrogance.

These rules, in other words, have weaknesses, limitations, shortcomings; they neither enjoy universal approval nor apply without exception. Even so, they have been unusually effective in strengthening Japan's industrial performance. What, then, lies behind their acceptance and success?

The Case for Tradition

The most common answer given in Japan as well as in the West is that these rules represent uniquely Japanese traditions and values. But this is surely not the whole answer; in fact, it is largely the wrong answer. Of course, rules of social and political behavior are part of a culture and have to fit it or at least be acceptable to it. How the Japanese implement their rules is very Japanese indeed, but the rules themselves represent *a* rather than *the* Japanese tradition. They represent a choice among widely different, but equally traditional, alternatives.

Some of the rules, moreover, have only a questionable foundation in Japanese tradition. The present industrial harmony of Japan, though usually attributed to long-standing cultural values, is in sharp contrast to the ofttimes violent history of relations between Japanese superiors and subordinates. As late as the 1920s (that is, through the formative stage of modern Japanese industry), Japan had the worst, most disruptive, and most violent labor relations of any industrial country in the world.

For the 150 years before modern Japan was born in the Meiji Restoration of 1868, relations between the lords and their military retainers, the samurai, on one side the peasant labor force on the other meant at least one bloody peasant rebellion per year. There were more than 200 such rebellions during the period, each of them suppressed just as bloodily.

"Government by assassination" rather than the careful attempt to find common ground was still the rule for relationships among competing groups in the 1930s. Nor is it entirely coincidental that student violence and terrorism began in Japan in the 1960s and took their most extreme form there. If it is meaningful to speak of a Japanese cultural tradition, violence and internecine warfare are every bit as much a part of it as the quest for harmony and mutuality of interest.

The Business Heritage

These rules of economic life did not evolve in a vacuum. They were strongly opposed when first propounded and were considered quite unrealistic for a long time. The greatest figure in Japanese business history is not Eiichi Shibusawa, the man who formulated the ethos of modern Japanese society. It is Yataro Iwasaki (1834–1885), the founder and builder of Mitsubishi, who was to 19th-century Japan what J. P. Morgan, Andrew Carnegie, and John D. Rockefeller combined were to the United States. Stoutly denying Shibusawa's claim that business leaders should take responsibility for the national interest and for embedding conflict in a bond of common interest, Iwasaki rejected out of hand Shibusawa's vision of society. Shibusawa was greatly respected, but his teachings had little influence on practical men of affairs, who were far more impressed with Iwasaki's business success.

As a guide to industrial behavior, these rules won general acceptance only after the Second World War. When a defeated, humiliated, and almost destroyed Japan began painfully to rebuild, it asked the question "What are the proper rules for a complex modern society, a society that must participate in a competitive world economy and be dependent on it?" Only then did the answers that Shibusawa had given 60 years earlier come to be seen as right and relevant.

The Historical Context

Historians will long debate why Shibusawa's answers, having failed to discover a receptive audience before the war, found one so soon after it. Indeed, historians will be as busy trying to explain what happened in Japan in the 1950s as they have been for years trying to explain what happened in Japan at the time of the Meiji Restoration. In both cases the central questions are much the same: How did a humiliated Japan organize itself to become a modern commercial nation while remaining profoundly Japanese in its culture? How were the appropriate elements of that culture mobilized without violating the rest?

One might speculate that the shock of total defeat and the humiliation of being occupied by foreign troops—especially since no foreign soldiers had ever before landed on Japanese soil—created a willingness to try things that had never been tried before. One might speculate further that, although there was no single leader, no one great figure, to put Japan on a new path, the pressing needs of Japanese workers supplied some of the motivating force.

The workers—many of them the unemployed, discharged veterans of a defeated army—desperately required a new sense of "home" and "community." They needed a defense against the strong pressures put upon them by the liberal labor experts of the American occupation, pressures to join left-wing unions and to become a revolutionary force in Japanese society. Having lost economic and, in many cases, emotional security, they looked to conserve as much as possible of their former lives, yet to conserve it in terms appropriate to the changed world about them.

Facing Up to a Pluralist Society

Why Japanese management was able to respond to these needs in such an effective manner no one yet really knows. The form that response took—Shibusawa's four habits, or rules, of economic behavior—did not draw on exclusively Japanese sources. In fact, the habits could just as well be explained with reference to purely Western teachings and traditions.

That business leaders are responsible for thinking in terms of the national interest was preached in the West around 1900 by such un-Japanese leaders as Walter Rathenau in Germany and Mark Hanna in the United States. That an enemy who cannot be destroyed must never be defeated or humiliated but must be made into a friend was first taught around 1530 by Niccolò Machiavelli. And that conflict must be embedded in a web of shared interests is also to be found in Machiavelli. It is to be found as well in the work of Mary Parker Follett, that most proper of proper Bostonians who made much the same argument in the 1920s when she first applied political theory to management and to conflict resolution.

All these Westerners—Rathenau and Hanna, Machiavelli and Follett—asked the same basic questions: How can a complex modern society, a pluralist society in an era of rapid change, be effectively governed? How can it make productive use of its tensions and conflicts? How can it evolve a unity of action out of the diversity of interests, values, and institutions? And how can it derive strength and cohesion from being surrounded by, and even dependent on, a multitude of competing powers?

Though the West has asked these questions, it has not taken them seriously enough. Why not? Perhaps the Great Depression had something to do with it, for before the depression a number of leaders did take them seriously. Both Herbert Hoover and Heinrich Brüning, the last chancellor of democratic prewar Germany, saw the common interest of all groups as the catalyst of a genuine national unity. In contrast, Roosevelt's New Deal saw the principles of countervailing power and adversarial relations as the basis for a very different kind of unity. Compromises acceptable to all because they do not offend any one group too much offer a promise of national unity based on the least common denominator, not the largest view of national interest.

But this is speculation. What is fact is that the secret behind Japan's economic achievement is not a mysterious Japan, Inc., a creation that belongs, if anywhere, in some Hollywood grade B movie. Far more likely, it is that Japan—at present alone among the major industrial nations—has addressed herself to defining the rules for a complex, pluralist society of large organizations in a world of rapid change and increasing interdependence.

Better than the best

In the feudal days of Japan, it was the ambition of every samurai or warrior to serve his lord better than did any of his fellow samurai, and every local lord made efforts to stand higher in the favour of the Shogun and the Emperor than did any other lords in the country. Now that she has entered the world arena, it is her greatest ambition to be better than the best in the world in any line of culture. In the prewar days the world charged Japan with exporting commodities cheaper than their manufactures would cost in other countries. She was not dumping them at all, but, on the contrary, she endeavoured to supply the world with cheaper articles than were supplied by any other countries in the world. In art, science, literature, trade, industry and what-not does every single Japanese aspire to stand higher in his own profession and occupation than anybody else, and in her effort to be better than the best lies indeed the secret of the great progress that Japan has made and will make to rise up from her defeated ruins.[2]

---

[2] From "Secret of Japan's Progress," *We Japanese, Being Descriptions of Many of the Customs, Manners, Ceremonies, Festivals, Arts and Crafts of the Japanese* (Miyanoshita, Hakone, Japan: Fujiya Hotel, Ltd., 1934).